D1122005

Developing Country Debt
and Economic Performance

A National Bureau
of Economic Research
Project Report

Developing Country Debt and Economic Performance

Volume 1

The International Financial System

Edited by   Jeffrey D. Sachs

The University of Chicago Press

Chicago and London

JEFFREY D. SACHS is a professor of economics at Harvard
University and a research associate of The National Bureau of
Economic Research.

The University of Chicago Press, Chicago 60637
The University of Chicago Press, Ltd., London
© 1989 by The National Bureau of Economic Research
All rights reserved. Published 1989
Printed in the United States of America

98 97 96 95 94 93 92 91 90 89   5 4 3 2 1

Library of Congress Cataloging-in-Publication Data

Developing country dept and economic performance / edited by
Jeffrey D. Sachs.
    p.   cm.—(A National Bureau of Economic Research
project report)
    Papers presented at a conference held in Washington, D.C. on
Sept. 21–23, 1987.
    Bibliography: p.
    Includes indexes.
    Contents: v. 1. The international financial system.
    ISBN 0-226-73332-7 (v. 1)
    1. Debts, External—Developing countries—Congresses.
2. Developing countries—Economic conditions—Congresses.
3. International finance—Congresses.   I. Sachs, Jeffrey.
II. Series.
HJ8899.D4815 1988
336.3'435'091724—dc19   88-20866
                                                            CIP

Relation of the Directors to the
Work and Publications of the
National Bureau of Economic Research

1. The object of the National Bureau of Economic Research is to ascertain and to present to the public important economic facts and their interpretation in a scientific and impartial manner. The Board of Directors is charged with the responsibility of ensuring that the work of the National Bureau is carried on in strict conformity with this object.

2. The President of the National Bureau shall submit to the Board of Directors, or to its Executive Committee, for their formal adoption all specific proposals for research to be instituted.

3. No research report shall be published by the National Bureau until the President has sent each member of the Board a notice that a manuscript is recommended for publication and that in the President's opinion it is suitable for publication in accordance with the principles of the National Bureau. Such notification will include an abstract or summary of the manuscript's content and a response form for use by those Directors who desire a copy of the manuscript for review. Each manuscript shall contain a summary drawing attention to the nature and treatment of the problem studied, the character of the data and their utilization in the report, and the main conclusions reached.

4. For each manuscript so submitted, a special committee of the Directors (including Directors Emeriti) shall be appointed by majority agreement of the President and Vice Presidents (or by the Executive Committee in case of inability to decide on the part of the President and Vice Presidents), consisting of three Directors selected as nearly as may be one from each general division of the Board. The names of the special manuscript committee shall be stated to each Director when notice of the proposed publication is submitted to him. It shall be the duty of each member of the special manuscript committee to read the manuscript. If each member of the manuscript committee signifies his approval within thirty days of the transmittal of the manuscript, the report may be published. If at the end of that period any member of the manuscript committee withholds his approval, the President shall then notify each member of the Board, requesting approval or disapproval of publication, and thirty days additional shall be granted for this purpose. The manuscript shall then not be published unless at least a majority of the entire Board who shall have voted on the proposal within the time fixed for the receipt of votes shall have approved.

5. No manuscript may be published, though approved by each member of the special manuscript committee, until forty-five days have elapsed from the transmittal of the report in manuscript form. The interval is allowed for the receipt of any memorandum of dissent or reservation, together with a brief statement of his reasons, that any member may wish to express; and such memorandum of dissent or reservation shall be published with the manuscript if he so desires. Publication does not, however, imply that each member of the Board has read the manuscript, or that either members of the Board in general or the special committee have passed on its validity in every detail.

6. Publications of the National Bureau issued for informational purposes concerning the work of the Bureau and its staff, or issued to inform the public of activities of Bureau staff, and volumes issued as a result of various conferences involving the National Bureau shall contain a specific disclaimer noting that such publication has not passed through the normal review procedures required in this resolution. The Executive Committee of the Board is charged with review of all such publications from time to time to ensure that they do not take on the character of formal research reports of the National Bureau, requiring formal Board approval.

7. Unless otherwise determined by the Board or exempted by the terms of paragraph 6, a copy of this resolution shall be printed in each National Bureau publication.

(Resolution adopted October 25, 1926, as revised through September 30, 1974)

Contents

Preface

This volume includes eight papers that were prepared as part of a research project by the National Bureau of Economic Research on Developing Country Debt. These papers examine other debt crises that occurred before World War II, the role of the banks during the current crisis, the effect of developed country economies on the debtors, as well as possible solutions to the debt crisis. The findings of NBER's Debt project were presented at a conference for government officials of lending and debtor countries, economists at international organizations, and representatives of banks and other private firms with interests in the debtor countries. The conference was held in Washington, D.C., from 21 through 23 September 1987.

In addition to the papers in this volume, the project also included case studies of Argentina, Bolivia, Brazil, Indonesia, Mexico, the Philippines, South Korea, and Turkey. These country studies will be published in two additional volumes. A fourth book will contain shorter and slightly less technical summaries of the eight papers in this volume and the eight country studies.

We would like to thank the Agency for International Development, The Ford Foundation, Mr. David Rockefeller, the Rockefeller Brothers Fund, and The Tinker Foundation for financial support of this work. The success of the project also depended on the efforts of Deborah Mankiw, Yasuko MacDougall, Kirsten Foss Davis, Ilana Hardesty, Robert Allison, and Mark Fitz-Patrick.

Jeffrey D. Sachs

1   Introduction

Jeffrey D. Sachs

1.1   Introduction

The Project on Developing Country Debt undertaken by the National Bureau of Economic Research in the past two years seeks to provide a detailed analysis of the ongoing developing country debt crisis. The focus is on the middle-income developing countries, particularly those in Latin America and East Asia, though many lessons of the study should apply as well to the poorer debtor countries in sub-Saharan Africa.

The urgency of the NBER study should be self-evident. For dozens of developing countries, the financial upheavals of the 1980s have set back economic development by a decade or more. Poverty has intensified in much of the developing world as countries have struggled under an enormous external debt burden. Moreover, the world financial system has been disrupted by the prospect of widespread defaults on the foreign debts of the developing world. More than six years after the onset of the crisis, almost all of the debtor countries are still unable to borrow in the international capital markets on normal market terms.

Table 1.1 shows several aspects of the ecomomic crisis of the major debtor countries in recent years. Since the dramatic outbreak of the crisis in 1982, economic growth has slowed sharply or has been negative. Per capita incomes in the most indebted countries are still generally well below the levels of 1980. And ominously, debt-export ratios are higher today than at the beginning of the crisis.

Future growth prospects are clouded by a sharp drop in the share of capital formation in GDP. At the same time, inflation has risen to remarkable levels throughout Latin America. The mechanisms behind the epidemic of high inflations are basically the same that caused the

1

Table 1.1   The Economic Crisis in the Heavily Indebted Countries

	Average 1969–78	1979	1980	1981	1982	1983	1984	1985	1986
Per capita GDP (annual change)	3.6	3.6	2.6	-1.6	-2.7	-5.5	-0.1	0.9	1.4
Inflation (annual rate)	28.5	40.8	47.4	53.2	57.7	90.8	116.4	126.9	76.2
Gross capital formation (percent of GDP)	n.a.	24.9	24.7	24.5	22.3	18.2	17.4	16.5	16.8
Debt-export ratio	n.a.	182.3	167.1	201.4	269.8	289.7	272.1	284.2	337.9

Source: All data refer to the fifteen heavily indebted countries: Argentina, Bolivia, Brazil, Chile, Columbia, Ivory Coast, Ecuador, Mexico, Morocco, Nigeria, Peru, Philippines, Uruguay, Venezuela, Yugoslavia. Data are from the IMF *World Economic Outlook*, April 1987. Inflation refers to the consumer price index.

n.a. = not available.

hyperinflations in Central Europe after World War I, with foreign debts now playing the role that reparations payments played in the post-World War I crisis.

The NBER Project analyzes the crisis from two perspectives, that of the individual debtor country, and the international financial system as a whole. This volume contains the studies of the international financial system as a whole. The country studies are contained in two companion volumes, *Developing Country Debt and Economic Performance: Country Studies* (volumes 2 and 3). A major goal of the country studies is to understand why some countries, such as Argentina or Mexico, succumbed to a serious crisis, while others, such as Indonesia or Korea, did not. Another important goal is to understand why most of the debtor countries have been unable to overcome the crisis despite many years of harsh economic adjustments. To analyze such questions, the NBER commissioned eight detailed country monographs, covering four countries in Latin America and four countries in the Middle East and East Asia. Each study was prepared by a team of two authors, a U.S.-based researcher and an economist from the country under study: Argentina, by Rudiger Dornbusch and Juan Carlos de Pablo; Bolivia, by Juan Antonio Morales and Jeffrey D. Sachs; Brazil, by Eliana A. Cardoso and Albert Fishlow; Mexico, by Edward F. Buffie, with the assistance of Allen Sangines Krause; Indonesia, by Wing Thye Woo and Anwar Nasution; the Philippines, by Robert S. Dohner and Ponciano Intal, Jr.; South Korea, by Susan M. Collins and Won-Am Park; and Turkey, by Merih Celâsun and Dani Rodrik.

The individual country studies can answer only some of the questions about the crisis, since global factors have undoubtedly been key to many of the developments in the past few years. Indeed, as Lindert and Morton stress in their contribution to this volume, international debt crises have been a recurrent part of the international financial landscape for at least 175 years, in the 1820s, 1870s, 1890s, 1930s, and 1980s. It is important to understand the fundamental properties of the international macroeconomy and global financial markets which have contributed to this repeated instability.

The NBER studies in this volume cover a wide range of topics. Peter Lindert and Peter Morton study the history of sovereign debt from 1850 until the present, offering us a sweeping historical panorama and several important new findings. Perhaps most important is their conclusion that some form of debt relief (i.e., a renegotiation of the foreign debt that reduces the present value of the repayment stream below the original contractual level) has been a central feature of most "workouts" of past debt crises. Barry Eichengreen reviews in detail the history of U.S. capital market lending to sovereign borrowers in the

20th century, and arrives at several conclusions in accord with Lindert and Morton.

Three papers in this volume take up the issues of adjustment problems in the debtor countries. As the country case studies amply document, adjustment to the debt crisis in the 1980s has been anything but smooth! Six years after the onset of the crisis, inflation in Latin America was averaging more than 150 percent per year, and no major debtor country had restored normal access to borrowing on the international capital markets. The papers by Sebastian Edwards, Jeffrey Sachs, and Stephan Haggard and Robert Kaufman, all complement the country studies in shedding some light on the adjustment problems of the debtor countries.

Edwards emphasizes the profound difficulties of combining macro-economic policies (e.g., reductions in the public-sector deficit) with structural policies (e.g., tariff reductions). Sachs emphasizes the limitations in IMF and World Bank conditionality, and argues that debt relief should play an important role in many of the programs supervised by the international institutions. Haggard and Kaufman focus on the *political* requirements for successful stabilization, and suggest that the political design of adjustment programs is as important as their economic design.

The final three papers in this volume focus on various global aspects of the problem. Paul Krugman examines the relationship of debtor governments and their private bank creditors. Rudiger Dornbusch discusses the linkages of industrial country macroeconomic policies and debtor country economic performance. Stanley Fischer, in the final paper of the volume, examines various proposals for global solutions to the debt crisis.

1.1.1   The Creditor and Debtor Interpretations of the Debt Crisis

The international debt crisis has already given rise to many oversimplified interpretations, most of which can be dismissed on the basis of the studies in the NBER project. Simple ideas abound on this topic, often because they serve particular vested interests. Creditors want to blame the crisis on the policy mistakes of the debtor governments. Debtors want to blame the crisis on the macroeconomic and trade policies of the creditor governments. Both sides are keen to neglect the more nuanced historical record.

The mainstream creditor interpretation (as expressed variously by the United States government, the international institutions, and the commercial banks) can be summarized as follows. The debt crisis emerged largely because of the policy mistakes of the debtor governments. Loans were wasted by inefficient state enterprises, or were squandered in capital flight. "Successful" governments were those like

South Korea, which pursued free-market economic policies, while unsuccessful governments smothered economic growth with government regulations. With sufficient economic reforms, including trade liberalization and an encouragement of foreign direct investment, the debtor countries will be able to grow out of the current crisis.

Most creditors have also maintained that the only proper way to manage the current crisis is to insist that the debtor governments honor their debts in full, since to do otherwise would threaten the international financial system. To grant debt relief to the debtors, they also suggest, would hurt the debtors more than it would help them, because it would cut the debtors off from future borrowing from the world financial markets, and thereby hinder their economic growth.

The debtor perspective of course differs at key points. Debtor governments hold that the crisis erupted because of the rise in world interest rates, the fall in commodity prices, and the collapse of world trade at the beginning of the 1980s. They blame the macroeconomic policies of the creditor governments, particularly the U.S. fiscal policies, for many of the global shocks. Debtor governments typically downplay the role of debtor country policies in the crisis, and often state that advocates of "free market policies" are responding to the crisis by serving foreign interests (e.g., multinational firms) at the expense of domestic interests.

Many debtor governments argue that successful adjustment will require some debt relief. One reason for this pessimism is the view that attempts to honor the debt burden through increased exports would merely promote offsetting protectionist pressures in the creditor economies. Another reason is the view that the austerity required to service the debts on the original terms would generate political and economic instabilities that would be self-defeating, and ultimately detrimental to the creditors as well as to the debtors.

The evidence from the NBER study belies many of the points commonly made by both the creditors and the debtors. The NBER study offers fresh evidence on several important issues: the sources of the debt crisis (and of debt crises in the past); the patterns of economic adjustment in a debtor country after a debt crisis gets underway; the nature of bargaining between debtors and creditors; and the role for public policy in easing or eliminating the global crisis. These subjects are taken up in detail in the following sections.

1.2. Origins of the Debt Crisis

The debt crisis arose from a combination of policy actions in the debtor countries, macroeconomic shocks in the world economy, and a remarkable spurt of unrestrained bank lending during 1979–81. The "unsuccessful" adjusters (all but Indonesia and South Korea among the countries in the NBER study) fell prey to a common pattern of policy actions: chronically large budget deficits; overvalued exchange rates; and a trade regime biased against exports in general, and agriculture in particular. These policies would have hindered economic performance in most circumstances, but they provoked a deep crisis when combined with severe shocks to world interest rates, exchange rates, and commodity prices, in the early 1980s. The crisis was greatly exacerbated because for many years the commercial banks provided financial support for the bad policies of the developing countries, particularly during 1979–81, and then abruptly withdraw new credits starting in 1982.

1.2.1 The Role of Global Shocks

The importance of global macroeconomic changes in provoking the current debt crisis has been widely noted (see Sachs 1987 for a review of this issue). The growth of the Eurodollar market and the OPEC price shocks of 1973–74 put in motion a period of rapid bank lending to the developing countries. During the period 1973–79, the export proceeds of the developing countries boomed, while nominal interest rates on the loans were low, contributing to the happy state of affairs that debt-to-export ratios remained modest despite heavy borrowing by the developing countries. Indeed, for the non-oil LDCs as a whole, the debt-export ratio was lower in 1980 than in 1973, while for the western hemisphere LDCs it was only marginally higher in 1980 compared to 1973, as can be seen in the data in table 1.2.

At the end of the 1970s, therefore, the pace of international lending did not seem to pose a serious danger to the commercial banks or to the world economy. But few observers fully appreciated how much this happy state of affairs depended on nominal interest rates remaining below the growth rate of dollar exports of the borrowing countries (put another way, *real* interest rates remaining below the growth rate of *real*

Table 1.2	Debt-Export Ratios, 1973 to 1986, as a Percentage, Selected Years							
(percent)	1973	1980	1981	1982	1983	1984	1985	1986[a]
Non-oil LDCs	115.4	112.9	124.9	143.3	152.8	148.3	162.0	162.2
Western Hemisphere LDCs	176.2	178.4	207.9	273.1	290.4	275.2	296.2	331.3

Source: International Monetary Fund, *World Economic Outlook*, April 1986 and October 1986 editions.

[a]Preliminary.

exports). Even worse, almost nobody foresaw that the era of high export growth and low interest rates would come abruptly to an end at the end of the 1970s.

In the happy case that interest rates are below export growth rates, borrowers can borrow all the money needed to service their loans without suffering a rise in the debt-to-export ratio (since exports will grow faster than the debt). In other words, the borrower does not have to contribute any of its own resources to servicing its debts. Once the interest rate rises above the export growth rate, however, then the country cannot simply borrow the money to service its debts without incurring a sharply rising debt-to-export ratio. Sooner or later, the country will be cut off from new borrowing, and it will have to pay for its debt servicing out of its own national resources, i.e., by running trade surpluses vis-à-vis the rest of the world.

The remarkable fact is how abruptly the interest rate–growth rate relationship was reversed as of 1980, as shown in figure 1.1. Extremely tight monetary policies in the industrial countries, designed to fight inflation, provoked a sharp rise in interest rates, an industrial country recession, and a steep fall in the export prices and terms of trade of the developing countries. The debt crisis followed relentlessly upon the resulting rise in interest rates and the collapse in developing country export earnings. All of a sudden, all of the debt warning signs started to fly off the charts, as seen by the rapid increase in the debt-export and debt-service ratios after 1980. Commercial bank lending dried up once the debt-export ratios started to soar. Total gross bank lending to the non-oil developing countries rose by 24 percent in 1980 over 1979, 18 percent in 1981, and only 7 percent in 1982.

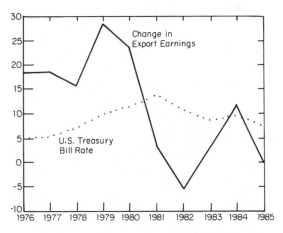

Fig. 1.1   Interest rates and annual change in non-oil export earnings

1.2.2   The Role of Bank Lending Behavior

Few observers perceived the risks of international lending as of the end of the 1970s, least of all the lenders themselves. Lindert and Morton, as well as Eichengreen, suggest that in earlier historical experiences as well, lenders lost sight of the inherent risks of cross-border lending. In the late 1970s, bankers adopted the credo of the world's leading international banker, Citicorp Chairman Walter Wriston, who justified the heavy international lending with the declaration that "countries never go bankrupt." In the mid- and late 1970s, the commercial banks were making enormous profits on their cross-border lending to the developing countries. In Citicorp's case, overall international operations accounted for 72 percent of overall earnings in 1976, with Brazil alone accounting for 13 percent of total bank earnings, compared with 28 percent for all U.S. operations! (Cited in Makin 1984, 133–34.)

The banks had the recent loan experience to back them up. As already pointed out, the combination of high export growth rates and low interest rates meant that debt-to-export ratios remained under control despite the heavy lending. There was no real evidence, of course, that the countries would be willing or able to pay back their loans, or even service them, *with their own resources,* but that did not seem to matter: new lending to repay old loans made sense in the circumstances.

One can fault the banks severely for not looking more deeply into the quality of economic management in the developing countries during this period. Few banks, apparently, were concerned with the question of whether the debtor countries would be willing and able to service their debts if debt servicing had to come out of national resources rather than out of new loans. This issue seemed to be an abstract concern, at least through the end of the 1970s.

What is truly remarkable about the bank behavior is not the lending during 1973–79, but rather the outpouring of new lending during 1980–81, even after the world macroeconomic situation had soured markedly. In table 1.3 we see the astounding fact that in a mere two years, 1980 and 1981, net bank exposure to the major debtor countries nearly doubled over the 1979 level. Thus, in the two years *after the rise in real interest rates,* the commercial banks made about as many net loans to the major debtors as during the entire period 1973–79.

This late burst of lending is all the more remarkable, and difficult to justify, in light of the enormous capital flight that was occurring at the same time, as shown in table 1.4. In the case of Argentina, of the tremendous rise during 1980 and 1981 in the overall gross debt of the country, 84 percent was offset by the outflow of private capital, according to the estimates of Cumby and Levich (1987). For Venezuela, the offset is well over 100 percent. I will discuss the origins of the capital flight in more detail below.

Table 1.3   **Net Liabilities of Countries to International Banks in the BIS Reporting Area ($ billion)**

Country	December 1979	December 1981
Argentina	5.3	16.3
Brazil	28.8	44.8
Mexico	22.5	43.4
Subtotal	56.6	104.5
Indonesia	−0.1	−1.5
Malaysia	−1.3	0.2
South Korea	7.2	13.7
Thailand	1.6	1.8
Subtotal	7.4	15.2

Source: Bank for International Settlements, "The Maturity Distribution of International Bank Lending," various issues.

Table 1.4   **Capital Flight and Change in External Debt during 1980 and 1981 for the Major Debtors**

	Capital Flight (1980 and 1981)	Change in Gross Debt	Ratio: (1)/(2)
Argentina	12.8	10.8	0.84
Brazil	19.8	1.9	0.10
Mexico	35.1	15.6	0.44
Venezuela	7.8	13.0	1.67

Source: Cumby and Levich (1987), tables in data appendix. The capital flight variable is according to the World Bank definition reported by the authors.

New market-based lending by the commercial banks to the developing countries virtually disappeared after 1982. Even where lending continued, the transfer of net resources to the country (i.e., new lending minus total debt servicing on existing debt) was almost everywhere negative: the debtor countries paid more to the commercial banks than they received in new funds. Some countries received so-called "involuntary loans" as part of financial workout packages, usually linked to an IMF program. In such involuntary lending, the banks agreed to contribute new funds on a pro rata basis, relative to their exposure at an initial date. Even in this case, however, the new lending was invariably less than the amount of debt service payments due from the country to the bank creditors, so that the net resource transfer to the country remained negative.

The heavy commercial bank lending, particularly during 1979–81, certainly created the potential for a serious international banking crisis.

As shown in table 1.5, the cross-border exposure of the U.S. money-center banks at the end of 1982 to all of the developing countries equalled nearly three times total capital, and to Latin America alone amounted to almost two times bank capital. This exposure was very highly concentrated: about three-fourths of all U.S. commercial bank lending to more than 40 LDCs was centered in just four countries— Argentina, Brazil, Mexico, and Venezuela. The usual prudential rule of limiting exposure to any single borrower to 10 percent of bank capital was also ignored. The 10 percent rule was skirted by major U.S. banks by counting all different types of public sector borrowers in one country (e.g., state enterprises, central government, etc.) as distinct borrowers, even though they were all backed by the same "full faith and credit" of the central government and therefore reflected nearly identical credit risks.

1.2.3   The Role of Debtor Country Policies

In the easy-money period of the 1970s, commercial banks did not seriously consider the policies of the debtor countries. As loans were not serviced out of the country's own resources, but rather out of fresh borrowing, the countries were never put to the test of whether their loans were well used and their economic policies sound. Nor were there many complaints about the policies of most of the debtor countries, with the exceptions of Jamaica, Peru, and Turkey, which rescheduled ahead of the rest of the other countries.

It is only with the emergence of the debt crisis itself that banks began to examine the soundness of the earlier borrowing. Which countries

Table 1.5   **U.S. Bank Assets in the Debtor Countries, Nine Major Banks**

	End-1982	Mid-1984	March 1986
Total Exposure ($ billion)			
All LDCs	83.4	84.0	75.6
Latin America	51.2	53.8	52.2
Africa	5.6	4.9	3.6
Exposure as Percentage of Bank Capital			
All LDCs	287.7	246.3	173.2
Latin America	176.5	157.8	119.7
Sub-Saharan Africa	19.3	14.3	8.1

Source: Federal Financial Institutions Examination Council, "Country Exposure Lending Survey," various statistical releases. End-1982 from statistical release of 15 October 1984; March 1986 from release of 1 August 1986. Exposures are calculated using data for "Total amounts owed to U.S. banks after adjustments for guarantees and external borrowing." Total exposures are calculated for all LDCs (OPEC, Non-oil, Latin America (Non-oil Asia, Non-oil Africa); Latin America (Non-oil Latin America plus Ecuador and Venezuela); and Africa (Non-oil Africa plus Algeria, Gabon, Libya and Nigeria).

could service their debts without a crushing blow to the domestic economy? Which countries would lack the economic or political stamina to maintain debt servicing? To some extent, of course, the answer turned on the amount of the borrowing itself relative to national income. But many other features were of crucial significance: the extent to which the debt was held by the public versus the private sector; the distribution of production between tradables and nontradables; the uses to which the earlier borrowing had been put (consumption, fixed investment, financing of private capital flight); and so forth. In all cases, these various issues depended integrally on the types of policies that the various borrowing governments had been following, and on the motivations for the foreign borrowing in the first place.

The NBER studies suggest that two fundamental dimensions of policy require emphasis: fiscal policy and trade policy. Moreover, the studies suggest that while certain patterns of policymaking were both dysfunctional and deeply rooted, the specific policies pursued during 1980–82 (after the shift in the world macroeconomic environment) were often pivotal. Did the government adjust to the changed international environment effectively, or did it continue to behave as if nothing had happened?

The differences across countries in response to the challenges of 1980–82 are striking. As Collins and Park made clear in their study of South Korea (see the country studies volumes), the South Korean government adjusted strongly to the global shocks after 1979: budget deficits were cut, the exchange rate was devalued, and a policy of heavy investment in highly capital intensive industries was scaled back. Nineteen eighty was a year of economic and political crisis, but by 1981 the economy was already readjusting to the new global environment. Indonesia and Turkey similarly adjusted early on. Indonesia had devalued substantially in 1978, which helped it greatly in the subsequent adjustment. Turkey in fact had fallen into economic crisis already by 1977–78, and political crisis soon thereafter. Strong adjustment measures, backed by the international official community, were already being set by early 1980. When a military coup intervened, the military government continued the adjustment policies that the preceeding civilian government had set in motion, and even retained as deputy prime minister Mr. Turgut Ozal, who had originated the reform effort in the previous civilian government.

The contrast with the other five countries in the NBER study could not be more stark. In Brazil, for example, when the planning minister, Mr. Mario Simonsen, began to apply budget-tightening measures in 1979, the policies were vigorously attacked as "recessionist," and Simonsen was soon replaced by another minister, Mr. Antonio Delfim Netto, whose response to the external shocks was an *acceleration* of foreign borrowing. Rather than restraining spending at the crucial moment, Brazil stepped on the accelerator, a choice that still haunts the economy today. In neighboring Bolivia, political chaos effectively blocked any coherent response to the global economic shifts. Bolivia had no less than eleven heads of state between 1978 and 1982, as the economy drifted towards hyperinflation.

In Argentina, policies went similarly awry. At almost the moment that world real interest rates began to soar, Argentina embarked on a disasterous policy of pegging the Argentine peso to the dollar, with the result of discouraging exports and encouraging capital flight and imports, and thereby contributing to an enormous bulge in foreign borrowing. In Mexico, the critical period from 1979 to 1982 was approached not with restraint and a sense of caution, but with the greatest increase in government spending in Mexico's entire history. Despite the warning signs in the world economy, the Portillo government increased government expenditure as a share of GNP from 32 percent in 1979 to an astounding 47 percent in 1982, and raised the public sector deficit to 17.6 percent of GNP in 1982.

Finally, in the Philippines, the political business cycle crashed against the international business cycle. The most significant excesses in Marcos's now legendary cronyism were being set in place as the world economic environment seriously deteriorated.

1.2.4 The Role of Fiscal Policy

Many of the policy actions in the debtor countries are not "mistakes" or technical misjudgments, but were the result of deeper political instabilities. The economies in Latin America, in particular, are deeply riven by great inequalities of income, which in turn prompt fierce political conflicts. The chronically large budget deficits in these countries are a reflection of these political conflicts. In some of the cases under study, the governments were too weak to resist the demands for spending from various highly mobilized social groups. In the most pathological cases, the political battle degenerated into a battle of "ins" versus "outs," with the ins using the apparatus of the government for narrow personal gain. The worst excesses of this sort are seen in the Philippines under Marcos, and in several Bolivian regimes in the late 1970s and early 1980s.

At the same time, the governments either could not, or chose not to, raise taxes on the economic elites. On both the spending and revenue sides, therefore, political institutions repeatedly failed to keep the demands for government spending in line with the government's limited tax collections. Foreign borrowing in the 1970s and early 1980s provided a short-term way out of these political dilemmas, by allowing governments to finance large budget deficits without incurring high inflationary costs in the short term. Simply put, the governments could borrow from abroad, rather than face the monetary consequences of borrowing directly from the central bank. Once the net capital inflows ceased in the early 1980s, and governments had to start making net payments abroad, the inflationary consequences emerged, as governments were not able to reduce expenditures and raise revenues sufficiently in response to the shift from net inflows of foreign capital to net outflows. They instead turned to printing money to make up the shortfall in foreign lending.

One of the most talked about, and misunderstood, phenomena in the debt crisis is that of "capital flight." Capital flight refers to the accumulation of foreign assets by the private sector of an economy, often at the same time that the public sector is incurring sharply rising external debts. As an example, while the Mexican government accumulated debts of approximately $75 billion to foreign creditors, the Mexican private sector accumulated claims abroad in the amount of perhaps $40 billion. This phenomenon of heavy public debts and large private assets is mainly a reflection of the loose fiscal policies that we have been emphasizing.

The predominant mechanics of capital flight in the late 1970s and early 1980s were as follows: Suppose that the government increases transfer payments to the private economy. In order to finance these transfer payments, it borrows from the central bank. The central bank financing causes an incipient rise in the money supply as the government spends the borrowed funds. The higher money balances lead to a weakening of the exchange rate as the private sector, flush with cash, attempts to convert some of the increased transfers into foreign currency. This creates the tendency towards higher inflation (the weakening of the currency would tend to raise the domestic prices of imports, exports, and import-competing goods). In order to stabilize the price level, the central bank keeps the exchange rate from depreciating by selling foreign exchange in return for the domestic currency (the excess money balances are thereby drained from the economy). The central bank runs down its reserves, and the private sector increases its foreign asset holdings.

To maintain an adequate level of resources, the central bank itself might then turn to world capital markets for a foreign loan to replenish its reserves. Over time, the result would be the growing foreign debt of the central bank, and growing private sector claims held in the form of foreign currency (and perhaps actually held abroad). The phenomenon is labelled "capital flight," but is simply the consequence of (1) large fiscal deficits, and (2) an anti-inflationary policy of pegging the nominal exchange rate.

As noted below, the fiscal consequences of the foreign borrowing in the 1970s were exacerbated by a common pattern of policy actions after the debt crisis erupted. When the financial crisis hit in 1981 and

1982, many *private* firms that had borrowed heavily from abroad were put into financial distress. In country after country, governments took over the private debt on favorable terms for the private sector firms, or subsidized the private debt service payments, in order to bail out the private firms. This "socialization" of the private debt resulted in a significant increase in the *fiscal* burden of the nation's foreign debt.

1.2.5   The Trade Regime

To the extent that foreign borrowing finances efficient investment in an economy above the level that would otherwise be financed with domestic savings, the foreign borrowing could well be prudent and welfare enhancing. The key condition is that the investment project yield a return that is above the world cost of capital, when the project's costs and returns are measured at appropriate shadow prices (i.e., at prices that take into account the distortions in incentives in the borrowing economy). Of course, much of the heavy foreign borrowing did not finance investment at all. It was used, instead, to finance current consumption spending as well as capital flight by the private sector.

It is well known from trade theory that strongly protectionist policies drive an important wedge between market prices and shadow prices, and thereby tend to lead to important distortions in the allocation of investment spending. In particular, investment is allocated too heavily towards nontradables and import-competing goods, and too little towards exportables. The result is that investments that may be profitable at market prices may be unprofitable at appropriate shadow values. Brecher and Díaz-Alejandro (1977), among others, demonstrated that foreign borrowing to support such misallocated investment is almost surely welfare worsening.

There is considerable evidence from the studies of Bhagwati (1978), Krueger (1978), Balassa (1984), Sachs (1985), and others, that economies with heavily protectionist trade regimes fare less well in overall economic performance than economies with more balanced trade regimes. The superior performance of so-called "outward-oriented" regimes appears to involve not only a better allocation of investment spending along the lines just suggested, but also other factors that are more difficult to quantify (such as improved technology transfer from abroad, higher savings rates, more market competition, and a tendency towards better exchange rate management).

The country studies in the NBER project support earlier findings on the superiority of outward-oriented regimes. By far the most successful performer in the NBER study is South Korea, the quintessential outward-oriented economy. Outward-orientation is generally measured by the overall incentives of the trade regime on the production of exportables relative to import-competing goods. The evidence described by Collins and Park suggests that the overall effect of trade incentives in Korea is to favor exportables, as opposed to the trade regimes in Latin America which have typically been anti-export (and favorable to import-competing sectors). As shown by Woo and Nasution, the Indonesian trade regime under Soeharto seems to lie between the outward orientation of the South Korean case, and the inward orientation of the Latin American cases. In Turkey, the trade regime became much more outward oriented during the 1980s.

In addition to tariffs and quotas, the management of the nominal exchange rate can have an important bearing on the relative profitability of exports versus import-competing goods. When the nominal exchange rate is overvalued, to the extent that the central bank *rations* the sale of foreign exchange for current transactions, the result is typically an implicit tax on exports, even if no tariffs or trade quotas are imposed. A black market for foreign exchange results from the rationing, allowing a rise in the domestic price of import-competing goods (which at the margin are imported at the black market rate). Exporters, on the other hand, typically must surrender exchange at the overvalued official rate. The typical result of the foreign exchange rationing, therefore, is to lower the relative price of exports, and to bias production away from the export sector.

As shown in Sachs (1985), and confirmed again by the country studies, the East Asian economies (South Korea and Indonesia in the NBER sample) never allowed a substantial black market premium to develop during the 1970s and 1980s, while the Latin American economies all had phases of substantial black market premia on their currencies.

Another dimension of policy is the balance of incentives between tradables as a whole relative to nontradables (e.g., construction and services). Even when foreign exchange is not rationed, so that a black market premium does not arise, the failure to devalue the nominal exchange rate in line with domestic inflation can result in the fall in tradables prices relative to nontradables prices, with the result that production of both exportables and import-competing goods (at least those import-competing goods not protected by quotas), are hurt relative to the production of nontradables. The Korean authorities clearly managed the nominal exchange rate throughout the 1970s and 1980s with a close eye on maintaining a rough constancy in the price of tradables relative to nontradables. Indonesia, as well, stands out as a rare case in which devaluations of the exchange rate (in 1978, 1983, and 1986) were undertaken explicitly in order to keep tradables goods in line with rising nontradables goods prices, even before a balance of payments crisis occurred.

Turkey provides a particularly interesting example regarding the trade regime, as documented by Celâsun and Rodrik. During the 1970s, Turkey was afflicted by a chronically overvalued exchange rate (with a large black market premium), import rationing, and an overall anti-export bias. After the onset of the debt crisis at the end of the 1970s, the government moved to a strategy of export-led growth. This policy was based initially on a significant depreciation of the nominal exchange rate, which succeeded in raising the relative price of tradables, and of nearly unifying the black market and official exchange rate. Later, during the 1980s there was a progressive liberalization of the trading system. The results were impressive: nontraditional export growth was rapid, and provided the basis for overall growth of the economy in the 1980s. In their paper, Celâsun and Rodrik discuss at some length the contribution of the Turkish policy changes versus other special factors (e.g., the Iran-Iraq war) in promoting the export boom.

As already noted, the Latin American regimes have all been characterized by a considerable degree of import protection and general anti-export bias. In many cases, the exchange rate was allowed to become severely overvalued in real terms (with a considerable black market premium on foreign exchange), with the exchange rate moved only in the midst of an extreme balance of payments crisis. As with the budget, the exchange rate policy appears to reflect political conditions in Latin America as much as technical mistakes. The chronically overvalued exchange rate favors urban workers and the protected manufacturing sector at the expense of the agricultural sector, which has been politically weak in most countries since the Great Depression.

There are some additional lessons regarding the trade regime that are raised by the country studies. Contrary to a common view, outward orientation in the NBER sample of countries is not at all the same thing as a free-market trade policy (see Sachs 1987 for a further elaboration of this distinction in the experience of the East Asian economies). The outward-oriented countries in the study, South Korea, Indonesia (to some degree), and Turkey in the 1980s, all had successful export growth with continued import restrictions and heavy government involvement in managing trade. The key instruments in stimulating exports was not import liberalization, but rather (1) a realistic and unified exchange rate; (2) heavy investment in the exporting sectors, often spurred by government subsidies and direct credit allocations; and (3) an array of additional financial incentives for exporters.

More generally, the South Korean case belies the simple position often taken by the United States government and the IMF and World Bank, that "small" government, as opposed to effective government, is the key to good economic performance. As the study by Collins and Park makes clear, the government of South Korea played a leading role in organizing economic development. The government was sufficiently powerful, however, to be able to generate significant budget surpluses to finance domestic investment, and to pursue a long-term policy of export-led growth. Also, given Korea's relatively equal distribution of income (the result in large part of extensive land reform in the late 1940s and early 1950s), the government was able to devote its attention to matters of efficiency rather than redistribution.

Another interesting aspect of the experience of South Korea and Turkey is the blurring of the distinction over time between import-competing firms and exporting firms. It is notable that in both countries much of the export boom of the 1980s was based on investments during the 1970s in heavily protected industries, which became profitable for exports in the 1980s. Moreover, at the time that the investments were made, they were decried by economists as an inefficient allocation of investment spending, with the incorrect argument (in hindsight) that such industries could not be expected to export in the foreseeable future. As it turned out, productivity improvements together with a modest depreciation of the real exchange rate and an export-promoting regulatory environment were enough to make these sectors profitable for export in the 1980s.

This finding is both good news and bad news for those who are hoping for a major export boom in the Latin American debtor countries. On the one hand, formerly protected industries can probably become exporting industries with only moderate changes in the real exchange rate. On the other hand, export promotion did not come out of thin air in South Korea and Turkey, but rather out of heavy investment expenditure during the 1970s. Since the burden of debt servicing is now causing a major drain on investment spending in the heavily indebted countries, the base for future export promotion is jeopardized. The authors of the studies for Argentina, Bolivia, Brazil, and Mexico all highlight this dangerous situation with regard to current investment spending.

1.3 Adjustment to the Debt Crisis

The NBER case studies examined in great detail the process of adjustment once a debt crisis begins. The patterns of adjustment in the eight countries under study certainly belie the easy optimism of the creditor community in the years after 1982. An external debt crisis sets in motion a process of economic deterioration that is extremely difficult to limit in the short term. Early optimistic forecasts of a rapid recovery in the debtor countries, such as by Cline (1984) or by Rimmer DeVries, relied on models that projected debtor country performance purely on the basis of external variables (e.g., world growth, interest rates, etc.). These studies entirely neglected the internal economic disarray in the debtor countries that is caused by a sudden cutoff in foreign lending, combined with a sharp fall in commodities prices and a sharp rise in world interest rates.

The creditor community forecast a relatively smooth transition for economies that fell into debt crisis. Since the inflow of net capital declined sharply after 1982, the debtor economies had to shift from a position of current account deficits (i.e., net foreign borrowing) to a position closer to current account balance. Initially, it was felt, this would be brought about through a reduction of imports; subsequently, exports would grow over time in line with the growth in the markets in the industrial economies. The debtor economies would shift smoothly to a trajectory of export-led growth. Along this path, exports would exceed imports to the extent necessary to finance interest servicing on the foreign debt.

According to forecasting models such as Cline's (1984), the success of this strategy depended centrally on the external variables facing the debtor country: industrial country growth, world commodity prices, and world interest rates. Assuming an adequate trajectory for these variables (3 percent OECD growth, gently rising commodities prices, and gently declining world real interest rates), the recovery would take care of itself. Economic growth and world interest rates turned out to be close to Cline's estimates, though the economic recovery in the debtor nations did not materialize. Part of the discrepancy in Cline's forecast and the actual historical outcomes may have resulted from the decline in commodities prices after 1984, but a much larger part of the failure of Cline's model resulted from his neglect of the internal economic effects of an external debt crisis.

Remember that the debtor economies were hit by three simultaneous shocks: a cutoff in lending, a rise in world interest rates, and a fall in most commodities prices. The cutoff in new lending required that the current account balance move from deficit to near balance, and that the trade balance move from deficit to surplus (with the surplus required to finance the sharply higher interest payments on the foreign debt). Cline stressed the required adjustment in trade flows, but not the equivalent required shifts in savings and investment. Since the net foreign capital inflows before 1982 were financing domestic investment in excess of domestic savings, the cutoff in lending required a fall in investment relative to savings. As was shown in table 1.1, the common pattern was a sharp fall in the national investment rate after 1982. This fall in investment expenditure was bound to have deleterious effects on future growth prospects.

The cutoff in lending had particularly destabilizing effects since most of the foreign funds had been financing government deficits. All of a sudden, governments had to start making significant net resource transfers abroad. The sudden shift *in the public sector* from positive to negative net resource transfers is shown in table 1.6, and is most dramatic for Argentina, Bolivia, and Mexico. The shift for Brazil is delayed until 1985–86, as is the case in Indonesia and the Philippines. (Note that the shifts in net transfers would tend to be higher if short-term debt were also included in the calculations.) Governments were therefore required to cut their non-interest deficits sharply, or to shift the method of their finance. Most of the governments undertook harsh cuts in public sector investment, but dramatic as those cuts were, they were insufficient to eliminate the financing gap left over by the shift from net capital inflows to net capital outflows.

Governments shifted to new forms of financing. Increased domestic bond finance tended to raise real interest rates substantially, while domestic money finance tended to raise inflation. Usually, governments struggled with some combination of lower public-sector investment, higher internal real interest rates, and higher inflation. These adverse developments often undermined the fiscal situation even further. Higher inflation reduced the real value of tax collections, while higher real interest rates increased the burden of servicing the stock of internal public debt. As recessions developed in the debtor countries, under the weight of higher real interest rates, reduced commodities prices, and falling public spending, the tax base fell in line with shrinking national income.

By 1987, as a result of a pandemic fiscal crisis, very high inflation was deeply entrenched in the major debtor countries in Latin America. In Argentina, Brazil, Mexico, and Peru, inflation was well into the

Table 1.6   **Net Resource Transfers to the Public Sector (medium- and long-term debt, public and publicly guaranteed)**

	Averages for period, percentage of GNP:		
Country	1981–82	1983–84	1985–86
Argentina	2.2	−1.5	0.1
Bolivia	0.0	−5.1	0.6
Brazil	0.2	0.8	−2.2
Mexico	1.8	−3.5	−0.8
Indonesia	1.4	1.9	−0.4
Philippines	2.0	2.0	−0.6
South Korea	1.3	0.7	−1.6
Turkey	0.0	−0.4	−0.6

Sources: Net resource transfers are defined as net loans minus interest payments, on medium- and long-term debt on public and publicly guaranteed debt. Data are from the World Bank, *World Debt Tables, 1987–88,* and earlier for 1979–81. GNP data are from the IMF, *International Financial Statistics Yearbook, 1987.* Note that the shift from positive to negative net transfers would tend to be even larger if short-term debt were included in the calculations.

triple-digit levels, as shown in table 1.7. In Bolivia, a hyperinflation during 1984–85 was brought under control, in part through a suspension of interest servicing on the foreign bank debts of the Bolivian government. Even countries that had traditionally maintained very low inflation rates, such as Venezuela, were suffering with inflation many times the country's norm.

The adverse effects of the cutoff in lending were greatly exacerbated by the simultaneous deterioration in the terms of trade for most of the debtor countries. It *cannot* be claimed, as some have tried, that the commodity price decline was the major cause of the debt crisis, since some countries such as Bolivia and Mexico fell into crisis even though commodity prices were strong by historical standards. Nonetheless, for almost all countries, prices for commodity exports fell in real terms after 1981, and thus exacerbated the capital market shocks. The decline in export prices lowered national income, and further squeezed government revenues, since the revenue base in most of the debtor countries was either directly or indirectly tied to commodity exports (directly through exports by state enterprises, as in Bolivia and Mexico; indirectly through export taxes, as in Argentina).

A successful strategy of debt servicing with growth requires the development of new exports. In general, however, major new export sectors require heavy investment. A devaluation can sometimes produce a rapid increase in exports (as happened in South Korea and Turkey after 1980, and Brazil after 1983), but only if there is substantial excess capacity resulting from earlier investments (or if there is a sharp domestic recession, which may free up domestic capacity for export

Table 1.7   **Inflation Rates, 1985–87, Selected Latin American Debtor Countries**

Country	Inflation Rate[a]		
	1985	1986	1987[b]
Argentina	385.4	81.9	175.0
Bolivia	8,170.5	66.0	10.5[c]
Brazil	228.0	58.4	366.0
Ecuador	24.4	27.3	30.6
Mexico	63.7	105.7	159.2
Peru	158.3	62.9	114.5
Venezuela	5.7	12.3	36.1

Source: Economic Commission for Latin America and the Caribbean (ECLAC), "La evolucion economica en America Latina en 1987," January 1988 (Santiago, Chile).
[a]Consumer Price Index, variations of December over December of previous year.
[b]Preliminary.
[c]November to November.

if the country produces tradables that are consumed domestically). Also, increasing the capacity of export industries often requires both public and private investment. New export sectors generally require new infrastructure in transport, communications, and perhaps port facilities, that usually are in the domain of public investment. Unfortunately, public sector investment has been among the hardest hit areas of government expenditure in the crisis countries of Argentina, Bolivia, Brazil, Mexico, and the Philippines.

1.3.1   Further Adverse Feedbacks in Adjusting to the Crisis

Adjustment to the external shocks has required enormous relative price changes within the debtor economies, but contrary to simple theory, those relative price changes have often intensified the crisis itself—at least in the short term. The inevitable effect of the cutoff in foreign lending, higher world interest rates, and adverse commodity price shocks, was a significant decline in domestic demand in the debtor economies, and therefore a sharp fall in the price of nontradable goods relative to tradable goods (i.e., a sharp depreciation of the real exchange rate, defined as the price of tradables relative to nontradables). This rapid shift against nontradables is, in principle, the motive force behind the desired shift in resources to tradables production. In practice, however, the rapid collapse of nontradables production had several highly deleterious effects in the economies under study, that in fact may have impeded the longer term reallocation of resources.

Most important, the collapse of nontradables prices led to financial distress for much of the nontradables sector. Not only did the profitability of nontradables production suffer when the real exchange rate depreciated, but nontradables firms that had incurred dollar-denominated debts found themselves unable to service their debts (the decline in the relative price of nontradables meant that nontradables output prices failed to keep pace with the rising cost of foreign exchange, which has to be purchased to service the debts). In many cases, the domestic commercial banks had borrowed internationally and then re-lent the borrowed funds in dollar-denominated loans in the domestic capital markets to firms in the nontradables sector. When firms in the nontradables sector could not pay back their debts, much of the banking system was put in jeopardy in Argentina, Bolivia, and Mexico. Note that firms in the tradables sector were typically better prepared to service their dollar-denominated debts, since tradables output prices moved in tandem with the price of foreign exchange.

In turn, the collapse of the banking system disrupted financial intermediation more generally. With banks at risk, domestic residents demanded a significant risk premium over foreign interest rates in order to maintain funds in the national banking system. Several governments in Latin America were forced to take over many banks directly, or at least to take over the bad loans of much of the banking system. With many large conglomerates (known as *grupos* in Latin America) in financial distress, even the export-sector parts of the conglomerates were unable to attract new credits. (See Galbis 1987 for a further discussion of the role of the *grupos* in the Latin American financial system.)

Note that the central government faced the same problems as an overindebted firm in the nontradables sector. Since the public-sector debts were heavily dollar-denominated, while much of the tax base was effectively linked to nontradables production, the shift in the terms of trade against nontradables tended to exacerbate the fiscal deficits. Put another way, the domestic currency value of the government's external debt rose sharply relative to the domestic currency value of the government's tax revenues. Thus, in Brazil, for example, what looked like a moderate fiscal burden of foreign debt suddenly became enormous after the real exchange rate depreciations during 1980–82.

Once a government's fiscal situation has seriously deteriorated, a fiscal crisis can become self-fulfilling, as argued recently by Guillermo Calvo (1987). The fear of high future inflation, for example, can raise nominal interest rates, and thereby raise the interest costs for the government. Higher interest costs in turn widen the fiscal deficit and make inevitable the high future inflation. This kind of adverse feedback has apparently contributed to the sustained high interest rates in many of the debtor countries in recent years.

Despite the centrality of the public-sector budget in the origin and development of the crisis, there are profound difficulties in measuring and forecasting the fiscal position. Even the IMF auditing of the fiscal accounts, as recorded in the IMF's *Government Finance Statistics,* are inadequate to the task.

There are several kinds of measurement problems, many with economic significance. First, actions with fiscal consequences (e.g., actions that increase the public debt or the money supply) are made not only by the central government, but also by regional governments, parastatal enterprises, development banks, and the central bank. Often, the finance minister has little ability to measure, much less control, the consolidated public sector accounts. In most of the countries under study, the various governmental entities outside of central government can gain direct access to the central bank, or can get government guarantees for foreign borrowing, without the authorization of the finance minister.

Another problem is that private-sector obligations often quickly become public-sector obligations when a financial crisis hits, a point that we have already noted several times. Domestic firms cry for bailouts, and foreign creditors often insist as well that the central government make good on the private-sector debts. The government takeover of the debt can be partially disguised (or at least hard to measure) if the takeover comes in the form of special exchange rates for debt repayments, subsidized credits, or other off-budget means of bailing out private debtors.

The net result of this fiscal complexity is that many countries are forced to rely heavily on inflationary finance even when the measured central government budget seems close to balance. Cardoso and Fishlow discuss, for example, the data problems in Brazil, where several years of triple-digit inflation were accompanied by measured deficits near zero. The small measured deficits led some to conclude that the inflation was purely an "inertial" phenomenon. This view was tested in the ill-fated Cruzado Plan, which attempted to use a wage–price–exchange rate freeze to break the inertia. After the collapse of the Cruzado Plan, most observers now concede that large fiscal deficits are the driving force of the high Brazilian inflation.

1.4   Renegotiating the Foreign Debt

The historical record, and the country experience, speak strongly on another point. To get out of a debt crisis, countries have almost always required a sustained period of time in which the debt-servicing burden is sharply reduced or eliminated. This financial "time out" has come about through a combination of a negotiated reduction of payments (as in the case of Indonesia during 1966–71), a substantial increase in official lending (as in the case of Turkey during 1979–81), or a unilateral suspension of debt-servicing payments (as in the case of Bolivian commercial bank debt, 1986–87). In recent years, most countries have not been able to achieve a significant "time out" through conventional negotiations. The Turkish bailout in 1979–81, for example, is a key exception that proves the rule. The generous official lending to Turkey during 1979–81 came mainly because of Turkey's geopolitical significance as a NATO ally on Iran's border, rather than as the result of conventional debtor country negotiations.

The NBER historical studies also make clear that debt relief has played an important role in the resolution of earlier crises. Relief has come in many forms (e.g., debt repurchases at a discount and conversions of debt into new debts with a lower servicing burden) that might prove to be relevant in the present circumstances. The studies by Lindert and Morton, and Eichengreen, both demonstrate that previous debt crises have usually ended in some forgiveness. A compromise is typically reached in which the debtors service some, but not all, of the debt that is due. *A partial writedown of the debt is the norm, not the exception.* In the past, the compromise was typically reached as the result of bilateral negotiations between debtors and creditors. Lindert and Morton suggest that the involvement in the 1980s of third parties (mainly the creditor governments and the international financial institutions) has hindered the effective (though often messy) process for arriving at a solution to excessive debt.

The creditor view that debt relief would be harmful even for the recipient debtor countries, because these countries would be closed out of capital markets for many years in the future, is not supported by the historical experience. Both Lindert and Morton, and Eichengreen, find that countries that have achieved partial debt relief have not lost access to the markets to any greater extent than countries that continue to pay their debts. In the aftermath of global debt crises, neither "good" debtors nor "bad" debtors have been able to borrow. To quote Lindert and Morton,

> Defaulting debtors were not consistently punished. Only a few cases of countries trying to default in visible isolation led to direct sanctions and discriminatory denial of future credit. Most of the defaults occurred in the worldwide crises of the 1930s—and possible the 1980s— when uncooperative debtors suffered no more than cooperative ones.

Eichengreen similarly concludes that, "If there were costs of default, they did not take the form of differential credit-market access in the first postwar decade."

History offers many clear examples why. Argentina, for example, was the only country in South America to service the federal debt in the 1930s, under terms laid down by onerous treaties with Great Britain. The nationalist backlash against foreign influence helped to sweep Peron into power. Peron's populist policies more than undid any beneficial reputational effects that Argentina might have garnered from its debt repayments in the 1930s.

1.4.1 Debt Management during 1982–87

The management of the crisis since 1982 has so far differed from the historical experience, at least in the sense that negotiated debt relief has so far played little role in the resolution of the crisis. Indeed, because of creditor government fears over the possibility of an international banking crisis, the whole thrust of creditor government policies since the crisis began has been to *avoid* debt relief, by pressuring the debtor countries to remain current on their interest servicing. (See Sachs 1986 for an elaboration of this interpretation of creditor government policies.)

The standard form of debt management was set in the aftermath of the Mexican crisis in mid-1982. The events in Mexico prompted strong and almost immediate actions in support of Mexico from the official financial community, under the leadership of the United States. Within days of Mexico's announcement that it would be unable to meet its debt-servicing obligations, the U.S. government arranged for several forms of emergency official finance. On the other hand, the United States pressed hard on Mexico to maintain interest servicing to the commercial banks. In November 1982 an agreement was reached between Mexico and the IMF.

One novelty of the Mexican agreement was to link the IMF financing with new "concerted" lending from Mexico's bank creditors. The IMF declared that it would put new money into Mexico only if the existing bank creditors also increased their loan exposure. The requisite agreement with the commercial banks (involving a loan of $5 billion, which covered a portion of Mexico's interest costs in 1983) took effect in early 1983. Additionally, the Mexican debt was rescheduled. Crucially, while the rescheduling called for a postponement of repayments of principal, the rescheduling also provided for *the continued and timely payments of all interest due.* In fact, the spread over LIBOR (The London interbank offer rate for dollar deposits) on Mexican debt was increased in the agreement, so that in present-value terms, there was no sacrifice by the banks in the debt-rescheduling process.

The Mexican agreement was quickly improvised, but it nevertheless became the norm for the dozens of reschedulings that followed. Like the Mexican program, virtually all of the debt restructurings have had the following characteristics:

1. The IMF has made high-conditionality loans to the debtor government, but such loans have been made contingent on a rescheduling agreement between the country and the commercial bank creditors.
2. The commercial banks have rescheduled existing claims, by stretching out interest payments, but without reducing the contractual present value of repayments.
3. The debtor countries have agreed to maintain timely servicing of interest payments on all commercial bank loans.
4. The banks have made their reschedulings contingent on an IMF agreement being in place.
5. The official creditors have rescheduled their claims in the Paris Club setting, and have also made such reschedulings contingent on an IMF agreement.

In the original conception of the debt management strategy, the concerted lending was to play a key role in guaranteeing that countries receive an adequate amount of international financing in order to stabilize and recover. In fact, after 1984, the amounts of concerted lending dropped off sharply. Moreover, as shown in table 1.8, only the *largest* debtors, with the greatest bargaining power vis-à-vis the commercial banks, have been able to obtain concerted loans with any regularity. In the table, Sachs and Huizinga (1987) measure the size of concerted loans in a given year as a proportion of disbursed debt at the end of the preceeding year. On average, this ratio is far higher for the large debtors (Argentina, Brazil, Chile, and Mexico) than for the rest of the countries. Indeed, the fifteen smallest debtors in the table had 3.4 percent of the debt at the end of 1983, but received only 0.3 percent of the concerted loans during 1984–86.

We should stress as well that the whole notion of "new" money in the concerted-lending agreements is misleading, in the sense that most "new money" packages after 1982 have involved considerably less in new loans than was due to the same creditors in interest payments. Thus, even when Mexico or Argentina gets a new concerted loan, the check is still written by the country to the creditors, since the new loan only covers a fraction of the interest that is due to the creditors. The fact of negative net resource transfers points up one of the fallacies in a popular argument as to why debtor countries should not default. It is sometimes said that if a country defaults, it will not be able to attract new bank money. This is obviously not a major concern to a debtor country if the reduction in interest payments achieved by default systematically exceeds the amounts of new money that the country is able to borrow by not defaulting.

1.4.2   The Default Decision

It remains to ask why the debtor countries have by and large continued to service their debts fully in the 1980s, despite the fact that this has resulted in large net resource transfers to the creditors, at considerable economic cost to the debtor countries. In part, the answer may be simply one of time. In the first years of the crisis, most countries accepted the creditors' arguments that the crisis could be quickly resolved. As that has not come to pass, more and more countries are taking unilateral actions with respect to debt servicing. By the end of 1987, several Latin American countries had unilaterally suspended at least part of the interest servicing of the debt, including Bolivia, Brazil, Costa Rica, Dominican Republic, Ecuador, Honduras, Nicaragua, Panama, and Peru.

Another aspect of the debt servicing policies involves the balance of power between debtors and creditors. Debtor governments fear the retaliation of the commercial banks, especially in the form of a cutoff in trade credits. In fact, many of the countries that have suspended interest payments in recent years (e.g., Brazil, Ecuador, and Peru), have been able to maintain their trade credit lines, though often at the cost of a sharply higher risk premium on the short-term borrowing.

Table 1.8   **Medium-Term Concerted Lending as a Percentage of Debt**
Outstanding and Disbursed from Financial Markets[a]

	1983	1984	1985	1986	Average 1983–1986
Argentina[b]	12	18	0	0	8
Bolivia	0	0	0	0	0
Brazil	11	14	0	0	6
Chile	35	16	9	0	15
Colombia	0	0	29	0	7
Congo	0	0	0	9	2
Costa Rica	0	0	0	0	0
Dominican Rep.	0	0	0	0	0
Ecuador	20	0	0	0	5
Gabon	0	0	0	0	0
Guatemala	0	0	0	0	0
Honduras	0	0	0	0	0
Ivory Coast	0	0	4	0	1
Jamaica	0	0	0	0	0
Liberia	0	0	0	0	0
Madagascar	0	0	0	0	0
Malawi	0	0	0	0	0
Mexico	11	6	0	8	4
Morocco	0	0	0	0	0
Nicaragua	0	0	0	0	0
Nigeria	0	0	0	4	1
Panama	0	0	3	0	1
Peru	16	0	0	0	4
Philippines	0	18	0	0	5
Senegal	0	0	0	0	0
Sudan	0	0	0	0	0
Togo	0	0	0	0	0
Uruguay	18	0	0	0	5
Venezuela	0	0	0	0	0
Yugoslavia	41	0	0	0	10
Zaire	0	0	0	0	0
Zambia	0	0	0	0	0

Sources: World Bank, *World Debt Tables, 1986–87;* IMF, *International Capital Markets, 1986.* Taken from Sachs and Huizinga (1987).

[a]For each year t, we calculate the ratio of the concerted loan CL_t, to the disbursed debt in year $t - 1$, $D_t - 1$.

[b]In 1987 Argentina received a concerted loan amounting to 6 percent of its 1986 outstanding loans.

Another kind of retaliation that is feared is a reaction by the creditor governments (especially the United States), either within the financial sphere or more generally in other areas of foreign relations. Countries fear that if they suspend interest servicing, they may lose access to support from the IMF, the World Bank, the Paris Club (for a rescheduling of debts with official bilateral lenders), foreign aid agencies, and export credit agencies. Moreover, debtor governments fear that the leading creditor governments might withdraw other forms of foreign policy support (e.g., involving trade policy, security assistance, etc.), and might even back political opponents of the regime.

The United States government has repeatedly warned would-be re-calcitrant debtors that nonpayments of interest on the foreign debt constitutes a major breach of international financial relations, and a major breach of normal relations with the United States. Countries that choose default with their bank creditors are forced into the position of simultaneously choosing a hostile action vis-à-vis the United States government. Most finance ministers, and their presidents, do not have the stomach for such a confrontation, which takes steady nerves and a considerable capacity to explain the crisis to the domestic populace.

A final, and often overlooked reason that countries do not default involves the domestic political economy of the debtor country. In the case of a unilateral suspension of debt payments, some sectors and classes of the economy will tend to gain and others will tend to lose. Gainers from tough bargaining will usually include the nontradables sectors, urban workers, and landless peasants producing for the domestic market. Losers will include the tradables sectors (both because of repercussions on the exchange rate, and because of possible retaliation), and the domestic financial community, which has a stake in harmonious financial relations with the foreign banks. Left-wing governments, such as Alan Garcia's in Peru, are therefore more likely to please their working class constituency by taking a hard line on the debt than are governments oriented to exporters and the banking community. Most developing country governments, however, have sufficiently close ties with leading bankers (domestic and foreign) and leading exporters, that they are unwilling to run the risk of an overt international confrontation.

1.5 New Approaches to Managing the Debt Crisis

The unsatisfactory economic performance of most of the debtor countries in the past five years has led to continued suggestions for new approaches to international debt management. The NBER studies by Fischer, Krugman, and Sachs consider several alternatives that have been widely discussed, as well as some new proposals. Edwards and Sachs discuss the appropriate role of the international institutions, and the appropriate kinds of policy reforms, for overcoming the crisis.

All of the authors stress that a workable solution to the debt crisis will differ across countries. Some countries, such as Bolivia, Sudan, or Zaire, clearly can service only a small fraction of their debt on market terms. When Bolivia tried to meet its debt-servicing obligations during

1982–84, the result was a hyperinflation (the links between debt servicing and hyperinflation are explained by Morales and Sachs). Other countries can service some, but perhaps not all of their debts at normal market terms. Thus, a real case-by-case approach would recognize the need for substantial debt relief for some of the poorest and weakest economies, and perhaps some lesser degree of relief for the other debtor countries.

1.5.1   The Case for Debt Relief

Krugman and Sachs both illustrate the efficiency case for debt relief (See also Sachs 1988 for a further analysis). A heavy debt burden acts like a high marginal tax rate on economic adjustment. If the economy successfully imposes austerity, much of the benefit accrues to the foreign creditors. Partial debt relief can therefore be Pareto improving (i.e., to the benefit of *both* creditors and debtors), by improving the incentives for the debtor country to take needed adjustment actions. In political terms, partial debt relief can strengthen the hand of moderates, who would pay some but not all of the debt, against the hand of extremists, who would like to service little or none of the debt.

Debt relief is extremely difficult to negotiate, for several reasons. First, because each debtor country has many types of creditors, and the various creditors have the incentive to let the *others* grant the debt relief while they individually try to hold on to the full value of their claims. Second, the linkage between debt relief and improved economic policies is not sufficiently tight to make debt relief an obvious proposition for the creditors, a point stressed by Sachs. Even if creditors understand that the existing overhang of debt acts as a major disincentive to policy reform in the debtor countries, they might be skeptical that debt relief alone would be sufficient to lead to policy reforms. The creditors tend to view debt relief as throwing away money, i.e., giving up the potential of getting fully repaid, with little tangible benefit. As Sachs points out, the strongest case for debt relief can be made if the relief can be explicitly conditioned on particular policy reforms in the debtor countries.

Fischer offers an analysis of a broad range of proposals for modifying the current management of the crisis, dividing his analysis between those alternatives that would merely restructure the debt, and those that would effectively cancel part of the debt. In the first group, he considers debt-equity swaps, and echoes the conclusions of Krugman that debt-equity swaps are unlikely to be a major vehicle for resolving the crisis. Indeed Krugman shows how such swaps can very easily be detrimental to the debtor country.

Among proposals that would offer partial forgiveness to the debtor countries (i.e., an explicit write-down of part of the present value of the debt), Fischer focuses heavily on the idea of creating an International Debt Discount Corporation (IDDC). The IDDC would buy developing country debt from the banks in exchange for claims on the institution, and in turn collect from the debtor countries. The basic idea is that the IDDC would buy the debt at a discount, and then cancel some of the debt due from the debtor country. Calculations in Sachs and Huizinga (1987) show that the IDDC, far from hurting the commercial banks, could actually raise their market value, because the bank stock prices have *already* been deeply discounted in view of their LDC debt exposure.

Fischer stresses, however, that the most likely scenario is that partial relief will result from bilateral negotiations between creditors and debtors (as in the historical examples described by Eichengreen, and by Lindert and Morton) rather than through a single international relief operation.

Krugman analyzes in detail one purported remedy to the current crisis: the use of so-called debt-equity swaps. Upon close analysis, these transactions are much less attractive to the debtor country than they first appeared when the debt-equity schemes were introduced. In a typical debt-equity swap, a foreign direct investor purchases, at a discount, some sovereign debt in the secondary debt market (e.g., it pays a commercial bank $50 for $100 in face value claims on the government of Mexico). It then returns the debt to the central bank of the debtor country, in return for local currency that must be used for a direct investment in the country. The price that the central bank pays for the debt will generally lie between the second market price, expressed in local currency, and the full face value of the claims. To the extent that the central bank pays more (in the local currency equivalent) for the debt than the secondary market price, the government is effectively offering a subsidy to the firm making the foreign investment that is equal to the spread between the secondary market price and the repurchase price.

In essence, then, the debt-equity swap amounts to a cash repurchase of debt by the government combined with a fiscal subsidy for foreign investment in the country. The main problems with debt-equity schemes are (1) that either piece of this transaction (the debt repurchase or the investment subsidy) might be disadvantageous from the country's point of view and (2) the debt-equity schemes link these two pieces, often in a confusing and arbitrary way, even though the country might be better off to pursue just one aspect of the policy (e.g., to repurchase its debt, but without a link to foreign direct investment).

A cash repurchase of debt may or may not make sense. On the one side, it may well be highly inflationary, since a large cash outlay is made to repurchase debt that would otherwise have been rescheduled (and therefore not amortized for several years). The advantage of undertaking such a repurchase depends on the price of the repurchase. If the debt can be repurchased at a deep discount, it might make sense for a government to repurchase its debt.

In typical debt-equity programs, however, the price paid by the central bank for the debt has been close to the face value of the bonds, so that the foreign direct investor rather than the debtor government gets the spread between the secondary market price of debt and the face value. In effect, the discount on the bonds is used as a subsidy for direct investment. This is almost always a subsidy that the debtor country can ill afford, since almost by definition, the government is strapped for cash, and is very ill-placed to be offering a large subsidy to foreign firms for direct investment. Like most subsidy schemes, this kind of arrangement is likely to give most of the subsidy to firms that *would have invested in any case,* so that the incremental investment that is generated by the subsidy is likely to be very small.

From the country's point of view, therefore, it may make sense to engage in repurchases of debt, but it is less likely to make sense to link such repurchases to foreign investment in the country. However, as Krugman points out, there may be contractual barriers to a government's repurchase of its own debt, in which case a debt-equity scheme may be a way to overcome such contractual barriers. In such cases, however, it still makes sense to design the scheme to emphasize the debt repurchase (by having the central bank repurchase the debt at the secondary market price), and to play down the investment subsidy component.

1.5.2   Breaking the Cycle of Failed Reforms

We have stressed that policy "mistakes" in the debtor countries are often not mistakes (in the sense that the government misunderstands the implications of its actions). Rather they are often symptoms of deeper political or economic problems in the debtor countries. The diagnosis that a budget deficit is too large, and therefore should be reduced, is not a complete diagnosis. In the abstract, most finance ministers understand that excessive inflation, or excessive foreign borrowing, result from excessively large budget deficits. At the same time, they are often unable or unwilling to do much to reduce the deficits. In order to improve the design of stabilization programs, and to improve the effectiveness of conditionality, we must therefore give greater emphasis to why the political process produces the excessive deficits. The papers by Haggard and Kaufman, Sachs, and Edwards, as well as the country monographs in the companion NBER volumes, all emphasize the political context in which various economic policies are pursued.

The basic ideas in most stabilization programs supported by the IMF and World Bank are quite straightforward, and aim to reduce budget deficits, achieve a real exchange rate depreciation, and open the economy to international trade. The sobering point is that programs of this sort have been adopted repeatedly, and have failed repeatedly, in the countries under investigation during the past 30 years. A major goal must be to understand why such programs typically fail.

Consider the cases of Mexico and Argentina, for example. As the Mexican case study by Buffie and Krause makes clear, the "standard" package has been attempted in 1971, 1977, and 1983. In the first two cases, at least, major parts of the package were abandoned early on. Similarly, in Argentina, the "orthodox" package has been tried under Peron, in 1951; Ongania, in 1967 (the so-called Krieger-Vasena program); Viola, in 1977–81 (with Martinez de Hoz as finance minister); and to some extent, Alfonsin, since 1985. Again, the staying power of the orthodox program has been very weak in Argentina. (In late 1987 this weakness was again underscored, by the electoral losses of Alfonsin's Radical party, and the electoral resurgence of the Perónists.)

We have already noted that part of the problem with program implementation lies in the deep political and class cleavages that afflict most of the countries under study, combined with weak political institutions and fragmented political parties that fail to keep pace with rapid increases in political and social mobilization. The result, as pointed out by Samuel Huntington in an influential treatise, is that "cliques, blocs, and mass movements struggle directly with each other, each with its own weapons. Violence is democratized, politics demoralized, society at odds with itself" (Huntington 1968, 262). This is certainly an apposite sketch of Argentina, Bolivia, Brazil, the Philippines, and Turkey at various times in recent history. In the end, governments alternate rapidly between civilian and military regimes, and budgets are exploited for short-term political advantage rather than long-term economic strategy.

Interestingly, Huntington suggested that political stability in modernizing societies can best be achieved through an alliance of an urban ruling elite with the rural masses. Ideally, according to Huntington, that alliance is cemented through agrarian reform and the organization of party support in the countryside. Among the countries under study in the NBER project, Indonesia and South Korea most closely fit Huntington's characterization, as the governments have sought stability through an important base of rural support. (In the case of Indonesia, however, Soeharto's stress on his rural constituency was combined, early in his rule, with violent repression of his rural opposition.) In none of the Latin American countries in the NBER study have governments recently looked to the rural sector as the principal locus of political support. An apparent exception to this rule in Latin America is Colombia (unfortunately not studied in the NBER project), which is also the only major South American economy to have avoided a debt crisis.

Haggard and Kaufman identify several other features of the political landscape which affect a government's capacity to carry out necessary economic adjustments, including the administrative capacity of the governments, the pattern of trade union organization, and the susceptibility of the political institutions to electoral business cycles.

Sachs stresses that the normal problems of carrying out a reform program are greatly exacerbated by the overhang of foreign debt. Not only is the economic adjustment process made more difficult, but the political difficulties of reform are deepened as well. To the extent that the reforms serve mainly to raise the amount of foreign debt servicing, and so act as a tax on the domestic economy, they will find little political support domestically. Indeed, the government will be heatedly attacked for caving in to the interests of the foreign creditors. Adding debt relief as a part of the package of reform and adjustment could greatly enhance the likelihood that the economic program will in fact be carried out and sustained.

Sachs also explores whether changes in the nature of IMF/World Bank conditionality could increase the chances of compliance with programs monitored by these institutions. He argues that the nature of negotiations between the IMF and the debtor countries seems almost programmed to undermine the political legitimacy of Fund programs, thereby reducing their chance of success. In recent years, IMF programs have been unrealistically harsh, as they reflect the priorities of the private creditors rather than the realities of economic adjustment. Though the IMF has not yet acknowledged the possibility, there are times when debts to private-sector creditors cannot or will not be paid in full. Automatically designing programs based on the opposite assumption is bound to lead to frustration and failure.

Moreover, the style of negotiations seems problematic. Most IMF programs are negotiated between a technocratic team in the debtor government and the IMF staff, under conditions of secrecy. The letter of intent with the IMF is generally not made public by the debtor government. The result is that the agreement with the Fund often has little internal political support, and calls for actions by parts of the government (e.g., the legislative branch) or the private sector (e.g., the union organizations) that were not parties to the agreement. Since the actions are typically things that the government must do "down the road," the programs are signed, and then not adequately implemented.

With regard to the substantive design of adjustment programs, Edwards disputes the notion that dramatic liberalization is helpful in the context of a debt or stabilization crisis, suggesting that dramatic liberalization has little basis in either theory or history. Edwards argues that rapid trade liberalization is likely to generate adverse employment effects in the short term, as occurred in the liberalization programs in

Argentina, Chile, and Uruguay in the 1970s. Similarly, abrupt devaluations are likely to result in output losses and unemployment in the short run.

1.5.3   The Global Macroeconomic Setting

Even with debt relief, political resolve in the debtor countries, and well-designed economic reform programs, the chances for economic recovery in the debtor countries will depend on an adequate international economic environment. Dornbusch suggests that the probability of a "soft-landing" as the United States reduces its external deficits is rather low. In Dornbusch's view, a successful adjustment path for the U.S. will require a period of progressively tighter fiscal policy combined with expansionary monetary policy, with a strong likelihood of rising inflation in the U.S. as the dollar continues to weaken. Dornbusch suggests that "the monetary authorities would have to be sufficiently accommodating and impervious to inflation, and asset holders would have to be patient, sitting out the dollar depreciation without a stampede." He concludes that "this does not seem to be a high-probability scenario."

Dornbusch's emphasis on interest rates and monetary policies suggests one point of optimism regarding the debt crisis in future years. The crisis broke out decisively in the early 1980s when interest rates shot up above export growth rates. There are some good reasons for believing that real interest rates may now be in a steady decline (because of declining U.S. budget deficits, a fall in U.S. consumption spending, and the apparent room for continuing ease in U.S. monetary policy, as of late 1987). If this turns out to be the case, the fall in interest rates could significantly meliorate the crisis, in the same way that the sustained rise in real interest rates at the beginning of the 1980s was a decisive international shock that helped usher in the crisis.

References

Balassa, Bela. 1984. Adjustment policies in developing countries: A reassessment. *World Development* 12 (September): 955–72.
Bhagwati, Jagdish. 1978. *Anatomy and consequences of exchange control regimes*. Cambridge, Mass.: Ballinger Publishing Company.
Brecher, Richard, and Carlos Díaz-Alejandro. 1977. Tariffs, foreign capital, and immiserizing growth. *Journal of International Economics* 7(4): 317–22.
Calvo, Guillermo. 1987. Servicing the public debt: The role of expectations. Philadelphia, Penn.: University of Pennsylvania. Mimeo.
Cline, William. 1984. *International debt: Systemic risk and policy response*. Washington, D.C.: Institute for International Economics, July.
Cumby, Robert, and Richard M. Levich. 1987. On the definition and magnitude

of recent capital flight. NBER Working Paper no. 2275 (June). Cambridge, Mass.: National Bureau of Economic Research.

Galbis, Vincente. 1987. La liberalizacion del sector financiero bajo condiciones oligopolicas y las estructura de los holdings bancarios. In *Estabilizacion y ajuste estructural en America Latina,* ed. Santiago Roca. Lima, Peru: IDE/ESAN. [English language version is published in *Savings and Development* 21 (1986), Milan, Italy.]

Huntington, Samuel. 1968. *Political order in changing societies.* New Haven, Conn.: Yale University Press.

Krueger, A. 1978. *Foreign trade regimes and economic development: Liberalization attempts and consequences.* Cambridge, Mass.: Ballinger Publishing Company.

Makin, John. 1984. *The global debt crisis.* New York: Basic Books.

Sachs, Jeffrey. 1985. External debt and macroeconomic performance in Latin America and East Asia. *Brookings Papers on Economic Activity* 2: 523–73.

———. 1986. Managing the LDC debt crisis. *Brookings Papers on Economic Activity* 2: 397–432.

———. 1987. Trade and exchange-rate policies in growth-oriented adjustment programs. In *Growth-oriented adjustment programs,* ed. Vittorio Corbo, M. Goldstein, and M. Khan. Washington, D.C.: International Monetary Fund and The World Bank.

———. 1988. The debt overhang of developing countries (paper presented at memorial conference, WIDER, Helsinki, Finland, 1986). In a conference volume in memory of Carlos Díaz-Alejandro, ed. Ronald Findlay and Jorge de Macedo. Forthcoming.

Sachs, Jeffrey, and Harry Huizinga. 1987. The U.S. commercial banks and the developing-country debt crisis. *Brookings Papers on Economic Activity* 2: 555–601

I   History of Debt Crisis

2 How Sovereign Debt Has Worked

Peter H. Lindert and Peter J. Morton

2.1 Introduction

The international financial community has often preferred to repeat the past rather than study it. Since 1974 international lending has passed through another cycle of enthusiasm followed by nonrepayment and creditor revulsion, repeating a pattern that has recurred several times since the eighteenth century.

The process is costly. Relative to ordinary private lending, lending to sovereign debtors[1] brings costs to either side or both sides, and often to third parties. The unenforceability of debt service obligations sooner or later breeds lasting creditor distrust and cuts the supply of capital to countries where its marginal product is generally high. One such net capital cost takes the form of credit disruptions and other penalties levied by creditors, with greater damage to the debtors than gain to the creditors. The debtors' macroeconomies are destabilized by the borrowing boom and later bust, especially when the bust brings unforeseen austerity.

Peter H. Lindert is a professor of economics and Director of the Agricultural History Center at the University of California at Davis. Peter J. Morton is an assistant professor of economics at Hofstra University.

The authors wish to thank the National Science Foundation and the Institute of Governmental Affairs, University of California at Davis for financial support, and Wendy Eudey, Kara Hayes, and Hai Wen for research assistance. They have also benefitted from comments on preliminary partial drafts at the University of California (Davis, Berkeley, Los Angeles, Santa Cruz), Harvard University, the University of Illinois, the University of Michigan, the Washington Area Group in Economic History, and Williams College, and by Thomas Mayer and Mira Wilkins. A much fuller set of appendixes is available as a separate working paper from the Institute of Governmental Affairs, University of California, Davis CA 95616, and the underlying bond data set is available in either hard copy or floppy disk from the authors at cost.

Those caught in the current lingering debt crisis cannot blame their innocence on an absence of historical literature. The recurrence of default has been pointed out by scholars and by bondholder protective councils for a century (Fenn 1874–98; Corporation of Foreign Bondholders, annually from 1873; Clarke 1879; Fitch 1918; Foreign Bondholders' Protective Council, annually from 1935; Kimber 1925 and 1933; Winkler 1933; Borchard 1951; Mintz 1951; Wynne 1951; Cameron 1961, chaps. 13–16; Bittermann 1973; Kindleberger 1978; Cizauskas 1979). Scholars have added a comparative anatomy of debt crisis, finding what kinds of trends trigger debt crises and what kinds of borrowers are less likely to repay (Díaz-Alejandro 1984, Edwards 1984, Fishlow 1985, Sachs 1985, Eichengreen and Portes 1986). We know that the problem inheres in sovereign debt, that the timing of the crises is related to unforeseen deflation, and that countries with runaway government budgets and less commitment to trade are more likely to have recurring repayment crises.

The remaining uncertainties are how the lending waves unfold and what can be done once a crisis is in full swing. This chapter addresses these two issues at the start and end of the lending cycle. In section 2.2, we shall argue that past lending to foreign governments has brought high private returns in the aggregate, but with curious patterns that suggest (but cannot prove) an unprofitable "bubble" dynamic of excessive investment followed by excessive revulsion. Investors seem to pay little attention to the past repayment record of the borrowing governments. They may or may not have been wise in ignoring the past. Their inattention, at any rate, reveals that they do not punish governments with a prior default history, undercutting the belief in a penalty that compels faithful repayment.

Section 2.3 turns to historical experience with the different policy options available in the wake of a major debt crisis. Noting the necessary imperfections in any policy approach, we discuss some arguments in favor of the older bond-era direct confrontation between problem debtors and their creditors, an approach that usually led to partial default. The more recent approach of bringing the IMF and the World Bank into tripartite debt-crisis negotiations has brought extra costs relating to moral hazard, delays, and macroeconomic adjustment.

It is fair to ask whether history should be consulted at all as a guide to present debt-crisis options. As a statistician might put it: "If history is supposed to be the sample, what is the population? And are we really sampling from the same population today as in the past?" That is, is there really a probability distribution of outcomes likely to be shared by the past and the present? A cautious affirmative answer can be ventured in this particular case. The merits of comparison and contrast with the past are greatest when there is a durable mechanism at work.

Such is the case with sovereign debt, which is subject to that inherent defect of unenforceability and which reveals its basic repayment and relending dynamic only over a long period of time. In such cases, deductive modeling quickly reaches barriers that only a longer empirical view can push back.

2.2   Sovereign Debt Repayment since the Early 19th Century

It has been suggested that it would be far better were the national capital employed in home works instead of being lent to foreign countries. So far as an individual is concerned, whether he loses £1,000 in a [domestic] bubble company or in a swindling foreign loan, the operation and the sequel are the same. (Hyde Clarke 1879, 21.)

If there were no rescuer, no International Monetary Fund, how would sovereign debt work? How well would creditors and debtors be likely to fare? How far below the ex ante contracted rates of return were the rates eventually realized by the whole chain of debtholders? Were the returns either so excessive or so low that they suggest a case for special policy intervention in defense of either debtors or creditors? While the future need not match past patterns, there is a long and varied history to tap in forming guesses. In what follows, we offer an extensive menu of results, allowing readers to choose which results to emphasize.

2.2.1   Background

Fresh lending to foreign governments followed the same wave-like pattern as other international lending in the nineteenth and early twentieth centuries. There was a post-Napoleonic wave in the 1820s, including loans to most of the newly independent nations of Latin America, followed by widespread default. Gross lending to governments, like international lending in general, returned to high tide in the 1850s, in the late 1860s and early 1870s, in the late 1880s, in 1904–14, and again in the late 1920s. The wave of lending to foreign governments in the late 1920s, like that of 1974–82, exceeded any before World War I in real absolute value and even as a share of lender-country GNP. Each wave ended with at least some occurrence of repayments breakdown, sometimes due to international trade depression, sometimes due to government budget crises, and sometimes due to the revelation of financial abuses.[2]

The timing and magnitude of the lending waves is illuminated differently by figure 2.1. We cast a particular light on the long-noted waves by measuring the net real investment flow, rather than the gross flow. Setting aside the "spike" of 1894, caused by heavy Russian borrowing (not all of it truly external), figure 2.1 singles out the 1906–14 and 1973–81 waves as the greatest. These two would probably stand out even if all figures

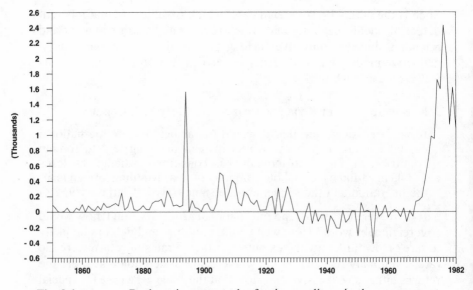

Fig. 2.1   Real net investment by foreign creditors in the government debt of ten countries, annually, 1850–1982. *Notes:* The vertical axis measures the real value of fresh lending to ten governments—Argentina, Australia, Brazil, Canada, Chile, Egypt, Japan, Mexico, Russia, and Turkey—by foreign creditors, predominantly private, minus retirements on the same external debt in the same year. The figures are in millions of dollars at 1913 prices, with flows in other currencies converted at the 1913 exchange rates. Payments of interest are not included, nor are changes in the real value of outstanding debt due to movements in the consumer-price deflator.

The large "spike" of 1894 was a loan package of $1,489.5 million to the Russian government, much of which may have been purchased by Russian creditors. On the foreign-domestic mixture in subscriptions to Russian hard-currency loans see Anan'ich and Bovykin (forthcoming, section 2).

The genuine rise after 1973 is slightly exaggerated in relative terms by a change in series. For developing countries the post-1970 data cover not only bonds but the other types of lending captured in the World Bank's loan disbursements data.

were divided by real national product or real wealth. The famous wave of the 1920s is less impressive on this net investment measure. It was, to a large extent, a refinancing wave in which fresh loans, most of them in dollars, largely covered service on prewar, mostly sterling, loans. It was also, of course, an era in which international lending was partly preoccupied with trying to induce German recovery and reparations.

Who defaulted, and when? It is not easy to summarize the frequency or percentage of nonrepayment. We begin by noting the countries that defaulted outright, in whole or in part, at one time or another, here and in table 2.8 in appendix B.

Soon after the lending wave of the 1820s most Latin American governments defaulted to some degree. Several southern states in the United States defaulted in the 1830s–40s and again in the Reconstruction era. Latin America and the Eastern Mediterranean (Greece, Turkey and, momentarily, Egypt) figured prominently in the default waves of the mid–nineteenth century. The end of the late–1880s lending wave featured relatively few defaults, the most notable being Argentina's partial nonrepayment (on which more later) and lingering difficulties with Colombia's debt service. Brazil's good record was finally compromised with repayment lapses necessitating refunding loans in 1898 and 1914. The 1910s brought wholesale defaults in the Mexican Revolution, the Russian Revolution, and the fall of the Ottoman Empire. The greatest wave, however, came in the early 1930s (Eichengreen and Portes 1986; Eichengreen, chap. 3 of this volume), in which essentially all of Latin America, most of Eastern Europe, Turkey, and China defaulted. In the early postwar years, with bond finance dried up and most of the trickle of loans coming from governments or with their guarantees, outright default was replaced with a murmur of repeated concessionary refundings for problem governments, notably Turkey, Latin America, and some newly independent nations (Bittermann, 1973). The list of countries needing concessionary refundings in the 1970s and 1980s is more extensive but similar, still featuring Latin America, Eastern Europe, and now much of Africa (Watson et al. 1986).

Other areas always repaid. One was Western Europe outside of Germany and Spain. Another consisted of the sovereign Arab nations, with only slight exceptions. Asia east of the Persian Gulf consistently repaid, except for China in the 1930s, Japan between 1941 and 1952, and the independent Philippines. So did the white Commonwealth nations.

The list of incomplete repayers by itself conveys only very limited information, however. Foreign governments had to offer higher interest rates than creditors' home governments, precisely because nonrepayment was feared. To judge their repayment behavior or to judge the lenders' behavior, one needs a careful accounting of their borrowings and debt-service outflows.

To capture the overall tendency in sovereign debt repayment, one needs to examine as long a period as possible, in order to avoid overemphasis on either good or bad times. One must also take care to sample loans or countries fairly, to avoid picking a sample of particularly problematic borrowers or particularly faithful ones. The desired goal is equiprobable sampling of all constant-price dollars ever lent by private parties to foreign governments that were expected to remain sovereign, and to pursue the mean and variance of repayment of that population of constant dollars. In practice, one samples in some more convenient way that does not sacrifice representativeness to any serious degree. Eichengreen and Portes (1986) drew a random sample of loans from the 1920s, giving equal sampling chance to each loan, not far from equal sampling of each constant dollar. We intend different coverage here, encompassing only loans to governments but spanning a much longer period of time. The longer time span means a diversity of sources, preventing our sampling individual loans from all times and nations.

To span as long a time period as was practical, we began with the bonds outstanding in 1850, and those floated between 1850 and about 1970, following them all the way to settlement or to the end of 1983. In choosing bonds to follow, we exploited the historical concentration of sovereign debt into a small number of borrowing governments. Specifically, we follow the experiences of ten borrowing governments: Argentina, Australia, Brazil, Canada, Chile, Egypt, Japan, Mexico, Russia, and Turkey. We follow their foreign bond debt, drawing on bondholder annuals, periodic compendia of foreign investments (Fenn, Fitch, Kimber, Dominick and Dominick, etc.), and country studies. We concentrate on bond lending, with separate later treatment of the brief bank-loan wave of 1974–82.

Table 2.1 ranks the top external-debtor governments by their debts on three benchmark dates. As can be seen, our ten-country sample accounted for a large share on each date. Our ten were almost, but not quite, the top ten borrowers over the last 130-odd years. As appendix A elaborates, we included Chile, a more interesting but less important borrower, in lieu of New Zealand or South Africa. The use of Chile may slightly bias the ten-country sample toward a low-repayment result from a worldwide perspective, but the conclusions that follow take this possible bias into account.

The procedures used to process 1,552 external bonds from the history of the ten countries are laborious and complex. One has to judge which debtors were truly "sovereign" in the sense of being able to evade the usual legal recourses faced by ordinary private defaulters. Though one could extend the term to cover anybody borrowing from a foreign source, we have followed only government borrowers, including local governments but excluding private borrowers backed by government guarantee. One must also judge which government debts were truly external. Our judgments rested on the place of issue, the currency of account, and hints about the residence of most holders. Appendix A offers a guide to our treatment of such complexities.

2.2.2   Choosing Summary Measures

Summarizing the flows of real resources between creditors and debtors calls for three related measures. One is the internal rate of return on the loans, with all flows converted into real consumable resources.

The resources in question are consumables of the lending countries, since (a) these mattered directly to lenders, (b) the loans were in lending-country currency, and (c) appropriate price deflators are harder to derive for the debtor countries.

The second measure is the real rate of return on an alternative asset, used for comparison with the real (and realized) internal rate on foreign sovereign debt. Any choice of an alternative asset implies a degree of riskiness, which may or may not be comparable with the risk on lending to a foreign government. The main quantitative results all compare sovereign foreign debt with home-country bonds. For foreign debt re-payable in sterling, the home-country alternative was to buy consols. For foreign debt repayable in dollars, the home-country alternative was long-term U.S. government bonds.[3] We follow an unconventional pro-cedure, however, in specifying the term structure of the investment in the alternative asset, as explained more fully in appendix A. To min-imize the influence of inflation and deflation on the difference in the real ex post rates of return on foreign sovereign debt and home-country debt, we match the stream of repayments on the hypothetical holdings of home-country debt to the actual repayments on the foreign sovereign debt in question. The alternative real rate of return is thus an average of real ex post rates on a mixture of holdings of home-country gov-ernmental bonds maturing at the times dictated by the actual repay-ments of foreign sovereign debt.

The third summary measure is a net present value of the foreign sovereign debt vis-à-vis home country debt. Specifically, it is the pres-ent value of the repayments on the mixture of home-country bond holdings, discounted back to the time of purchase, minus the amount actually lent to a foreign government with the same realized repayment stream. It is thus the amount by which lenders to foreign governments were able to *lend less* to foreign governments than they would have had to lend to the home government to get the same repayments (again, see appendix A for details).

How should we deal with the fact that the loans occurred at different times? How should a loan made in 1850 be weighed against a loan made in 1950? The answer depends on the question being asked. One might wish to know how much better or worse the whole chain of investors would have fared ex post if they had chosen the alternative asset, instead of the sovereign foreign debt, starting from a moment in history. To find out, one would use the first kind of procedure:

1. All investments are discounted to the same year (e.g., 1850), at the alternative-asset interest rate ($\bar{\rho}$).

This first procedure will give heavy weight to early experience (e.g., loans in 1850), regardless of the date to which all flows are discounted. A more important question, however, is what probability distribution

Table 2.1   Top Governments Ranked by Gross External Debt to Private Creditors, 1913–14, 1930, and 1979

Rank	1913–14 Country	%	End of 1930 Country	%	End of 1979 Country	%
	Top 10 externally-indebted governments at each date					
(1)	Russia	35.7	Australia	17.0	Mexico	12.0
(2)	Australia	9.0	Canada	9.7	Brazil	9.6
(3)	Japan	6.7	Brazil	8.1	Canada	9.2
(4)	Brazil	5.8	Japan	6.6	Norway	7.6
(5)	Argentina	5.1	Union of South Africa	5.4	Australia	5.1
(6)	Turkey	4.8	New Zealand	5.4	Venezuela	4.6
(7)	Union of South Africa	4.3[a]	Rumania	5.3	South Korea	4.3
(8)	Mexico	3.5	Belgium	5.2	Algeria	4.3
(9)	Canada	3.4	Argentina	3.9	Turkey	3.7
(10)	Egypt	3.4	Chile	3.1	New Zealand	3.6
	Other sample countries					
	(15) Chile	1.4	(12) Egypt	3.0	(12) Argentina	2.4
			Mexico, in default[b]		(17) Chile	1.4
			Russia, in default[b]		(23) Egypt	1.3
			Turkey, in default[b]		(47) Japan	0.1
					Russia, in default[b]	
	All countries	100.0	All countries	100.0	All countries	100.0
Share owed by 10 sample countries:		78.8		51.5		44.8
Total value ($ billion):		12.6		14.4		83.0
Number of countries covered:		42		47		108

Sources: For 1913–14, we preferred Kimber (1925) and our detailed estimates for the ten sample countries, but made sparing use of United Nations (1948). For 1930, we preferred Royal Institute for International Affairs (1937) and our detailed estimates, but also made use of United Nations (1948). For 1979, we used Moody's *Manual of municipals and governments* for bonds issued by governments of developed countries, and the World Bank's *World debt tables* for gross disbursed borrowings (not just bonds) of developing-country governments from private foreign creditors. The difference in coverage may elevate the ranks of less developed countries.

[a]Total public debt, not just external.

[b]The outstanding amounts on Mexican, Russian and Turkish external loans are disregarded here as they were effectively repudiated, in order to give balances that were more representative of borrowing activity in the 1920s (for 1930) and the 1970s (for 1979).
Excluded from this table are foreign borrowings of financial-center countries, which debts were not "external" in the sense that a strictly external repudiation was made more difficult by their ready salability in the borrowing country. In the absence of comprehensive exchange controls, any repudiation would have to apply to all public debt.

of outcomes the past suggests for future experience. Here the reader has free range of choice. Is the more peaceful experience of the mid–nineteenth century the best lesson that the past has to offer the future? If so, one could be content with the first procedure. But if one (plausibly) considers more recent experience more relevant, one can choose from these three workable procedures:

2. "all loans at once"—give the same weight to every constant-price dollar of fresh lending, regardless of when it occurred, starting all loans at the same hypothetical year. This gives somewhat greater weight to the heavy gross flows of the 1920s than to the smaller gross volume of prewar lending;
3. do the same as in (2), but weight each loan by its share of lending-country wealth at the time of the loan instead of deflating by consumer prices; or
4. insist that only the interwar and postwar experience is a valuable guide to the future.

We consider the second—"all loans at once"—the fairest offering from the pre-1973 past to the future, but our results can also be used to infer the results of procedure (4).

The available data allow us to compare realized flows with those originally contracted, and to compare nominal flows with real (price-deflated) ones. Three of the following four kinds of flows, with their corresponding rates of return, are presented:

	Contracted (ex ante)	Realized (ex post)
Nominal	Table 2.2	Table 2.10
Real	Not calculated	Table 2.3

Table 2.2 sets the stage by introducing national average ex ante returns and capitalized values contracted at the time of bond issue. In the bond era, investors asked for premia ($v - \bar{\rho}$) on foreign government bonds that were usually between 1.5 and 2.6 percent. These premia will serve as a yardstick for several comparisons to follow. We will find, first, that the real realized returns were well below these ex ante premia. Virtually all of the shortfall in real realized returns was due to defaults, not to ex post inflation, which affected both home-bond and foreign-bond returns similarly. Second, the ex ante rates in table 2.2 did not differ across countries in any way that consistently foretold the international differences in ex post returns. True, the market guessed "right" in charging lower premia to Canada and Japan before World War II, and in charging more to prerevolutionary Mexico and Turkey.[4] But the market was unable to foresee the enforced full repayment by Egypt or the massive default by czarist Russia. The wide differences in realized returns were unpredictable.

Table 2.2   **Contracted Nominal Returns on Bond Lending to Ten Foreign Governments, 1850–1983**

Borrowing Nation	n	Rates of Return (%)			(Millions of $)		Risk-Neutral Expected % of Capital Loss
		v	$\bar{\rho}$	$v - \bar{\rho}$	NPV	L_0	
A. All marketed bonds, 1850–1983							
Argentina	181	5.92	3.47	2.45	561.4	2,476.6	2.31
Brazil	129	6.19	3.64	2.55	572.3	1,517.4	2.40
Chile	60	6.89	3.94	2.95	274.5	637.5	2.76
Mexico	48	5.83	3.11	2.72	376.8	843.8	2.57
Four Latins	418	6.09	3.52	2.57	1,785.0	5,475.4	2.43
Australia	439	5.60	4.52	1.09	1,358.7	9,836.9	1.03
Canada	488	4.51	2.82	1.69	925.9	1,635.6	1.61
Egypt	20	6.71	3.29	3.43	222.9	513.9	3.21
Japan	60	5.75	3.51	2.24	525.1	1,682.4	2.11
Russia	48	4.94	2.92	2.01	1,952.2	3,456.4	1.92
Turkey	46	5.86	3.33	2.53	744.9	1,300.1	2.39
These six	1,101	5.44	3.86	1.59	5,729.7	18,425.3	1.50
All ten	1,519	5.59	3.78	1.81	7,514.7	23,900.6	1.72
B. Bonds issued 1850–1914 (or outstanding in 1850)							
Argentina	110	5.07	2.91	2.15	295.4	930.5	2.05
Brazil	77	4.86	2.95	1.91	270.6	843.4	1.82
Chile	32	5.39	2.98	2.42	100.7	251.1	2.30
Mexico[a]	33	5.78	2.91	2.87	325.1	578.1	2.71
Four Latins	252	5.19	2.93	2.26	991.8	2,603.1	2.15
Australia	232	4.35	3.01	1.34	539.2	1,567.0	1.28
Canada	62	4.47	3.17	1.30	50.1	81.8	1.24
Egypt	17	7.18	3.11	4.07	227.8	443.8	3.80
Japan	32	4.36	2.90	1.47	217.5	896.9	1.41
Russia[b]	48	4.94	2.92	2.01	1,952.2	3,456.4	1.92
Turkey	34	7.39	3.16	4.23	737.8	752.3	3.94
These six	425	5.13	2.98	2.15	3,724.6	7,198.3	2.04
All ten	677	5.32	2.97	2.36	4,716.5	9,801.4	2.24
C. Bonds issued 1915–1945							
Argentina	69	5.81	3.78	2.05	184.9	1,231.7	1.94
Brazil	52	7.85	4.51	3.34	301.7	674.0	3.10
Chile	28	7.86	4.56	3.30	173.7	386.4	3.06
Mexico[a]	0	0	0	0	0	0	0
Four Latins	149	6.76	4.13	2.63	660.4	2,292.1	2.46
Australia	114	5.16	4.00	1.16	510.0	3,425.6	1.10
Canada	243	4.51	3.94	0.64	127.0	489.1	0.61
Egypt[c]	3	3.75	4.40	−0.65	−4.9	70.1	n.a.
Japan	9	7.71	4.48	3.24	243.3	516.8	3.00
Russia	0	0	0	0	0	0	0
Turkey	3	4.30	3.30	1.00	3.8	51.6	0.96
These six	372	5.35	4.05	1.30	879.3	4,553.2	1.24
All ten	521	5.82	4.07	1.75	1,539.7	6,845.3	1.65

(continued)

Table 2.2   (continued)

Borrowing Nation	n	Rates of Return (%)			(Millions of $)		Risk-Neutral Expected % of Capital Loss
		v	$\bar{\rho}$	$v - \bar{\rho}$	NPV	L_0	
D. Bonds issued after 1945[d]							
Argentina	4	8.88	3.95	4.93	81.1	314.4	4.52
Brazil	0	0	0	0	0	0	0
Chile	0	0	0	0	0	0	0
Mexico	15	5.94	3.56	2.39	51.7	265.7	2.26
Four Latins	19	7.53	3.77	3.76	132.8	580.1	3.50
Australia	93	6.32	5.37	0.95	309.5	4,844.3	0.90
Canada	183	4.51	2.28	2.23	748.8	1,064.7	2.13
Egypt[e]	0	0	0	0	0	0	0
Japan	19	6.61	3.70	2.91	64.2	268.7	2.73
Russia	0	0	0	0	0	0	0
Turkey	9	3.69	3.58	0.11	3.3	496.1	0.11
These six	304	5.85	4.68	1.17	1,125.7	6,673.8	1.11
All ten	323	5.99	4.61	1.38	1,258.5	7,253.9	1.30

Notes:

n = the number of bonds covered here.

v = the internal rate of return implied by the bond issue price and repayment terms.

$\bar{\rho}$ = the rate of interest on bond lending to the home government (U.K. consol rate or U.S. Treasury long-term bond rate, depending on the place of issue).

NPV = net present value, defined in the following special way: the amount investors were able to save by buying the same promised repayment stream from a foreign government at higher interest instead of from the British or U.S. government.

L_0 = the gross value initially lent to the foreign government.

The "risk-neutral" expected % of capital loss" = $(v - \bar{\rho})/(1 + v)$ is a suggestive hypothetical measure used here as in Feder and Just (1984). If bond purchasers were risk-neutral, the coexistence of the two rates of return, v and $\bar{\rho}$, would imply the stated percentage of expected nonrepayment on the higher-yielding foreign bonds. To the extent that purchasers are risk-averse, $(v - \bar{\rho})/(1 + v)$ overstates their expectation of capital losses and instead reflects their aversion to the asset with the higher contracted yield.

[a]Two unsuccessful conversion loans to Mexico in 1943 (valued at £293,000) have been included in the 1850–1914 sample, to make them part of the aggregate prerevolutionary experience here as in table 2.3. Including them causes a very slight understatement of the ex ante contracted returns on prerevolutionary bonds.

[b]Two dollar loans to the Czarist government in 1916 have been included in the prewar totals.

[c]The three interwar Egyptian bonds are actually Ottoman debt settlements loans, not true market loans.

[d]Our sample excluded bonds issued in the 1970s and 1980s, except for those issued by Australia and Canada. We sought to follow all external bond issues up to about 1970. The general inactivity of the postwar bond market meant that our bond populations stopped with bonds issued in the following final years: Argentina, 1968; Australia, 1978; Brazil and Chile, 1930; Canada, 1982; Egypt, Japan, and Turkey, 1965; Mexico, 1966; and Russia, 1916. All subsequent flows were followed through 1983, after which the remaining small balances were assumed to be paid off.

[e]The 1965 Egyptian bond issued in Kuwait has been excluded for want of sufficient information.

The 488 Canadian bonds have been handled differently from others. To save time developing computer routines for these well-behaved bonds, we aggregated their payment flows on separate spreadsheets, one for each province or the Dominion and each of the two currency categories

Table 2.2   (continued)

(US-dollar and non-dollar). Each Canadian "loan" entered into the ten-country data processing is therefore a set of aggregate payments streams resulting from many loans issued and maturing at different times. For the period breakdown of parts B, C, and D of this table, the accumulated Canadian balances were assumed to be paid off at the ends of 1914, 1945, and 1983. The different treatment of Canada causes understatement of the value of Canadian loans relative to those issued by other countries, but should not affect the rates of return greatly.

The total numbers of loans are often below those of table 2.3 below, because table 2.2 is supposed to focus only on bonds accepted by the marketplace, not conversion loans forced on dissatisfied holders of problem debt.

Reminder: nominal values from periods of very different commodity price levels have been aggregated together. This otherwise inappropriate aggregation facilitates comparison with the more relevant real-value aggregations in table 2.3 below.

Real realized returns are summarized in Table 2.3, first for all bonds, then for the largely-sterling prewar bonds, then for the largely-dollar interwar bonds, and finally for a few postwar bonds, with values in sterling at 1913 prices converted into 1913-price dollars at $4.86. The results in table 2.3 are best understood by surveying individual-country results first, before discussing possible inferences about the efficiency of the overall sovereign-debt portfolio.

2.2.3   Repayment Experience for Individual Borrowing Governments in the Bond Era

The credit histories summarized in table 2.3 cover the whole spectrum from perfectly faithful repayers to governments that have defaulted massively enough to give their foreign creditors negative rates of return. Let us scan the spectrum, from the best repayers to the worst.

Some governments have repaid all their foreign bond debts faithfully since the mid–nineteenth century. One in particular ended up having no choice in the matter. By 1879 Egypt had been teetering on the brink of default for several years. On 22 April that year the Khedive Ismail, in a final defiance of his European creditors, issued a decree amounting to a unilateral partial default on outstanding bonds. In response the British and French governments pressured the Ottoman sultan to depose Ismail and replace him with Tewfik, his more compliant son. British and French officials took over control of Egyptian government revenue, managing it in the interests of the private creditors (Wynne 1951, 598–611; Landes 1958, 302–18; Feder and Just 1984). Egypt lost national sovereignty, which was not regained until after World War II.

It cost her dearly. Egypt fully repaid at a high interest rate reflecting her ex ante ability to default. She obtained a few more loans before World War I, but none thereafter until midcentury. Table 2.3 shows the premium she paid, in the form of a real realized rate of 6.41 percent on prewar bonds, well above the 3.49 percent realized on the alternative streams of consol loans. The combination of ex ante sovereignty and ex post nonsovereignty brought Egypt's private creditors an extra 2.92 percent per annum.[5]

Three other governments were faithful repayers, at less cost than Egypt bore because the market trusted them a bit more from the start. Australia, Canada, and Japan have faithfully serviced their sterling and U.S. dollar bonds, with the exception of Japan's nonpayment of any debt service between Pearl Harbor and the end of the occupation in 1952. Perhaps in exchange, Australia and Canada were also heavy gross borrowers, able to return to the market repeatedly since 1850. Each of these governments had slight limitations on its sovereignty before World War I, though none to the degree of Egypt's subjugation under

Table 2.3   Realized Real Returns on Bond Lending to Ten Foreign Governments, 1850–1983

Borrowing Nation	n	Rates of Return (%)			($ mill. at 1913 prices)	
		v	$\bar{\rho}$	$v - \bar{\rho}$	NPV	L_0
A. All marketed bonds and conversion bonds, 1850–1983						
Argentina	187	3.52	1.56	1.96	405.9	1,943.4
Brazil	143	2.97	2.14	0.83	156.5	1,278.5
Chile	60	1.66	1.88	−0.22	−3.9	501.3
Mexico	52	−0.21	1.72	−1.92	−140.1	564.6
Four Latins	442	2.65	1.79	0.86	418.4	4,287.7
Australia	439	3.00	1.97	1.03	669.6	4,873.6
Canada	488	1.91	0.35	1.56	512.3	969.1
Egypt	21	6.21	3.68	2.53	219.5	408.8
Japan	60	2.90	1.33	1.58	290.3	1,346.5
Russia	48	1.31	2.94	−1.63	−691.1	3,340.9
Turkey	54	1.29	2.58	−1.29	−174.0	919.1
These six	1,110	2.40	2.14	0.26	826.6	11,858.0
All ten	1,552	2.47	2.05	0.42	1,245.0	16,145.8
B. Bonds issued, 1850–1914 (or outstanding in 1850)						
Argentina	113	3.52	1.81	1.71	251.6	928.1
Brazil	79	2.27	1.38	0.89	1223.5	841.8
Chile	32	2.79	1.31	1.48	55.0	249.7
Mexico[a]	37	−0.74	1.98	−2.72	−157.3	475.7
Four Latins	261	2.21	1.65	0.57	272.8	2,495.0
Australia	232	3.02	2.01	1.01	319.2	1,525.2
Canada	62	4.77	3.50	1.27	39.9	65.7
Egypt	18	6.41	3.49	2.92	222.4	367.9
Japan	32	1.85	0.60	1.25	190.3	914.9
Russia[b]	48	1.31	2.94	−1.63	−691.1	3,340.9
Turkey	42	1.61	3.17	−1.56	−166.9	695.4
These six	434	2.09	2.48	−0.39	−86.1	6,910.0
All ten	695	2.12	2.26	−0.14[c]	186.6[c]	9,405.0

Table 2.3   (continued)

Borrowing Nation	n	Rates of Return (%)			($ mill. at 1913 prices)	
		v	$\bar{\rho}$	$v - \bar{\rho}$	NPV	L_0
C. Bonds issued 1915–1945						
Argentina	70	3.34	1.39	1.95	135.3	928.0
Brazil	64	4.31	3.61	0.70	32.9	436.7
Chile	28	0.54	2.44	−1.90	−58.9	251.6
Mexico	0	0	0	0	0	0
Four Latins	162	3.17	2.15	1.01	109.3	1,616.3
Australia	114	4.18	2.97	1.21	279.3	2,165.1
Canada	243	3.41	2.76	0.65	93.9	379.1
Egypt[d]	3	4.41	5.41	−0.73	−2.9	40.9
Japan	9	5.89	3.62	2.26	83.2	340.2
Russia	0	0	0	0	0	0
Turkey[e]	3	−3.16	−2.27	−0.88	−3.4	47.2
These six	372	4.16	2.97	1.20	450.2	2,972.5
All ten	534	3.81	2.68	1.13	559.5	4,588.8
D. Bonds issued after 1945						
Argentina	4	5.51	0.81	4.70	19.0	87.3
Brazil	0	0	0	0	0	0
Chile	0	0	0	0	0	0
Mexico	15	2.67	0.35	2.31	17.2	89.1
Four Latins	19	4.08	0.58	3.50	36.2	176.4
Australia	93	0.81	0.09	0.72	71.1	1,183.3
Canada	183	0.47	−1.78	2.25	378.5	524.3
Egypt	0	0	0	0	0	0
Japan	19	2.32	0.06	2.25	16.8	91.4
Russia	0	0	0	0	0	0
Turkey	9	1.21	1.55	−0.34	−3.7	176.5
These six	304	0.83	−0.28	1.10	462.6	1,975.5
All ten	323	1.09	−0.21	1.30	498.8	2,151.9

Notes: The algebraic symbols are defined as in table 2.2, except that real rates replace nominal. The rates of return v and $\bar{\rho}$ now contain subtractions for the ex post rate of consumer-price inflation in the lending country, and every flow is deflated by a lending-country consumer price index.

[a]As in table 2.2, two unsuccessful Mexican conversion loans from the 1915–45 period have been shifted to the pre-1914 period.

[b]Two dollar loans to czarist Russia in 1916 have been shifted to the pre-1914 period.

[c]The aggregate rate spread ($v - \bar{\rho}$) for the ten countries is negative, despite a positive NPV, because it is artificially calculated as an L_0-weighted average from the rates for the ten countries. If the rates of return had been properly derived from a computer run specific to the ten-country total, ($v - \bar{\rho}$) would have been positive.

[d]Three loans unsuccessfully aimed at settling Egypt's Ottoman debt.

[e]Three bonds issued by Turkey in 1933–35, just before commodity prices rebounded from their trough. Hence the negative $\bar{\rho}$.

The present figures are based on a larger set of bonds than in table 2.2. Conversion bonds, aimed at reviving payments on previous problem bonds, are now included. In some cases these were attached to the records of the previous problem bonds, while in other cases they were entered as separate bonds, possibly in a later period.

the British occupation. The imperial and Commonwealth tie presumably restrained Australian and Canadian temptation to avoid repayment. Japan feared heavy borrowing, especially early in the Meiji reign, and repaid faithfully until 1941 out of fears that arrears would be used as a pretext for foreign intervention.

Argentina also compensated foreign creditors for the tangible risk of her default. The federal government did refuse full repayment in the 1820s and again in the early 1890s, and provincial and municipal governments defaulted in the 1930s. Yet the defaults of the nineteenth century were never complete, and the federal government retired all its debt on time through the 1930s and 1940s. On balance, foreign bondholders got an average real interest premium of 1.96 percent per annum on all Argentine bonds since 1850.

Brazil's record was mixed, though positive on balance. She repaid her sterling (and franc) debts very faithfully, most of them being retired before the crisis of the 1930s. Her dollar debt, however, was largely repudiated in that crisis. Brazil unilaterally offered partial repayments later, leaving an ex post interest premium of 0.83 percent as bond-era legacy.

Chile is the marginal case. Until 1930 she was a perfect repayer, at an elevated interest rate. But her default in the 1930s was so complete, with so little offered creditors out of later nitrate revenues, that her overall repayment only about matched what lenders would have received by lending to their home governments.

Turkey, by contrast, declined repayment on two major occasions, the default of 1876–81 and the refusal of the Nationalist government to repay Ottoman debts after World War I and Versailles. The former episode well illustrates what Fishlow has called "revenue default" (Fishlow 1985; Wynne 1951, 393–453). Turkey's default was virtually assured by a pattern of overspending, corruption and inefficiency of tax collection dating back at least to the Crimean war loan of 1854. Turkey's creditors received only some of the generous interest rates initially offered them, with the result that the whole package of Turkish bonds has yielded a lower present value than the corresponding amounts of less risky consols, as shown in table 2.3.

The net gain from lending to Mexico was clearly negative. Table 2.3 shows, in fact, that even the *gross* realized internal rate of return was negative in the case of Mexican bonds since 1850, ignoring the net default on bonds before our 1850 starting point.

Mexican experience pitted the default incentive against gunboats, with default the ultimate victor, after an interlude of financial health. Throughout her first half-century of independence, a series of Mexican governments borrowed desperately and defaulted regularly. The crisis peaked during 1859–61, when the governments of Britain, France, and

Spain intervened in an attempt to seize control of the customs collections previously promised to private creditors. In the shuffle France installed Maximilian, who floated new loans, part of which financed partial repayments on old debt.[6] After Maximilian fell, the government of Benito Juárez refused to repay debts or honor customs-revenue pledges, from Maximilian or earlier. Later, in 1885–86, favorable negotiations with Porfirio Díaz ushered in a whole generation of financial rehabilitation and renewed foreign borrowing, to be stopped by the revolution in 1911. Thereafter, the old pattern returned: tentative debt agreements, each promptly breached (Lill 1919; Turlington 1930; Wynne 1951, 3–108; Bazant 1968). Thus ended Mexico's bond era, her credit not restored until the famous 1974–82 wave of bank lending.

The most negative experience was that tied to the government that borrowed from foreigners the most before World War I. By some outward indicators, czarist Russia might have seemed creditworthy. The imperial government had repaid loans faithfully, even to the extent of paying out more in debt service than it received in fresh loans between 1900 and 1913. Her trade and production were also growing apace (Fishlow 1985, table 3). Not far under the surface, however, the Russian government bonds were used in ways that did not promise repayment to the bondholders, revolution or no revolution. The investors, particularly those in France, were the ones who lost sovereignty in this case, deceived by the French and Russian governments in concert. Russia was building railways, to be sure, but at least from 1888 on the routes were being chosen for military purposes in consultation with the French government and French armaments suppliers (Feis 1930, 218–23). The main form of repayment was thus the political-military benefit reaped by the Allied governments, as Hawtrey has stressed:

> [T]he investor . . . was induced to hand over his money directly to pay for an allied country by way of preparation. The investor lost his money, because when the war came, the ally could not stand the strain. The strategic railways were not finished, the munitions were inadequate, the government was inefficient and corrupt. Still the investment was not wholly fruitless. Russia, at any rate, kept seventy divisions occupied for three years (as cited in Feis 1930, 220–24).

Other parts of the loan proceeds were also used by the imperial government to manipulate the lending governments and the investors. The French financial press was bribed by the czar's agents to give glowing descriptions of Russia's financial prospects on the eve of new bond flotations (Raffalovich 1931). Russian officials also maneuvred their large deposits among foreign banks so as to embarrass any bank or central bank squeezing the flow of credit to Russia. In the monetary tightness of the Moroccan crisis of 1911, for example, banks that tried to shut off their ordinary trade credits to Russian firms found that the Russian government pulled out still other deposits in large amounts, payable to other banks for new loans to the inconvenienced Russian firms (Lindert 1969, 29–31). Thus in a variety of ways, Russia made any attempt to stop lending costly to her creditors.

2.2.4 Global Returns to Lenders, in the Bond Era and since 1973

Combining the ten countries' diverse experiences, table 2.3 shows that investors made more on bond lending to foreign governments than on safer home governments, despite the revolutions and the Great Depression.[7] Foreign bondholders got a net return premium of 0.42 percent per annum on all bonds outstanding anytime between 1850 and 1970 (with payments carry-over traced through 1983). Curiously enough, the bonds issued in the troubled years between 1915 and 1945 fared better (for creditors) than those issued back in the prewar golden age. The bonds issued between 1850 and 1914 barely broke even with home-government bonds in the ex post measures used here, while those from 1915–45 realized a premium of 1.13 percent.

Were the realized returns on foreign bonds better or worse than those on lending to private domestic corporations? The only suitable comparison at hand is with W. Braddock Hickman's landmark study of U.S. corporate bonds (1958, 75–138; 1960). Our ten foreign governments repaid a nominal interest rate of 4.68 percent, versus 3.85 percent on home-government bonds, between 1850 and 1983 (table 2.10). In the troubled era 1900–43, Hickman's large U.S. corporate bonds repaid a lifetime return of 5.4 percent, versus an average return on home-government bonds somewhere near the 1850–1983 average. At face value, this would suggest that foreign government debt paid a bit less well than gambling on the fortunes of U.S. corporations. But Hickman's measures may be too optimistic about U.S. corporate bonds. He gives them generous subsequent-market valuations, both by following bonds across an era of declining nominal interest rates and by assuming that defaulted bonds were later redeemed at the favorable prices that only some of them fetched in the 1940s. For now, pending more detailed research, one should say only that there is no clear evidence of a systematic difference in the realized returns on foreign-government and domestic-corporate bonds.

Have creditors fared better or worse on loans to foreign governments since 1973? We must first note that lending institutions have changed. Bond lending has been very modest, even in the 1974–82 wave of optimism. Far more important are direct bank loans to governments. The maturities are generally shorter than those on the earlier bonds, and interest rates are quoted as premia over the variable London Interbank Offer Rate (LIBOR). The quoted interest rates ran a little over

1 percent above LIBOR (as table 2.6 will show below), but LIBOR is not the most relevant alternative rate. More appropriate are rates on U.S. government bonds of the same maturity. The contracted (ex ante) premium on Third World loans, like the earlier bond-era premia, was about 2 percent over interest rates on U.S. government bonds.

Are the loans of the 1974–82 wave being fully repaid? So far, despite the landmark Brazilian suspension of payments in February 1987, the answer is "maybe." The flurry of reschedulings in the period 1982–86 has had little effect on the realized rates of return. Borrowers repaid private creditors on contract, and were given little relief. To be sure, financial markets have come to *expect* a breakdown of debt service. As of mid-1987, the informal secondary market for banks' loans to problem debtors tended to discount these loans by about one third in most cases, with a much steeper discount on Bolivian debt. Top U.S. banks have posted over $16 billion in reserve-addition loss, much of it an expected loss on foreign debt. Similarly, the initial fears after the Mexican crisis of 1982 and later shocks depressed bank stocks (Kyle and Sachs 1984, Ozler 1986). Yet these expectations have not yet been reflected in any great shortfall of realized debt service.

How much default would it take to make the realized returns on recent loans match the realized return on bonds between 1850 and 1970? Table 2.4 quantifies the real rates of return realized on Third World debt since the end of 1973, under various assumptions about the extent of default. The three rate-of-return columns show the rates implied by actual experience up to the end of the year in question and by full repayment at the end of that year. The two columns at the far right measure the percentages of default that would bring the overall rate of return down to meet two norms. The first norm is simply the real rate of return on U.S. Treasury bonds of about the same maturities. The second is "history," or the historical premium of 0.42 percent a year over home-country bonds that was derived from table 2.3 above.

Had debtor countries fully repaid their public external debts at the end of 1982, private creditors would have reaped a premium of 2.81 percent a year over the (negative) real returns on having lent to the United States over the previous nine years. As of 1982, table 2.4 further implies, they could have collectively lost 15.3 percent of the total balance and still have earned the historical-average premium over loans to a creditor-nation government. This did not happen, of course. Instead, the debtors made partial net transfers to private creditors, while most of the debt was rescheduled and enlarged. Curiously, the net transfers to creditors of 1983–86 have been offset by a growing inconvenience to them. By being locked into rescheduled debts, instead of investing in now-more-competitive U.S. bonds, creditors have experienced a drop in their maximum possible premium on loans to the

Table 2.4   Private Real Rates of Return and Possible Default Losses on Public External Debt of Developing Countries, 1973–86, under Various Assumptions about Repayments in the 1980s

Outstanding Debts Paid or Defaulted at End of Year	If All Debts were Fully Repaid			Default Variations		
	Internal Rate of Return(v_f)	Real Rate of Return on U.S. Bonds($\bar{\rho}$)	Spread ($v_f - \bar{\rho}$)	Percent Capital Loss to Make Returns Match		Complete Default → Internal Rate $v_o =$
				U.S. Bonds ($v = \bar{\rho}$)	"History" ($v = \bar{\rho} + 0.42$)	
1982	0.77%	−2.04%	2.81%	17.9%	15.3%	−54.16%
1983	1.56	0.06	1.50	11.8	8.6	−39.69
1984	1.97	0.47	1.50	13.6	10.0	−28.25
1985	2.34	1.44	0.90	10.4	6.0	−20.96
1986	2.66	2.05	0.61	9.2	4.0	−15.68

Notes: We followed the actual performance of all public and publically-guaranteed external debt for all the 97 Third World nations included in World Bank, *World Debt Tables*, latest available estimates deflated by the U.S. consumer price index. Each row in the table represents a different year in which the debts were assumed to be completely settled, with the indicated degrees of default. Rates of return were defined as in table 2.3 above. All estimates refer to rates earned by private creditors, with initial loan fees apparently netted out of the amounts lent.

The internal rates of return (v_f) were calculated using the end-of-1973 disbursed debt outstanding as the initial flow to the borrowing country. For the purpose of calculating v_f, the debt outstanding at the end of the stated year was assumed to be repaid in full.

The alternative rate of return ($\bar{\rho}$) is the average of the real rates of return on seven-year U.S. Treasury bonds (ρ_t) held, and rolled over, from year t to the end of the year listed above, as an alternative to the net transfers to the developing country in year t. The average $\bar{\rho}$ thus corresponds to its formula in appendix A, except that discounting is forward to the end of a final year between 1982 and 1986, rather than backward to an initial loan date. (More precisely, ρ was calculated from the ρ_t's for 1973–81 only, leaving alone the ρ_t's unaveraged for the net-repayment years from 1982 on.)

The amount of default at the end of 1982 (or 1983, . . . , 1986) that would bring the internal rate of return (v) down to match the alternative rate of return ($\bar{\rho}$) equals the end-of-1982 value gained by capitalizing, at the ρ_t real rates, all actual flows between the private foreign creditors and the debtor country. The same procedure is repeated to calculate how much default would make the ex-post returns match a premium earned by earlier generations of international investors. Table 2.3 found that premium to be on the order of 0.42 percent per annum.

An additional technicality had to be addressed for correct use of the data in *World debt tables*. The starting point was the set of tables on "long-term public and publicly guaranteed" (hereafter "PG") debt to private foreign creditors. Dealing with these data alone would have given a biased picture of the returns to lenders. It seems that each year's flow data (new lending, repayments, and interest) refer to the population of loans classified as PG at the start of that year. Unfortunately, that population kept changing from year to year. The key to adjusting for this inconsistency was to note that the change in the amount outstanding failed to match the difference between new loan disbursements and principal repayments. The discrepancy equalled (apart from small exchange-rate adjustments and rare write-downs) a net inflow of loans into the PG category from other categories (short-term or non-guaranteed), on which we lack detailed data. The data discrepancy made it possible to sketch a profile of the earlier loans that became converted into PG loans, and to include both the earlier loans and the PG loans in the results shown here.

Third World ($v_f - \bar{\rho}$). As of the end of 1986, everything still hung in the balance: the creditors would suffer great losses if they received only the secondary-market discounted values for their loans, but if they were eventually bailed out, they would have received a better return than their pre-1973 bondholding predecessors got.

2.2.5   No Systematic Creditor Errors?

Despite the positive ex post returns overall, those recurring waves of international debt crisis tempt us to look for irrationality in investors' behavior. We take only a few steps in that tempting direction here. Like persons trying to pose for an interesting photograph in front of Niagara Falls, we want to get close enough to a subject of general interest to attract the viewer. But not too close.

Even if table 2.3 had shown overall returns below the safe-asset rate, economists are not willing to infer irrationality from ex post bad results. We generally insist on a tougher test of asset-market inefficiency. The market is inefficient—it is guilty of *systematic* forecasting errors—only to the extent that one can prove that some information available to investors could have improved their forecasts beyond their revealed valuations of assets in competitive asset markets. The appropriate test, then, is a regression test in which other available information significantly improves rate-of-return or asset-price forecasts from a sample when it is added to a regression already including the whole history of the market price of the asset. Could the holding of foreign government bonds "pass" this inefficiency test? No such test has been run. An obvious point to pursue in later regression-based research is: should not investors have noted the level of lending itself? The periods of highest gross lending, in relation to macro-aggregates, were the periods just before returns dropped. In this respect, the time pattern resembles the cross-sectional significance of debt ratios noted by Edwards (1986).

Indirect clues can be gained by exploring some circumstantial evidence. Note, in particular, the consistency in the identities of the defaulters. The set of borrowing countries defaulting (wholly or partially) before World War I had a higher probability of default in the 1930s than did other countries receiving loans in the 1920s. Again, the set of borrowing countries defaulting either before 1930 or in the 1930s had a higher probability of needing concessionary "rescheduling" of loans since World War II.

Figure 2.2 and table 2.5 summarize the historical consistency in the identities of the defaulters and reschedulers. The shares of countries falling into problem-debtor status (default, arrears, or, in the 1980s, signing rescheduling agreements) are contrasted between two kinds of countries: those with and those without such status in an earlier period. We chose periods long enough so that a wave of defaults had time to

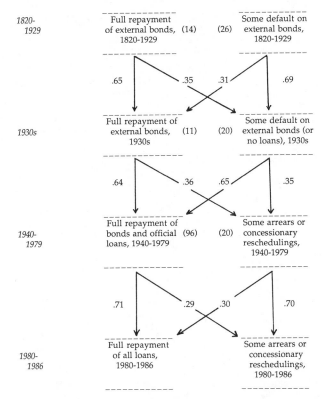

Fig. 2.2   Historical transition rates between repayment behaviors, governments of developing countries only, 1820–1986. *Notes:* Figures in parentheses are the numbers of countries at each starting point. The numbers are affected by historical changes in whether a country is considered less developed. For more detail, see tables 2.5 and 2.8. Countries listed in table 2.8 as "no loans" in the starting period of a transition are not counted. Russia/USSR is included in the first transition, but not in later ones.

abate, allowing a renewal of lending. There is a striking pattern of statistical significance. In either worldwide lending crisis (the 1930s and 1980–86), the problem debtors tended to be those who had had problems earlier. The pattern holds whether one looks across all countries or just across large samples of developing countries. We can reject the notion that repayments breakdown in crises is uncorrelated with the same nation's distant debt history. Two questions immediately arise: Why should such patterns exist, and have international lenders taken due note of them?

We can only begin to suggest reasons for the significant legacy left by a country's history of repaying, or not repaying, foreign creditors.

Table 2.5   **Historical Rates of Transition into Problem-Debtor Status, among Five Periods, 1820–1986**

Earlier → Period	Later Period	Among Earlier Full Repayers		Among Earlier Problem Debtors		Difference in Transition Rates	
		n	δ_r	n	δ_d	$\delta_d - \delta_r$	(Signif.)
A. All debtors							
1820–79 →	1880–1929	19	.105	23	.696	.591	**
1880–1929 →	1930s	32	.313	20	.800	.487	**
1820–79 →	1930s	23	.217	26	.692	.475	**
1930s →	1940–79	22	.182	22	.364	.182	
1940–79 →	1980–86	118	.237	21	.666	.429	**
1820–1929 →	1980–86	24	.167	25	.640	.473	**
1930s →	1980–86	25	.200	24	.625	.425	**
B. Developing-country debtors only							
1820–79 →	1880–1929	9	.222	23	.696	.473	*
1880–1929 →	1930s	22	.409	20	.800	.391	*
1820–1929 →	1930s	14	.357	26	.692	.335	*
1930s →	1940–79	11	.364	20	.350	.014	
1940–79 →	1980–86	96	.292	20	.700	.408	**
1820–1929 →	1980–86	8	.500	23	.696	.196	
1930s →	1980–86	9	.556	22	.682	.126	

Notes: "Sovereign debtor governments" are national or local governments in those countries whose national government was recognized as sovereign in budget setting and contract law in both the earlier and the later period, and which actually received foreign loans within both periods. Excluded (as nondebtors) are four usually-creditor nations: U.S., U.K., France, Germany. "Problem debtors" are those whose national or local governments did not repay contracted external debt in full, whether through repudiation or through recorded arrears lasting more than a year or (1980–86 only) signing rescheduling agreements with creditors. See Table 2.8.

n = number of countries covered.

δ = share of sovereign debtor governments becoming problem debtors in the later period.

* = difference is significant at the 5% level with a two-tailed test.

** = difference is significant at the 1% level with a two-tailed test.

To avoid sloppy references to "national character," later research on this issue should stick to exploring four paths. One argues that certain countries, by stint of economic history and geography, continue to be vulnerable to external shocks that trigger frequent debt crises. Another stresses the transmission of political forces from one regime to another causing such macro-policy distortions as hyperinflation, repeatedly triggering general financial crises. A third is that the very experience of not having repaid all debts in the past adds to the national political legitimacy of nonrepayment in the future. Finally, creditor jitters may invite the repetition of crises in the same countries, through higher interest premia and quicker flight when repayment problems loom (though we now turn to evidence against this fourth possibility).

Whatever the cause of the consistency of national repayments behavior, have creditors taken notice? They have indeed rationed credit to the Soviet bloc and China, and have continued to lend heavily to high-income good repayers like Australia and Canada. But among Third World borrowers, they have taken little note of history in their lending in the 1970s. Given the findings shown in figure 2.2 that default history raised the probability of rescheduling, both in 1980–86 and earlier, one would expect major banks to charge higher premia, or lend at shorter term, or lend less, to governments with a default history. They did slightly the opposite in 1976–79, according to table 2.6. Governments with histories of default and rescheduling paid about 0.04 percent *less* in interest, on slightly longer-term loans, than governments with unblemished repayment records. Repayments history, which helps predict subsequent repayments crises in the international cross-section, was ignored.

2.2.6   Were Defaulters Punished?

A clearer result from the history of rates of return on sovereign debt relates to the ex post treatment of those who fell into arrears: The only ones punished were a few countries defaulting in isolation before 1918. Before World War I, creditor-country military power could punish an individual borrowing country. Such was the fate of Egypt in 1880, as noted above. Venezuela also capitulated to gunboat pressure, in 1902. The Dominican Republic's attempt to default led to an invasion of the U.S. Marines and a takeover of the country's customs revenue in 1905. Nicaragua also lost her sovereignty to the Marines and to U.S. customs supervisors in 1911–12. Mexico, Turkey, and the Soviet Union were denied new credits after their repudiations around World War I.

Yet surprisingly few debtors have been punished since the 1920s, either with direct discriminatory sanctions or with denial of future credit. A correct reading of the relevant history is that the majority of nonrepayers "escaped" punishment during global crises. In the 1930s, debtors may have seemed to suffer cutoffs and trade retaliation, but the impression misleads. In that crisis and its early-postwar aftermath, the United States and other creditors were indiscriminate in their denial of fresh credits: Almost *no* governments in less developed countries got fresh loans, whether they were repaying old ones or not. A temporary gesture toward credit discrimination was the U.S. passage of the Johnson Act in April 1934 prohibiting private loans to foreign governments in default. But for the rest of the decade no loans were forthcoming even to governments exempt from the Act, and in July

Table 2.6   Debtor History vs. Interest Premia, 1976–79

| Country | Borrowing Experience, 1976–1979 | | | | Repayment Record, 1980–86 |
	Interest Premium	No. of Loans	Amount Lent ($ mill.)	Weighted Term (yrs.)	
A. Countries with no defaults or reschedulings before 1980					
Algeria	1.46%	46	2,822	7.5	—
Côte d'Ivoire	1.88	9	362	6.6	r '84–'86
Jordan	1.30	9	340	6.9	—
Korea, South	1.03	17	2,519	9.0	—
Malaysia	0.92	10	1,188	8.2	—
Morocco	1.21	13	2,070	7.6	r '83, '85
Portugal	1.02	22	1,506	7.6	—
Thailand	1.03	11	460	7.5	—
Tunisia	0.94	7	427	8.2	—
These nine	1.20%	144	11,694	7.9	
B. Countries with pre-1940 nonrepayments, none 1940–1979					
Bolivia	1.73	8	494	6.5	r '80,'81
Colombia	0.95	12	1,089	9.6	—
Costa Rica	1.16	11	521	9.5	d '83,r '83,'85
Ecuador	1.10	21	1,395	8.8	r '83, '85
Greece	0.79	13	1,497	9.4	—
Mexico	1.10	66	14,539	7.7	d '83,r '83,'84
Panama	1.52	12	871	8.4	r '85
Spain	1.02	75	5,511	7.7	—
These eight	1.09	218	25,916	8.0	
C. New post-1940 countries with reschedulings by 1979					
India	0.86	4	155	6.2	—
Indonesia	1.19	17	2,773	8.2	—
Philippines	1.24	28	2,953	8.7	r '84
These three	1.21	49	5,881	8.4	
D. Countries defaulting before 1940 and rescheduling 1940–79					
Argentina	1.36	41	4,398	8.2	r '82–'85
Brazil	1.38	116	10,191	9.5	r '83, '84
Chile	1.41	16	1,475	8.1	r '83–'85
Uruguay	1.45	7	357	8.5	r '83–'85
Venezuela	0.82	27	6,170	7.4	r '85
Yugoslavia	1.27	10	458	7.5	r '84, '85
These six	1.23	217	23,048	8.6	
E. All 26 countries	*1.16*	*628*	*66,538*	*8.2*	
F. Classified by later repayment record (1980–86)					
12 repaying on schedule	1.09	243	20,286	8.1	—
14 reschedulers	1.20	385	46,252	8.2	r

Sources: The data summarizing borrowing experience for 1976–79 were kindly supplied by Professor Sebastian Edwards. They underlie Edwards (1986, 574–77), and draw on data published by the World Bank. The repayments record is from table 2.8.

Notes: Interest premium = percent premium over London Interbank Offer Rate (LIBOR) on public and publically-guaranteed borrowings from banks in the Eurobank market.

r = rescheduling.

d = default, as defined in table 2.8.

— = repayment on schedule.

1945 exemptions were granted to every government belonging to the IMF and the IBRD (International Bank for Reconstruction and Development)—in effect, to every government outside the Soviet bloc (Lewis 1948, 140–5, 204–6).

Even trade policy, which had the chance to discriminate in the bilateralism of the 1930s, was not used to discriminate against defaulters or in favor of faithful repayers. Protectionism was too sweeping. Britain's Imperial Preference system might be viewed as an exception, inasmuch as it favored Commonwealth countries, who happened to have been faithful repayers, but even here repayment history was not the organizing principle. The United States, for its part, concluded reciprocal trade agreements after 1934 that favored defaulting countries as often as not (Tasca 1938, 274–75, 330–35; Tasca 1939, chaps. 1 and 2). The Export-Import Bank was restructured in 1936 in a way facilitating new loans to good neighbors, many of whom were Latin American defaulters on dollar bonds (Felix 1987, 31).

In the postwar era U.S. lending again failed to discriminate against defaulters among Third-World governments. Barry Eichengreen (chap. 3 in this volume) has shown as much for the lending of 1945–55. And, as we have seen in table 2.6, defaulters paid no extra premium when borrowing in 1976–79.

In the 1980s, too, the signs of discrimination against problem debtors remain weak, at least among developing countries. Bond lending has virtually dried up, and the revival of bank lending has been very meager, for countries who have repaid faithfully as well as for those demanding repeated rescheduling. Whatever the private wisdom of the pervasiveness of creditor pessimism, the external cost of repayments breakdown seems as evident in the 1980s as in the 1930s: Some faithful repayers (e.g., Colombia, Egypt) have suffered credit contraction along with problem debtors.

Thus the seeming irrelevance of repayments history in creditors' eyes is itself a lesson of history. It predicts that borrowers will not suffer much by following the lead of Peru and Bolivia in 1984 and Brazil and Ecuador in 1987 in cutting repayments and demanding partial writedowns of debt—at least if they do so collectively.

2.3.   Options for Handling Debt Crises: Some Suggestions from History and Theory

A combination of history and theory offers tentative lessons on dealing with a repayment crisis once it has already broken. History's contribution in this case is not based on the assumption that the present resembles the past, but on our belief that present crisis management differs from that of the bond era in an instructive way. What is special about the lingering crisis of the 1980s is official third-party intervention, led by the IMF. To understand what difference this option makes in a debt crisis, we need to use a framework that includes the main stylized crisis-management options.

2.3.1 Overview

The starting point for analysis of a debt crisis is to define the crisis. The present definition is straightforward: A debt crisis exists *if in the absence of a better offer, the debtor would rather impose unilateral nonrepayment than repay fully.* While there may be some incentive to bluff in such matters, let us accept insistent statements by a debtor government that it "cannot" repay fully without help or concessions from others as good prima facie evidence that it will not repay fully without such help. That is, as a rule of thumb, a debt crisis exists if the debtor says it does.

The options for minimizing the costs of a debt crisis are unilateral, two-party, and three-party. The creditors have two unilateral options (subject to the problem of getting organized as a group). They can impose penalties on the debtor if he does not repay, or they can lend more to the debtor on the current terms. Such a net transfer of resources will surely be satisfactory to the debtor. If no such unilateral aid is forthcoming, the debtor also has a unilateral alternative to full repayment: full or partial nonrepayment. The two-party option is one with a long history: The debtors and creditors can reach a compromise, each side bringing its own threat to the bargaining table. The two-party category includes cases in which the debtor unilaterally imposes a partial-repayment offer that creditors cannot refuse. The three-party options are more complex, typically involving financial aid and other policy measures by an official agency such as the IMF, the World Bank, or the government of the United States.

The options are conveniently judged with the help of table 2.7, which gives a schematic overview of the distribution of gains an losses from eah course of action. The simplicity of the framework may deceive. It is *not* based on a one-period view of debt negotiations. Rather it stems from a model of sequential multi-period decisionmaking described elsewhere (Lindert 1986). Its effects on different parties are based on capitalizations of the values of options for the future conditioned on this year's behavior. While policy recommendations are proscribed here, we describe the likely effects of each option on world wealth. We turn to the options in the order in which they are listed in the columns of table 2.7.

2.3.2 By Definition, Direct Full Repayment Is Out

A debt crisis has been defined as a situation in which V_t^D, the maximum social welfare attainable by the debtor by defaulting in this year,

t, exceeds V_t^R, the maximum welfare attainable by faithfully repaying this year, with the option to repay or default next year.[8] The welfare inequality $V_t^D > V_t^R$ is a direct translation of an inequality in the resources available for intertemporal consumption, as detailed in a companion paper (Lindert, 1986). Repaying this year means giving up principal and interest. In the framework used here, all of a loan is viewed as repayable at the end of the same year, with a new loan to be negotiated. If D_t is the borrower's debt at the start of the year, the debt service given up is $(1 + r_t)D_t$, where r_t is the interest rate on the loan. The countervailing advantage of faithful repayment is the avoidance of any penalty or loss of future access to credit. We can use P_t to represent the capitalized direct sanctions penalty for nonrepayment, taking such forms as foreign-policy reprisals, disruption of the debtor's foreign trade and seizure of his assets in the creditor country (Kaletsky 1985). P_t may vary with the size of the defaulted debt. The other cost avoided by repayment is B_t, the capitalized value of the borrower's surplus on all future borrowing made possible by the better repayment record. The definition of a debt crisis assures that the debtor would lose from repayment: $P + B < (1 + r)D$, if we drop the time subscripts. Unfortunately, the lender would gain more by avoiding default than the borrower would lose. In imposing penalties, the lender realistically recaptures only a fraction, α, of the penalty imposed. The rest of the penalty $(1 - \alpha)P$, is a deadweight loss from default, or a world wealth gain from repayment. Yet the borrower can impose this net cost by choosing default. Full repayment is ruled out in a debt crisis.

Note that the condition defining a debt crisis does not hinge critically on whether or not the debtor is bankrupt. Bankruptcy is a sufficient but not a necessary condition for a debt crisis. If the debtor is sovereign, meaning that direct seizure of collateral and similar penalties are less than the debt service owed, $[P < (1 + r) D]$, there can be a default incentive (i.e., a debt crisis, with $P + B < (1 + r) D$) even with debtor solvency (the debtor's assets, K, greater than $(1 + r) D$).

2.3.3 Relending Versus Default

A Theorem

The point brought out in the second column of table 2.7 is that extra lending at the same interest rate in a debt crisis does not remove the default incentive, but rather raises the amount defaulted on. If more is lent by the start of this period (D raised), the value of the debt service to be defaulted on at the end of the same period is raised by more than the costs to the debtor of defaulting.

This result states that more debt raises the net national welfare gain, and the net national wealth gain, from defaulting: $\partial(V^D - V^R)/\partial D > 0$ and $1 + r > \partial(P + B)/\partial D$. It follows from (a) the definition of a debt

Table 2.7   **Debt Crisis: Options for the Morning After**

Given that the debtor would prefer (or "be forced to") default without a rescue package, the following options bring the listed capital-value payoffs relative to complete default on the original loans:

Party	Unilateral Options		Two-Party	Third-Party Rescues	
	(1) Direct Full Repayment	(2) Extra Loans (ΔD), Same Terms	(3) Partial Debt Write-down	(4) Fully Repay Easy Rescue Loan	(5) Next-Year Default on Easy Rescue Loan
Debtor	$P + B - (1 + r)D < 0$	$\Delta(D - P - B) > 0$	$P + B - (1 + \lambda)D \geq 0$	$P + B - (1 + e)D - MAC \geq 0$	$P - P^e - eD \geq 0$
Lenders	$(1 + r)D - \alpha P > 0$	$\Delta(\alpha P) - \Delta D < 0$	$(1 + \lambda)D - \alpha P \geq 0$	$(1 + r)D - \alpha P > 0$	$(1 + r)D - \alpha P > 0$
Third party (rescuer)	—	—	—	$(e - r)D < 0$	$(e - r - 1)D + \alpha P^e < 0$
World wealth	$(1 - \alpha)P + B > 0$	$-(1 - \alpha)\Delta P - \Delta B$	$(1 - \alpha)P + B > 0$	$(1 - \alpha)P + B - MAC -$ moral hazard costs	$(1 - \alpha)(P - P^e)$, with moral hazard costs
Punch lines:	Debtor won't allow this.	Greater default.	Workable, though untidy.	May be dominated by (3).	Possible, dominated by (3).

where α   = share of default penalty recoverable by creditor as collateral (asset seizure),
   B = capitalized benefits to debtor from future credit rations,
   D = initial outstanding loan from banks to debtor,
   e = interest rate on concessionary ("easy") rescue loan ($e < r$),
   λ   = revised interest rate forced onto lenders ($\lambda < r$),
   MAC = macroeconomic adjustment costs imposed on debtor as part of the rescue package,
   P = penalty inflicted on the debtor for default on initial loan,
   P^e = penalty inflicted on the debtor for default on initial rescue loan,
and r = interest rate on original loan.

Note: The results under (1) and (2) are derived at length, and those under (3)–(5) are hinted at, in a multi-period model in Lindert (1986).

crisis (i.e., a situation in which $(1 + r)D > P + B$), and (b) the plausible condition that the elasticity of default costs with respect to the amount of debt be less than unity that:

$$\frac{\partial(P + B)/\partial D}{(P + B)/D} < 1.$$

This is almost surely true. For one thing, $\partial B/\partial D < 0$: Allowing extra lending to take place reduces the untapped borrower's surplus by increasing the ration of credit toward the unattainable complete-trust amount of lending where the borrower's surplus stops growing with the ration of credit. In addition, the direct penalties against defaulters have a fixed-cost component. It is plausible to assume that the first little bit of debt repudiation damages the debtor's standing substantially, leaving less increment in penalty available for punishing extra levels of default. In other words, $\partial P/\partial D < P/D < (P + B)/D$.[9]

Once these premises are granted, the inadvisability of extra lending follows. Relending in a debt crisis magnifies the Ponzi-scheme aspect of overlending to a sovereign debtor. Whether it raises or lowers the cost to the world cannot be said with certainty, but it cannot reverse that net cost, a cost made more certain by the raising of the debtor's default incentive.

Myths about Relending and "Panic Risk."

Is there no case in which creditors in the aggregate can gain by lending more in a debt crisis? No, not with *sovereign* debt.

Earlier defenses of the idea of relending to debtors threatening nonrepayment are either flawed or inappropriate to the case of sovereign debt. One flawed view stresses an ability-to-pay dynamic. The simplest variant dates back at least to Domar:[10] If only the debt can grow faster than the rate of interest, every individual loan can be repaid. A more popular variant argues that all is well if the debt/export ratio is kept from rising by having export growth outstrip the interest rate (Cline 1983, 46–72; Cline 1985, 36–45; Avramovic 1985; Dornbusch 1985, 343–83; Dornbusch and Fischer 1985, 60–65; Feldstein 1986). It is used with favor in writings by the World Bank and policymakers in debtor countries (e.g., World Bank 1985, 50–53; Simonsen 1985). But as shown elsewhere (Lindert 1986, 3–6), the popular variant is just Domar's variant in disguise, since the export terms cancel out. Both variants fail to note or correct the fact that infinite relending to a sovereign debtor in a debt crisis is a Ponzi scheme. Nor do they note that even on this view's own terms, the crisis is avoided *only if* the lenders are chained to repaying themselves *forever*.

The best theoretical case for relending at the brink of default is one presented by Hellwig (1977). In Hellwig's model, the borrower goes for some time without income, then gets a random income that might allow repayment. Once the stream of lending has begun, moral hazard sets in. The borrower overconsumes in the initial period, running low on funds and demanding more. Despite the clear danger of bankruptcy, the creditor rationally yields and relends to save at least the possibility that the borrower will get rich and repay. Hellwig assumes that bankruptcy settlements hold such clubs over the borrower that he will want to repay if at all possible (1977, 1883–85). Since the issue becomes whether or not the borrower is able to repay, involuntary relending is indeed rational (given the questionable decision to start lending in the first place). But Hellwig's model, while correct, cannot be applied to the case of sovereign debt, since his key assumption rules out debtor sovereignty. The sovereign debtor would still ask whether he had an incentive to repay, even after becoming rich. The present result is not contradicted.[11]

The present result also challenges the usual description of "panic risk," the danger that individual lenders will stampede to stop lending when a default incentive looms and triggers a capital loss for all creditors. The usual story is that their pursuit of individual security ruins the collective creditor interest. The formation of lending syndicates is one device for solving the "free-rider" problem among already exposed creditors.[12] There is reason to question, however, whether the "panic risk" or "free-rider" problem really exists during a rush to stop lending. It could exist, of course, if those who panicked were misjudging the ability of the borrower to repay all debts. But if they are fleeing because they correctly perceive that the debtor has an aggregate default incentive, panic by individual lenders does not impose any special cost, any "panic risk," on the whole community of creditors.[13] What is wrong with the usual discussion of panic risk and free riding in the context of sovereign debt is its assumption that creditors' collective interest is served by continuing to relend in a debt crisis. It is not. If the debtor has a default incentive, those creditors why continue to relend are not averting the capital loss that panic would bring. They are only pretending it does not exist—and are magnifying its present discounted value by relending.

2.3.4 Two-Party Debt Renegotiation

As a Game

The debtor and creditor(s) can reach a compromise that gives each side something better than its unilateral alternative. Each can use its unilateral option as a threat point. The debtor has the default option, precluding full repayment as a debt crisis outcome. Column (3) of table 2.7 lists the bargaining outcome that gives the debtor least, one in which he gets just enough reduction in interest rate (from r down to λ) to match the perceived gains of default. The creditors gain by avoiding default, recapturing enough of their investment, $(1 + \lambda)D$, to outweigh the seizure value of the debtor's assets, αP. The latter (αP for them, costing the debtor P) defines their threat point. The lower it is, the more the informed debtor can force creditors to write down debt obligations.[14] The two parties are likely to find a bargaining solution between the two threat points. In at least one formal model, they do find such a compromise under special assumptions (Bulow and Rogoff 1986), but there is no general theorem establishing a smooth bargaining solution.

How It Worked in the Bond Era

The two-party approach worked as well as could be expected before World War I. The exact outcomes varied with circumstances. At the benign noncrisis extreme, there were uncontroversial reschedulings that preserved the contractual capitalized value of debt while postponing (and magnifying) nominal service obligations to meet a pure-liquidity problem.[15]

Of the cases involving real give and take, three prewar Latin American examples illustrate the flexibility of two-party bargaining. One solution was reached between Mexico and her creditors in 1885–86. Eager to attract fresh foreign capital, incoming President Díaz signed three decrees on 22 June 1885 cutting government spending and offering a partial repayment of old foreign debts, but refusing to pledge any special government revenue to creditors. A year later these terms were accepted by the Corporation of Foreign Bondholders, and other arrangements were soon worked out regarding Mexico's non-London debts. Lending resumed until the revolution (Turlington 1930, 171–211; Wynne 1951, 30–47).

The Romero Plan (Arreglo Romero) of July 1893 revised Argentina's foreign public debts along similar principles.[16] Argentina was excused from 30 percent of interest payments for five years and from all amortization for eight years. Still in arrears despite a funding loan in 1891, Argentina was able to convince her private creditors that this was the best they would be offered. Creditworthiness, fresh inflows, and faithful repayment ensued. Financial rehabilitation owed less to fiscal belt-tightening then to a revival in demand for Argentina's exports from the late 1890s on (possibly helped by undervaluation of the peso after its stabilization).

The Brazilian funding loans of 1898 and 1914, organized by the Rothschilds, showed how private-bank conditionality differed with circumstances. The 1898 loan required that Brazil retire some of her note issue, which had grown too rapidly in the mid-1890s. In exchange,

Brazil got very little debt reduction, the loan calling primarily for value-preserving postponement of service, akin to the pure "rescheduling" packages of the 1980s. As Fishlow (1985 and 1987) has noted in this context, "[f]unding loans were not all finance and no adjustment," and in 1898 Brazil was prepared to take little direct financial relief and some adjustment for the sake of regaining creditworthiness. In 1914 she gave up less. In the eyes of creditors as well as her own, Brazil's troubles were not self-inflicted, but stemmed from a sudden plunge in her terms of trade on world markets, warranting renewed credit after a minor rescheduling.

The same workability could not be recaptured, of course, in the wake of the Mexican and Russian revolutions. In both aftermaths, creditors held no effective clubs over the postrevolutionary governments—no extra sanctions (P) that were not being imposed anyway, and no credible promise of generous future credits (bringing borrower surplus B) to compensate repayment of large past debts. No system was likely to succeed in averting default in these cases.

The same applies to the 1930s. Bargains were struck repeatedly, but each settlement was promptly breached by the debtors. As the present analysis of debtor incentives implies, repayment collapsed because, in effect, P and B plunged to zero. Threats of penalties against a debtor country were not credible, given that so many countries defaulted and that international trade and trade finance could hardly be made worse by vindictive creditors. Nor was there any reasonable prospect of renewed lending large enough to tempt most debtors into faithful repayment. The breakdown of the 1930s shows only that a worldwide collapse, which was not due in any large degree to the international debt defaults, posed a problem so great that no bargaining solution could work, no matter who helped out.

2.3.5 The Three-Party Approach

By contrast, international debt settlements in the postwar world are governed in part by international agencies ready to intervene in the debt-bargaining process—the International Monetary Fund, the World Bank, the Paris Club—and by the hegemonic lobbying efforts of the United States government on behalf of sound international finance. Outright repudiation has largely been replaced by those other "re-" words: rescheduling, refinancing, restructuring, renegotiation. The consensus is that this intervention has helped avoid the instability of the 1930s. Yet there are reasons to question the consensus. The imperfect bilateralism of the bond era may have been a more realistic approach to the inherently untidy problem of sovereign debt than the new third-party interventionism.

Its Postwar Evolution

The evolution of the three-party approach can be divided into three postwar stages for expositional purposes. Before about 1955, when governments borrowed abroad mainly from other governments, rescheduling was also bilateral. The troubled debtor got assistance directly from an agency of the lending government, such as the export-import bank. Concessionary refinancing, like Marshall Plan aid, was an American affair. The IMF and World Bank still concentrated on their initial priority tasks, the balance of payments and development loans, respectively. This earliest phase resembled the two-party approach of column (3) in table 2.7.

Between about 1955 and about 1979 the supply curve of concessionary third-party financing shifted out. The Fund and Bank began to assume a greater and greater third-party role in debt refinancing (Bittermann 1973, chap. 3). In some cases, they merely provided good offices, as an informed catalyst in negotiations between other governments. In others, they, especially the IMF, laid out formulas for macroeconomic adjustment in the borrowing country. And in some cases, they actually contributed to the refinancing package, with loans on their own separate terms. Their supply of concessionary financing may have been raised by the establishment of explicit Fund conditionality between 1952 and 1955, a move that may have raised the contributions of their conservative main subscriber, the United States (Dell 1981, 9–12). Essentially the same policy guidelines for the supply of concessionary finance have remained intact since.

After 1979, and especially after the debt crisis broke in mid-1982, the demand curve for refinancing shifted far to the right. Debtors' first recourse was, as usual, to their immediate creditors. By 1979, however, these creditors were private banks whose exposure had risen to heights not approached since the 1920s. The private banks were more reluctant than the earlier government creditors to write down the debt obligations due them. They suffered greater exposure, lacked any foreign-policy motivation to make concessions to a foreign government, and (in the United States) were (and still are) constrained by law to declare any loan with interest arrears to be "nonperforming," forcing a write-down of net worth. What private creditor banks have sought in the crisis since 1982 is an extension of third-party rescue, the policy that was emerging in the 1955–79 period. The surge in demand for third-party help posed a delicate policy issue.

Third-Party Rescues in Principle

To judge the potential and the perils of third-party rescue packages, let us first describe this approach as an ideal type and then compare it with actual practice in the debt crisis of the 1980s.

A stylized third-party rescue would lead to the cost-benefit accounting sketched in column (4) of table 2.7 above. The third party (e.g., the IMF or World Bank) grants a rescue loan at the lower interest rate, e, which the debtor uses to pay off private creditors at the higher interest rate, r. The private creditors recapture their money in full, and the debtor gets a reduction in its external liability. The rescuer, with money ultimately raised from taxpayers, subsidizes the combination of the first two parties, giving interest-rate relief ($e < r$) that is split between the debtor government and its private creditors.[17] The two parties thus gain, relative to the bond-era institutions forcing them to bargain only with each other. The world benefits in exactly the same way as with two-party negotiations: It saves the deadweight loss from the retaliatory penalties, or $(1 - \alpha)P$, subject to subtler costs discussed below.

Which side tends to capture the subsidy—the debtors or the creditors? No simple answer can be firmly given, but there is reason to suspect that the creditors are the larger proximate beneficiaries. Their gain is the more tangible, at least: They get repaid the full risk-elevated interest rate (r) on their loans, whereas two-party bargaining would have forced them to accept a write-down ($\lambda < r$). The debtors are given enough to forestall default (though it could return, as column (5) in table 2.7 warns).

Three Extra Costs

Subsidizing international lending on insufficient collateral would not seem so costly if one just looked at the subsidy wedge and the likely elasticity of long-run overlending response as a percentage of world product, calculated on the back of an envelope. The effect on world wealth could be as low as that in the two-party settlements of column (3). There are three subtler costs, however: moral hazard costs, macroeconomic adjustments costs, and costs of delays in settlement.

A third-party rescue involves an extra moral hazard not present in the two-party case.[18] That subsidy tied to the write-down ($e - r)D$ encourages the type of lending wave that creates debt crises. Yet it captures only those immediate world gains, $(1 - \alpha)P + B$, that two-party settlements could have captured without the extra moral hazard.

Rescue packages involving the IMF also impose macroeconomic austerity on the debtor countries (via conditionality). Austerity is not a bad in itself. In fact, given the frequent bias toward inflated government payrolls, monetized deficits, and inflation, austerity can be its own reward from the viewpoint of the adjusting nation. The IMF could continue to offer incumbent policymakers its services as the classic "ogre of first resort," taking blame for short-run adjustment costs and giving them the extra political chance to survive until the whole nation reaps the longer-run gains from austerity.

The issue here is not the idea of conditionality, but its current marriage to repayment of private creditors. In the 1980s, IMF conditionality has imposed macroeconomic adjustments in relation to the debt hangover, not just in relation to the macroeconomic need for austerity in the debtor country. Some countries might be pressured too much, others too little. To the extent that there is merit in correcting debtor-country macropolicies just to encourage international creditworthiness, that is a task that might be left to private conditionality (Friedman, in Williamson 1983), just as it was in the two-party bargaining before World War I. The Fund has the option of concentrating its conditionality on the seriousness of macroeconomic overheating in the debtor country.

A third subtle cost of the three-party approach is a cost of delay, which has become evident in the wave of reschedulings in the 1980s. Unlike the ideal concessionary third-party relending of column (4) in table 2.3, the involvement of the IMF and the World Bank has not brought significant relief to debtors and has not resolved the uncertainties of the debt overhang. To be sure, dozens of rescheduling and refinancing agreements have been signed. Yet the terms involve no clear write-down of debt. While debtors' demand for liquidity has been assisted by debt rollovers with grace periods, the rescheduling loans tend to involve a *higher* interest-rate spread over LIBOR. Of the fourteen leading debtors whose rescheduling in 1980–86 was noted in table 2.4 above, nine are slated to pay clearly higher spreads over LIBOR than those at which they borrowed in 1976–79; four (Argentina, Panama, Mexico, Yugoslavia) are paying spreads both above and below, but averaging above, their 1976–79 rates; and only the B-loan to Côte d'Ivoire is below the 1976–79 average rate (Watson et al., 1986, 106–22). While one could argue that the rescheduled rates over LIBOR might be below the shadow price of funds given the debt crisis, they do not concede any write-down of existing debt.

Why has little or no debt relief yet been offered to debtors in the negotiations of the 1980s? While the issue must remain open to debate, we hypothesize that the intervention of the Fund and the Bank has impeded the striking of bilateral bargains between debtor governments and the creditor banks. Debtor countries seeking debt relief are also shopping for concessionary new loans from the Fund and the Bank. Under current practice, an impasse arises—or is imposed by creditor resistance. IMF policy generally proscribes agreement with a debtor country for concessionary finance in exchange for domestic belt-tightening until the country has reached an agreement restoring good standing with private foreign creditors. The link between creditor satisfaction and official financing is explicit in the Fund's pursuit of "co-financing" packages since 1982. Knowing this, the main banks have the option of holding out for repayment at or near the original high interest rates. With official aid held hostage, the debtor resorts to buying time, remaining current on debt service and signing short-run rescheduling agreements involving little or no relief. The delays continue, and cloud capital formation, until the debtor gives up on the process—a resignation seemingly signalled by Brazil in February 1987.

The three-party approach thus has extra problems, the magnitudes of which depend on whether the approach is truly followed or only simulated. A genuine rescue, by reducing debt service, poses a moral hazard. It subsidizes the combination of debtors and lenders, inviting future waves of overlending. It also distributes costs of macroeconomic austerity according to foreign debt outstanding, rather than according to the severity of domestic macroeconomic disequilibrium. If the three-party approach is only simulated, as in the indecisive reschedulings of 1980–86, time is wasted, prolonging uncertainties that may depress capital formation. One way or the other, the three-party approach seems to offer lower world wealth than the two-party approach.

2.3.6   A Note on Creditor Distress

An obvious fear about the suggestion just raised is that leaving lenders to their own devices threatens financial instability. In an unlikely extreme case, if their full Third World exposure were a capital loss, the nine top U.S. banks would be insolvent. Is there not a case for an official bailout to avert the financial panic that might attend their bankruptcy?

The issue of financial panic definitely cannot be resolved in the space available here. It is one on which reasonable people may differ. Yet we would be remiss if we did not indicate our own views on this issue, an issue naturally raised anew by our interpretation of the evidence above.

We suggest three reasons why such a concern does not make a case for policies rescuing shareholders and managers of the troubled banks. One minor reason is that panic probabilities can be invoked only when the kind of default possible exceeds lenders' exposure and the lenders are major financial institutions. In most cases, the two-party bargaining process would predictably yield an outcome in which the creditors suffered only a partial default. Neither they nor the debtor countries on the other side of the table have an incentive to let the main creditors fail. A second restraint on the fear of financial destruction is that a major U.S. bank in serious trouble can be purchased by any of several already-willing suitors (e.g., First Interstate, Sumitomo, etc.), with its operating units intact. Its accumulation of knowledge, customer relations, and physical capital need not be dismantled and auctioned off in uneconomical parts.

Above all, history reminds us that a key line of defense for avoiding financial panics stemming from bank insolvency (whether bank investment policies are at fault or not) is to protect the nonequity *claimants* on the insolvent banks. Given a capital loss on the banks' (or other private creditors') assets, the central bank or other rescuer bears only the same or less cost by defending nonequity claimants as it would bear by sheltering shareholders' net worth against any capital loss at all. The U.S. bank failures of the early 1930s did not show that the "lender of last resort" needed to protect banks' shareholders, but that it should have protected depositors and other claimants, calming more fears with less official loss and less moral hazard. And, back in the international sphere, the Bank of England followed a similar strategy in the Barings Crisis of 1890. When Barings was threatened with insolvency because of its Argentine investments, it was liquidated and reorganized with some loss of partners' equity. The claimants on Barings were rescued first, with the Barings partners' equity left at market risk. No tidal wave of panic resulted (Clapham 1958, 2:325–39).

2.4   Conclusions

There is a growing body of literature in which lessons are carefully drawn from comparisons of the 1980s debt crisis with earlier crises involving international lending to sovereign debtors. This chapter concentrates on two sets of issues: the long-run patterns of behavior toward international lending, and the policy options for dealing with debt crises after they have hit.

On the private returns to such lending, we get a mixture of results:

1. On the whole, lending to foreign governments has brought investors a higher real rate of return than the alternative of lending to their own governments, despite foreign defaults. Between 1850 and about 1970, lenders were promised about a 2 percent ex ante premium on the bonds of ten foreign governments, and ended up with about a 0.42 percent ex post premium. In the wave of lending since 1973 the ex ante premia were again about 2 percent over home-government bonds. The ex post returns still depend heavily on future repayments, subject to the constraints quantified in table 2.4. Debaters over the need for official intervention into the international-debt sphere cannot yet cite any past aggregate shortfall in investors' private returns.

2. For a subset of major government borrowers, the crises of nonrepayment have been deep enough or frequent enough to make their bond debt an inefficient part of foreign portfolios for over a century.

The foreign bond debts of Chile, Mexico, Russia, and Turkey have offered negative net returns. Investors had foreseen some likelihood of default in three of these four cases, charging higher than average ex ante interest premia (Russia is the exception here).

3. There is a significant historical consistency in the identities of the countries defaulting. Countries that had defaulted before 1929, for example, were more likely to default in the 1930s than were others. Similarly, countries that had defaulted or needed concessionary refinancing before 1980 were more likely to be in arrears or get rescheduling agreements in the 1980s.

4. Defaulting debtors were not consistently punished. There were only a few early cases where countries trying to default in visible isolation led to direct sanctions and discriminatory denial of future credit. Most of the defaults occurred in the worldwide crises of the 1930s—and possibly the 1980s—when uncooperative debtors suffered no more than cooperative ones.

For international debt crises in full swing, there is no tidy solution, because of the inherent defects of unenforceable lending. We rank the available options according to their likely world-wealth effects, arguing from a mixture of history and theory that

5. In a debt crisis, merely relending to the same borrower on the same terms (pure "rescheduling") must lower creditor and world wealth, given that it was necessitated by the borrower's credible threat to cut repayments unilaterally if no lending occurred.

6. The older direct two-party bargaining of the bond era, in which debtors and creditors turned to partial repayment plans, had a mixed record. Revolutions and the Great Depression brought sweeping debt repudiation and credit cessation, but other cases were resolved much more smoothly. Direct two-party bargaining can be said to be workable, if untidy.

7. The modern three-party approach, with international agencies intervening in debt crisis negotiations, introduces three further complications beyond those of the imperfect two-party bargaining of the bond era. First, the experience of the 1980s finds that the three-party approach has produced short-run cosmetic agreements with little clear resolution of the underlying disagreement over resource transfer. The attending delays may have prolonged investment uncertainty. Second, if truly concessionary rescue loans had been forthcoming, they would have brought moral hazard, inviting further waves of private gambling on foreign sovereign debt. Finally, further work is needed to determine whether third-party (e.g., IMF) pressure for macroeconomic adjustment has become less correlated with the need for such adjustment because the pressure is attached to the extent of external debt.

Appendix A
Data Sources and Data Processing for the Bond Sample

Overview of Data Sources

Bondholders' Watchdog Annuals

The most important of these were the annual reports of the British Corporation of Foreign Bondholders (CFB). The series dates from 1873, and the approximate period of full detail covers the half-century from 1885 to 1935. During this interval, the typical issue comes in three parts: a brief narrative account of such country-specific important events as new issues, negotiations, defaults and consolidations; a more quantitative series of country appendices; and finally, a brief summary of "Principal Loans in Default." CFB tries to report all obligations of debtor governments, but its coverage of sterling issues is of higher quality than its coverage of other European and American-based lending activities. The country appendixes try to provide summary measures of debt outstanding and total debt service for some countries, but the terms of aggregation cannot be relied upon to be consistent from one year to the next. For the purposes of this project we did not make any use of aggregated information from CFB or any other source, but instead applied our own aggregation methods to the information on individual issues. During the late 1930s the quality of the reporting deteriorates rapidly. The editors blame the manpower demands of World War II, but the timing of the decline suggests that the real cause may be demoralization and shortage of funds associated with the massive wave of default of the early 1930s. Reports continue to issue until at least the mid-1970s, but are usually inferior in quality to other sources available for this period.

By the 1930s several other annual publications are available to supplement those of the CFB. The American-based Foreign Bondholders' Protective Council (FBPC) was patterned after the CFB, and provides very good coverage of American issues outstanding during the 1930s and 1940s. FBPC data have been of special value in tracing the details of patchwork funding arrangements for Latin American debt during the 1930s and its subsequent liquidation during the 1940s. It is also of great value in tracing the arrangements made to adjust Japanese debt during the post–World War II period. By comparison to CFB, however, it gives less attention to issues of foreign (here, non-American) origin.

The best American annual source of debt information is that provided by the Moody's annual reports. We began to rely on these as a main source of information for debts to all countries around the year 1930, creating a period of overlap with the CFB coverage. Fortunately, the Moody's and CFB figures reconcile quite well during this period.

Occasional Compendia

Certain other publications which were not issued on an annual basis also contributed extensively to the data base. For the interval 1850 to 1885, before the period of greatest reliance on CFB data, the chief sources were Hyde Clarke (1879) and Fenn (1874, 1889, and 1898). Thereafter, we consulted the American compendia Fitch (1918), Kimber (1925), Kimber and Nagel (1933), and Dominick and Dominick (1934, 1936). These sources constituted the most detailed summaries of debt outstanding at points of time, and the preferred research strategy was, where possible, to jump from one compendium to the next, falling back upon the annual publications only when necessary to resolve conflicts or focus on particular years of interest.

Country Studies

The third most important class of information source for this project consisted of special studies, usually devoted entirely to a single country. Perhaps the best of these were those included in Wynne (1951). From this work we made use of chapters devoted to Egypt, Mexico, and Turkey. Three other important resources were Peters (1934), Turlington (1930), and Ludwig (1985), devoted respectively to Argentina, Mexico, and Brazil.

For each country, coverage typically moved from one dominant source to another. In trying to keep the reader informed about the passing of dominance from one source to the next, we do not mean to imply that the secondary sources were disregarded; only that in most cases they were found to be redundant.

Sample Design Strategy

Definitions of "Sovereign" and "External" Debt

The mass of data available from the sources mentioned above was assembled for the benefit of contemporary investors, not subsequent scholars. Definitions and categories shift over time and make it necessary to apply some criteria in deciding what to include and what to leave out. The most important case in point here is that of government guaranteed railroad debt. In many sample countries this category of investment was at least as important an avenue of capital inflow as direct government bond issue, but it is not included in this study because technically there is presumed to have been some recourse available against nonsovereign private borrowers before any guarantee could be invoked. Also, these sorts of flows are very poorly documented until their failure makes them direct government obligations. When this happens, it is usually necessary to treat them as new inflows at the time of the activation of the guarantee. Where possible, of course, we tried to include as much of the original issue information as could be retrieved.

In the same sense it was not always clear which issues should be considered truly external. The general criterion employed here is that real foreign debt should be issued and serviceable abroad, and should be redeemable in foreign currency. In some cases such as that of Argentina, this test is met by certain bonds explicitly denoted "internal," because of the need to circumvent a legislative ceiling on interest payable on "foreign" debt. These were included in the study, while the Argentine mortgage instrument known as a "cedula," which was apparently popular in European portfolios during the last century, was left out except where service was specified to be made in gold values.

Throughout the process of data collection, we were mindful of the fact that some international lending is motivated more by strategic considerations than by expectation of financial return. Thus we excluded all government-to-government transactions associated with the two world wars. In the post–World War II regime, however, the dividing line was not so obvious, given a proliferation of international financial intermediaries who were subject to some degree of manipulation on behalf of the global interests of the lending country governments. Here the sorting task became very difficult. In one case, that of Turkey, we observed some surprisingly low ex post rates of return on post–World War II dollar debt, which were not due to default. Whether they were due to unanticipated dollar inflation, or whether the loans were semiconcessionary from their inception, remains unclear. For some purposes the reader may wish to exclude them from the sample, which is easily done because there were no pre–World War II dollar denominated loans to Turkey.

Choices of Sample Countries

Our strategy, as mentioned in the text, was to sample the greatest value share of all loans since 1850 at the least research cost by tracking the whole population of external bonds issued by the ten top foreign-borrowing countries. The "top" countries were to be those with the greatest real gross borrowing over the whole 130-odd years. Lacking world data on total borrowings by country, we had to make an initial guess based on the secondary literature. The ten countries followed here were thus chosen by hunch, even before we could construct the estimates in table 2.1 of the stock of outstanding external debt at three dates. Table 2.1 reveals that we probably did not pick the top ten. In particular, Chile should have been replaced with New Zealand if we were to get as close as possible to the top ten borrowers over the whole period.

Yet by picking up a Latin American that defaulted in the 1930s and is again a problem debtor in the 1980s, we at least made the sample and the task of data-gathering more interesting than if we had followed the history of yet another good repayer, such as New Zealand. Chile, we expect, will interest more readers. The switch means that our sample is slightly biased toward nations with troubled histories, a slight bias that helps firm up some of this paper's finding but not others.

Choice of Sample Period (1850–1983)

We originally intended to build a continuous data set embracing both bonded (largely pre–World War II) lending and direct bank lending (largely post-1970) in a unified format. It did not take long, however, to discover that the best data available for the former category of lending activity took the form of information about individual issues, whereas the information on the more recent wave of bank lending took the form of aggregated flows into and out of each borrowing country. Thus, an apparent regime shift in lending practices was accompanied by an apparent regime shift in reporting practices.

The main reason for this recent emphasis on aggregate flows is probably the fact that individual loan contracts had become too small relative to the whole, too short in their term and too flexible in the determination of interest rates (i.e., indexation to LIBOR), to permit reporting on the specifics of each individual issue. It may also be significant that when sovereign loans became permanent features in the portfolios of the lending banks and ceased to be traded on public financial markets, information on individual issues became proprietary to the banks themselves in a way that it had not been previously. At any rate, in a project such as ours, it is apparent that such a change in reporting conventions was not accomplished without the loss of important information. One is faced with the anomaly that in spite of the technical advances in data handling which had taken place during the period since World War II, the quality of the available data deteriorated. Any merger of the two data sets would have necessitated discarding the additional information available for the earlier set, making it impossible to draw conclusions about "anticipated" returns as well as realized returns. We decided to maintain the separation in order to take full advantage of the richness of the data on bonded lending. The reader will note that bonded lending tends to "taper down" throughout the post–World War II period as it is supplanted by the new practices, while the direct lending by banks explodes into prominence in the mid-1970s.

In fact, the temporal distribution of bonded lending may be said to show almost symmetric tails, accelerating from about 1850 to 1890, and with a phaseout period from about 1940 to 1980. It is far from a smooth curve, since it covers many cycles of boom and bust, and in fact there is some overflow at either end. We initiated the investigation at 1850 largely because the preceding two decades were almost totally quiescent. Several large issues were floated in the 1820s to Latin America and Russia, and we used the expedient of treating the outstanding balances as cash inflows in the year 1850. Similarly, we assumed where no evidence of default existed, that all outstanding issues were paid off at par in 1983, our final year of coverage. The bulk of these loans were to Australia and Canada and Japan, so this was probably a very safe assumption. (In contrast, the outstanding balances for defaulted loans to czarist Russia were *not* assumed to be repaid in 1983).

The Collating Algorithm

The Data Records

The relative abundance of information about individual bonded issues made its demands upon the available technology of aggregation, particularly because of the emphasis to be placed on stacking all loan contracts together as if they had a common inception year. It is precisely here that data on aggregate cash flow totals will not suffice. In order to stack loans to a common origin date it is necessary to treat the aggregate debt service annuity payable by a sample country to its creditors as being composed of many substreams traceable to different origin dates and thus subject to different discounting schemes. For this purpose, we employed a system of breaking down the history of each loan into annual data on debt service, retirement, and balance outstanding, so that the information could then be reassembled for the purpose of stacking. This will henceforth be referred to as a "collation algorithm," since its primary function is to sort and arrange data for convenient analysis. In all cases except that of Canada, we made use of the same general approach to the collating of data. The number of issues considered per country borrower varies widely, from 22 in the case of Egypt, to 439 in the case of Australia. There is great variance in the size of the issues, because countries differ in the extent to which their various subdivisions have borrowed on their own account. Canada represents the extreme case in this regard, where the number of tiny issues overwhelms the means of assimilating them into the data base.

For this reason all the results for the 488 Canadian bonds are pre-aggregated into aggregate cash flows with a spreadsheet program, without any ability to stack by origin year.

The typical pre–World War II bond issue by a sample country specified repayment in a fixed annual sum for a specified number of years in return for an inflow generated by the flotation of bonds of specified face value. The ability to hold the entire principal outstanding until maturity appears to be an option that was available chiefly to white commonwealth borrowers, although Japan also borrowed according to this model. When the United States began lending in the 1920s, its mode of operation sometimes called for repayment in specific blocks of outstanding debt leading to a staggered repayment stream, but fortunately these instances are uncommon. Other exceptional forms sometimes occurred when there was lending to a sovereign under stress. Here interest may escalate in stages or a sinking fund may not commence until a specified future year. Loan contracts may vary as to whether or not specific revenues were pledged as security, and the degree of choice to be exercised by the creditor in specifying the currency of service. The agreement may contain provisions about how bonds were to be selected for payoff; whether the borrower could retire ahead of schedule; and the price, not necessarily par, at which outstanding debt must be retired.

All the above features might be considered contractual between borrower and lender at the time of the capital inflow. Having entered into the loan agreement, the creditor then faced not only the risk of imperfect fulfillment of the contract by the debtor, but also the risk of imperfect fulfillment of expectations about prices and exchange rates. In order to capture the rest of the story, source materials must be scanned for reference to ensuing irregularities, balances outstanding, and dates of final retirement. New issues may give rise to new inflows, or consolidations may replace one issue with a successor issue. The desired objective is to follow the payment history generated by a given loan transaction until it was extinguished at maturity, completely defaulted, or paid off in some market-mediated transaction. Consolidations or refinancing operations or settlement agreements that did not involve the public marketing of fresh debt were not considered sufficient reason to "restart the clock," and the descendant issues in these cases were treated as originating in the year of the initial capital inflow. With the good data available for most publicly offered issued during the bond-lending era, this goal was generally attainable.

The "Collator" Program

The "collator" program was used to construct a schematic representation of the year-by-year history of each loan qualifying for inclusion in the study. The program accepts information on the contract specifications and subsequent changes in performance for each loan, and targets outstanding balances for particular downstream years. It interpolates between the fixed points in the history of the loan to provide a continuous track on interest, retirement, and balance outstanding for each year of the loan's life. One-time flows which come at the beginning or the end of the loan's life are recorded in a fourth payment category reserved for lump-sum capital flows.

This stage of creation of annual breakdowns for all loans manages to capture almost all types of performance risk faced by the lender, with the possible exception of disputes involving currency of service. First, it takes note if the original issue price of the bonds differs from par, because this results in an increase of face value outstanding which is not the same as the amount of the associated capital inflow. In addition, the collating procedure captures intervals of complete or partial default, or the payment of interest with retirement suspended. It can show changes in terms or face value, or the issuance of cash bonuses which may come as part of a negotiated settlement. Most subtly, it incorporates an iterative procedure which uses a downstream year balance outstanding together with other information on the loan history to estimate the average price at which bonds are being retired by the action of a contractual sinking fund. This is useful in cases where countries are specifically permitted to retire their debt through purchase on the open market if it is circulating below par. When prices are low, countries may be able to retire debt much faster than anticipated without spending more than is called for in the contract, and this is captured by the procedure. Unless specific mention is made to the contrary it is assumed that no more is being allocated to retirement than is called for by the contract, and when retirement is observed to lag behind schedule it is assumed that the loan is not being fully served.

The original schematic loan record also includes an index section in which are stated some of the particulars of the loan such as its title, if any, its currency and power of 10, source references, and notes about its eventual disposition. The selection of the service currency is sometimes confused by language which appears to permit the bearer to select service in a currency of choice, from among several possibilities. There was no clear way to resolve problems of this sort, and almost universally it is simply assumed that the currency of service is that of the major lending country associated with the flotation of the loan. When a loan issues in more than one currency tranche, each tranche is considered to be served in its own currency of origin. Purported gold clauses were assumed not to be enforced in the absence of mention to the contrary, because in practice they seldom proved binding. The lack of certainty about service currency is of limited consequence in light of the predominance of dollar and sterling issues. The exchange rate questions arise most urgently in the case of French franc loans which depreciated drastically in value along with the franc after World War I. Most franc lending, however, was concentrated in Turkey, Brazil, and most importantly Russia. Of these, Turkey and Russia paid little and nothing, respectively, after the abandonment of the gold standard. Brazil paid in paper francs during the 1920s despite a decision of the World Court in favor of the gold clause. Before the decision could be fully implemented, the Brazilian debt too was in default.

The creation of the initial loan profiles is in no instance completely straightforward, although it approached this state most closely in the case of the best-behaved borrowers. Many of the sample countries have very contorted borrowing histories, and no array of programming tools can eliminate the need for spot judgment and improvision. The most noteworthy of these exertions are mentioned briefly in an unpublished appendix giving country histories. In general, one goal was achieved and one was abandoned. Each country history has been assembled out of individual loan records in such a way as to be a coherent whole, but the same cannot be said for each individual loan record. Often a consolidation or a settlement plan would be captured only by the inclusion of loan records drawing together fragments of many original issues under one heading. Where this happened, neither the original issue records nor the record specifically dedicated to, say, a consolidation plan, tells a complete story about the stream of payments arising from an original market offering. Only when taken together do the records produce meaningful net present values and rates of return on bonds born in the marketplace.

To compute the ex ante contracted returns of tables 2.2 and 2.10, the loan profiles for each country are then subjected to a "masking" program which creates a new hypothetical loan record showing perfect performance on the part of the borrower, regardless of how bad was the actual outcome. This was done by discarding all information about any decreases in the service flow. In these "idealized" loan records, the borrower is presumed never to reduce the amount remitted from one year to the next until the whole balance is retired. (This procedure is possible solely because of the observed rule that in *no* case was any loan contract observed to specify in advance a decrease in the annual service prior to the full repayment of the loan.) Consolidation issues emerging from periods of interrupted service were eliminated, since under perfect performance they would never have occurred. The result is a new record base which can be used to calculate hypothetical "contracted" yields, and thus by contrast separate the ex post impact of contract nonfulfillment from the impact of movements in exchange rates and prices.

Summary Measures for Rates of Return and Net Present Value

To judge the net profitability of holding foreign sovereign debt, we need to compute its real internal rate of return, v, the real rate of return on alternative assets, $\bar{\rho}$, and the net real present value, *NPV,* of the sovereign debt over and above the value of a comparable investment in the alternative asset. The real rate of return measure, v, must take into account all departures from the contracted payments schedule, and not be just the real equivalent of the stated coupon rate.

Measuring real rates of return for alternative assets requires a treatment of inflation, given that all loans are repaid in currency. There is no consensus model of price expectations. Nor is one particularly appropriate here, since the present study seeks to determine the ex post record rather than ex ante expectations. Our choice of price inflation measure is accordingly straightforward: We use the ex post rate of price inflation from one period to another to convert the nominal interest rate on alternative assets, n, into an ex post real rate of interest, $\bar{\rho}$. The real rates v and $\bar{\rho}$ are calculated by discounting debt service flows that have already been deflated into constant (1913) dollars or pounds.

What alternative assets? To highlight the distinctive property-rights feature of foreign sovereign debt, one might want to contrast it with domestic private debt backed by full collateral. It is hard, however, to find a long time series on such private debt with no changes in its own riskiness. We resort instead to a comparison of foreign sovereign debt with the rates of return on government debt of the main lending countries, the United Kingdom and the United States. (These convenient time series on relatively safe debt might make the return to foreign sovereign debt look good in the eyes of readers forgetting about the risk differentials.) The main type of risk associated with holding U.K. or U.S. governments is the hard-currency inflation risk shared by the foreign government debt.

To compare foreign sovereign debt with domestic (lending-country) government debt from the private creditor's viewpoint, we shall not compare the flows of returns on two equal loan outflows. To keep accidents of the ex post timing of commodity-price movements from seeming to affect the relative return on foreign government debt, we adopt the reverse strategy of comparing the different present valuations of the same stream of debt service on home and foreign government debt. The basis for this choice should be evident from the following algebra and discussion.

We define three summary measures:

(1) The real *internal rate of return* on foreign sovereign debt is v, as defined by the equation

$$0 = \Sigma_{t=0}^{T} (S_t/p_t) (1 + v)^{-t} - L_o/p_o ,$$

where

time T = the number of years to full maturity;

S_t = the actually-repaid nominal debt service in year t, consisting of both interest and principal-repayment;

p_t = the level of consumer prices in the lending country (countries) in year t;

L_o = the initial nominal loan outflow at market price (not necessarily par), here assumed to take place fully in the initial year 0.

(2) The real *net present value* of the foreign sovereign debt relative to home-country government debt is *NPV*, as defined by the equations

$$NPV = \Sigma_{t=0}^{T} (S_t/p_t) (1 + \rho_t)^{-t} - L_o/p_o$$
$$= \Sigma_{t=0}^{T} (S_t/p_t)(1 + \pi_{ot})^t (1 + n_o)^{-t} - L_o/p_o ,$$

where the real rate of interest from the initial year 0 to year t (or ρ_t) depends on the nominal rate on t-year government bonds at year 0 (or n_o) and the geometric-average rate of inflation from year 0 to year t (or π_{ot}):

$$1 + \rho_t = (1 + n_o)/(1 + \pi_{ot}), \text{ so that } \rho_t \approx n_o - \pi_{ot} .$$

In other words, the net present value (*NPV*) measures how much more the lenders would have to lend their own governments, beyond L_o/p_o, to get the same stream of real service payments they could get from lending just L_o/p_o to the foreign government. Of course, *NPV* can be of any sign.

(3) The rate of return on the alternative asset is summarized in the *effective real rate of discount,* or $\bar{\rho}$, defined by the equation

$$0 = \Sigma_{t=0}^{T} (S_t/p_t) (1 + \bar{\rho})^{-t} - \Sigma_{t=0}^{T} (S_t/p_t) (1 + \rho_t)^{-t} .$$

The effective real rate of discount is thus a geometric average of the real rates of return, the ρ_t's, on lending to a lending-country government. A simplification will be adopted in the measurement of ρ_t. As is implicit in its definition above, ρ_t uses data on a single long-term nominal size of interest, n_o, as the rate that lenders could get by buying the whole service stream, instead of combining different rates on different maturities. This simplification seems appropriate to the degree of commitment that lenders make in buying foreign long-term (usually 30- or 40-year) government debt.

All three summary measures are thus shaped by the time-path of real ex post debt service (the S_t/p_t's). The alternative asset, a loan to the British or U.S. government, is imagined to pay back the same complicated time-stream of real debt service that lenders experienced on their lending to sovereign foreign governments. The two kinds of assets differ only in the real values initially lent to get the same complicated debt-service stream.

To see why such an approach should be preferred to just using an ordinary government bond as the alternative asset, consider the case of a 40-year loan to the government of Chile in 1878. On the typical pattern, Chile would pay back a fixed debt service each year with a somewhat larger outpayment in the final year, 1918. With what time-profile of British or U.S. debt service should this foreign loan be compared? If we chose a 40-year government bond that was completely end-loaded, with all service coming in the final year 1918, the high prices of that year would greatly depress the rate of return on lending to, say, Her Majesty back in 1878. On the other hand, if we chose a British bond with a fixed nominal debt service each year for 40 years, we would find a relatively high real rate of return on lending to Her Majesty in 1878, because returns in the high-price year 1918 would play a smaller role in the British debt service than in the Chilean debt service. It is desirable to free the rate-of-return gap between Chilean and British government debt from any spurious dependence on the accidents of the timing of inflation. This can be done with the formulas outlined above, which compare different present values or different rates of return on the same time-profile of debt service.

Extra inflation in any i^{th} year cannot reverse the sign of NPV or the rate-of-return gap $v - \rho_i$. Starting from the initial rates v and $\bar{\rho}$, raising p_i and π_{oi} ex post inflation will affect the present values of foreign debt (L_o/p_o) and home government debt ($NPV + L_o/p_o$) in the same ways: deflating the real value of the ith year's debt service and discounting it less rapidly by lowering the ex-post real rate of return $\rho_i \approx n_o - \pi_{oi}$. Before any price increase in year i, that year's contribution to the NPV gap is

$$NPV_i = (S_i/p_i)(1 + \rho_i)^{-i} - (S_i/p_i)(1 + v)^{-i}$$
$$\approx (S_i/p_i)(1 + n_o - \pi_{oi})^{-1} - (S_i/p_i)(1 + (v - \rho_i) + n_o - \pi_{oi})^{-i}.$$

The inflationary shifts dp_i and $d\pi_{oi}$ will shift NPV_i as follows:

$$dNPV_i = -(S_i/p_i^2)(1 + n_o - \pi_{oi})^{-i} dp_i - (iS_i/p_i)(1 + n_o$$
$$- \pi_{oi})^{-i-1} d\pi_{oi} + (S_i/p_i^2)[1 + (v - \rho_i) + n_o - \pi_{oi}]^{-i} dp_i$$
$$+ (iS_i/p_i)[1 + (v - \rho_i) + n_o - \pi_{oi}]^{-i-1} d\pi_{oi}.$$

The only thing keeping $dNPV_i$ from cancelling out to zero is the appearance of the discount-rate gap $v - \rho_i$ in the formula. Given that dp_i and $d\pi_i$ have the same sign,

$$\text{sign}(dNPV_i) = -\text{sign}(v - \rho_i) = -\text{sign}(NPV).$$

Ex-post inflation cannot reverse the initial signs of the rate-of-return advantage, or the net-present-value advantage, of foreign debt. This desirable property led us to choose the summary measures described here.

Stacking and Aggregation.

The procedure for "stacking" loans into aggregations for summary measures is much the same whether it is the contracted (ex ante) or the realized returns that are being summarized. One by one, the loan records for a particular sample country are taken from storage. They are filtered to discard any loan records to be defined out of the subsample in question (e.g., a subsample defined by borrowing country and time period). Qualifying loans were reduced to two currencies, the U.S. dollar and the pound sterling. In the runs reported here, the U.S. dollar stacks consisted only of loans issued and repayable in U.S. dollars, while flows in all other currencies of issue and service were converted into pounds sterling at the current exchange rates. Once all figures were in either dollars or pounds, they were converted into real 1913 consumer bundles by following the conventional consumer price indexes of the United States of the United Kingdom. These real 1913 values were reaggregated into dollars or pounds at the 1913 exchange rate, \$4.86656 = £1. Of course, if the results in question are nominal rather than real, the deflation step is omitted.

For stacking into aggregates, each loan's capital inflows, interest and retirement are netted into a single net cash flow, year by year. The net cash flows are then added across all loans. For reasons presented in the text, we have chosen to present results that are based on starting all bonds at the same abstract year of issue. Stacking therefore involves adding together all the net cash flows for the same number of years since each bond's issue, not the same historical year. Obviously, this means that most of the inflows occur in the same initial year for all loans. As we had hoped, such all-at-once stacking reduced the incidence of multiple sign reversals in the net flow, which could have led to multiple roots for the same internal rate of return. Experimentation showed that even when we did not follow the all-at-once rule, an iterative computer routine seemed to converge on a clear and sensible value for the international rate of return.

The all-at-once rule for stacking was not followed for one particular country, Canada. Having already slaved to enter 439 Australian loans, we were daunted by the prospect of tracking what would have been over 600 external-currency Canadian bonds, issued by all levels of government down to the Saskatoon School District. We resolved to try time-saving short-cuts for Canada, knowing that hers was a dull story of good repayment (except for Alberta and a few cities). The first was to throw out the subprovincial borrowers (school districts, Ontario Hydro, etc.), bringing us down to 488 external bonds issued by the

Dominion and the provinces. Then we saved a little time (alas, not much) by aggregating loans historically on spreadsheet files—historically, rather than all at once, to save on file space by overlaying loans onto the same record. Each "loan" for Canada, as it was later entered on the computer, was in fact the whole stream for a province or the Dominion in a particular external currency (either U.S. dollar or all others, aggregated into the pound sterling). By keeping most Canadian loans from starting as early as the others in the stacks, we lowered the present value of Canadian borrowing, and weighted Canada's rates of return toward those earlier in history. To view separate eras in tables 2.2 and 2.3, we diced the Canadian profiles into period-specific flows, assuming full repayment at the end of each period.

Appendix B
Additional Tables

(Tables 2.8–2.10 follow on pages 92–100.)

Table 2.8   A Summary of Default and Reschedulings on Government Debts to Foreign Creditors since 1820

Nation	Privately Held Bonds, 1820–1929	Privately Held Bonds, 1930s	Loans, Mainly Official, 1940–79	Privately Held Loans, 1980–86
Abu Dhabi			—	—
Afghanistan			—	no loans
Algeria			—	—
Antigua & Barbuda				
Argentina	d 1830, '88–'93,'15(locals)	d local gov'ts only	r'51,'56,'62,'65	r'82–'85
Australia	d'68	d'32	—	—
Austria			—	—
Bahama Islands			—	—
Bahrain				
Bangladesh			r'74	
Barbadoes				
Belgium	—	—	—	—
Belize				
Benin				
Bhutan			no loans	no loans
Bolivia	d'74–'75	d'31	—	r'80(2),'81
Botswana				
Brazil	r'98,'14,d'17 (locals)	d'31	r'61,'64	r'83,'84
Bulgaria	d'15	d'32	no loans	no loans
Burma			—	—
Burundi			—	—
Cameroon			—	—
Canada	—	d Alberta, locals only	—	—
Cape Verde Islands			—	—

Central African Republic				
Chad	d 1826	d'31	—	r'81,'85
Chile	d'13	d'38	—	r'83,'84,'85
China/Taiwan		no loans	r'61,'63,'65,'72,'74,'75	—
China/PRC	d'79,'00		no loans	—
Colombia		d'32	—	—
Comoro Islands				
Congo, PR				
Costa Rica	d 1827,'74,'95	d'37	—	d'83,r'83,'85
Côte d'Ivoire		d'33	—	r'84,'85,'86
Cuba			—	r'83,'85
Cyprus	—			
Czechoslovakia	—	—	no loans	—
Denmark		—	—	
Djibouti				
Dominica				
Dominican Rep.	d'69,'99	d'31	—	d'82,r'83,'85
Ecuador	d'68,'11,'14,'27	—	—	r'83,'85
Egypt	d'76,[a]	—	—	
El Salvador	d 1827, '21	d'32	—	
Equat. Guinea	—	—	—	r'85
Estonia				
Ethiopia	no loans	no loans	—	—
Fiji			—	—
Finland	—		—	—
France	—		r'78	—
Gabon				—

(*continued*)

Table 2.8 (continued)

Nation	Privately Held Bonds, 1820–1929	Privately Held Bonds, 1930s	Loans, Mainly Official, 1940–79	Privately Held Loans, 1980–86
Gambia				—
Germany/FRG	d reparations	d	—	—
Germany/DDR			no loans	—
Ghana			r'66,'68,'70,'74	—
Greece	d 1824,'93	d'32	—	—
Grenada				—
Guatemala	≈6 d's	d'32	—	—
Guinea			—	r'86
Guinea-Bissau				
Guyana			—	r'82,'83,'84(2)
Haiti	d 1827,'73,'14	—	r'52,'65	—
Honduras	—	d'31	—	d'81–83,r'82,'84
Hungary	—	—	no loans	
Iceland				—
India			r'58,'69,'72–'76	—
Indonesia			r'66–'70	—
Iran			—	
Iraq	—		—	
Ireland	—	—	—	
Israel	—		—	r'81,'84,'85
Italy			r'70,'79	
Jamaica			d'41–'52	—
Japan				
Jordan				

Kampuchea			r'72	no loans
Kenya			—	—
Korea, North			—	—
Korea, South			—	—
Kuwait			—	—
Laos			—	—
Lebanon			—	—
Lesotho			—	—
Liberia	d'74	—	r'63,'68	r'80,'81,'82
Libya	—	—	—	—
Luxembourg				
Madagascar				r'81(2),'82,'83,'84,d'84
Malawi				r'83
Malaysia				—
Maldives				—
Mali				—
Mauritania				r'85,'86
Mauritius				—
Mexico	d 1827,'67,'14	no loans		d'83,r'83,'84(2)
Morocco				r'83,'85
Mozambique				r'85
Nepal				—
Netherlands	—	—		—
New Zealand	d 1827, pre-1911	—		—
Nicaragua		—		d'80,'81,r'80,'81,'82,'84
Niger				r'84,'85
Nigeria				r'83(2)
Norway	—			—
Oman				—
Pakistan			r'72,'73,'74	r'81

(continued)

Table 2.8 (continued)

Nation	Privately Held Bonds, 1820–1929	Privately Held Bonds, 1930s	Loans, Mainly Official, 1940–79	Privately Held Loans, 1980–86
Panama		d'32	—	r'85
Papua New Guinea			—	—
Paraguay	d 1827,'20	d'30–'33	r'68,'69,'78(2)	r'80,'83,'84,d
Peru	d'75–'84	d'31	r'69	r'84
Philippines			—	d'82,r'82(2),'83,'84,'85
Poland		d'36	—	—
Portugal	—[b]		—	
Qatar				
Romania	d WWI	d'33	—	d'81,r'82,'83
Russia/USSR	d 1839,'17	no loans		no loans
Rwanda				
St. Lucia			no loans	no loans
St. Vincent			no loans	no loans
Sao Tome & Principe			no loans	no loans
Saudi Arabia				
Senegal			—	r'81,'84,'85
Seychelles				
Sierra Leone			r'77	r'80,'84
Singapore				
Solomon Islands				
Somalia				
South Africa		—		
Spain	d's pre–'79			
Sri Lanka		—		
Sudan			—	r Dec.'79,'81,'82,'83,'84

Suriname	—	—	—	—
Swaziland	—	—	—	—
Sweden	—	—	—	—
Switzerland	—	—	—	—
Syria	—	—	—	—
Tanzania	—	—	—	—
Thailand	—	—	—	—
Togo	—	—	—	d'79,'82,r'80,'83,'85
Trinidad & Tobago	—	—	—	—
Tunisia	—	—	r'56,'58,'63,'79(2)	—
Turkey	d'76–'81, WWI	no loans	—	r'80,'81,'82
Uganda	—	—	—	r'81
U.A. Emirates	—	—	—	—
U.K.	—	—	—	—
U.S.	d several states	—	—	—
Upper Volta/BF	—	—	—	—
Uruguay	d'76	d	r'65	r'83,'84,'85
Vanuatu	—	—	—	—
Venezuela	d'34,'47,'64,'78,'92,'98c	—	d'60	r'85
Vietnam	—	—	—	—
Western Samoa	—	—	—	—
Yemen Arab Rep.	—	—	—	—
Yemen, PDR	—	d'37	—	—
Yugo./Serbia	—	—	r'65–'69	r'84,'85
Zaire	—	—	r'76,'77,'79	r'81,'83,'85,'86
Zambia	—	—	—	r'83,'84,'86
Zimbabwe	—	—	—	—
Totals				
Countries covered	56	57	157	157
Problem debtors (d,r)	29	24	22	42
No loans	1	4	9	8

(*continued*)

Table 2.8 (continued)

Sources: Clarke (1879); Corporation of Foreign Bondholders, various years; Foreign Bondholders' Protective Council, various years; Winkler (1933); United Nations (1948); IBRD annual reports, various years; Bitterman (1973); Hardy (1982); Watson et al. (1986); Moody's *Municipal and governments manual*; Dillon and Oliveros (1987).

Notes:

d = unilaterally defaulted, or simply went into arrears, on at least part of the foreign debt of national or local (provincial, city) governments or utilities starting in the year listed. No attempt is made here to record when a past default was settled.

[blank] = not a sovereign nation anytime in this period.

r = negotiated refinancing on terms at least partly concessionary.

— = fully met all service obligations without rescheduling that lowered creditors' capital value.

no loans = no lending, or negligible lending, recorded in the sources cited here.

[a]Egypt attempted default, but instead lost her national sovereignty.

[b]Brief mention has been made of temporary nonrepayment by Portugal, before 1855 and 1891–93, but the sources listed here offer no specifics.

[c]Venezuela attempted default in 1898, but by 1902 military threats had forced her to repay on contract.

Not counted as defaults are the breakdowns in war debts between allies, or the nonpayment of foreign debt service by countries occupied in war. Not counted in any totals, though listed here, are the governments of four usually-creditor countries: U.S., U.K., France, and Germany.

Table 2.9   **Annual Real Net Investment by Foreign Creditors in the Government Debt of Ten Countries, 1850–1982** (In millions of dollars at 1913 consumer prices and exchange rates. Gross new lending minus retirements. Excludes interest payments and changes in real value of outstanding debt due to changes in consumer prices.)

Year	Net Inflow	Year	Net Inflow	Year	Net Inflow	Year	Net Inflow
1850	89.44	1884	141.01	1918	19.67	1952	− 3.04
1851	52.36	1885	140.04	1919	23.35	1953	17.40
1852	4.40	1886	163.47	1920	28.11	1954	− 0.16
1853	− 0.61	1887	67.10	1921	175.49	1955	− 414.45
1854	8.80	1888	272.90	1922	200.53	1956	84.45
1855	51.91	1889	191.48	1923	− 24.98	1957	− 62.55
1856	− 0.49	1890	78.45	1924	308.72	1958	− 18.30
1857	− 0.78	1891	91.65	1925	− 5.97	1959	85.40
1858	50.54	1892	67.11	1926	154.41	1960	− 71.93
1859	25.56	1893	85.35	1927	327.34	1961	− 0.49
1860	96.78	1894	1,563.03	1928	176.33	1962	26.54
1861	− 1.52	1895	6.39	1929	3.19	1963	3.01
1862	81.87	1896	148.66	1930	− 11.87	1964	− 63.62
1863	36.49	1897	58.14	1931	− 121.33	1965	47.38
1864	18.03	1898	41.72	1932	− 155.94	1966	− 128.95
1865	76.47	1899	5.05	1933	− 4.67	1967	13.40
1866	29.03	1900	89.75	1934	112.51	1968	− 59.64
1867	114.67	1901	110.27	1935	− 152.54	1969	132.78
1868	62.60	1902	26.33	1936	20.81	1970	150.28
1869	68.10	1903	16.27	1937	− 123.73	1971	191.71
1870	92.09	1904	108.51	1938	− 41.25	1972	426.86
1871	112.01	1905	510.68	1939	− 40.15	1973	668.07
1872	81.40	1906	473.55	1940	− 280.28	1974	982.61
1873	246.87	1907	141.19	1941	− 51.98	1975	953.01
1874	27.31	1908	253.16	1942	− 122.21	1976	1,719.55
1875	66.17	1909	414.07	1943	− 210.33	1977	1,601.01
1876	194.25	1910	366.30	1944	− 214.20	1978	2,427.78
1877	35.06	1911	122.92	1945	16.10	1979	2,062.21
1878	17.07	1912	76.96	1946	− 136.52	1980	1,136.42
1879	40.33	1913	258.62	1947	− 93.04	1981	1,617.86
1880	82.77	1914	223.55	1948	13.29	1982	1,093.50
1881	35.35	1915	131.56	1949	9.39		
1882	28.58	1916	95.25	1950	− 310.30		
1883	114.44	1917	148.76	1951	117.75		

Table 2.10   Realized Nominal Returns on Bond Lending to Ten Foreign Governments, 1850–1983.

Borrowing Nation	n	Rates of Return (%)			(Millions of nominal $)	
		v	$\bar{\rho}$	$v - \bar{\rho}$	NPV	L_0
Argentina	187	5.71	3.53	2.18	516.3	2,631.3
Brazil	143	4.39	3.57	0.81	190.6	1,517.0
Chile	60	3.62	3.90	−0.28	−27.7	637.5
Mexico	52	3.42	4.25	−0.83	−68.6	923.2
Four Latins	442	4.76	3.70	1.06	610.6	5,709.1
Australia	439	5.60	4.52	1.09	1,358.7	9,836.9
Canada	488	4.51	2.82	1.69	925.9	1,635.6
Egypt	21	6.00	3.20	2.80	305.1	423.9
Japan	60	5.48	3.86	1.61	407.8	1,873.6
Russia	48	1.48	2.98	−1.50	−654.3	3,386.8
Turkey	54	2.28	3.54	−1.26	−207.3	1,645.4
These six	1,110	4.47	3.91	0.56	2,135.9	18,802.2
All ten	1,552	4.54	3.86	0.67	2,746.5	24,511.2

Note: The procedures used here are the same as for table 2.3, except for omitting the price deflation.

Notes

1. Sovereign debt is defined as any financial claim that is unenforceable by seizure of debtor assets matching the debt in value. This paper takes a conventional narrow focus on the interest-earning nonmonetary claims of private creditors on foreign governments. It ignores such sovereign claims as unbacked paper money and the debt and equity obligations of private parties who can take refuge behind the ineffectiveness of contract laws.

2. For a further summary of the lending waves and an analysis of the incidence of default in terms of trade shocks and fiscal policies, again see Fishlow (1985).

3. For the years before World War I, we used the widely-publicized railroad bond rate. Splicing the two different rates of return together might cloud the comparison with foreign sovereign debt. However, the prewar railroad bond rate is hardly used in our calculations, since very little of the foreign sovereign debt was in dollars before World War I. The returns on the large amounts of interwar and postwar foreign sovereign debt in dollars were therefore compared with the U.S. government bond rate, as preferred.

4. As for the higher premia charged to Canada and Japan after World War II, these were elevated by the fact that Canada and Japan borrowed early in the postwar era, when fears about nonrepayment still lingered and when the interest rate on long-term U.S governments was pegged exceptionally low.

5. In November 1931 a mixed court went further, ruling that Egypt had to continue to repay creditors in sterling at its gold-standard value, even though this meant doubling the British commodity value of the service payments. The protectorate government refused, however, and soon won higher-court deci-

sions in favor of its insistence on merely repaying the sterling value (Wynne 1951, 629–31).

6. In summarizing Mexico's credit history, we have counted the Maximilian service on old loans, but have omitted any other aspect of Maximilian's loans on the ground that they do not refer to Mexico. After Maximilian's fall, the French government took the unprecedented step of repaying French creditors half of their investments in the Maximilian loans, on the grounds that the government had encouraged them to take such a risk. The same procedure was not followed after the Russian Revolution, however, even though the French government had knowingly deceived private investors on the quality of czarist Russian government bonds.

7. Two other kinds of conclusions by conventional rate-of-return studies are not pursued here. First, by following the returns to holding a bond over its entire lifetime, we do not disaggregate into the annual (or other short-term) gains that would hypothetically be realized by an investor buying, holding, and selling within that year. For an excellent example of the annual rate-of-return approach, with its heavier use of market price data, see Edelstein (1977 and 1982). We have suppressed this disaggregation into individual years by summarizing the returns to the whole chain of holders of each bond.

Second, we offer little view of the variance of returns. The perceived variance across possible outcome states exists, of course, only in the ex ante eyes of the potential investor, and is only indirectly revealed in ex ante returns like those in table 2.2. Yet other studies have shown an interest in commenting indirectly on the unobservable perceived variance by measuring ex post variation in returns (1) across debtors, (2) across creditors, (3) across the lifetimes of a cross-section of individual securities, (4) across individual holding years for a cross-section of securities, and (5) across the years of existence of a single security. Of these, our table 2.3 sheds only a little light on the first. With additional work, our data set could yield variances (2) and (3). For studies of variance (4), see Fishlow (1987) and again Edelstein (1977 and 1982).

8. The sudden reference to abstract social welfare, so soon after a discussion of real-world debtor governments, may surprise. Yet the charitable assumption that governments maximize some social-welfare analogue to individual utility suits the present debating purpose. If officials' goals are narrower and less worthy of the "social" label, then the present paper's warnings about rescue operations will be reinforced.

Another element of realism that is missing at this point is soon to be introduced: The borrower often has an incentive for only partial, rather than complete, debt repudiation.

Our definition of a debt crisis is narrower than our definition of debtor sovereignty:

a debt crisis exists $<=> (1 + r)D > P + \text{ B} <=> V^D > V^R$;
the debtor is sovereign $<=> (1 + r)D > P$.

9. We should deal with two other ways in which one might suspect that extra lending could somehow raise P and B faster than D, making debt more enforceable and allowing a reduction in the interest rate. First, one might suspect that a better collateral mechanism could be devised, e.g., developing stronger trade dependence, raising P more than D. But if so, then why was this option not already taken? Second, one might imagine that a third party, such as the IMF, could raise B more than D by offering new loans at so low an interest rate that the borrower's surplus from continued faithful repayment, B, is raised more than D is raised. But this proposal, discussed below, can only raise B by writing down debt service. It is a form of partial default.

10. Domar (1950). Domar's reasoning was repeated recently by Niehans (1985). This reasoning has been criticised for overlooking the default implications of its treatment of the infinite horizon (Lindert 1971, 1976). See also the 1928 quotation from Auld in Felix (1987, 20). Note that this frequent argument would have been correct if it had been confined to the case in which D remained below the enforceable limit on prudent lending, the limit $h = (P + B)/(1 + r)$.

11. A model that might seem to contradict the present result in the context of sovereign debt is that of Krugman (1985), which explicitly argues (on pp. 88–89) that defensive relending is rational for creditors. But Krugman's formal model (pp. 84–88) implies the opposite, i.e., that extra lending raises the (second–period) incentive to default. The alleged case for defensive relending is not based on his formal model, and makes some questionable assumptions: (a) that postponing default somehow prevents it; (b) that a small fresh loan would entice borrowers to repay debt service exceeding the fresh loan; and (c) that offering submarket interest rates to a problem borrower is a way of avoiding default (in fact, it is a way of acquiescing in partial default).

12. The issue is noted in Sachs (1984, 29–37) and Eaton, Gersovitz, and Stiglitz (1986, 496–98).

13. Panic could ruin the collective ability of *already exposed* creditors to hide the likelihood of default from new lenders, who might somehow have been induced to take over their exposure. Such a successful deception would not, however, have raised the wealth of all creditors.

14. The B term is included in column (3) under the simplifying assumption that successful negotiation of partial debt reduction restores the credit ration that the borrower would have had with full repayment. The assumption seems reasonable. While the debtor's record is tainted, lowering debt from $(1 + r)D$ to $(1 + \lambda)D$ can convince creditors that the rewards from further default have been lowered enough to warrant safe relending up to the prudence limit $h = (P + B)/(1 + r)$.

15. There were also pure unilateral refinancings permitted by contract, in which the debtor took advantage of a dip in market yields to retire old high-interest debt.

16. For further background, see Peters (1934), Ferns (1960), Ford (1962), and Fishlow (1985).

17. And, apparently, the taxpayers take a capital loss equal to $(e - r)D < 0$. One might argue that the lower interest rate is not below market, and thus not a loss, given that repayment is more certain than on the other debt in the marketplace. This argument would presumably rest on the perception that a debtor always tries to remain faithful to the IMF, the "lender of first resort." Yet the same would hold for loans to other debtors not on the brink of default, suggesting that the rescue does indeed impose a risk-adjusted loss on the taxpayers relative to their other (via-IMF) lending opportunities.

18. Here we echo a theme sounded by Vaubel (1983), among others, though with more emphasis on the international private lending hazards and less on macro-policy hazards.

References

Anan'ich, B. V., and V. I. Bovykin. Forthcoming. Foreign banks and foreign investments in Russia. In *International banks, investment and industrial finance, 1870–1914*, ed. Rondo E. Cameron and V. I. Bovykin. We are indebted to Mira Wilkins for this reference.

Avramovic, Dragoslav. 1985. Debts in early 1985: An institutional impasse. *Journal of Development Planning* 16: 105–19.

Bazant, Jan. 1968. *Historia de la dueda exterior de Mexico*. Mexico, D.F.: El Colegio de Mexico.

Bittermann, Henry J. 1973. *The refunding of international debt*. Durham, N.C.: Duke University Press.

Borchard, Edwin. 1951. *State insolvency and foreign bondholders. Vol. 1, General principles*. New Haven: Yale University Press.

Bulow, Jeremy I., and Kenneth Rogoff. 1986. A constant recontracting model of sovereign debt. Typescript.

Cameron, Rondo. 1961. *France and the economic development of Europe, 1800–1914*. Princeton: Princeton University Press.

Cizauskas, Albert. 1979. International debt renegotiation: Lessons from the past. *World Development* 7: 199–210.

Clapham, Sir John. 1958. *The Bank of England: A history*. Cambridge: Cambridge University Press.

Clarke, Hyde. 1879. *Sovereign and quasi-sovereign states: Their debts to foreign countries*. London: Effingham Wilson, Royal Exchange.

Cline, W. R. 1983. *International debt and the stability of the world economy*. Washington, D.C.: Institute for International Economics.

————. 1985. International debt: Analysis, experience and prospects. *Journal of Development Planning* 16: 25–55.

Cohen, Daniel, and Jeffrey Sachs. 1986. Growth and external debt under risk of debt repudiation. *European Economic Review* 30 (June): 529–58.

Cooper, Richard N., and Jeffrey D. Sachs. 1985. Borrowing abroad: The debtor's perspective. In *International debt and the developing countries*, ed. Gordon W. Smith and John T. Cuddington. Washington, D.C.: The World Bank.

Corporation of Foreign Bondholders. *Annual Reports*, 1873 on.

Dell, Sidney. 1981. *On being grandmotherly: The evolution of IMF conditionality*. Essays in International Finance no. 144 (October). Princeton: Princeton University, International Finance Section.

Díaz-Alejandro, Carlos F. 1984. Latin American debt: I don't think we are in Kansas anymore. *Brookings Papers in Economic Activity* 2: 355–89.

Dillon, K. Burke, and Gumersindo Oliveros. 1987. *Recent experience with multilateral official debt rescheduling*. Washington, D.C.: International Monetary Fund.

Domar, Evsey. 1950. The effects of foreign investment on the balance of payments. *American Economic Review* 40, no. 5, part 1 (December): 805–26.

Dominick and Dominick. 1934–37. *Dollar bonds issued in the United States*. New York: Dominick and Dominick.

Dornbusch, Rudiger. 1985. Policy and performance links between LDC debtors and industrial nations. *Brookings Papers in Economic Activity* 2: 303–68.

Dornbusch, Rudiger, and Stanley Fischer. 1985. The world debt problem: Origins and prospects. *Journal of Development Planning* 16: 57–81.

Eaton, Jonathan, Mark Gersovitz, and Joseph Stiglitz. 1986. The pure theory of country risk. *European Economic Review* 30 (June): 481–514.

Edelstein, Michael. 1977. Realized rates of return on U.K. home and overseas portfolio investment in the age of high imperialism. *Explorations in Economic History* 13, no. 3 (July): 283–329.

————. 1982. *Overseas investment in the age of high imperialism: The United Kingdom, 1850–1914*. New York: Columbia University Press.

Edwards, Sebastian. 1984. LDC borrowing and default risk: An empirical investigation. *American Economic Review* 74, no. 4 (September): 726–34.

——. 1986. The pricing of bonds and bank loans in international markets. *European Economic Review* (June): 565–89.

Eichengreen, Barry, and Richard Portes. 1986. Debt and default in the 1930s: Causes and consequences: *European Economic Review* 30 (June): 559–640.

Feder, Gershon, and Richard E. Just. 1984. Debt crisis in an increasingly pessimistic international market: The case of Egyptian credit, 1862–1876. *Economic Journal* 94, no. 2 (June): 340–56.

Feis, Herbert. 1930. *Europe, the world's banker, 1870–1914*. New Haven: Yale University Press.

Feldstein, Martin. 1986. International debt service and economic growth: Some simple analytics. NBER Working Paper no. 2076 (November). Cambridge, Mass.: National Bureau of Economic Research.

Felix, David. 1987. Alternative outcomes of the Latin American debt crisis: Lessons from the past. *Latin American Research Review* 22, no. 2: 3–46.

Fenn's compendium of the English and foreign funds and *Fenn on the funds*. 1874–1898. Various editions, London.

Ferns, H. S. 1960. *Britain and Argentina in the nineteenth century*. Oxford: Clarendon Press.

Fishlow, Albert. 1985. Lessons from the past: Capital markets during the nineteenth century and the interwar period. *International Organization* 39, no. 3 (Summer): 383–439.

——. 1987. Lessons of the 1890s for the 1980s. Working Paper no. 8724 (January). University of California, Berkeley, Department of Economics.

The Fitch record of government finances. 1918. 3d ed. New York: Fitch Publishing.

Ford, Alec G. 1962. *The gold standard, 1880–1914: Great Britain and Argentina*. Oxford: Oxford University Press.

Foreign Bondholders' Protective Council. *Annual Report*, 1935 on. New York.

Friedman, Irving S. 1983. Private bank conditionality: Comparison with the IMF and the World Bank. In *IMF Conditionality*, ed. John Williamson. Washington, D.C.: Institute for International Economics.

Hardy, Chandra S. 1982. *Rescheduling developing-country debts, 1956–1981: Lessons and recommendations*. Washington, D.C.: Overseas Development Council.

Hellwig, Martin F. 1977. A model of borrowing and lending with bankruptcy. *Econometrica* 45, no. 8 (November): 1879–1906.

Hickman, Walter Braddock. 1958. *Corporate bond quality and investor experience*. Princeton: Princeton University Press.

——. 1960. *Statistical measures of corporate bond financing since 1900*. Princeton: Princeton University Press.

Kaletsky, Anatole. 1985. *The costs of default*. New York: Twentieth Century Fund.

Kimber, Albert W., ed. 1925. *Kimber's record of government debts and other foreign securities, 1925*. 9th annual ed. New York: Exporter's Encyclopedia Corp.

Kimber, Albert W., and Alfred Nagel, eds. 1933. *Kimber's record of government debts, 1932–33*. New York: Overseas Statistics, Inc.

Kindleberger, Charles P. 1978. *Manias, panics, and crashes: A history of financial crises*. New York: Basic Books.

Krugman, Paul. 1985. International debt strategies in an uncertain world. In *International debt and the developing countries*, ed. Gordon W. Smith and John T. Cuddington. Washington, D.C.: The World Bank.

Kyle, Steven, and Jeffrey Sachs. 1984. Developing country debt and the market value of large commercial banks. NBER Working Paper no. 1470. Cambridge, Mass.: National Bureau of Economic Research.

Landes, David. 1958. *Bankers and pashas*. Cambridge: Harvard University Press.

Lewis, Cleona. 1948. *The United States and foreign investment problems*. Washington, D.C.: Brookings Institution.

Lill, Thomas R. 1919. *National debt of Mexico, history and present status*. New York.

Lindert, Peter H. 1969. *Key currencies and gold, 1900–1913*. Princeton Studies in International Finance no. 24. Princeton: Princeton University Press.

———. 1971. The payments impact of foreign investment controls. *Journal of Finance* 26, no. 5 (December): 1083–99.

———. 1976. The payments impact of foreign investment controls: Reply [to Guy. V. G. Stevens]. *Journal of Finance* 31, no. 5 (December): 1505–8.

———. 1986. Relending to sovereign debtors. Working Paper (September). University of California, Davis, Institute for Governmental Affairs.

London Stock Exchange. 1882–1933. *The stock exchange official index*. London: T. Skinner.

———. 1882–1933. *Weekly official intelligence*. London.

———. 1934–1983. *Yearbook*. London.

Ludwig, Armin K., ed. 1985. *Brazil: A handbook of historical statistics*. Boston: G. K. Hall.

Mintz, Ilse. 1951. *Deterioration in the quality of foreign bonds issued in the United States, 1920–1930*. New York: Columbia University Press.

Moody's. Various years. Relevant title varies: *Moody's investments, Moody's municipal and governments manual, Moody's foreign governments, Moody's bond record*. New York: Moody's.

Niehans, Jurg. 1985. International debt with unenforceable claims. *San Francisco Federal Reserve Bank Review* (February): 64–79.

Ozler, Sule. 1986. The motives for international bank rescheduling, 1978–1983: Theory and evidence. UCLA, Department of Economics Working Paper no. 401.

Peters, H. E. 1934. *The foreign debt of the Argentine republic*. Baltimore, Md.: Johns Hopkins University Press.

Raffalovich, A. 1931. *L'abominable vénalité de la presse*. Paris: Librairie du Travail.

Royal Institute for International Affairs. 1937. *The problem of international investment*. Oxford: Oxford University Press.

Sachs, Jeffrey D. 1984. *Theoretical issues in international borrowing*. Princeton Studies in International Finance, no. 54. Princeton, N.J.: Princeton University Press.

———. 1985. External debt and macroeconomic performance in Latin America and East Asia. *Brookings Papers in Economic Analysis* 2: 523–74.

Simonsen, Mario Henrique. 1985. The developing-country debt problem. In *International debt and the developing countries*, ed. Gordon W. Smith and John T. Cuddington, Washington, D.C.: The World Bank.

Tasca, Henry J. 1938. *The reciprocal trade policy of the United States*. New York: Russell and Russell.

———. 1939. *World trading systems*. Paris: League of Nations.

Turlington, Edgar. 1930. *Mexico and her foreign creditors*. New York: Columbia University Press.

United Nations, Department of Economic Affairs. 1948. *Public debt, 1914–1946*. Lake Success, New York: United Nations.

Vaubel, Roland. 1983. The moral hazard of IMF lending. *World Economy* 6: 291–303.

Watson, Maxwell, Russell Kincaid, Caroline Atkinson, Eliot Kalter, and David Folkerts-Landau. 1986. *International capital markets: Developments and prospects* (December). Washington, D.C.: International Monetary Fund.

Williamson, John, ed. 1985. *IMF conditionality.* Washington, D.C.: Institute for International Economics.

Winkler, Max. 1933. *Foreign bonds: An autopsy.* Philadelphia: Roland Swain. Reprinted, New York: Arno Press, 1976.

World Bank. 1985. *World development report 1985.* New York: Oxford University Press.

———. 1980–86. *World debt tables.* Washington, D.C.: World Bank.

Wynne, William H. 1951. *State insolvency and foreign bondholders. Vol. 2, Case histories.* New Haven: Yale University Press.

3   The U.S. Capital Market and Foreign Lending, 1920–1955

Barry Eichengreen

3.1 Introduction

In happier times (the 1970s), countries were thought to pass through stages of indebtedness analogous to the stages of the international product cycle. According to the stages theory (e.g., de Vries 1971), countries in the initial phases of the process (before "takeoff into indebtedness") lack the political stability and economic infrastructure required for borrowing abroad. Once these preconditions are met, foreign borrowing commences and proceeds at an accelerating pace. With capital inflows come development, rising exports, and steadily increasing capacity to service foreign obligations. With rising domestic incomes come increased savings, diminishing the need to borrow abroad. A point of inflection is reached after which a country's indebtedness begins to decline. The rise of domestic incomes ultimately permits the debtor to liquidate its foreign obligations and to transform itself into an international creditor capable of lending to countries in the early phases of the cycle. The paradigmatic case is the United States, which seemed to pass through these stages in the century after 1820.

In these less optimistic times, a typical stages of indebtedness model would look rather different (e.g., United Nations 1986). Countries' initial inability to borrow would be ascribed not to the absence of domestic preconditions but to caution and pessimism in international

Barry Eichengreen is a professor of economics at the University of California at Berkeley and a research associate of the National Bureau of Economic Research.

The work reported here is related to research conducted jointly with Richard Portes and supported by a World Bank research grant on LDC debt. I thank seminar participants at Tel Aviv University, where an earlier version of this paper was presented. Stanley Fischer and Peter Lindert provided valuable comments on section 3.3.

capital markets, often themselves a legacy of previous defaults. Only when some exogenous event such as an intergovernmental loan or domestic monetary expansion has a catalytic effect on the market does foreign lending commence. Undue pessimism gives way to excessive optimism as competing lenders jump on the bandwagon, pushing loans upon reluctant borrowers and failing to distinguish between good and bad credit risks. Indiscriminate lending culminates in default, recrimination, and retaliation as lending collapses and international trade is disrupted at the expense of economic growth in the capital-importing regions. Developing countries are unable to borrow for an extended period, returning in effect to the initial stage of the indebtedness cycle. Here the paradigmatic case is the half-century commencing in 1920, when hesitancy gave way to a burst of foreign lending after 1923, default after 1930, and a considerable diminution of private external portfolio lending until the 1970s.

Both characterizations of the process of foreign lending are oversimplified and overly mechanistic. In some instances, foreign lending has taken place in response to promising development prospects, foreign funds have been profitably invested, and debts have been repaid, as posited in the stages-of-indebtedness model. In others, funds have been provided indiscriminately, invested unproductively, and written off by the lenders. The question is what mix of the two phenomena characterizes the operation of the market. Similarly, the impact of default on the growth prospects of the indebted nations is less clear-cut than most would have it. The impact of default on economic performance in indebted regions hinges in part upon its implications for access to the international capital market. If nonpayment damages the debtor's reputation sufficiently to impede its ability to borrow for an extended period, default may have serious economic consequences. Moreover, if the consequences spill over to other nations by leading to the collapse of the international capital market, default may have externalities, the costs of which are incurred by third parties.

In this chapter, I view these issues through the lens of the last complete debt cycle, that spanned by the half-century from 1920. I start in section 3.2 by considering the factors that ignited the process of foreign lending, focusing on the case of the United States. During the early twenties, in sharp contrast to the second half of the decade, relatively little U.S. foreign lending took place. This raises the question of what first discouraged the floatation of loans and then initiated the burst of lending. Was the outlook of capital-market participants transformed by a newfound ability of sovereign debtors to satisfy the preconditions for foreign borrowing, as stages-of-indebtedness models would suggest, or by developments largely exogenous to the debtors? I conclude that lending was restrained initially by the debt overhang associated with reparations and by the disruption of international trade—i.e., as much by conditions in the world economy as by conditions in debtor countries. I suggest that the policies of the creditor governments—specifically, the Dawes Plan, the League of Nations loans to Central Europe, and reconstruction of the gold standard system—had a catalytic effect on the market. I consider also the monitoring and moral suasion exercised by the U.S. Commerce and State Departments, and ask how they influenced the flow of funds.

In section 3.3, I consider the behavior of the market once foreign lending was underway. At stake is the effectiveness with which the market allocated funds among competing borrowers. Did market participants discriminate adequately among good and bad risks? Did they take into account factors affecting the likelihood of default? To address these questions I analyze the pricing of foreign bonds, considering the determinants of spreads over the risk-free interest rate and the default probabilities they imply. The impression conveyed by this evidence is that lenders discriminated among borrowers and demanded compensation for the danger of default, but to a limited extent. Neither an efficient-markets nor a fads-and-fashions model provides a wholly adequate characterization of the operation of this market.

In section 3.4 I consider the consequences of default from the perspective of relending. Did countries which serviced their loans through the 1930s reap the benefits of favored access to the capital market? If not in the 1930s then subsequently, did defaulting nations pay a price in the form of reduced access to international capital markets?

3.2 Initiating the Debt Cycle: The U.S. Capital Market in the 1920s

Current judgments on American experience with the foreign loans of the 1920s might be refined and corrected if more attention were paid to the general economic situation at the time of their issue and its influence on their character and soundness. (Mintz 1951, 4)

3.2.1 Overview

The United States is the paradigmatic example of a country which appears to have passed through stages of indebtedness, transfiguring itself from international debtor to international creditor in the span of 100 years. Foreign capital played an integral role in the development of American industry and in the opening of the West. Although the U.S. remained an attractive destination for foreign capital even as the economy matured, by the turn of the century American investors had already begun to direct their attention abroad. In the 15 years prior to World War I, U.S. foreign liabilities increased by approximately 4.6 percent per annum, but U.S. foreign assets increased at more than twice that rate.[1] (See table 3.1.) Three-quarters of U.S. foreign lending in this period took the form of direct investment, primarily in railways, sugar mill machinery and mining and drilling equipment. Although on the eve of World War I the U.S. remained a net foreign debtor, the position already was beginning to shift.

Wartime exigencies accelerated America's transition from debtor to creditor nation. Between 1914 and 1919, largely as a result of loans floated on behalf of the French and British governments and the liquidation of foreign holdings of U.S. securities, America's net debtor position of $3.8 billion was transformed into a net creditor position of comparable magnitude.[2] There followed a surge in peacetime lending matched previously only by the United Kingdom in the period 1900–13. U.S. investors lent more than $10 billion to foreigners in the 11 years ending in 1930, 40 percent in the form of direct foreign investment, 45 percent through the purchase of long-term foreign securities. Contemporaries were struck by the growth of U.S. portfolio investment abroad, given the predominance of direct investment in American lending over previous decades. The earliest estimates, for 1897, show more than 90 percent of U.S. foreign investment to have been direct, while estimates for 1914 suggest that the share of direct investment in the total was still more than 75 percent; by 1930 the share of direct investment had fallen to less than half.

This overview of early 20th century U.S. experience suggests three questions. First, what explains the magnitude of U.S. foreign lending in the 1920s? Second, what explains the composition—specifically, the rise in portfolio investment? Third, what explains the timing—specifically, the surge in the period 1925–28?

3.2.2 Magnitudes

A country's foreign lending is, by definition, the excess of domestic saving over domestic investment:

$$(1) \qquad \text{NFI} = S \cdot \text{GNP} - I \cdot \text{GNP},$$

where NFI is net foreign investment (U.S. investment abroad net of foreign investment in the United States), GNP is Gross National Product, S = Gross Saving/GNP, and I = Gross Investment/GNP. Differentiating yields:

$$(2) \qquad d\text{NFI} = \text{GNP} \cdot dS - \text{GNP} \cdot dI + (S-I) \cdot d\text{GNP}$$

The first term on the right-hand side is the contribution of changes in saving to U.S. investment abroad, the second the contribution of changes in investment, the third the contribution of GNP growth. In table 3.2 this decomposition is applied to U.S. data for the early 20th century. In contrast to the 1970s, when fluctuations in investment were

Table 3.1 International Investment Position of the United States 1897–1939 (Excluding War Debts) ($ billions)

Item	End of 1897	1 July 1914	1919	End of Year 1930	1933	1939
United States investments abroad (private account)						
Long-term:						
Direct	0.6	2.7	3.9	8.0	7.8	7.0
Portfolio	0.1	0.9	2.6	7.2	6.0	3.8
Total long-term	0.7	3.5	6.5	15.2	13.8	10.8
Total short-term	—	—	0.5	2.0	1.1	0.6
Total long- and short-term	0.7	3.5	7.0	17.2	14.9	11.4
Foreign investments in the United States						
Long-term:						
Direct	{3.1	1.3	0.9	1.4[a]	1.8[b]	2.0
Portfolio[c]		5.4	1.6	4.3[a]	3.1[b]	4.3
Total long-term	3.1	6.8	2.5	5.7	4.9	6.3
Total short-term	0.3	0.5	0.8	2.7	0.5	3.3
Total long- and short-term	3.4	7.2	3.3	8.4	5.4	9.6

(*continued*)

Table 3.1 (continued)

Item	End of 1897	1 July 1914	1919	End of Year		
				1930	1933	1939
Net creditor position of the United States						
On long-term account	−2.4	−3.3	4.0	9.5	8.9	4.5
On short-term account	−0.3	−0.5	−0.3[d]	−0.7[d]	0.6	−2.7[d]
On long- and short-term account	−2.7	−3.8	3.7	8.8	9.5	1.8
U.S. wholesale prices (1897 = 100)	100	146.7	299.6	185.8	141.7	165.8

Sources: Lewis (1938), Lary (1943), U.S. Department of Commerce, *Historical Statistics of the United States* (1976).

Note: All data for 1919 and data for 1929 on foreign long-term investments in the United States are unofficial estimates; other data are as estimated by the Department of Commerce.

[a] 1929 data.

[b] 1934 data.

[c] Includes miscellaneous investments.

[d] Net debtor position.

Table 3.2   **Change in U.S. Net Foreign Investment and Its Proximate Determinants, 1904–1928 ($ million)**

	Change in Net Foreign Investment	Change Due to Saving	Change Due to Investment	Change Due to Growth
1904–13 to 1909–18	376	642	−306	37
1909–18 to 1914–23	317	−5	123	197
1914–23 to 1919–28	−56	−546	329	168

Source: Calculated from Ransom and Sutch (1983), appendix tables A-1, col. 5, and E-1, cols. 2 and 8.

Note: Components do not sum to totals because of the residual (a small interaction term).

mainly responsible for driving the current account (Sachs 1981), during this earlier period punctuated by war savings fluctuations generally played the more important role.

If we compare the prewar decade (1904–13) with that encompassing the war years (1909–18), the increase in the net capital outflow is more than accounted for by the wartime surge in saving. The resulting capital outflow was moderated, in fact, by the concurrent rise in investment. In contrast, the growth of GNP accounts for a relatively small share of the growth in U.S. foreign investment. The net capital outflow is even larger in the subsequent period, 1914–23. Since the savings rate was almost identical immediately before and after the war, it contributes little to changes in U.S. foreign investment. About a third of the increased capital outflow is due to the fall in gross private investment after the war, some two-thirds to the growth of nominal incomes.

Moving from 1914–23 to 1919–28, net foreign investment falls. This reflects the fact that net foreign investment was actually greater during the war than during the boom period of foreign lending in the second half of the 1920s. Wartime lending took different forms, notably the repurchase of American obligations held by foreigners. And U.S. foreign lending in the second half of the 1920s vastly exceeded that in any previous peacetime period. But it is striking that the volume of net lending in the second half of the 1920s was by no means historically unprecedented. The decline in the capital outflow between 1914–23 and 1919–28 is fully accounted for by the tendency of savings to return to its pre-1909 level.

A full explanation for U.S. foreign lending must also consider the question from the perspective of the borrowing countries. The excess of U.S. savings over investment had as its counterpart a shortfall of foreign savings over foreign investment. In analyzing that shortfall, it is important to distinguish Europe from other parts of the world, as in table 3.3. In the first half of the twenties, Europe's savings-investment balance reflected both a drastic decline in savings and exceptional returns to investment. Wartime destruction of plant, equipment, and infrastructure had reduced European industrial production and national income below prewar levels.[3] Since this decline in income was recognized as temporary, Europeans wished to reduce their savings to smooth consumption. Moreover, the quick returns to be reaped from repairing industrial and commercial capacity provided exceptional incentive to invest.

In addition to the impact of the war on productive capacity and utilization and its direct implications for European savings and investment, there was the recycling associated with reparations. Although great play has been given to similarities between German reparations in the 1920s and the OPEC surpluses of the 1970s (see, for example, Balogh and Graham 1979), the parallels should not be pushed too far.

Table 3.3   Distribution of American Foreign Security Issues, 1919–29 (percentages of total, total in millions)

Year	Europe (%)	Canada (%)	Latin America (%)	Asia (%)	Total ($m)	Total in Constant 1929 Prices ($m real)
1919	60.3	30.4	8.9	0.2	377.5	259.6
1920	51.5	38.2	10.1	0.0	480.4	334.4
1921	26.2	32.5	38.6	2.5	594.7	580.5
1922	29.5	23.5	31.2	15.6	715.8	704.3
1923	26.1	29.0	27.7	17.0	413.3	391.0
1924	54.7	15.7	19.4	9.9	961.3	934.7
1925	58.9	12.8	14.8	13.2	1,067.1	983.0
1926	43.5	20.3	33.1	2.8	1,110.2	1,056.4
1927	44.2	18.1	26.0	11.5	1,304.6	1,299.3
1928	48.0	14.8	26.5	10.5	1,243.7	1,221.3
1929	21.5	44.0	26.5	7.8	658.2	658.2

Source: Computed from U.S. Dept. of Commerce, *American Underwriting of Foreign Securities* (various issues). The final column deflates the current price total by U.S. wholesale prices, from U.S. Department of Commerce, *Historical Statistics of the United States* (1976).

Note: Components may not sum to 100 because of rounding.

So far as U.S. foreign lending was concerned, the essence of the reparations question was Germany's need to shift resources into sectors producing traded goods and her desire to defer large resource transfers until productive capacity, financial balance, and political stability had been restored. In addition, because the German authorities pursued a tight monetary policy in the wake of hyperinflation, there was a persistent high demand for working capital, further increasing the incentive to borrow abroad. Each of these factors contributed to Germany's demand for foreign funds. A separate question is whether it was sensible for American lenders to willingly provide the supply, given the ongoing dispute over reparations.[4]

In contrast to Europe, the economies of Latin America and the Far East had been less severely disrupted. Hence incentives for investment in Latin America were rather different from those in the United States and Europe. American investors were attracted by the prospects for exploiting raw material endowments and aiding government programs to promote industrialization. Outside Europe, Americans were particularly attracted to investments in infrastructure (public utilities, railways, etc.). Between 1917 and 1924, U.S. investment in Latin America and the Far East remained small by the standards of subsequent years, although there were exceptions to the rule: $230 million and $224 million of Latin American issues were offered in 1921 and 1922 and $100 million of bonds were floated on behalf of the Netherlands East Indies in 1922. There then followed a dramatic surge in the share of U.S. foreign investment destined for Latin America. Between 1925 and 1929, Chile, Argentina, Brazil, and Colombia together accounted for a quarter of U.S. foreign lending.

3.2.3 Composition and Timing

Although the dominance of portfolio investment was the most striking aspect of international capital market experience in the 1920s, direct investment continued to make up a significant share of the U.S. total. Over a third of U.S. direct foreign investment between 1924 and 1929 took the form of purchases of and investment in public utilities, nearly quadrupling U.S. holdings in this sector. Primary production (agriculture, mining, and petroleum production) accounted for 28 percent of the total, manufacturing for 26 percent.[5] Direct foreign investment was disproportionately destined for South America, in contrast to portfolio investment, which was most heavily directed toward Europe.

Relative rates of return played some role in allocating U.S. savings between domestic and foreign uses. Foreign bonds were attractive for their yields, which exceeded those on U.S. government securities and high-grade corporate bonds, if not always those on domestic medium-grade bonds. Despite sterilization by the Federal Reserve, a steady gold influx in conjunction with the expansion of bank credit depressed the returns on domestic assets. After 1921 the rate on bankers' acceptances declined to less than 4 percent, while call money rates fluctuated between 2 and 5 percent. Domestic bond yields declined from 1923 through 1928. In a period such as 1927–28 when medium-grade domestic bonds yielded only 5.5 percent, foreign bonds which might yield seven or eight percent were understandably attractive.

Figure 3.1 shows the relationship of the yields on domestic and foreign dollar bonds over the 1920s. The yield on domestic medium-grade bonds is Moody's Baa rate, that on foreign bonds Lary's (1943) sample of 15 foreign issues. Also plotted is the value of new capital issues on behalf of foreign government and corporate borrowers.[6] The figure shows that, as the yield on domestic medium-grade bonds declined between 1923 and 1927 and that on foreign bonds grew increasingly attractive, U.S. foreign lending increased. The fall in U.S. foreign lending after 1927 coincides similarly with a fall in the spread of foreign over domestic yields. Yet rates of return by themselves account for little of the variation in the volume of foreign lending. The role of other factors—specifically risk—is especially evident before 1924, when many U.S. investors seem to have been unwilling to lend to foreigners at any price. Foreign lending rises thereafter despite the absence of any noticeable change in relative rates of return.[7]

The risks which deterred foreign lending in the early 1920s are most evident in Central Europe. So long as the level of their reparations obligations remained uncertain, it was unclear whether the nations of this region would have the resources needed to service additional debt. If they had the resources, it was not evident that they would succeed

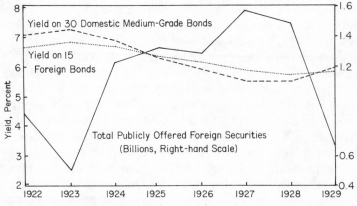

Fig. 3.1   Relative interest rates and foreign issues, 1922–1929

in mobilizing them. In Germany and many of the newly-created nations of Eastern Europe, the stability of governments remained in doubt. The successor states of the Austro-Hungarian Empire had no tax systems in place. Hyperinflation was evidence of their failure to balance government budgets through conventional means. In effect, the inability of these countries to borrow in the early 1920s reflected the operation of two factors also impeding borrowing in the 1980s: a large debt overhang in the form of existing obligations (which in the 1920s mainly took the form of war debts and reparations), plus questions about ability of governments to mobilize export earnings in order to service external debts.

Yet the perception that foreign lending was risky was not limited to Central Europe. It applied also to countries with relatively small debts and relatively stable governments. Compared to the levels achieved in the second half of the twenties, lending to Latin America remained depressed. In the immediate postwar years, foreign issues consisted primarily of high-quality Canadian bonds and loans to the governments of Norway, Sweden, and Switzerland, nations that had remained neutral during the war and whose credit was beyond reproach. Other countries obtained long-term loans from the United States only under unusual circumstances and at exceptional cost: at 7.7 percent, yields to maturity on long-term loans issued in 1920–21 were nearly 50 percent higher than yields on issues floated during the early war years and 15 percent higher than they were to become in 1922–24.[8]

Why did countries find it so difficult to borrow in the first half of the 1920s? The immediate postwar years were overshadowed by the Bolshevik revolution. In many countries, labor movements and affiliated political parties had gained new influence during hostilities, and it was unclear how radical their programs might prove if and when they took office. Governments deadlocked over the question of who should pay for the war were left with no alternative but the inflation tax. The option of a capital levy was seriously considered in every major European country, surely discouraging investors, domestic and foreign alike, from holding claims on governments.[9] "Postwar Europe," in the words of Stoddard (1932, 85), "could hardly be rated as an 'A-1' investment opportunity."

But the dominant factor was surely the depressed level of world trade and uncertain prospects for its recovery. Export volumes worldwide remained depressed relative to 1913 levels, as many governments retained tariffs and quantitative restrictions imposed during the war. Unless trade recovered, the ability of countries to generate foreign exchange receipts and service external debts would be permanently reduced. Contemporaries saw monetary stabilization—specifically a return to the gold standard—as a necessary condition for the restoration of domestic prosperity and the reduction of restrictions needed for the recovery of trade. Only with the termination of Central European hyperinflations, capped by Germany's stabilization in 1923–24, and the international movement back onto the gold standard did investors conclude that trade ultimately would recover and did the capital markets take heart.

The recovery of international trade hinged, in the view of observers, on the financial restoration of Central Europe, notably of Germany, the region's leading industrial and commercial power. Hence the 1923–24 League of Nations loans to Austria and Hungary and the 1924 Dawes loan to Germany, by cementing that restoration, had a catalytic impact on U.S. lending to the region. (Details on the League loans are provided in table 3.4.) If a lesson for the 1980s is to be drawn from the initiation of this earlier debt cycle, it is that when disruptions to trade and a debt overhang interrupt the flow of lending, outside intervention by governments or international institutions may serve to restart it.

Why were the League loans successfully placed? First, they offered exceptionally attractive returns. The 1923 League loan to Austria bore a yield to maturity of 7.8 percent. The 1924 League loan to Hungary offered a yield to maturity of 8.6 percent; on the day it was floated in London, British Consols were yielding only half that amount.[10] But while a risk premium of 100 percent eliminates much of the mystery, it does not provide the entire answer. Insofar as risk increases with the premium charged, there may be no interest rate at which the market takes up the loan. An important part of the explanation must lie, therefore, in governmental supervision and sponsorship. Before the loans received League of Nations support, governments engaged in discussions with the League's Financial Committee, involving plans to eliminate the fiscal deficit, to reform the central bank, and to strictly control future expenditures. In both the Austrian and Hungarian cases, the League appointed a commissioner-general, resident in the country, who was granted extraordinary access to government officials and vested with responsibility for supervising the collection of loan service and verifying the government's adherence to the protocols negotiated with the League. Thus, very extensive measures were taken not only to eliminate domestic sources of fiscal imbalance but to establish an institutional means whereby the borrowing country's progress might be monitored. It is no surprise that potential investors viewed the League loans differently from ordinary bond issues. Moreover, in the case of the Austrian loan, the sponsoring governments effectively collateralized the loan by depositing bonds in its amount in earmarked accounts. In the case of other League loans, such as that to Hungary, although no such collateral was provided, investors were left with the impression

Table 3.4   **League Loan Debtors and Creditors, 1923–28**

Date	Name	Amount (£ millions)
1923	Austrian Government Guaranteed Loan	33.6
1924	State Loan of the Kingdom of Hungary	14.2
1924	Greek Government 7 percent Refugee Loan	12.2
1925	Municipality of Danzig 7 percent Mortgage Loan	1.5
1926	Kingdom of Bulgaria 7 percent Settlement Loan	3.4
1927	Free City of Danzig 6½ percent (Tobacco Monopoly) State Loan	1.9
1927	Republic of Estonia 7 percent (Banking and Currency Reform) Loan	1.5
1928	Greek Government 6 percent Stabilization and Refugee Loan	7.5
1928	Kingdom of Bulgaria 7½ percent Stabilization Loan	5.4
	Total	81.2

Creditors for League Loans

	Percent of Total Loans
Austria	3.2
Belgium	1.2
Czechoslovakia	4.8
France	3.0
Great Britain	49.1
Greece	3.3
Holland	1.8
Hungary	0.4
Italy	5.9
Spain	2.6
Sweden	1.6
Switzerland	4.0
United States	19.1
	100.0

Source: League Loans Committee, *Third Annual Report,* (London, June 1935), 60–61.

that the sponsoring governments would take whatever steps proved necessary to insure continued debt service.

Unlike Austria and Hungary, Germany did not negotiate a foreign loan under the League of Nations' aegis. Because of her entanglement with the reparations issue, the loan emerged instead from an American plan to assemble a committee of business experts to deal with the external problem. The Dawes Plan announced to the public in April 1924 included a loan in the amount of 800 million RM, half to be floated in the United States, a quarter in Britain, and the remainder in France,

Belgium, Holland, Italy, Sweden, and Switzerland. As with the League loans, the market's response was overwhelming. The issue was oversubscribed in Britain by a factor of 13, in New York by a factor of 10.

The enthusiasm with which American investors took up the Dawes loan is striking in the light of earlier skepticism about European floatations. Even the bankers had greeted the plan with considerable skepticism. In part, success resulted from propitious financial market conditions. The Federal Reserve discount rate had been reduced in the spring of 1924 by an exceptionally large amount, from 4.5 to 3 percent, rendering foreign investments attractive for their return.[11] The American tranche was sold to the public at 92, to be redeemed at 105; together with a nominal interest rate of 7 percent, this meant that it yielded 7.6 percent. In addition, the U.S. government and New York banks had pressed for British and French involvement, partly to create domestic interests in those countries that would oppose giving priority to reparations over commercial liabilities. Involving foreign investors increased U.S. confidence that Dawes loan obligations would not be subordinated to reparations. A final explanation for the success of the loan lies in the aggressive publicity campaign launched in its support. Even President Coolidge urged patriotic American investors to subscribe.

These measures were used to buttress financial stability in Europe and to ensure the restoration of international trade, and once launched they continued to operate on their own. For many investors, foreign dollar bonds had been until recently an unfamiliar instrument. But American investors grew accustomed to holding bonds through the good offices of the U.S. Treasury, which aggressively administered the Liberty Loan campaign during World War I. Under the Liberty Loan Act of 1917, the Secretary of the Treasury was authorized to purchase obligations of foreign governments at war with enemies of the United States. U.S. purchases of foreign securities were financed by selling the American public dollar-denominated securities in matching amounts. The rate of interest charged the European borrowers was simply the rate required by American investors plus a small spread to cover costs. American investors encouraged to subscribe by extensive publicity campaigns did so in the amounts shown in table 3.5. "Millions of individuals who had never clipped a coupon or owned a share of stock, now became "investment-minded" for the first time in their lives."[12]

American investors' appetite for foreign bonds having been awakened, changes in the scope and structure of U.S. financial markets helped to satisfy it. Sales of foreign dollar bonds were buoyed by the growth of the investing public. In 1914, by one estimate, there were no more than 200,000 American bond buyers in a market limited largely to Boston and its environs.[13] But by 1922, when an income of $5,000

Table 3.5   **Loans by the United States Government, under the Liberty Loan Act, 1917–22[a] (millions of dollars, calendar years)**

Borrower	1917	1918	1919	1920–22	Total
Belgium	75.4	141.6	121.7	8.5	347.2
Cuba	—	10.0	—	−2.3	7.7
Czechoslovakia	—	5.0	49.3	7.7	62.0
France	1,130.0	966.4	801.0	35.9	2,933.3
Great Britain	1,860.7	2,122.0	287.4	−133.6	4,136.5
Greece	—	—	5.0	10.0	15.0
Italy	400.0	776.0	444.9	27.1	1,648.0
Rumania	—	—	25.0	−1.8	23.2
Russia	187.7	—	—	—	187.7
Serbia	3.0	7.8	16.0	−0.7	26.1
Total	3,656.8	4,028.8	1,750.3	−49.2	9,386.7

Source: Lewis (1938, 362).

[a]Compiled from data given in the *Combined Annual Reports of the World War Foreign Debt Commission, Fiscal Years 1922–26* (1927, 2, 318–25). For 1919 the British figure and the total are both net, after deductions have been made to take account of 7.6 million dollars repaid by Great Britain during that year. The minus signs used in the 1920–22 column indicate repayments in excess of cash advances.

a year was required to participate in the bond market, according to reputable investment bankers, the annual incomes of nearly 600,000 Americans exceeded this amount, and by 1929 there were more than one million such individuals.[14]

Both the wartime and postwar transformation of American commercial banking and the growth of the investment trust reinforced these trends. Before World War I, few national banks had engaged in the securities business. Only in exceptional instances did they do more than provide their customers information. But the banks became heavily involved in the wartime campaign to distribute Liberty Bonds. Following the war's conclusion, they attempted to retain purchasers of Liberty Bonds as clients by offering them foreign obligations. Many investors who developed a newfound interest in the bond market grew accustomed to buying and selling through the bond departments of commercial banks, which expanded dramatically in consequence. Between 1922 and 1931, the number of national banks engaged in securities operations through their bond departments increased from 62 to 123.

By establishing a security affiliate, banks could engage in the entire range of bond-market activities without the restrictions of federal or state banking laws. A security affiliate also permitted them to circumvent the barriers to interstate branching. Between 1922 and 1931, the number of national bank security affiliates grew from 10 to 114. By 1919 National City Bank's underwriting and brokerage affiliate, the

City Company, had opened branch offices in 51 cities, often on the ground floor to encourage walk-in business. It publicized the attractions of a bond portfolio through advertisements in popular magazines such as *Harper's* and *Atlantic Monthly*.

Banks and their affiliates took an active role not only in retailing but in the origination of foreign bond issues. In the 1920s American banks for the first time expanded overseas on a significant scale. Prior to the passage of the Federal Reserve Act, national banks had been prohibited from branching abroad. Although private banks and some state banks were permitted to do so, as late as 1914 there existed only 26 foreign branches of American banks. The Federal Reserve Act relaxed the constraint on foreign branching, however, and World War I, by disrupting the ability of European banks to extend export credits, provided the impetus for American banks to move overseas. Although some retrenchment occurred in the years to follow, by 1920 the number of foreign branches of U.S. banks had increased to 181. These branches provided a steady stream of contacts between American bankers and potential foreign borrowers.[15]

The need for a diversified portfolio, impressed upon potential purchasers by responsible salesmen, limited the involvement of the small investor.[16] Increasingly, however, this constraint was relaxed by the growth of the investment trust. A forerunner of the modern mutual fund, the investment trust pooled the subscriptions of its clients, placed their management in the hands of specialists, and issued long-term securities entitling holders to a share of the organization's earnings. The modern investment trust originated largely in Britain, where it traditionally specialized in foreign bonds.[17] When the investment trust first appeared on a significant scale in the United States after 1921, many of the new institutions followed British example by investing heavily in foreign bonds.[18]

Thus, in the 1920s as in the 1970s, the surge in foreign lending was greatly facilitated by financial innovation. The rapid development of retailing and underwriting activities and the proliferation of investment vehicles provided financial organizations both incentive and opportunity to increase their participation in foreign bond markets. While the growth of the investing public and the low yields on domestic bonds created an incipient demand for foreign assets, competition among financial institutions provided the supply. It has been asserted, following Hiram Johnson, head of the Senate's 1931–32 Foreign Bond Investigation, that these institutions competed excessively, pushing loans on inexperienced foreign governments and forcing bonds on naive domestic investors.[19] The banking community counters that established firms with reputations to protect had no incentive to promote questionable investments, since "such securities would damage the underwriter's credibility with investors, making it more difficulty for the underwriter to sell securities in the future."[20] While this logic is impeccable, it may apply imperfectly to the 1920s by virtue of the fact that many institutional participants in international bond markets were recent entrants with little if any reputation to protect. The model fits better in Britain, where the underwriting of foreign securities was handled almost exclusively by a small number of long-established firms that agreed to limit the extent of competition, dividing the field "among themselves and develop[ing] more or less permanent financing arrangements with various foreign issuers."[21] In the United States, a distinctive feature of the market environment in the 1920s was the extent of entry. Mintz (1951) notes that the loans issued by various groups of banking houses in the 1920s fared very differently, with only 14 percent of the (non-Canadian) loans issued by three participants ultimately defaulting, but nearly 90 per cent of the loans issued by six other banking houses falling into default. Although Mintz is careful not to identify the banking houses, the timing of their loans suggests that the first group was composed of long-time participants and the second of recent entrants. One might speculate that firms in the second group were simply less well managed, but it is also likely that their managements were more inclined toward risky issues since they had less reputation to lose in the event of default. If, in the long run, track record in comparison with incumbants will drive unsuccessful entrants out of the market, there is no reason to suppose that these forces had much effect between 1921 and 1929.

Critics blamed loan pushing on lax regulation by public authorities. Until 1933 many of the operations of securities affiliates remained unregulated. The popular argument, especially after the Wall Street crash and the onset of default, was that the establishment of bank security affiliates brought into conflict the bank's obligation to provide prudent advice to its depositor-investors and its desire to sell the security issues it originated. Even if the affiliate did not unduly favor the securities of its customers, with a bond distribution network in place the affiliates had an interest in promoting the sale of bonds even when the supply of high-quality issues declined. This notion that the establishment of affiliates led the banks to encourage reckless investment in foreign bonds contributed to the passage in 1933 of the Glass-Steagall Act outlawing the security affiliate.[22]

The U.S. State and Commerce Departments also can be criticized for inadequately screening individual loans. Banks originating foreign loans were asked only to consult the State Department prior to offering an issue to American investors. The State Department then consulted with the Treasury and Commerce Departments before announcing whether or not it had an objection. While the program was voluntary, bankers hesitant to cooperate risked incurring the wrath of the administration and losing its assistance in the event of default. Critics such as Senator Carter Glass of Virginia complained that the program was at the same time insufficiently stringent to prevent dubious foreign loans and insufficiently clear to prevent potential investors from interpreting a statement of "no objection" as the government's seal of approval.[23]

The government's activities involved both education and data gathering. Its agents furnished information on particular enterprises and investment projects, which the department mailed to hundreds of American banks. These agents were sometimes able in their official capacity to obtain financial information to which the bankers did not have access. Hence many U.S. banks came to rely on assessments by Commerce Department agents of potential foreign investment projects as part of normal business practice.[24]

The principal instances in which the U.S. authorities made use of their oversight of foreign lending were in connection with foreign governments owing war debts to the United States.[25] A strict loan embargo was imposed against the Soviet Union. Washington disapproved a prospective Romanian loan in 1922 because of the absence of a war debt funding agreement. It disapproved of refunding issues for France until that country negotiated a war debt settlement. Naturally, this policy proved unpopular in Europe, the French threatening for example to impose a tariff on U.S. automobiles, which led in 1928 to permission to float French industrial securities on the American market.[26] This was only a particular instance of a general phenomenon, that "[i]n almost all cases where the government entered an objection, it could be gotten round or in time removed" (Feis 1950, 13).

Compared to their attitude toward other countries, U.S. authorities were surprisingly lenient in their treatment of German loans. While Commerce Department agents in Berlin continually reminded Washington of the magnitude of the reparations burden and of the danger that Germany would be unable to both pay reparations and service municipal and corporate loans, the position of the U.S. authorities remained ambiguous. Commerce continued to supply the leading investment houses with information on the finances of municipalities and even the prospects for specific investment projects. While the warnings of its agents were passed on to the U.S. investment banking community, few if any German loan applications met with formal objection. Starting in 1925, the Commerce and State Departments issued somewhat ambiguous warnings to the bankers. The State Department alluded to the possibility of an embargo on loans to German states and municipalities in instances where such loans might hamper transfers under the Dawes Plan.[27]

While the Department of State raises no objection to this flotation
. . . it feels that American bankers should know that the amount of
German loans has become so large, and the control of exchange on
behalf of the Allies is such, as to raise a question as to whether or
not it may be very difficult for German borrowers to make the necessary transfers.[28]

Why was German borrowing treated so leniently? It is not that
Commerce Department officials failed to recognize the danger of default. As early as 1925 internal memoranda warned of an investment
"debacle," and in 1928 the problem had achieved such proportions
that middle-ranking officials were warned to distance themselves from
German lending to protect the government in the event of default.[29]
But the State Department overrode the hesitations of Commerce out
of a desire to maintain German stability as a bulwark against Bolshe-
vism. Moreover, Andrew Mellon, secretary of the treasury for much
of the 1920s, actively represented the bankers' desire that German
lending be left unfettered. And ultimately, U.S. officials believed deeply
in the laissez-faire approach to foreign lending—that the market knew
best.

3.3 Pricing Foreign Debt

Why did these people lend money to Austria, or Japan, or Germany,
or Argentine, or Belgium? Here, statistics are of little value. Men
have not yet found a way of measuring the motives of other men.
(Morrow 1927)

A standard criticism of the international capital market in the 1920s
is that it failed to discriminate adequately among borrowers. Precisely
the same criticism has been leveled at U.S. creditors in the 1970s;
Guttentag and Herring (1985) argue that rates charged sovereign borrowers on bank loans could not have adequately incorporated the determinants of country-risk premia because they varied so little across
loans. Edwards (1986) has attempted to test this hypothesis formally
for both bank loans and bonds, using regression to analyze the relationship between ex ante spreads and correlates of the country-risk
premium such as debt, reserves, investment, the current account, and
imports as shares of GNP, the ratio of debt service to exports, the rate
of economic growth, the real exchange rate, and characteristics of the
borrower and the loan. His results for the bond market were mixed:
rates charged borrowers were found to rise with the debt/GNP ratio,
to fall with the investment/GNP ratio, and to decline with the maturity
of the loan. The first two of these results are consistent with the notion

that bondholders distinguished among good and bad credit risks. The coefficients on the other variables were uniformly insignificant, however, suggesting that investors paid little attention to other plausible indicators of country risk when pricing foreign bonds.

These results provide a benchmark for comparison with my analysis of the bond market in the 1920s. To analyze the determinants of the ex ante rate of return required by bondholders in the 1920s, I employ data on the yield to maturity on issue for bonds floated in the United States between 1920 and 1929. These data, compiled by Lewis (1938), include all foreign securities issued and taken in the United States, both securities publicly issued and privately taken. They exclude portions of such issues sold on foreign markets (so far as could be determined) and securities of American-controlled enterprises (which are considered direct investment), thereby differing from other sources of information on the subject such as the Department of Commerce's lists of foreign loans. (Both public and private issues are similarly included in modern studies such as Edwards's.) The par value of loans and the yield to maturity are provided by year of issue, domicile of borrower, maturity (long-term loans versus short-term loans of five years or less), and type of borrower (national and provincial, municipal or corporate). For the 1920s the required information is provided for 383 categories of bonds. These data were then linked to information on the characteristics of the borrowing countries. It was not possible to obtain information on all of the independent variables used in modern analyses, regrettably insofar as this renders the results to follow imperfectly comparable. But just as estimates of national income, investment and related variables for the 1920s are not available to historians, such estimates were not available to bondholders and hence were unlikely to be used in pricing foreign bonds. The readily-available indicators of policy stance were foreign trade and public finance statistics.[30] I therefore use the trade and budget balances as measures of domestic policy. Contemporaries argued that a balance-of-trade surplus should have been related negatively to the required rate of return on bonds, as the larger the surplus the greater the export receipts available for debt service. Similarly, a government budget surplus should have been negatively associated with the required rate, as any budget surplus could be used to retire domestic debt and reduce the government's total debt burden.[31] Data on these variables were drawn from publications of the League of Nations for 221 of Lewis's 383 observations.[32] Trade and budget surpluses are measured as shares of imports and government expenditures, respectively.

The dependent variable is the spread over domestic risk-free rates, defined as the foreign yield minus the yield on securities rated Baa by Moody's (annual averages). The value of the loan is divided by the value of exports to control for country size.[33] Regression results are reported in table 3.6. The omitted alternatives (1929, Venezuela, and corporation) are picked up by the constant term.[34] The spread varies considerably, with a mean of 0.46 and a standard deviation of 1.20. According to the regressions, the yield on short-term loans averaged 73 basis points below that on long term loans. Although this result contrasts with that obtained by Edwards for the 1970s, who found the yield on short-term bonds to be higher than that on long-term issues, it is consistent with the presumption that the yield curve should be positively sloped. The negative coefficients on public loans (both sovereign and municipal) indicates that the public demanded a smaller risk premium for them than on corporate bonds. This contrasts with Edwards's (1986) finding for the 1970s of no discernible difference.

The remaining variables are dummies for countries, trade and budget balances, and dummies for years prior to 1929. The first can be interpreted as proxies for national reputation, the second as proxies for current policy, the third as components of the spread not attributable to other characteristics of the loans. The coefficients on years indicate some tendency for the spread to rise over the course of the 1920s, as if market participants recognized the increasingly risky nature of foreign loans. According to the country dummies, the best bond-market reputations were enjoyed, not surprisingly, by Scandinavian countries (Denmark, Norway, Sweden), members of the British Commonwealth (Australia, Canada, Ireland), small Western European countries (Switzerland, the Netherlands), and small Central American republics economically or politically dependent on the United States (Cuba, the Dominican Republic, Haiti, Panama).[35] There were good reasons to expect these countries to service their obligations promptly; bondholders' willingness to lend to them at favorable rates indicates some significant ability to discriminate among potential borrowers. Conversely, high rates were charged the new nations of Eastern Europe (Bulgaria, Czechoslovakia, Hungary, Poland, Rumania), a country engaged in an international dispute (Greece), and Latin American nations with a history of debt service disruptions (Bolivia, Peru). Again, given the political and economic situation in these countries and, in the case of Latin America, their past record of servicing debt, bondholders' tendency to demand a risk premium indicates some ability to discriminate among borrowers. At the same time, the relatively small risk premia charged Germany, the leading borrower of American funds, and a number of the larger South American republics raise questions about whether bondholders discriminated adequately.

The coefficients on the trade and budget balances provide additional information relevant to this question. While the coefficient on the trade surplus is negative as anticipated, it differs insignificantly from zero.

Table 3.6   **Bond Spreads: Pooled Data 1920–29 (The dependent variable is spread over Moody's Baa bond yield.)**

Variable	(1)	(2)	Variable	(1)	(2)
Constant	0.82	0.71	Greece	2.26	2.39
	(4.56)	(5.94)		(5.05)	(6.35)
Value/Exports	−0.01	−0.01	Hungary	1.21	1.22
	(0.53)	(0.38)		(6.82)	(6.82)
National	−0.29	−0.28	Ireland	−0.82	−0.89
	(3.29)	(3.24)		(4.75)	(6.55)
Municipal	−0.12	−0.12	Italy	0.26	0.41
	(1.44)	(1.46)		(0.95)	(0.18)
Short-term	−0.73	−0.73	Netherlands	−0.73	−0.53
	(8.37)	(8.27)		(2.54)	(3.41)
Trade surplus	−0.23	—	Norway	−0.86	−0.67
	(0.96)			(3.45)	(6.27)
Budget surplus	0.09	—	Poland	1.66	1.81
	(0.26)			(8.71)	(16.03)
1920	−1.12	−1.09	Rumania	1.56	1.69
	(3.70)	(4.51)		(7.75)	(10.94)
1921	−1.89	−1.92	Sweden	−1.48	−1.38
	(3.82)	(4.01)		(8.13)	(10.51)
1922	−0.65	−0.67	Switzerland	−1.05	−0.87
	(3.16)	(3.30)		(4.27)	(6.20)
1923	−0.97	−1.00	Yugoslavia	0.96	1.11
	(5.47)	(6.05)		(2.99)	(4.01)
1924	−0.67	−0.70	Canada	−1.45	−1.35
	(4.65)	(5.00)		(9.78)	(11.17)
1925	−0.13	−0.14	Argentina	0.54	0.62
	(1.10)	(1.16)		(2.74)	(3.47)
1926	−0.05	0.01	Brazil	0.80	0.94
	(0.40)	(0.09)		(4.54)	(7.81)
1927	0.21	0.19	Bolivia	1.65	1.56
	(1.70)	(1.51)		(8.47)	(8.77)
1928	−0.18	−0.20	Chile	0.46	0.45
	(0.12)	(1.66)		(2.48)	(3.13)
Austria	0.75	0.97	Colombia	0.88	1.01
	(2.80)	(7.32)		(4.42)	(7.64)
Belgium	0.34	0.50	Peru	1.03	1.00
	(0.78)	(1.30)		(6.70)	(7.16)
Bulgaria	1.51	1.66	Costa Rica	1.01	1.11
	(4.76)	(6.32)		(5.38)	(8.41)
Czechoslovakia	1.21	1.31	Cuba	−0.57	−0.52
	(5.95)	(7.18)		(2.25)	(2.18)
Denmark	−1.26	−1.12	Dominican	−0.31	−0.21
	(6.82)	(10.38)	Republic	(2.24)	(2.55)
Finland	0.31	0.45	Haiti	−0.41	−0.28
	(1.51)	(3.58)		(2.05)	(2.11)
France	0.35	0.47	Panama	−0.28	−0.16
	(1.20)	(2.11)		(0.23)	(0.13)
Germany	0.26	0.42	Australia	−0.83	−0.71
	(1.25)	(3.90)		(2.43)	(2.75)

Table 3.6 (continued)

Variable	(1)	(2)	Variable	(1)	(2)
Japan	0.21	0.36	Number of	221	221
	(0.91)	(2.71)	observations		
			R^2	.88	.88

Source: See text.
Notes: White-corrected t-statistics in parentheses. The omitted alternatives are 1929, Venezuela, and corporations.

Moreover, the coefficient on the budget surplus is positive, although essentially zero. From this evidence, it does not appear that bondholders attached much weight to readily-available indicators of the current macroeconomic situation when determining the price at which to lend. It would seem that reputation more than current economic developments influenced bond market participants.

The remaining variable is loan size (scaled by exports). While its coefficient is negative, it differs insignificantly from zero, as in Edwards's sample of bonds issued in the 1970s. It seems curious that foreign borrowers were not charged a premium when floating larger loans, since the larger the loan, the greater the cost to the issuing house if the entire amount was not successfully placed and had to be absorbed by the sponsoring bankers, to be resold later at a loss. One possibility is that the bankers' commission rather than the price to the public responded to the size of the loan. Typically, foreign floatations in the United States in the 1920s were sponsored by a money center bank or issue house responsible for origination. Often shares of the issue were then sold to a syndicate of underwriting banks which shared responsibility for advertising, marketing and ultimately absorbing any residual amount of the bond issue which the public proved unwilling to purchase.[36] Hence the bankers' commission represented compensation for normal costs of marketing and advertising, compensation for underwriting risk, and possibly economic profit due to the relatively small number of issue houses active in the market.

Lewis (1938) provides information not only on the yield received by the public (the variable utilized in the regression analysis reported above) but also on that paid by the borrower; the difference measures the bankers' commission. That commission averaged 30 basis points on foreign bonds issued in the United States in the 1920s and could reach substantial levels; on Poland's 1925 national loan, for example, on which the price to the bankers was 86.3 and the price to the public 95.5, the commission amounted to nearly a full percentage point on a loan bearing a nominal interest rate of eight percent.[37]

The determinants of the bankers' commission are analyzed in table 3.7 using the same variables utilized to analyze the return required

Table 3.7   **Determinants of Bankers' Commission: Pooled Data, 1920–29 (The dependent variable is the difference between the interest rate to bankers and the interest rate to the public.)**

Variable	(1)	(2)	Variable	(1)	(2)
Constant	0.38	0.36	Greece	−0.13	−0.06
	(5.40)	(5.09)		(0.95)	(0.52)
Value	−0.01	−0.01	Hungary	0.42	0.45
	(2.22)	(1.63)		(3.51)	(3.38)
National	−0.08	−0.08	Ireland	0.09	0.04
	(2.32)	(2.00)		(1.33)	(0.86)
Municipal	−0.06	−0.05	Italy	−0.07	−0.04
	(1.42)	(1.09)		(0.59)	(0.36)
Short-term	−0.26	−0.25	Netherlands	−0.23	−0.05
	(8.02)	(7.41)		(1.89)	(0.50)
Trade surplus	−0.26	−0.27	Norway	−0.17	−0.11
	(2.31)	(2.23)		(1.62)	(1.07)
Budget surplus	0.21	0.12	Poland	0.12	0.15
	(1.72)	(1.22)		(0.68)	(0.88)
1920	0.24	—	Rumania	0.29	0.30
	(2.31)			(3.77)	(3.81)
1921	0.21	—	Sweden	−0.16	−0.18
	(2.30)			(2.40)	(2.52)
1922	0.15	—	Switzerland	−0.06	0.06
	(1.85)			(0.46)	(0.59)
1923	0.10	—	Yugoslavia	0.08	0.10
	(1.04)			(0.79)	(0.97)
1924	0.20	—	Canada	−0.11	−0.06
	(2.39)			(1.94)	(1.10)
1925	0.19	—	Argentina	0.04	0.02
	(2.25)			(0.67)	(0.39)
1926	0.01	—	Bolivia	0.29	0.25
	(0.23)			(5.01)	(4.72)
1927	−0.03	—	Chile	0.28	0.26
	(0.96)			(3.28)	(3.65)
1928	−0.02	—	Colombia	0.21	0.23
	(0.37)			(2.06)	(2.06)
Austria	0.22	0.27	Peru	0.41	0.38
	(1.31)	(1.46)		(7.14)	(7.82)
Belgium	−0.05	−0.04	Costa Rica	0.18	0.20
	(0.53)	(0.41)		(0.93)	(0.99)
Bulgaria	0.20	0.19	Cuba	−0.08	−0.09
	(2.33)	(2.24)		(1.54)	(1.88)
Czechoslovakia	0.32	0.45	Dominican	−0.04	−0.06
	(2.62)	(3.96)	Republic	(0.66)	(0.86)
Denmark	−0.22	−0.19	Haiti	0.24	0.40
	(2.52)	(2.41)		(0.74)	(1.36)
Finland	−0.02	0.06	Panama	−0.25	−0.27
	(0.28)	(2.04)		(1.69)	(1.74)
France	0.07	0.17	Australia	−0.04	−0.07
	(0.80)	(2.04)		(0.39)	(0.81)
Germany	0.03	0.03	Japan	0.03	0.08
	(0.38)	(0.38)		(0.29)	(0.86)

Table 3.7   (continued)

Variable	(1)	(2)	Variable	(1)	(2)
Brazil	0.05	0.04	Number of	221	221
	(0.59)	(0.48)	observations		
			R^2	.58	.52

Source: See text.

Notes: Ordinary least squares regressions with White-corrected *t*-statistics in parentheses. The omitted alternatives are 1929, Venezuela, and corporations.

by the public, except that loan value is not entered as a ratio to exports. Comparing tables 3.6 and 3.7 reveals that commissions moved very differently than rates to the public. Commissions rose gradually from 1920 through 1925 and fell back in 1926–27, before recovering in 1928–29. Mintz (1951, chap. 4) notes that a number of new banking houses entered the foreign lending business after 1924, which should have driven the commission down. Similarly, a number of houses withdrew from the market starting in 1928, permitting the commission to recover.

The commission on short-term loans was 25 basis points lower than that on long-term issues, presumably reflecting the smaller loss in the event that the issuing house was forced to absorb any portion not taken up by the market. This is consistent with Kuczynski's (1932) findings based on a sample of German bonds. Commissions on sovereign and municipal loans were slightly lower than on otherwise comparable loans to corporations. There is a negative association between the size of the loan and the bankers' commission, indicating that economies of scale associated with marketing large loans may have offset the extra risk to the issuing bankers.[38] In any case, there is no evidence in either table 3.6 or 3.7 that price was used to deter borrowers from floating larger loans.

The coefficients on the trade and budget-balance variables have the same signs as in the regressions explaining the spread, but in the commission regressions the trade-balance variable is significantly less than zero at standard confidence levels. There are at least three plausible interpretations of this difference between tables 3.6 and 3.7. My preferred interpretation is that specialists had more knowledge of bond market risks, recognized the danger that it might be difficult to market the loans of countries running trade deficits, and demanded compensation. Another possibility is that the bankers were less able than bondholders to diversify away the risks associated with a specific issue. Given the practice of forming syndicates to underwrite loans it would appear that considerable diversification was possible, however. Finally, it could be that simultaneity tending to bias the trade-balance coefficient upward (since countries charged low commissions could borrow more and hence were permitted to run large deficits) is less of a problem in table 3.7 than in table 3.6 (where a more important source of simultaneity would arise from the ability of countries charged low interest rates to borrow more and hence to run deficits).

In sum, this analysis provides some evidence that lenders discriminated among potential borrowers on the basis of reputation and political factors conveying information about the probability of default, but little evidence that they were responsive to current economic conditions in the indebted countries. Did they discriminate adequately? One way to approach this question is to compare ex ante and ex post returns. A simple model can be used as the basis for this comparison. The expected rate of return on risky loans, i_r, should exceed the risk free rate, i_f, by a risk premium:

$$(3) \qquad\qquad i_r = i_f + \delta\sigma$$

where σ is default risk so $\delta\sigma$ is the premium on risky loans. Ex ante (of default) the return on risky loans exceeds that required:

$$(4) \qquad\qquad i_{ex\ ante} = i_r + \beta\sigma$$

where $i_{ex\ ante}$ is the ex ante rate of return. The ex post return $i_{ex\ post}$ differs from that required by investors by their expectational error ϵ,

$$(5) \qquad\qquad i_{ex\ post} = i_r + \epsilon.$$

Substituting and solving for the ex ante return gives:

$$(6) \qquad i_{ex\ post} = \frac{\beta/\delta}{1 + \beta/\delta} i_f + \frac{\delta + \beta}{\delta} i_{ex\ ante} + \epsilon.$$

If investors' expectational errors have mean zero, in a regression of ex post on ex ante returns the constant term $\left(\frac{\beta/\delta}{1 + \beta/\delta} i_f\right)$ should be positive and the coefficient on $i_{ex\ ante}$ should be greater than unity.

Using the ex ante and ex post rates of return calculated by Eichengreen and Portes (1986) for a sample of 50 dollar bonds (national, provincial, municipal, and corporate) issued in the United States between 1924 and 1930, equation (6) can be estimated, yielding:

$$(7) \qquad\qquad i_{ex\ post} = 9.00 - 120.59\ i_{ex\ ante}$$
$$(0.94) \quad\ (0.89)$$

$$N = 50 \qquad R^2 = 0.016$$

with t-statistics in parentheses. Although the constant term is positive, the coefficient on $i_{ex\ post}$ is less than unity, which is inconsistent with the joint hypothesis of rational expectations and market efficiency. What kind of behavior does this imply? Instead of (4), posit an asset-pricing equation of the form:

$$(4')\qquad i_{ex\ ante} = i_r + (\beta - \alpha)\sigma,$$

which can be interpreted with $\alpha > 0$ as meaning that investors systematically underincorporate the cost of default into the ex ante prices of those bonds most at risk. Then it is possible for the coefficient on $i_{ex\ post}$ to be less than unity and, if $\alpha > \beta + \delta$, for that coefficient to be negative as in (7).

Thus, these results suggest that investors incompletely incorporated differential default risk into the spreads they demanded of foreign borrowers. This is surprising in light of the observed tendency (see table 3.6) of bond-market participants to demand low-risk premia of many borrowers that did not default (Scandinavian and Western European nations, members of the British Commonwealth, dependent Central American republics) and high-risk premia of many borrowers that did default (Eastern European nations, other small Latin American nations), since both tendencies should have given rise to a negative correlation between ex ante and ex post returns. But despite demanding risk premia in the appropriate instances, it nonetheless appears that they received inadequate compensation. This is particularly evident in the comparison between loans to Western European nations that performed well ex post and loans to Germany that performed disastrously, and between loans to Argentina and Brazil.

If default risk was imperfectly perceived at the time of issue, did bondholders recognize and act upon it subsequently? If risk-neutral investors are faced with the choice between two assets, only one of which is subject to default risk, the return on the risk-free asset should be a weighted average of the return on the other asset in instances in which default does and does not take place, where the perceived probability of default is the weight. Using γ to denote the share of interest and principle lost in the event of default:

$$(8)\qquad (1 + i_r) \cdot (1 - P) + (1 - \gamma)(1 + i_r) \cdot P = 1 + i_f,$$

where P is the probability of default, and i_r and i_f are the risky and risk-free rates of return respectively. The expected capital loss γP (default probability times percent capital loss given default) can be derived from the spread,[39]

$$(9)\qquad \gamma P = [(i_r - i_f)/(1 + i_r)].$$

Moody's Aaa bond rate and the yield to maturity on the sample of 50 dollar bonds, each at the end of the calendar year, are used as measures of the riskless and risky rate. Several expected losses from the sample of 50 dollar bonds described above are depicted in figures 3.2–3.7. Figures 3.2 and 3.3 for Colombia and Brazil show that through 1929 the market's expectation of capital loss was low (4 percent or less). Thereafter, the expected loss due to default began to rise. Since the first defaults occurred in 1931, while the spreads on Colombian and Brazilian bonds rose in 1930, there is some indication that the danger of default was anticipated by market participants. Was this a perceived increase in the probability of default by those countries that ultimately suspended debt service, or did market participants revise their expectations for all Latin American bonds? Figure 3.4 suggests the latter, although the timing and rate of growth of the expected loss differed across issues. Argentine central and provincial government debt fell

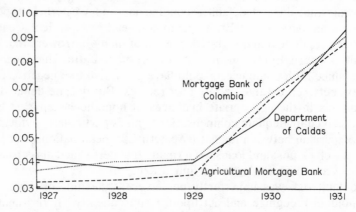

Fig. 3.2   Implicit expected capital losses: Colombian bonds

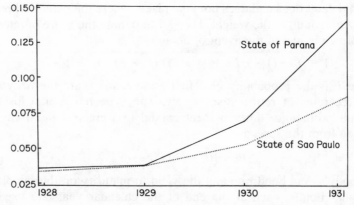

Fig. 3.3   Implicit expected capital losses: Brazilian state debt

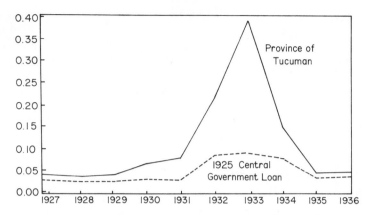

Fig. 3.4   Implicit expected capital losses: Argentine national and provincial debt

to discounts even in instances where no default ultimately occurred. The expected capital loss on the 1925 Argentine loan had risen by 1932 to the levels achieved by Brazilian and Colombian bonds in 1931. But Argentina's expected loss rises later and declines once it is clear that the national government intends to maintain service on the debt. The 1927 Province of Tucuman issue behaves very differently: The expected loss begins to rise as early as 1930 and reaches high levels in 1932–33 as default takes place on other state and municipal Argentine loans. Once it becomes clear that debt service will be maintained, spreads return to their initial levels.

Figures 3.5 through 3.7 provide information on the pricing of European bonds. They suggest that the externalities associated with the initial Latin American defaults were limited largely to Latin America; significant discounts on the German, Austrian, and Hungarian bonds depicted in figures 3.5–3.6 do not appear until 1932, despite the spread of Latin American defaults from early 1931. It is remarkable that more serious doubts about Central European bonds did not materialize as early as 1930, when the Young Plan rescheduling of reparations was needed to prevent Germany from falling into arrears. Even at this late date National City Company was still suggesting that "[I]t is reasonable to believe that the new loan . . . marks the beginning of a widening demand for German bonds, both in this country and abroad. And the present, therefore, would seem to be an opportune time for their purchase."[40]

Figure 3.7 depicts the behavior of spreads on three Scandinavian loans serviced promptly throughout. Before 1932, spreads on these loans remain exceptionally low. They then rise in 1932 as default spreads to Eastern Europe, although to nowhere near the levels of the German, Austrian, and Hungarian bonds in figures 3.5–3.6. As in Latin America,

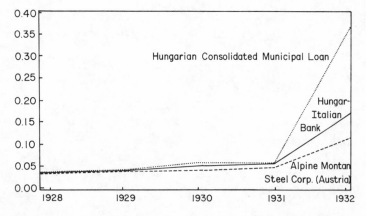

Fig. 3.5　　　　　Implicit expected capital losses: Central European bonds

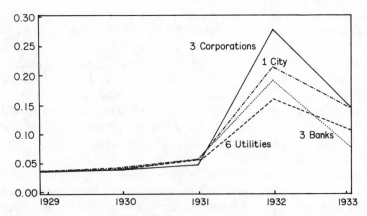

Fig. 3.6　　　　　Implicit expected capital losses: German bonds

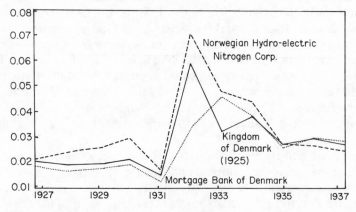

Fig. 3.7　　　　　Implicit expected capital losses: Scandinavian bonds

there is evidence that the German, Austrian and Hungarian defaults had contagion effects on the perceived credit-worthiness of other European borrowers.

Does this evidence suggest that default carried negative externalities by creating doubt about the credit-worthiness of even those nations which continuously maintained service on their obligations? In the 1930s, it appears that such externalities existed but were confined mainly to other countries in the same region. The first Latin American defaults did not have a discernible impact on the bonds of countries in other parts of the world. But when these effects occurred, they were persistent; it took four years, for example, for the initial impact on Argentine credit-worthiness to dissipate.

3.4   Default and Market Access

> The great depression that began in 1929 brought our first great venture in foreign lending to a sick end. There had been a thrill about this swift financial ascension over the oceans. It was gone, and seemingly for all time. . . . A general sign of resolve was to be heard over the United States: Never again should we lend or invest our money in foreign lands. (Feis 1950, 1)

The debt defaults of the 1930s were sobering for American investors. The performance of U.S. portfolio investments abroad, notably debts of foreign governments, was particularly disheartening. Approximately two-thirds of foreign securities held by American investors fell into default over the course of the Depression decade. Contemporaries believed that the experience of the thirties had a lingering impact on the attitudes of investors. The United Nations explained the postwar decline in private loans to governments on the basis of "losses resulting from default and only partly mitigated by subsequent agreements with the borrowers that bondholders have accepted in order to avoid more severe loss. . . ."[41] When transmitting to the Economic and Social Council of the United Nations in 1949 a study by the National Association of Manufacturers of the potential for U.S. capital exports following the conclusion of the Marshall Plan, Curtis E. Calder, Chairman of the Association's International Relations Committee, expressed this view as follows:

> We feel further that the relative undesirability of inter-governmental loans has been impressed equally upon grantors and recipients. After the experience of the thirties and the serious balance of payment difficulties now plaguing most of the world, the superiority of equity over loan financing has, we believe, a universal appeal. . . . We strongly recommend that no reliance be placed upon intergovernmental loans outside of the category of those qualifying within the

limits of the funds of Export-Import Bank and the Bank for Reconstruction and Development.[42]

Despite a proliferation of similar statements, it is not obvious that the experience of the thirties influenced investors' actions as well as their statements, particularly since a variety of other postwar disruptions might conceivably have exercised an even more powerful influence over the volume and pattern of foreign lending. Moreover, any new hesitancy to extend loans to foreign governments did not have a sufficient half-life to prevent the astounding growth of sovereign debt in the 1970s. Still, it seems plausible that repercussions of the debt defaults of the 1930s were felt by the capital markets in the 1940s and 1950s. One approach to this issue is to compare U.S. foreign lending in the ten years immediately succeeding World Wars I and II. Clearly, the second half of the 1940s and first half of the 1950s constitute a very special period in the history of the world economy, following as they do on the heels of a global conflagration. Since the years 1919–28 form an equally special period for many of the same reasons, they provide an especially useful basis for comparison. Admittedly, a study of the ten years immediately following World War II is not a complete analysis of the legacy—if any—of interwar debt defaults. But if no legacy of default can be discerned in the immediate postwar decade when interwar experience was so immediate and the parallels were so extensive, it seems unlikely that such evidence could be found for subsequent years.

In comparing U.S. foreign lending in the decades immediately following the two world wars, it is useful to distinguish three questions. First, was total U.S. foreign lending depressed in the wake of the debt defaults of the 1930s? Second, was the relative importance of direct and portfolio investment altered by the lingering effects of interwar defaults? Third, compared to countries that continuously serviced their debts, did countries that had defaulted find it more difficult to borrow abroad?

Table 3.8 summarizes the volume and composition of U.S. foreign lending in the two postwar decades. Lending from 1946 through 1955 is expressed in 1919–28 average prices. A first fact evident from table 3.8 is that U.S. capital exports actually were larger in the second postwar decade (more than three times as large at current prices, more than twice as large at constant prices). However, the difference is due almost entirely to unilateral transfers by government, notably the Marshall Plan. (The amount and direction of Marshall Plan aid are summarized in table 3.9.) Net of official transfers, U.S. foreign lending at constant prices remains almost exactly unchanged between the two postwar decades. At the most aggregated level, then, there is little

Table 3.8 U.S. Foreign Lending in the Two Postwar Decades, 1919–28 and 1946–55 (In millions of current dollars for 1919–28 and in 1919–28 average prices for 1946–55.)

	1919	1920	1921	1922	1923	1924	1925	1926	1927	1928	Decade Average
Public, long- and short-term	2,328	175	−30	−31	−91	−28	−27	−30	−46	−49	217
Private											
Direct, long-term	94	154	111	153	148	182	268	351	351	558	237
Other, long-term	75	400	477	669	235	703	603	470	636	752	502
Short-term	n.a.	n.a.	n.a.	n.a.	82	109	46	36	349	231	142
Unilateral transfers											
Private	832	634	450	314	328	339	373	361	355	346	433
Government	212	45	59	38	37	25	30	20	2	19	49

	1946	1947	1948	1949	1950	1951	1952	1953	1954	1955	Decade Average
Public, long- and short-term	2,705	3,079	690	462	106	96	265	139	−59	197	682
Private											
Direct, long-term	206	546	486	468	424	311	537	469	425	523	444
Other, long-term	−114	36	47	57	338	268	135	−118	204	153	107
Short-term	278	137	78	−133	102	63	59	−107	404	121	97
Unilateral transfers											
Private	603	497	470	377	310	258	279	321	321	290	368
Government	2,015	1,416	2,580	3,620	2,430	1,904	1,315	1,262	1,131	1,299	1,871

Source: U.S. Department of Commerce, *Historical Statistics of the United States* (1976, 198–201, 866–67).

Notes: n.a. indicates not available. Decade average short-term capital flow for the twenties is for the years 1923–28 only.

Table 3.9   European Recovery Program Direct and Conditional Aid, by Country: From Inception through 30 June 1951 ($million)

Country	Total	Grants Total	Direct	Conditional upon Aid Extended Under Intra European Payments Agreement[a]	Through European Payments Union	Credits
Total	10,260	9,128	7,537	1,355	236	1,132
Austria	492	492	488	5	—	—
Belgium-Luxembourg	537	484	8	447	29	52
British Commonwealth:						
United Kingdom	2,675	2,329	1,799	380	150	346
Denmark	231	200	191	9	—	31
France	2,060	1,869	1,807	61	—	191
Germany	1,174	1,172	953	219	—	2
Greece	387	386	386	—	—	1
Iceland	17	13	10	4	—	3
Ireland	139	11	11	—	—	128
Italy	1,034	959	873	86	—	74
Netherlands-Indonesia	893	743	711	32	—	151
Netherlands	809	659	628	30	—	151
Indonesia	84	84	83	1	—	—
Norway	199	164	153	11	—	25
Portugal	33	8	*	8	—	35
Sweden	103	82	*	77	5	20
Trieste	30	30	30	—	—	—
Turkey	89	17	*	17	—	71
International organization:	51	51	—	—	51	—
European Payments Union						
Unclassified areas	116	116	116	—	—	—

Source: U.S. Department of Commerce (1952, 60).

*Less than $500,000.

[a]Includes $3,500,000 extended by Iceland to Germany and $3,081,000 extended by Italy to Trieste outside of the intra-European payments plan.

evidence that the debt defaults of the 1930s had a damping effect on the volume of U.S. lending.

Only at the aggregate level, however, is there little change. Putting aside unilateral transfers, there is a reversal in the relative importance of lending by government and by the private sector, the public sector accounting for just 20 percent after World War I but for fully 51 percent after World War II. The real value of private lending at constant prices (long- and short-term combined) fell by nearly one third between the post–World War I and post–World War II decades. Within private lending, there are equally far-reaching changes in composition. While the share of short-term capital in U.S. private lending remains more or less unchanged, the relative importance of direct and portfolio investment is reversed. Where portfolio investment was more than double direct investment in the decade following World War I, it was less than a quarter of direct investment in the decade following World War II. Although there are other reasons why reliance on direct investment might have increased after World War II—such as the standard presumption that direct investment is relatively advantageous for firms engaged in the manufacture of goods produced with firm-specific technical knowledge, a type of production that tended to grow more important in international transactions as the century progressed—it seems implausible that these slowly-evolving factors rather than the repercussions of default were mainly responsible for the very dramatic rise in direct investment after 1945. Because of both the fall in the real value of private lending and the declining share of portfolio investment, the real value of the latter fell most dramatically between decades, by more than 80 percent. Overall, there was a dramatic decline in the willingness of Americans to accumulate portfolio investments abroad, precisely what one would expect had purchasers been deterred by defaults on foreign bonds.

While the United States was far and away the leading capital exporter of the post–World War II period, she had not been so dominant after World War I. In the period 1924–27, when U.S. capital exports fluctuated in the range of $1.2–$1.6 billion per annum, total capital exports of the industrial countries reached $2 billion annually and more.[43] It is noteworthy, therefore, that private capital exports of other industrial countries fell even more dramatically between the two postwar decades than did the capital exports of the United States. New issues for overseas account floated in London in the period 1947–52 amounted to £45 million per annum, less than 50 percent of the current-price value of the period 1920–25. Meanwhile, British investors steadily repatriated their foreign funds between 1946 and 1951. The nominal value of the overseas investments of U.K. residents in the form of securities quoted on the London Stock Exchange declined by £432 million.[44] The outflow of private capital from France over the period 1946–52 is estimated to have approached a total of $1 billion; in contrast, in the period 1920–26 the total outflow (excluding gold) had been more than $3.5 billion.[45]

Consistent country data on the extent of foreign borrowing after World War II are notoriously difficult to obtain. Fortunately, courtesy of Avramovic's (1958) massive study, reasonably consistent data on stocks of debt at three points in time are available for 36 countries. As summarized in table 3.9, these include disbursed and undisbursed long-term debt owned or guaranteed by public bodies in debtor countries (central and local governments, public agencies and state-owned enterprises) and exclude grants in aid (notably Marshall Plan aid), loans repayable in local currency, loans with a maturity of less than 12 months, and drawings on the IMF. Debt is valued as on the books of the borrowing countries.

In the raw data, no relationship between default in the 1930s and borrowing after 1945 is apparent. But reputational effects are only a subset of the factors affecting a government's willingness and ability to borrow abroad. The United Nations, when discussing external borrowing in this period, cited country size and the relative importance of imports in domestic consumption as factors positively associated with borrowing.[46] Standard borrowing models suggest in addition that countries whose exports are most variable will have the greatest tendency to borrow abroad in order to smooth fluctuations in export receipts and domestic purchasing power.[47] My analysis of the role of these factors and of past debt-servicing records in the extent of borrowing in the post–World War II decade builds on the data in table 3.10. Additional information on external debt was obtained from United Nations (1948) and the annual reports of the Council of the Corporation of Foreign Bondholders and Foreign Bondholders Protective Council, permitting Argentina, Bolivia, Costa Rica, Venezuela, Egypt, Germany, and Sweden to be added to the sample. Information on imports, exports, and GNP was obtained from International Monetary Fund (1978), supplemented as necessary by United Nations (1958) and Wilkie (1974). These were used to calculate measures of openness (the import/GNP ratio in 1955) and export variability (the variance of exports over the three years 1953–55). Finally, as a measure of the extent of interwar default, the percentage of dollar and sterling external governmental debt (all levels of government plus government-guaranteed loans to

Table 3.10   **External Public Debt Outstanding, 1945–55 (31 December of each year in thousands of U.S. $ equivalents.)**

	1945	1950	1955	Percentage Increase 1945–55	Percentage Increase 1950–55
Grand Total	*7,732,240*	*16,122,635*	*18,329,325*	*137.1*	*13.7*
Europe	3,594,809	12,225,248	11,726,205	226.2	−4.1
Austria	60,562	72,635	259,146[b]	327.9	256.8
Belgium	181,047	375,370	446,376	146.6	18.9

Table 3.10   (continued)

	1945	1950	1955	Percentage Increase 1945–55	Percentage Increase 1950–55
Denmark	272,135	389,493	251,984	−7.4	−35.3
Finland	147,998	326,742	292,177	97.4	−10.6
France	1,267,182	2,906,297	2,631,671	107.7	−9.4
Iceland	1,216	8,633	16,965	1,295.1	96.5
Italy	126,116	550,268	681,450	440.3	23.8
Luxembourg	5,310	19,502	17,342	226.6	−11.1
Netherlands	194,612	939,625	531,607	173.2	−43.4
Norway	222,456	286,523	347,476	56.2	21.3
United Kingdom	1,116,175	6,061,234	5,920,196	430.4	−2.3
Yugoslavia	n.a.	288,926[a]	329,815	n.a.	14.2
Africa	296,052	438,548	1,093,903	269.5	149.4
Belgian Congo	79,206	107,719	316,564[c]	299.7	193.9
Ethiopia	2,786	12,000	32,583	1,069.5	171.5
Federation of Rhodesia	69,157	169,806	368,410	432.7	117.0
Union of South Africa	144,903	149,023	376,346	459.7	152.5
Australia	1,760,514	1,288,118	1,400,084[b]	−20.5	8.7
Asia	495,764	429,461	1,426,125	187.7	232.1
Ceylon	37,918	26,345	59,470	56.8	125.7
India	47,467	58,998	486,378	924.7	724.4
Japan	402,945	309,121	627,855	55.8	103.1
Pakistan	—	—	181,785	—	—
Thailand	7,434	34,997	70,637	850.2	101.8
Latin America	1,585,102	1,741,260	2,683,008	69.3	54.1
Brazil	432,699	409,389	1,046,414	141.8	155.6
Chile	425,892	355,346	313,543	−26.4	−11.8
Colombia	171,447	157,545	281,079	63.9	78.4
Ecuador	24,222	31,944	59,254	144.6	85.5
El Salvador	13,383	22,367	28,263	111.2	26.4
Guatemala	878	378	21,172	2,311.4	5,501.1
Haiti	15,155	8,296	42,225	178.6	409.0
Honduras	5,430	1,260	4,200	−22.7	233.3
Mexico	200,577	509,099	478,944	138.8	−5.9
Nicaragua	5,776	4,640	22,730	293.5	389.9
Panama	15,641	13,000	20,463	30.8	57.4
Paraguay	15,781	15,287	17,974	13.9	17.6
Peru	104,842	107,176	215,366	105.4	100.9
Uruguay	153,379	105,533	131,381	−14.3	24.5

Source: International Bank of Reconstruction and Development, Economic Staff, Statistics Division; reproduced from Avramovic (1958, 163).
[a]30 June 1951.
[b]30 June 1955.
[c]30 June 1956.

enterprise) in default as to interest and/or sinking fund at the end of 1935 was calculated from the reports of the two bondholders' committees. The year 1935 is chosen for measuring interwar default as almost all of these defaults occurred between 1931 and 1934.[48] Admittedly, the share of debt in default is a crude measure of reputation; it might be desirable in future work to include the share of contracted debt service payments actually made, as computed by Jorgensen (1987) or Lindert and Morton (ch. 2, in this volume), or a measure of the outcome of debtor-creditor negotiations, such as the Foreign Bondholders Protective Council's endorsement.

The absence of information on one or more of the independent variables forced a number of countries to be dropped, leaving 32, of which 18 are Latin American.[49] Two types of regressions were run on this cross section. Those in table 3.11 analyze the determinants of net foreign borrowing by public authorities—the change in the external debt between 1945 and 1955. Those in table 3.12 follow other recent studies of sovereign debt by taking as the dependent variable not the net flow of resources over the decade but the terminal stock—the value of the external debt in 1955. An advantage of the stock formulation is that elasticities can be estimated directly by defining the 1955 debt

Table 3.11   Determinants of Foreign Borrowing, 1945–55 (Dependent variable is in millions of U.S. dollars.)

	(1)	(2)	(3)
Constant	413.89	−1,311.93	−1,169.87
	(1.69)	(3.98)	(3.88)
Share of debt in default, 1935	−171.39	644.37	557.65
	(0.47)	(3.14)	(2.91)
GNP	—	0.88	0.07
		(7.00)	(10.34)
Import/GNP ratio	—	3,955.93	3,497.55
		(3.29)	(3.10)
Debt in 1945	—	−24.15	−0.32
		(1.25)	(1.41)
Export variability	—	−0.01	—
		(0.60)	
Number of observations	32	32	32
R^2	0.01	0.82	0.82
F	0.22	23.35	30.38

Source: See text.

Note: t-statistics in parentheses.

Table 3.12 **Determinants of the Stock of Debt, 1955 (Dependent variable is in millions of U.S. dollars.)**

	(1) Log of Debt	(2) Level of Debt	(3) Log of Debt	(4) Level of Debt
Constant	−2.15 (1.25)	−1254.12 (3.78)	−2.65 (1.78)	−1,169.87 (3.88)
Share of debt in default, 1935	0.65 (1.27)	613.40 (2.89)	0.75 (1.56)	557.65 (2.90)
Log GNP	0.75 (4.21)	—	0.81 (5.50)	—
GNP	—	0.08 (7.04)	—	0.07 (10.34)
Import/GNP ratio	0.85 (0.31)	3,723.12 (3.12)	1.01 (0.38)	3,497.55 (3.10)
Log debt in 1945	0.16 (3.52)	—	0.17 (3.56)	—
Debt in 1945	—	0.67 (2.91)	—	0.68 (2.99)
Export variability	0.01 (0.62)	−0.01 (0.64)	—	—
Number of observations	32	32	32	32
R^2	0.74	0.88	0.74	0.88
F	15.16	37.39	19.29	47.67

Source: See text.

Note: t-statistics in parentheses.

stock in log form (which is not possible for the flow of borrowing, as that variable can be negative).

Consider first the value of borrowing. The first equation in table 3.11, in which borrowing is regressed on only a constant term and the share of debt in default in 1935, suggests at best a weak negative relationship between interwar default and external borrowing in the first post–World War II decade. The point estimate can be read to suggest that countries that defaulted (share in default = 1) borrowed $171.4 million less than countries that serviced their entire debt (share in default = 0). Since the mean of the dependent variable is $334 million, this point estimate is substantial. However, the next two equations indicate that this apparent difference among countries is due entirely to other respects in which defaulting and nondefaulting countries differed. Larger, more open countries borrowed more, while countries more heavily indebted at the beginning of the postwar decade borrowed less. These results are consistent with the observations of United Nations (1965) and the predictions of optimal foreign borrowing models. The only hypothesis not verified is the posited association between export variability and the volume of borrowing, which is nonexistent in this period. This variable is dropped, therefore, from the third equation. But the most striking finding is that inclusion of these additional determinants of borrowing reverses the association between interwar default and post-war borrowing, yielding a positive correlation between default and subsequent borrowing that is statistically significant at standard confidence levels. There is no evidence that countries that defaulted in the interwar period found it more difficult to borrow in the immediate post–World War II years.

An obvious suspicion is that the inclusion of 1945 debt is mainly responsible for reversing the coefficient on interwar default. Default in the 1930s, the argument would run, permitted countries to buy back their external liabilities at deep discounts and, by reducing their debt burdens, facilitated subsequent borrowing. This does not seem to have been the case, however, as dropping 1945 debt alters neither the sign nor the significance of the coefficient on 1935 default.

The results in table 3.12, concerned with variations in the terminal debt stock, are consistent with those just discussed. Again, the value of the external debt in 1955 is positively related to GNP and openness, insignificantly related to export variability, and related to the 1945 debt stock with an elasticity of less than unity (suggesting that countries heavily indebted at the start of the period borrowed less over the interim). Most important, interwar default is either positively associated or unrelated to postwar indebtedness. Again, there is no evidence that countries that defaulted in the 1930s found it more difficult to borrow in the 1940s and 1950s.

While the Avramovic data have the virtue of consistency, they have the problem of combining all types of external debt accumulated by governments, whether extended by international agencies, creditor country governments or private investors. There is no reason to expect public lenders, in particular the U.S. government at the beginning of the Cold War, to have responded to market incentives and reputational factors in the same manner as private investors. It would be desirable to analyze private portfolio lending (to both the public and private sectors) separately from lending by public agencies before concluding that no trace of interwar defaults can be discerned in the geographical distribution of postwar lending. Unfortunately, post–World War II balance-of-payments records of bond floatations and repurchases and of loans from private foreign banks are of dubious quality. Typically, they are derived as a residual from the balance-of-payments accounts by deducting from total long-term capital inflows the sum of loans granted by international agencies and foreign governments. Total long-term capital flows for this period are themselves exceptionally difficult to measure accurately because of the extent of security repurchases; while relatively good records are available of new floatations and bank loans, little reliable information is published on transactions in out-standing public or private securities held by foreigners.

Notwithstanding these difficulties, the United Nations (1965) has pub-lished estimates of private portfolio lending to the Latin American countries over the first postwar decade. These figures are shown in table 3.13. Table 3.14 combines them with the GNP, trade and default indicators described above to analyze the association of interwar de-fault with postwar portfolio capital inflows for the 18 Latin American countries included in the preceding analysis of the Avramovic data. The bivariate relationship between postwar portfolio borrowing and interwar default, shown in the first column, is positive but statistically insignificant. Once other correlates of the demand for debt are added to the equation, the coefficient on interwar debt turns negative, as the reputational hypothesis would predict, although the point estimate of the coefficient remains smaller than its standard error. While the sign of the coefficient on interwar default is somewhat sensitive to the com-bination of other variables included in the equation (only when both GNP and the curiously signed measure of export variability are in-cluded is the coefficient on interwar default consistently negative), its low level of significance is not. Once again, it is impossible to reject the null hypothesis that variations across countries in the severity of interwar default had essentially no impact on the relative ease with which countries secured private portfolio capital inflows during the postwar years.

Table 3.13   **Private Portfolio Capital Inflows to Latin American Countries, 1946–55 (in millions of U.S. dollars)**

Country	1946–50	1951–55	Country	1946–50	1951–55
Argentina	—	22.5	Guatemala	—	2.9
Bolivia	—	—	Haiti	—	—
Brazil	− 20.0	151.0	Honduras	—	—
Chile	− 0.5	− 1.8	Mexico	− 7.8	− 24.7
Colombia	8.7	82.9	Nicaragua	—	3.4
Costa Rica	− 0.4	6.7	Panama	− 3.3	− 0.1
Cuba	—	38.3	Paraguay	− 3.2	− 2.2
Dominican Republic	− 3.0	1.1	Peru	− 0.4	− 0.8
Ecuador	—	3.6	Uruguay	—	—
El Salvador	0.1	0.4	Venezuela	—	− 3.7

Source: United Nations (1965, annex table D).

Table 3.14   **Determinants of Private Portfolio Capital Inflow to Latin American Countries, 1946–55 (The dependent variable is in millions of U.S. dollars.)**

	(1)	(2)	(3)
Constant	−3.59	−3.14	7.11
	(0.18)	(0.12)	(0.18)
Share of debt in default, 1935	17.75	−14.31	−17.63
	(0.76)	(−0.81)	(0.86)
GNP	—	0.01	0.01
		(4.64)	(4.31)
Import/GNP ratio	—	46.00	5.63
		(0.38)	(0.03)
Debt in 1945	—	—	−0.013
			(0.35)
Export variability	—	−0.005	−0.005
		(3.22)	(3.13)
Number of observations	18	18	18
R^2	.04	.68	.69
F	0.58	7.01	7.15

Source: See text.
Note: t-statistics in parentheses.

The two central findings of this section—a much reduced volume of private portfolio lending and no greater difficulty of borrowing for countries that had defaulted previously—are not difficult to reconcile with one another. Recall the evidence from the previous section on the impact of one country's default on the market's expectation of capital losses on neighboring countries' bonds. That evidence suggests that some effects of interwar defaults were external to the initiating country, a conclusion consistent with the evidence from this section suggesting that the main legacy of interwar debt defaults was to depress the volume of private portfolio lending generally, not to divert it to faithful servicers from countries that had lapsed into default.

3.5   Conclusion

What picture of the capital market emerges from this study of the United States' first 35 years as a creditor nation? It is patently impossible to characterize the market as either perfectly rational or wholly irrational. Advocates of a return to the bond market as a panacea for recent difficulties with sovereign lending should take note of these conclusions. While switching back from bank loans to the bond market may divert some of the risk shouldered by creditor-country banking systems, bond market participants have shown no greater facility than bank loan officers historically in distinguishing good credit risks from bad. Nor were bond markets any more successful in smoothing the flow of capital to developing-country debtors.

What picture of the legacy of default for the subsequent behavior of the markets emerges from this study of the last complete debt cycle? Recent theoretical studies of sovereign lending in the presence of potential default have posited the existence of a default penalty, $\bar{P}$, usually interpreted as the costs of inferior access to international capital markets in the wake of default. The finding that, compared to countries that maintained debt service throughout, countries that lapsed into default in the 1930s were no less able to borrow in the 1940s and 1950s is difficult to reconcile with this simple view. If there were costs of default, they did not take the form of differential credit-market access in the first postwar decade. But this does not imply that default was costless. Evidence from bond prices in the 1930s and from the volume and composition of lending in the 1940s–1950s suggests that at least some of the costs of default spilled over among debtor countries. These costs took the form of reduced access to private portfolio capital flows for defaulting and nondefaulting countries alike.

To say that default had costs is not to say that it was necessarily welfare reducing. It may also have had benefits in the form of the spur to growth and adjustment provided by a lightened debt burden. Comparisons of economic growth and structural change in defaulting and nondefaulting countries will be needed before welfare conclusions can be drawn. But the fact that a substantial share of the costs were external to the individual country indicates that there may be gains to debtors from coordinating their decisions, whether or not that decision is to maintain service on their external debts.

Notes

1. Computed from Lewis (1938, 445).
2. If war debts are added to U.S. foreign assets, the U.S. net creditor position in 1919 exceeds $12 billion.
3. For figures, see Eichengreen (1986).
4. Fraga (1986, sec. 2). Some have suggested that the German authorities consciously wished to build up commercial liabilities as a way of impressing on American creditors the impossibility of making good both commercial and reparations obligations. For a discussion, see McNeil (1986).
5. See Lipsey (1988).

6. Foreign bond yields are annual averages, from Lary (1943, 204). Moody's Baa yields are from the U.S. Department of Commerce, *Survey of Current Business* (1937, 19). The value of total publicly offered foreign securities purchased in the United States (including refunding to Americans) is from Dickens (1932, 8). The picture for the other major creditor country, Britain, looks broadly similar although the fluctuations in lending are considerably damped; see Eichengreen and Portes (1986, sec. 2).

7. It is conceivable, of course, that the lending series is traced out not by movements of the supply curve along a stable demand curve but by shifts in borrowers' demand (down in 1923, up starting in 1924, and down after 1928). I argue, however, that demand remained relatively stable at high levels throughout the decade and that changes in quantities reflected mainly shifts in supply.

8. Lewis's (1938, 370) estimates of yields to maturity are 5.3 percent for 1915–April 1917 and 6.7 percent for 1922–24. The 1920 Belgian loan illustrates the difficulties encountered by borrowers at the beginning of the decade. It has been argued that Belgium managed to obtain these funds only because U.S. commercial banks had a special stake in the country. The banks had previously extended Belgium short-term credits in the amount of $50 million to purchase wheat and other essential commodities. Because of a deterioration in the country's external position, it quickly became evident that the government was in no position to repay. The authorities therefore approached the bankers, who agreed to float $50 million worth of 25-year bonds. The terms were highly favorable to investors: the bonds bore a nominal interest rate of 7.5 percent and were callable only at 115. Yet "the subscription books were kept open for three days, a very unusual procedure; every resource the bankers could command was used to induce subscription . . . ." Only after having taken these exceptional steps was the loan successfully floated. See Swan (1928), from which the above quotation is drawn.

9. As Lawrence Speaker wrote in 1924 (93), "From the political standpoint, Europe today presents a very uncertain outlook. Since most of Eastern Europe is in the hands of the radical socialists whose views on capital are quite incompatible with those held here, since Central Europe is threatened with political as well as economic breakdown, and the nations of Western Europe are torn apart by contending political influences, a policy of extreme caution in making investments in Europe seems highly advisable. It is possible that some of these countries, in their dire necessity, may be drawn to the confiscation of private property as well as wholesale repudiation of their internal debts. . . . Such tendencies on the part of governments are not at all conducive to the stability and soundness of investments."

10. *The Economist* (5 July 1924) described the return as follows, "The yield, allowing for redemption in twenty years, works out at approximately £8 16s. per cent. This is a high yield and indicates to some extent the measure of risk involved."

11. Costigliola (1976, 490) suggests that the Fed took this action in order to render investment in the Dawes loan more attractive.

12. Stoddard (1932, 43).

13. Stoddard (1932, 43).

14. Cleveland and Huertas (1985, 135).

15. When in 1919 National City Bank opened its Lima branch, for example, the president of Peru offered the National City Company the opportunity to become the nation's investment banker (Phelps 1927, 211; Cleveland and Huertas 1985, 177; see also Carosso 1970).

16. Cleveland and Huertas (1985, 137).

17. See Speaker (1924, chap. 2).

18. Robinson (1926, 327–28 and *passim*).

19. Both types of tales are too well known to require elaboration here. On selling the foreign borrower, one Department of Commerce expert told the Senate Finance Committee of a time at which there were at least 29 representatives of American investment banking firms in Colombia seeking to negotiate various loans. A Bavarian town initially wishing to borrow $125,000 was convinced to commission an issue of $3 million instead (U.S. Senate 1932, 845–48, 1279–80). On selling the small investor, Stoddard (1932, 106) writes, "Up to the slump of 1920, these new clients sought the branch-offices. After the slump, the branch-offices sought them. They did it through hosts of young salesmen, carefully schooled in 'high pressure' methods of breaking down 'sales resistance.' The keynote was pressure—all down the line. The home office kept the branch-offices 'on their toes' by a stream of phone-calls, 'flashes,' 'pep-wires,' and so forth. The branch managers kept the young salesmen all 'burned up' with 'pep-talks,' bonuses, and threats of getting fired. Everybody in authority demanded 'results'; which meant, more sales. Every salesman must sell his 'quota.' What he sold, how he sold it, and whom he sold it to, did not much matter. Verily, business had got into banking; or, rather, 'banking,' in the old sense of the word, had been kicked out of doors by business."

20. Cleveland and Huertas (1985, 177).

21. Madden, Nadler, and Sauvain (1937, 222).

22. The significance of this moral hazard problem is impossible to determine in the absence of detailed study of the operations of particular affiliates. But it is worth noting in this connection that White (1986) has found little empirical support for other criticisms of security affiliates.

23. Feis (1950, 13).

24. Brandes (1962, 128).

25. Dulles (1926, 35–37). There were also objections on other occasions, such as a loan for a Czech brewery, presumably on the grounds that this was inconsistent with a U.S. policy of Prohibition, and for a Brazilian coffee valorization scheme and a German potash syndicate, on the grounds that the higher prices which would result would be harmful to U.S. consumers. (Both borrowers ultimately succeeded in obtaining funds in London.) In addition, President Harding urged his secretary of state to discourage U.S. lending for foreign purchases of armaments.

26. Brandes (1962, 177–78) and Angell (1933, 101–2). France managed to circumvent U.S. restrictions to some extent before 1928. For example, Ivar Kreuger's Swedish Match Company loaned large sums to the French government soon after its U.S. subsidiary floated $50 million of bonds on the American market.

27. Williams (1929, 95).

28. Cited in Brandes (1962, 186). Extracts from the whole series of State Department letters are provided by Kuczynski (1932, 10–11).

29. Brandes (1962, 188).

30. Madden and Nadler (1929, 83), for example, in a manual on securities investment, instruct investors to consider trade and budget balances and natural resource endowments. (See also pp. 96–97). Madden, Nadler, and Sauvain (1937, 207) mention the trade balance, the budget balance, the position of the central bank, and the debt of the government.

31. Consistent with this hypothesis, Eichengreen and Portes (1986) found that government budget surpluses were negatively associated with the incidence of default in the 1930s.

32. Principal sources include the League's *Statistical Yearbook, Memorandum on Public Finance, Review of World Trade,* and *Balance of Payments and Foreign Trade Balances* (various years).

33. Regressions where loan value was entered alone rather than as a share of exports were virtually indistinguishable from those reported below.

34. These alternatives were omitted as the last year, country, and loan type included in Lewis's lists. The constant of 6.7 is to be interpreted, therefore, as the return that would have been required of a Venezuelan corporation in 1929 in percentage points on a small (value approaching zero) short-term loan had that country's trade and government budget been balanced.

35. In certain of the Central American countries, U.S. involvement had a military dimension with direct implications for creditworthiness. Under the Hay–Bunau-Varilla Treaty of 1904, the U.S. was permitted to intervene in Panama City and Colón to preserve order and to supervise the expenditure of Panamanian government loans placed in the United States. The Platt Amendment appended to the Cuban constitution in 1901 permitted the U.S. to object to what it regarded "improvident or otherwise objectionable fiscal policy." An American receiver-general was installed in the Dominican Republic in 1907 to collect customs revenues, and in 1912 revolution led to the landing of U.S. marines, followed by formal military administration in 1916. Even after the marines' withdrawal in 1924, the United States retained the right to object to changes in Dominican tariffs and public debt. Haiti was under U.S. martial law from 1916 to 1931, under the provisions of which the U.S. controlled the customs houses and all aspects of the public finances (see Angell 1933, 8–27).

36. For details on bond market organization, see Eichengreen and Portes (1986).

37. To be exact, 0.297 of a percentage point. This is an unweighted average of the commission on the dollar bonds for which Lewis provides information.

38. Kuczynski (1932, 88–89). See also Madden, Nadler, and Sauvain (1937, 228).

39. Yawitz (1977) shows that this formula applies equally to single and multiperiod bonds so long as i_f and i_r are constant.

40. Circular of 14 June 1930, cited in Feis (1950, 45).

41. The sentence continues, "but also the reduction in the real value of monetary claims through the rise in commodity prices . . . affecting domestic and foreign bonds alike" United Nations (1954, 41).

42. National Association of Manufacturers (1949, 2).

43. United Nations (1949, 17).

44. This amount would have been even greater if not for the capital gains of £84 million that resulted from the 1949 devaluation of sterling (United Nations 1954, 3).

45. The estimate for 1946–52 is from United Nations (1954, 4), that for 1920–26 from Royal Institute (1937, 200), correcting the typographical error for 1923, with a conversion to dollars using the annual average dollar/franc exchange rate. Much of the capital outflow from France in the 1920s was flight capital which was to return after the Poincaré stabilization in the second half of 1926.

46. United Nations (1965, 33–38, 119).

47. See, for example, Eaton and Gersovitz (1981).

48. Of course, this procedure neglects subsequent wartime developments. But as Mintz (1951, 43) points out, "The great majority of countries that serviced their loans in 1937 did so in 1949; most of the countries in default in 1937 were in default in 1949."

49. The countries included in the regression analysis are Argentina, Bolivia, Brazil, Chile, Colombia, Costa Rica, Ecuador, El Salvador, Guatemala, Haiti, Honduras, Mexico, Nicaragua, Panama, Paraguay, Peru, Uruguay, Venezuela, Belgium, Denmark, Finland, France, Germany, Italy, the Netherlands, Norway, Sweden, the United Kingdom, Australia, Japan, Egypt, and India.

References

Angell, James W. 1933. *Financial foreign policy of the United States*. New York: Council on Foreign Relations.

Avramovic, Dragoslav. 1958. *Debt-servicing capacity and postwar growth in international indebtedness*. Baltimore, Md.: Johns Hopkins University Press.

Balogh, Thomas, and Andrew Graham. 1979. The transfer problem revisited: Analogies between the reparations payments of the 1920s and the problems of the OPEC surpluses. *Oxford Bulletin of Economics and Statistics* 41: 183–92.

Brandes, Joseph. 1962. *Herbert Hoover and economic diplomacy: Department of Commerce policy 1921–1928*. Pittsburgh: University of Pittsburgh Press.

Carosso, Vincent P. 1970. *Investment banking in America*. Cambridge: Cambridge University Press.

Cleveland, Harold van B., and Thomas F. Huertas. 1985. *Citibank 1812–1970*. Cambridge: Harvard University Press.

Costigliola, Frank. 1976. The United States and the reconstruction of Germany in the 1920s. *Business History Review* 50: 477–502.

Council of the Corporation of Foreign Bondholders. Various years. *Annual Report*. London: Corporation of Foreign Bondholders.

de Vries, Barend. 1971. The debt-bearing capacity of developing countries— A comparative analysis. *Banca Nazionale del Lavoro Quarterly Review:* 12–18.

Dickens, Paul D. 1932. *American underwriting of foreign securities in 1931*. U.S. Department of Commerce, Bureau of Foreign and Domestic Commerce. Washington, D.C.: Government Printing Office.

Dulles, John Foster. 1926. Our foreign loan policy. *Foreign Affairs* 5: 33–48.

Eaton, Jonathan, and Mark Gersovitz. 1981. Debt with potential repudiation: Theoretical and empirical analysis. *Review of Economic Studies* 48: 289–309.

Edwards, Sebastian. 1986. The pricing of bonds and bank loans in international markets: An empirical analysis of developing countries' foreign borrowing. *European Economic Review* 30: 565–89.

Eichengreen, Barry. 1986. Understanding 1921–27 (Inflation and economic recovery in the 1920s). *Rivista di Storia Economica* 3: 34–66.

Eichengreen, Barry, and Richard Portes. 1986. Debt and default in the 1930s: Causes and consequences. *European Economic Review* 30: 599–640.

Feis, Herbert. 1950. *The diplomacy of the dollar: First era, 1919–1932*. Baltimore Md.: Johns Hopkins University Press.

Foreign Bondholders Protective Council. Various years. *Annual Report*. New York: Foreign Bondholders Protective Council.

Fraga, Arminio. 1986. German reparations and the Brazilian debt crisis: A comparative study of international lending and adjustment. *Princeton Studies in International Finance*. Princeton, N.J.: Princeton University Press.

Guttentag, Jack, and Richard Herring. 1985. Commercial bank lending to developing countries: From overlending to underlending to structural reform. In *International Debt and the Developing Countries*, ed. G. Smith and J. Cuddington. Washington, D.C.: The World Bank.

International Monetary Fund. 1978. *International financial statistics, 1978 supplement: Annual data 1953–1977*. Washington, D.C.: IMF.

Jorgensen, Erika. 1987. Default in Latin America in the 1930s: The borrowers' perspective. Unpublished, Harvard University.

Kuczynski, Robert R. 1932. *Bankers' profits from German loans*. Washington, D.C.: The Brookings Institution.

Lary, Hal B., and Associates. 1943. *The United States in the world economy*. Washington, D.C.: Government Printing Office.

Lewis, Cleona. 1938. *America's stake in international investments*. Washington, D.C.: The Brookings Institution.

Lipsey, Robert E. 1988. Changing patterns of international investment in and by the United States. In *The United States in the world economy*, ed. Martin Feldstein. Chicago: University of Chicago Press, 475–545.

McNeil, William C. 1986. *American money and the Weimer Republic: Economics and politics on the eve of the Great Depression*. New York: Columbia University Press.

Madden, John T. and Marcus Nadler. 1929. *Foreign securities*. New York: The Ronald Press.

Madden, John T., Marcus Nadler, and Harry C. Sauvain. 1937. *America's experience as a creditor nation*. New York: Prentice-Hall.

Mintz, Ilse. 1951. *Deterioration in the quality of foreign bonds issued in the United States, 1920–1930*. New York: National Bureau of Economic Research.

Morrow, Dwight. 1927. Who buys foreign bonds? *Foreign Affairs* 5: 219–32.

National Association of Manufacturers. 1949. *Capital export potentialities after 1952: An economic and statistical analysis*. Economic Policy Division Series no. 7. New York: National Association of Manufacturers.

Phelps, Clyde William. 1927. *The foreign expansion of American banks*. New York: Ronald Press.

Ransom, Roger, and Richard Sutch. 1983. Domestic saving as an active constraint on capital formation in the American economy, 1839–1928: A provisional theory. Unpublished, University of California, Berkeley.

Robinson, Leland Rex. 1926. *Investment trust organization and management*. New York: Ronald Press.

Royal Institute of International Affairs. 1937. *The problem of international investment*. London: Oxford University Press.

Sachs, Jeffrey. 1981. The current account and macroeconomic adjustment in the 1970s. *Brookings Papers on Economic Activity*, 201–68.

Speaker, Lawrence M. 1924. *The Investment Trust*. Chicago: A. W. Shaw.

Stoddard, Lothrop. 1932. *Europe and our money*. New York: Macmillan.

Swan, Joseph R. 1928. The world's present and future demand for capital. *Proceedings of the Academy of Political Science* (January).

United Nations. 1948. *Public debt 1914–1946*. Department of Economic Affairs. Lake Success, N.Y.: United Nations.

———.1949. *Capital movements during the Inter-war period*. New York: United Nations.

————. 1954. *The international flow of private capital.* Department of Economic Affairs. New York: United Nations.

————. 1958. *Statistical yearbook.* New York: United Nations.

————. 1965. *External financing in Latin America.* Department of Economic and Social Affairs, Economic Commission for Latin America. New York: United Nations.

United Nations, Committee for Development Planning. 1986. *Doubling development finance.* New York: United Nations.

United States Department of Commerce. 1937. *Survey of current business* (November).

————. 1952a. *Balance of payments of the United States, 1946–1951.* Washington, D.C.: Government Printing Office.

————. 1952b. *Foreign aid by the United States government, 1940–1951.* Washington, D.C.: Government Printing Office.

————. 1976. *Historical statistics of the United States: Colonial times to 1970.* Washington, D.C.: Government Printing Office.

————. Various years. *American underwriting of foreign securities.* Washington, D.C.: Government Printing Office.

United States Senate, Committee on Finance. 1932. *Sale of foreign bonds or securities in the United States.* 72 Cong. 1 sess. Washington, D.C.: Government Printing Office.

White, Eugene Nelson. 1986. Before the Glass-Steagall Act: An analysis of the investment banking activities of national banks. Unpublished, Rutgers.

Wilkie, James W. 1974. *Statistics and national policy.* Los Angeles: University of California.

Williams, Benjamin H. 1929. *Economic foreign policy of the United States.* New York: McGraw Hill.

Yawitz, J. 1977. An analytical model of interest rate differentials and different default recoveries. *Journal of Financial and Quantitative Analysis* 12. (Sept.): 481–90.

II Adjustment Problems in Debtor Countries

4 Structural Adjustment Policies in Highly Indebted Countries

Sebastian Edwards

4.1 Introduction

Mexico's announcement, in August of 1982, that it could no longer meet its international financial obligations took most of the world by surprise, sending shivers down the spines of bankers, politicians, and international bureaucrats. That fateful Friday the 13th of August 1982 marked the beginning of the worst international financial crisis since the Great Depression. What initially was thought to be an isolated case of temporary illiquidity soon spread to most of the developing world, placing the stability of the international financial system in serious jeopardy.

Five years after the eruption of the debt crisis most of the developing world is still struggling to get back on its feet. Although the collapse of the world financial system predicted by some overly pessimistic observers has not materialized, the debt crisis is far from over. In fact, when traditional creditworthiness indicators, such as debt-exports or debt-service ratios are analyzed, the highly indebted countries are now in an even weaker position than in 1982 (see table 4.1). It has now become apparent that a long-term resolution of the debt problems will be a painful and protracted process that will still require major additional adjustment efforts by the indebted countries, as well as extensive

Sebastian Edwards is a professor of economics at the University of California, Los Angeles, and a research associate of the National Bureau of Economic Research.

I have benefited from discussions with Marcelo Selowsky and am grateful to Alejandra Cox-Edwards, Edgardo Barandiaran, Pari Kasliwal, Miguel Savastano, Jeffrey Sachs and the participants of a meeting held in Cambridge, Mass., in May 1987 for helpful comments. Financial support from UCLA's Academic Senate and from the National Science Foundation is gratefully acknowledged.

Table 4.1   **Creditworthiness Indicators for Developing Countries: 1974–88**

	1979	1980	1981	1982	1983	1984	1985	1986	1987	1988
A. Ratio of External Debt to Exports of Goods and Services (%)										
All developing countries	90.8	81.6	94.6	120.1	133.3	133.7	147.8	167.5	168.6	160.7
15 highly indebted[a]	182.3	167.1	201.3	269.8	289.6	272.1	284.2	337.9	349.6	324.7
Western Hemisphere	197.7	183.5	210.3	273.8	290.3	277.1	295.5	354.7	367.6	342.2
B. Debt Service Ratios to Exports of Goods and Services (%)										
All LDCs	14.1	12.9	16.2	19.5	18.9	20.1	20.5	22.4	20.7	20.0
15 highly indebted[a]	34.7	29.6	39.0	49.4	42.5	41.1	38.7	43.9	40.7	39.5
Western Hemisphere	39.6	33.4	41.9	51.0	43.9	41.7	38.7	45.6	44.9	40.9

Source: IMF's *World Economic Outlook*, April, 1987.

[a]Argentina, Bolivia, Brazil, Chile, Colombia, Ivory Coast, Ecuador, Mexico, Morocco, Nigeria, Peru, Philippines, Uruguay, Venezuela, and Yugoslavia.

negotiations between debtor governments, creditor governments, the multilateral institutions, and the banks.

The adjustment approaches followed until now by most of the highly indebted countries can best be described as *emergency stabilization programs* geared towards generating very large trade balance surpluses in very short periods of time. Given the new circumstances and the sudden halt in external financing after 1982, these countries had little choice but to use every possible tool at their disposal to achieve the needed turnaround in their current accounts. As a consequence the adjustment process has been quite costly, generating drastic declines in real income and important increases in unemployment. In fact, as is reflected in table 4.2, in a number of Latin American countries in 1986 real per capita GDP was below its 1970 level!

A long-run solution to the debt crisis problem would entail (a) the regaining of creditworthiness by these countries, and thus the resumption of voluntary lending by the international financial community; and (b) the resumption of sustained growth.[1] Much of the recent policy literature on the debt crisis has focused on these issues, with some of the discussion dealing with the type of long-run structural reforms the debt-troubled countries should implement in order to attain the dual objective of improved creditworthiness and growth. Most of this literature has recommended very conventional measures, what economists had been advocating for a long time prior to the debt crisis, including trade liberalization, financial reform, major devaluations, and a reduced role for the government.[2] For example, this policy package is the core of the conditionality contemplated by the Baker plan. Surprisingly, there have been very few attempts to evaluate whether the design of these traditional policies, and in particular their speed and sequencing, should be altered in the presence of a major debt problem and, in some cases, still significant macroeconomic disequilibria.

Table 4.2   **Index of Real Gross Domestic Product Per Capita In Selected Latin American Countries (1970 = 100)**

	1970	1975	1980	1981	1982	1983	1984	1985	1986
Argentina	100	105.9	107.5	99.2	92.6	93.9	94.3	88.7	92.2
Bolivia	100	117.3	120.6	118.3	107.6	95.7	89.7	85.8	80.4
Brazil	100	145.1	179.5	172.8	170.4	161.5	165.0	174.7	184.7
Colombia	100	118.2	137.9	138.0	136.4	134.7	136.1	136.6	140.7
Chile	100	81.8	109.1	113.4	95.8	93.6	98.1	98.8	101.9
Mexico	100	116.8	139.8	146.8	142.3	131.3	132.4	132.6	124.3
Peru	100	108.9	104.7	105.9	103.6	89.9	91.8	90.9	96.2
Venezuela	100	106.5	105.7	102.3	100.0	91.8	88.3	83.7	82.9

Source: CEPAL, *Anuario Estadístico de América Latina y el Caribe, 1985* and CEPAL, *Balance Preliminar de la Economía Latinoamericana, 1986.*

The purpose of this chapter is to analyze a number of issues related to structural adjustment in the highly indebted developing countries. The chapter starts with a brief discussion of the main features of the adjustment process followed during 1982–87. I note that in spite of the major involvement of the IMF in this first phase of the adjustment, the actual policy packages implemented by most of the debt troubled countries differed markedly from what we can describe as an orthodox IMF-type stabilization program. I argue that the "unorthodox" elements of the stabilization programs, such as the imposition of exchange controls and trade restrictions, responded to the emergency nature of these programs. I then discuss at a more analytical level some longer-term aspects of structural adjustment reforms, focusing on the relation between outward orientation, export promotion, and trade liberalization. Emphasis is placed on the sequencing and speed of the structural reforms related to the external sector. Lessons drawn from the recent Southern Cone experiments with trade liberalization are incorporated into the analysis of the possible effects of tariff reforms on employment, income, and growth. I also discuss the role of devaluations in structural adjustment processes in the same section. Since the chapter focuses on the role of the adjustment programs implemented by the countries themselves, relatively little emphasis is given to the role of banks and the international financial community.

4.2 The Nature of the Adjustment, 1982–87

In this section I analyze the main features of the adjustment process followed by the highly indebted countries during 1982–87.[3] Given the great diversity of experience of the various countries, it is not possible to make sweeping generalizations; in fact, doing so would grossly over-simplify the discussion. When possible I point out the more important differences across countries.

4.2.1 Origins of the Crisis

During the second half of the 1970s and the early 1980s most of the developing nations embarked on a foreign borrowing binge. Between 1975 and 1982 the developing world's long-term foreign debt more than tripled, growing from $162.5 billion to $551.2 billion; in 1982 the *total* foreign debt of the developing world, including short-term debt and use of IMF credit, stood at $738.7 billion. Naturally, this huge increase in indebtedness was made possible by the liberal way in which, after the first oil shock in 1973, the international financial community and in particular the banks, provided funds to these countries. There is no doubt that the pace at which the developing countries were accumulating debt in the late 1970s and early 1980s—at a rate exceeding 20 percent per year—was not sustainable in the medium to longer run;

some type of adjustment was bound to take place. The world, however, was astonished by the severity of the crisis; instead of there being an orderly and slow reduction in the flow of borrowing, there was a major crisis that brought capital flows to a virtual halt.

The causes behind the spectacular growth in borrowing during the 1974–82 period varied from country to country. In Brazil, for example, it responded to a deliberate development strategy adopted after the 1973 oil shock. This policy was based on import substitution supplemented with a heavy reliance on foreign borrowing to finance major investment projects. In Turkey, the accumulation of foreign indebtedness responded mainly to the rapid growth of the public sector, which used most of the funds for investment purposes. The situation was greatly aggravated by the existence of the so-called "convertible Turkish lira deposits," which provided a defacto, evergrowing subsidy to foreign borrowing. Contrary to most other countries, Turkey entered into a crisis in 1977, even before the second oil shock. In Mexico, the populist policies of the Echeverria and Lopez Portillo administrations, with spectacular growth in the public sector and in the fiscal deficit, lay behind the crisis. The discovery of additional oil reserves generated a wave of optimism that greatly influenced the magnitude of the expenditure binge. It has been argued that approximately one half of the Mexican debt accumulated during the Lopez Portillo administration went to finance capital flight (Buffie and Sangines 1987). In Chile, on the other hand, fiscal policies played no role in the unleashing of the crisis; most of the huge increase in Chile's foreign debt was contracted by the private sector with no government guarantees. The opening up of the Chilean economy, as part of the overall project of economic liberalization of the Pinochet government, allowed the private sector to finance huge increases in consumption—especially of durables—with borrowing from abroad.[4] In spite of their different experiences during the 1970s, by late 1982 all these countries faced a severe cut in foreign financing; they had come to share the harsh reality of the debt crisis. In the years to follow their experiences would again differ, as they tended to follow somewhat different adjustment programs.

The behavior of the world economy during the early 1980s, and in particular the increase of interest rates, the decline in commodity prices, and the sluggish growth of the industrial countries, played an important role in determining the magnitude and timing of the crisis.[5] A recent study by CEPAL has estimated that for the Latin American nations, the deterioration of unit prices of non-oil exports and the hike in world interest rates "explain" almost 50 percent of the increase in the region's current account deficit during 1981 and 1982.[6]

The magnitude of external shocks can be better understood by analyzing the evolution of the *real* interest rate "relevant" for these countries, computed as nominal LIBOR (London Interbank offer rate for dollar deposits) deflated by the rate of inflation of their exports. This concept of real interest rate combines in one indicator the effects of both the higher international nominal interest rates and the lower commodity export prices. For the case of Latin America, this measure of the real interest rate jumped from an average of -3.4 percent during 1970–80 to 19.9 percent in 1981, 27.5 percent in 1982, and 17.4 percent in 1983. During the early 1980s even those countries with a large percentage of their debt contracted at fixed concessionary terms experienced dramatic increases in their interest bill. For example, as a result of the higher world interest rates, the Ivory Coast's interest payments increased from 3.1 percent of GDP in 1980 to more than 8 percent of GDP in 1983.

The adoption of inadequate exchange rate policies constitutes one of the most important domestic causes of the crisis; most of the countries that eventually experienced payments difficulties allowed their real exchange rates to become highly overvalued during the late 1970s and early 1980s.[7] The case of the countries of the Southern Cone of South America is a primary example of inadequate exchange rate policies. In Chile, for example, after a period with a passive crawling peg, and as a way to bring down a stubborn inflationary process, the currency was fixed to the U.S. dollar in June of 1979, at the same time as wages were indexed to past inflation and capital controls were relaxed. As a result, the real exchange rate appreciated by more than 30 percent between 1979 and mid-1982, provoking a major deprotection of the domestic tradables sector and a gigantic current account deficit that exceeded 14 percent of GDP in 1981.[8] Argentina and Uruguay adopted a declining preannounced rate of devaluation, also as a way to reduce inflation. However, contrary to the case of Chile, in Argentina and Uruguay the predetermined rate of devaluation was clearly inconsistent with the magnitude of their fiscal deficit. This resulted not only in a substantial real appreciation, but also in a steady loss of credibility in the sustainability of the stabilization and liberalization programs, and in major capital flight.[9]

In Mexico, as a result of a highly expansive fiscal policy, which was coupled with a quasi-fixed nominal exchange rate, the effective real exchange rate experienced a real appreciation that exceeded 40 percent between 1976 and February of 1982. In 1976–77 in an effort to put an end to an acute situation of real exchange rate overvaluation, the Mexican peso was devalued by almost 80 percent relative to the U.S. dollar. By 1981, however, the real value of the peso was already below its 1976 level; in less than 5 years more than 100 percent of the real effect of the devaluation had fully eroded. This case is particularly interesting since it clearly illustrates the difficulties that developing nations have many times faced when trying to engineer a real devaluation (see Edwards 1987).

The mismanagement of exchange rate policy was by no means a monopoly of the Latin American countries. For example, the Ivory Coast, the Philippines, and Nigeria, among the highly indebted countries, also experienced important degrees of real exchange rate overvaluation during the period preceding the crisis. In both the Ivory Coast and the Philippines real appreciation exceeded 15 percent between 1978 and 1982, while in Nigeria it boardered 10 percent during the same period.

The exchange rate policy was not inadequate in every developing country, however. In Colombia, Indonesia, and Korea, for example, the adoption of an active exchange rate management, including periodic devaluations, was an important component in overall strategies aimed at reducing the effects of world economic fluctuations. In that regard, Indonesia's exchange rate and macro policies were quite successful as a means to combat the Dutch disease effects associated with the oil booms. Also, Colombia's pragmatic approach towards exchange rate management allowed the country to avoid the deprotection effects of the coffee boom of 1975–79 and to maintain a reasonable macroeconomic equilibrium.[10]

Perhaps one of the most devastating effects of the generalized tendency towards overvaluation is that it fueled massive capital flight out of the developing world. In country after country, as it became increasingly apparent that the overvaluation was unsustainable in the longer run, the public began to speculate heavily against the central bank by acquiring foreign exchange and moving it abroad. Moreover, in some countries, such as Chile and Argentina, the overvaluation cast doubts on the continuity of an overall development strategy based on liberalization and open markets. In Chile the public began to expect a hike in import tariffs and tried to anticipate it by acquiring imported durables in record quantities (Edwards and Cox-Edwards 1987). Although because of its semi-illegal nature it is not easy to find official data on capital flight, most available estimates concur in suggesting that in most of the Latin American countries there was a significant increase in capital flight during the years surrounding the debt crisis. In a recent empirical study Cuddington (1986) found that there is a significant relation between overvaluation and capital flight. Table 4.3 contains estimates on capital flight for six developing countries. There is an interesting contrast between the Latin American and the Asian nations. In particular notice that in Korea, a country that by and large avoided the temptation of real exchange rate overvaluation, between 1979 and 1984 capital flight was, on average, *negative*.

4.2.2   The Adjustment

In August of 1982, immediately following Mexico's formal announcement that it was facing serious financial difficulties, the international

Table 4.3   Estimates of Capital Flight in Selected Developing Countries[a]
                 (billions of U.S.$)

	1979	1980	1981	1982	1983	1984
Argentina	2.2	3.5	4.5	7.6	1.3	−3.4
Brazil	1.3	2.0	−1.4	1.8	0.5	4.0
Korea	−0.5	−0.7	−0.8	0.5	−0.7	−0.6
Mexico	−1.1	2.2	2.6	4.7	9.3	2.6
Philippines	0.0	−0.1	1.3	0.0	−1.5	−1.8
Venezuela	3.0	4.8	5.4	3.2	3.1	4.0

Source: Cumby and Levich (1987).
[a]These estimates use William Cline's definition of capital flight as computed by Cumby and Levich.

financial community greatly reduced the amount of funds intermediated to the developing world. Even countries such as Colombia—which had not faced payments problems, had no serious macroeconomic dis-equilibria, and had not accumulated debt at a very fast pace—were affected by this reduction in foreign lending. In fact, it is fair to say that the availability of foreign funds was reduced in a brutal way. For the developing world as a whole external financing was reduced by almost 40 percent between 1981 and 1983. Moreover, the major debtors were forced to fully close a current account deficit, which in 1982 exceeded $50 billion, in less than 3 years. By 1985 the aggregate current account had reached virtual equilibrium (−$0.1 billion). In order to achieve this significant adjustment, these countries had to engineer a major turnaround in their trade balance, which went from an aggregate deficit of almost $7 billion in 1981 to a surplus of more than $40 billion in 1984. Table 4.4 contains data on exports, imports, the trade balance, and the current account, that very vividly capture the magnitude of the adjustment.

As can be seen from table 4.4 after reaching a record level in 1984 (almost $44 billion) the aggregate trade surplus of the major debtors has experienced a steady decline and it is expected that in 1988 it will be just over $22 billion. This rapid deterioration in the aggregate trade balance is to a large part a reflection of the Brazilian and Mexican situations.

Latin America was severely affected by the sudden unavailability of loans. Table 4.5 contains data on the net transfer of resources to the region from 1973 to 1986. As can be seen, starting in 1982 the net transfer of resources became significantly negative; between 1982 and 1986 the annual net transfer averaged −$26.4 billion, compared to a positive yearly average net transfer of more than $12 billion between 1976 and 1971. In real terms the net turnaround of resource transfers

Table 4.4   **Current Account and Trade Balance for 15 Highly Indebted Countries: 1979–88 (billions of U.S.$)**

Year	Export (FOB)	Imports (FOB)	Trade Balance	Current Account
1979	94.2	96.1	− 1.9	− 24.6
1980	127.1	122.7	4.4	− 29.5
1981	126.1	133.6	− 7.5	− 50.3
1982	111.5	108.3	3.2	− 50.6
1983	111.1	82.8	28.3	− 15.2
1984	123.4	80.2	43.2	− 0.6
1985	119.2	78.4	40.8	− 0.1
1986	98.6	75.7	22.9	− 11.8
1987	101.5	83.3	18.8	− 14.0
1988	112.2	90.3	22.3	− 10.5

Source: IMF's *World Economic Outlook* (April 1987).

Table 4.5   **Capital Inflows and Net Transfer of Resources in Latin America: 1976–86 (billions of U.S.$)**

Year	Net Capital Inflows	Net Interest Payments	Net Transfer of Resources	
1976	17.9	6.8	11.1	
1977	17.2	8.2	9.0	
1978	26.2	10.2	16.0	$\bar{X} = 12.3$
1979	29.1	13.6	15.5	
1980	29.4	17.9	11.5	
1981	37.5	27.1	10.4	
1982	20.0	38.7	− 18.7	
1983	3.2	34.3	− 31.2	
1984	9.2	36.2	− 27.0	$\bar{X} = -26.4$
1985	2.4	35.3	− 32.9	
1986	8.6	30.7	− 22.1	

Source: CEPAL (1986b, table 14).

exceeded $70 billion in the short period of three years between 1980 and 1983!

These very rapid adjustments in the current account and trade balance were achieved in all cases by reductions in imports and in investment. As can be seen from table 4.4 in the highly indebted countries the *nominal* dollar value of exports was lower in 1986 than in 1980, with the magnitude of this decline exceeding 15 percent. This drop was basically the result of a decline of almost 25 percent in the export prices of these countries between 1980 and 1986. In Latin America the deterioration of the terms of trade was so severe (see table 4.6), that in spite of an increase in the *quantity* of exports of 30 percent between 1980 and 1986, 100 percent of the net adjustment of the trade balance improvement has also been achieved by means of a reduction of imports.

Table 4.6 Terms of Trade in Latin America Between 1981 and 1986 (Index, 1980 = 100)

	Index				Rate of Change (%)					Cumulative Rate of Change (%)
	1983	1984	1985	1986	1982	1983	1984	1985	1986	1981–86
Latin America	87	92	88	80	−9.0	1.1	6.5	−5.0	−8.7	−20.0
Oil Exporters	95	97	93	63	−10.3	5.0	2.0	−3.4	−32.2	−36.9
Bolivia	97	112	110	86	4.0	2.7	16.4	−2.2	−21.5	−13.8
Ecuador	82	96	85	58	−1.3	−17.7	17.0	−10.8	−31.9	−41.9
Mexico	93	86	84	62	−13.9	6.7	−7.2	−2.3	−26.4	−38.1
Peru	96	94	89	77	−9.5	19.7	−2.8	−5.1	−12.8	−22.6
Venezuela	104	116	114	62	−7.9	8.9	12.1	−1.9	−45.5	−38.0
Oil Importers	82	89	83	94	−8.3	−0.1	9.4	−6.6	12.8	−6.0
Argentina	82	99	87	75	−11.7	−4.6	21.0	−12.1	−13.3	−24.9
Brazil	78	86	83	102	−6.0	−2.5	10.1	−3.4	22.6	1.6
Colombia	94	101	97	114	2.2	8.3	6.9	−3.9	17.6	13.9
Costa Rica	86	90	88	107	−2.0	2.8	5.2	−2.8	21.2	6.5
Chile	84	78	72	79	−13.2	9.6	−6.3	−8.0	9.3	−21.3
El Salvador	83	73	69	87	2.2	−11.8	−12.0	−5.0	26.6	−12.9
Guatemala	85	88	83	95	−5.5	3.4	3.4	−6.0	14.3	−5.5
Haiti	66	83	85	104	3.8	−10.7	26.1	2.7	22.5	4.4
Honduras	93	96	76	95	3.6	0.9	3.2	−20.9	24.8	−5.4
Nicaragua	83	105	97	119	−5.3	−3.3	26.9	−7.8	23.1	19.4
Panama	91	95	97	105	−10.3	9.7	4.6	2.2	8.2	5.0
Paraguay	90	134	110	102	−12.6	−3.9	49.8	−17.9	−7.2	2.3
Dominican Republic	77	85	72	83	−31.3	−5.5	9.7	−14.8	15.2	−16.9
Uruguay	99	99	93	96	6.9	6.9	0.4	−5.6	2.6	−4.0

Source: CEPAL (1986b).

For the major debtors as a group, investment declined from an average of 26 percent of GDP in 1973–77 to an average of 17.2 percent in 1983–86. Table 4.7 contains data on investment ratios for a selected group of countries. As can be seen, with the exception of Chile, which started from an exceedingly weak position, in all of these countries the gross investment ratio declined significantly after the crisis, with the cases of Nigeria, the Philippines, and Venezuela being particularly dramatic. In most cases public investment and investment in the construction sector were the components more severely curtailed. In the case of public investment this was a result of restrictive aggregate demand policies implemented immediately after the crisis. Naturally, this decline in investment has serious consequences for the prospects of renewed growth. Not only has the adjustment been costly in terms of current output and employment, but also in terms of future income.

Most countries faced the need to reverse the direction of the net transfers by resorting to a combination of expenditure-reducing and expenditure-switching policies, including devaluation, the imposition of capital controls, and import quotas. The adjustment required both a significant increase in real interest rates as well as major relative price changes or real devaluations. In most cases the selection of policy packages was based on the perceived "effectiveness" of these policies in the short run, rather than on efficiency, income distribution, or welfare considerations. As a result of the efforts made to implement rapidly effective policies, a number of trade-offs between different objectives—including improvement in the current account and inflation—emerged during the process.

In most countries the expenditure-reducing policies have been centered on efforts to cut public expenditure. In a number of cases the

Table 4.7   **Gross Investment as Percentage of GDP in Selected Debtor Countries**

	Average 1975–80	1984
Argentina	25.2	17.8
Bolivia	29.5	28.5
Brazil	25.9	17.0[a]
Chile	13.2	13.7
Ivory Coast	26.5	22.1[a]
Mexico	24.4	20.3[a]
Nigeria	25.3	14.4
Peru	16.6	16.0
Philippines	30.1	17.1
Venezuela	34.3	16.0

Source: International Monetary Fund.
[a]1983.

reduction of real public expenditure has been in fact very significant, with most of the cuts concentrating on public investment and government employees wages. According to CEPAL, in Argentina, Ecuador, Mexico, Uruguay, and Venezuela government expenditure was cut by more than 20 percent in real terms following the crisis.[11] Similarly, in Morocco real expenditure of the central government declined by 18 percent between 1982 and 1984, while in the Philippines this reduction exceeded 25 percent between 1982 and 1985.[12]

In spite of the effort to reduce overall public expenditures, government interest payments on the domestic and foreign debt increased quite significantly during the first five years of the adjustment process. This was a result of both the real devaluations engineered as part of the stabilization programs and of the deliberate policy of raising domestic interest rates in an effort to further curb aggregate expenditure. The negative effects of the devaluations on the interest bills of different governments are a good illustration of the trade-offs involved in the adjustment process. In the majority of the major debtors most of the foreign debt is owed by the government, either because the public sector originally contracted it, or because it took it over when the local private banking system collapsed, as in Chile.[13] What real devaluations do is raise the (real) domestic currency cost to the government of raising the required funds to pay the interest bill. This effect has been significant in countries like Argentina, Mexico, and Peru, where interest payments on public-sector foreign debt are a high proportion (i.e., approximately 20 percent) of total government expenditure.[14] In a number of countries, most notably in Argentina and Chile, the exchange rate policies followed during this period also became an important source of government expenditures. For example, in Argentina, the need to cover the exchange rate guarantee after the abandonment of the "tablita" generated staggering fiscal outlays. Similarly the adoption of a preferential (lower) exchange rate for foreign currency debtors in Chile resulted in an implicit subsidy that absorbed large amounts of foreign resources.[15]

In spite of the relatively successful efforts to reduce public expenditures, fiscal deficits increased in relation to the precrisis period in the major debtors as a group (see table 4.8). This was mainly due to the fact that in many of these countries total tax revenues were negatively affected by the recessions that followed the crisis. The steep increase in interest rates that took place in most countries also impacted negatively the fiscal accounts, by means of its effect on the public-sector domestic debt. Moreover, in most cases the sources of fiscal deficit financing were affected by the crisis. Up to 1982 in most instances the public-sector deficits were financed by foreign borrowing. The drying up of this source of funds forced the local governments to turn to the inflationary tax and to issuing additional domestic public debt.

Table 4.8   **Monetary Policy, Fiscal Policy, and Inflation in Highly Indebted Countries**

Year	Annual Percentage Change of Broad Money	Central Government Fiscal Deficits as Percentage of GDP	Average Percentage Change of CPI[a]
1979	51.8	0.8	40.8
1980	55.2	0.8	47.4
1981	64.0	3.7	53.2
1982	69.3	5.4	57.7
1983	86.7	5.2	90.8
1984	117.7	3.1	116.4
1985	125.4	2.7	126.9
1986	73.9	4.5	76.2
1987	n.a.	3.6	86.3
1988	n.a.	n.a.	87.2

Source: International Monetary Fund.
[a]Average annual inflation for 1969–78 was 28.5 percent.

The need to use inflationary financing placed pressure on the monetary and domestic credit policies which became significantly more expansive than the IMF, the World Bank, and the private bank officials felt they should have been. Table 4.8 contains summary data on monetary policy, the fiscal deficit, and the average rate of inflation in these countries. These data quite clearly illustrate some of the most interesting features of the emergency phase of the adjustment process. As is pointed out in more detail below, contrary to the historical experience with IMF sponsored programs, these have been stabilization programs with acceleration in monetary expansion, persistent high fiscal deficits that largely exceed the levels that prevailed before the crisis, and very high inflation.

The restraint of wage increases was, in most countries, another major component of the expenditure-reducing package. Table 4.9 contains data on the evolution of real wages in selected Latin American countries. As can be seen, with the exception of Argentina, Brazil, and Colombia, the decline in real wages has been significant.

In most countries the adjustment also relied on higher real interest rates, which helped keep expenditure, and in particular investment, in check. It should be noted, however, that in some cases the rise in real interest rates began some time before the "official" unleashing of the debt crisis in August of 1982. For example, in the countries of the Southern Cone, real interest rates began to climb quickly in mid–1981 as these economies were becoming clearly overheated; higher interest rates were in fact an early sign that in these countries the need for adjustment was quickly approaching. In Argentina the annual real lending rate had already reached 19.3 percent in 1981, a figure that was

Table 4.9   Evolution of Real Wages in Selected Latin American Countries
                 (percentage variation)

	1981	1982	1983	1984	1985	Present Crisis[a]
Argentina	− 10.6	− 10.4	25.5	26.4	− 15.2	7.8
Brazil	8.5	12.1	− 7.3	− 6.7	7.1	12.6
Colombia	1.4	3.4	5.2	7.4	− 2.9	13.4
Costa Rica	− 11.7	− 19.8	10.9	7.8	8.9	− 7.8
Chile	9.1	− 0.4	− 10.6	0.3	− 4.5	− 14.8
Ecuador	− 13.8	− 11.9	− 16.2	− 1.3	− 3.2	− 39.2
Mexico	3.6	0.8	− 22.7	− 6.2	1.2	− 26.1
Peru	− 1.7	2.3	16.8	− 15.2	− 15.3	− 38.9
Uruguay	7.5	− 0.3	− 20.7	− 9.2	14.1	− 18.1

Source: CEPAL (1986b).

[a]As the crisis did not begin simultaneously in all the countries included, cumulative variations have been calculated over different periods in order to reflect the impact of adjustment on real wages more accurately. Figures in this column thus show the variation registered between 1980 and 1985 for Colombia, Chile, Mexico, Peru, and Uruguay.

significantly higher than the average of 1.5 percent that prevailed during 1978–80. In 1982 and 1983, as the effects of the debt crisis per se were being felt, the real lending interest rates remained high (around 12 percent per annum) but not as high as the level attained in 1981. Chile presents a similar case, as in 1981 the annual real interest rate reached 58.1 percent, a figure much higher than the average of the previous two years (8.5 percent). During 1982 and 1983 the *real* lending rate declined to the still remarkable level of 16 percent per annum (Ramos 1986).

Although in the Southern Cone real interest rates began climbing almost a whole year before August 1982, the debt crisis further shocked the already weakened financial sector. In particular, in Chile the halt of capital inflows was partially responsible for the timing and magnitude of the financial debacle of late 1982 and 1983. By the end of 1982 the foreign debt of the Chilean banking system exceeded 6.6 billion in U.S. dollars, a remarkable figure when compared to the mere $0.6 billion (U.S.) of debt in 1978! These funds had been obtained without any government guarantee and had mainly been used to finance the operations of the large private conglomerates—the so-called *grupos*. By mid-1982 a large proportion of these loans were in fact bad loans, as owing to a number of factors including the real overvaluation of the peso, the *grupos* were facing very difficult financial times. During 1982 the amount of foreign funds available to the Chilean banks was reduced by more than 75 percent, generating a fatal blow to the troubled financial sector. As a result of these difficulties, in January 1983 the government stepped in, liquidating two banks and nationalizing others. Responding to pressures by the international banks the Chilean government decided to take over these banks' foreign debt, guaranteeing its payment. Paradoxically, at the end of 1983 the Chilean financial sector was in some ways at the same juncture as it had been ten years before, in the midst of the Allende socialist government. It had been nationalized and was tightly controlled by the state (see Díaz-Alejandro 1985 Edwards and Cox-Edwards 1987).

After August of 1982 most countries also relied on expenditure-switching policies. These consisted in most cases of a combination of nominal devaluations and, at least initially, of a major escalation in the degree of trade restrictions.

The extent of the devaluations varied from country to country and were particularly severe in Latin America. In an effort to assure that the effects of the nominal devaluations on the real exchange rate did not erode through inflation, most countries adopted some kind of active exchange rate management where the exchange rate continued to be adjusted after the initial parity change. In fact, as of July 1986, out of the 15 major debtors 12 had some sort of crawling peg regime consisting of periodical adjustments of the nominal rate somewhat related to the differential between internal and external inflation.

Another important feature of the exchange rate policy followed by many countries was the adoption of multiple exchange rates. This basically served three purposes. First, by implementing differential exchange rates for capital and current account transactions—as in Venezuela—the authorities hoped to separate real transactions from the supposed volatility of capital movements. More important, however, by imposing a free-floating exchange rate on unregistered capital flows the Venezuelan authorities tried to discourage capital flight without greatly affecting the current account. Second, multiple rates were also applied as a way to supplement the protective system. Indeed, when different exchange rates are applied to different commercial transactions, the resulting outcome is perfectly equivalent to a differentiated tariff schedule. This practice was again used by Venezuela, as well as by Mexico. And third, in some countries, such as Mexico, Chile, and Venezuela, a lower "preferential" exchange rate has applied to the private sector repayment of foreign debt. The rationale for this preferential rate was that in this way it would be possible to avoid the general bankruptcy of the private sector, which had borrowed heavily from foreign banks at the previously fixed nominal exchange rate.

Most countries were able to generate important real devaluations, which in some cases more than corrected the overvaluation that preceded the crisis. In Turkey, for example, between 1982 and 1986 there was a 24 percent real effective devaluation, while in the Philippines the real devaluation amounted to more than 8 percent. It was, however,

Table 4.10   **Real Effective Exchange Rate Indixes, 1980 = 100 (Trade Weight at 1980)**

	Argentina	Bolivia	Brazil	Chile	Mexico	Peru	Venezuela
1980	100.00	100.00	100.00	100.00	100.00	100.00	100.00
1981	99.11	79.75	84.06	85.52	87.97	85.77	89.00
1982	177.98	58.21	77.60	92.00	112.34	81.15	80.66
1983	188.62	71.15	91.10	115.91	132.97	85.59	75.51
1984	139.35	28.42	102.65	118.12	114.66	87.91	105.67
1985	173.78	9.5	103.85	145.52	106.22	101.91	104.81
1986	203.71	103.93	111.68	162.39	135.61	84.98	100.81

Note: An increase of this index indicates real devaluation, while a decline is a real appreciation. These real effective exchange rate indexes have been computed as the trade-weighted geometric average of the bilateral exchange rates adjusted by the ratio of domestic consumer price index to the corresponding trade partner wholesale price index.

in the Latin American countries that the more important turnarounds of real exchange rate behavior were achieved. As can be seen in table 4.10, in all of these countries the real effective exchange rate index shows that there have been significant real depreciations between 1982 and 1986.

As a result of these large nominal devaluations most countries experienced important increases in their price levels. As noted above, in an effort to avoid the erosive effects of these price increases the Central Bank authorities decided to resort to further devaluations as a means of maintaining a high real exchange rate. Naturally this practice added fuel to the already accelerated rates of inflation (see table 4.11).

Table 4.11   **Rate of Devaluation and Rate of Inflation in Selected Debtor Countries**

	Average Annual Devaluation (%)	Average Annual Inflation (%)
Argentina	301.2	366.5
Brazil	195.1	175.5
Chile	39.5	24.2
Ivory Coast	1.3	19.9
Mexico	81.5	76.9
Nigeria	18.9	21.9[a]
Peru	111.4	113.5
Philippines	24.3	19.6
Venezuela	17.1	10.3

Source: IMF, *International Financial Statistics.*
[a]1982–85.

Immediately following the crisis in many (but not all) of the major debtors the devaluation policies were supplemented by the imposition of trade restrictions. Table 4.12, for example, presents data on some of the policies implemented by four countries.

An important question is whether the use of quantitative restrictions (QRs) instead of tariffs or more substantial devaluations during the initial phases of the adjustment has introduced unduly high costs in terms of growth and efficiency. A well-known proposition in the theory of commercial policy is that, in terms of welfare and income distribution, tariffs are generally superior instruments than quotas as a means to restrict trade.[16] That type of analysis, however, is static and assumes perfect information on behalf of the authorities; according to this simple setting the relevant elasticities are known and thus it is possible to compute the exact height of the desired tariff. In reality, however, things are quite different, since the magnitudes of elasticities are only known in a very imprecise way. This means that in order to achieve a certain volume of imports with the use of tariffs, it is necessary to go through a trial and error process. This type of procedure may be very ineffective in cases such as the debt crisis where the foreign exchange value of imports has to be reduced very quickly, and where there are high penalties associated with surpassing that (much reduced) level of imports. For a small country that faces given foreign currency prices of imports, the use of quotas is an effective way of being sure that the value of imports (in foreign exchange) will not exceed a certain level.

Table 4.12		**Examples of Additional Trade Restrictions during the 1982–86 Period**
Argentina	1984:	Decree 4070. All imports require a permit. All imports competing with local production are subject to authorization (with consultations to domestic producers' associations).
	1985:	Tariff surcharge of 10 percent over imports and 9 percent for exports.
Chile	1982:	Import surcharges ranging from 4 to 28 percent imposed on more than 30 items. Also, two-tier exchange rate established.
	1983:	Import tariffs raised from 10 percent to uniform 20 percent.
	1984:	Import tariffs temporarily hiked to 35 percent.
	1985:	The uniform import duty system is stabilized at 20 percent (from the earlier uniform level of 10 percent).
Mexico	1982:	QRs were imposed on all imports (during the 1970–80 decade QRs only affected 60 percent of imports).
Venezuela	1983:	Foreign exchange controls and a two-tier official exchange-rate system. QRs on 70 percent of final consumption goods.

Source: The World Bank.
QRs = quantitative restrictions.

As long as countries need to establish credibility regarding their willingness to adjust, it is particularly important not to surpass the preestablished level of imports.

Although there is some justification for the (very) short-term use of QRs in the very first phase of the adjustment, there are no good reasons for maintaining their use for long periods of time. From an efficiency perspective QRs have well-known undesirable effects. For example, Buffie and Sangines (1987) have argued that the generalized use of QRs in Mexico in 1982–84 resulted in an unnecessary reduction of imports of intermediate inputs, which greatly hurt the Mexican economy.

Some countries have recently relaxed trade restrictions, while others have announced some easing up for the near future. In Chile, for example, tariffs were reduced to a 20 percent uniform level. Mexico has taken some steps towards reducing the coverage of licenses, while in Bolivia, as part of the stabilization program aimed at stopping hyperinflation, quotas have been abolished and tariffs reduced. As is discussed in more detail below, in many countries trade liberalization packages are being discussed as a part of conditionality agreements with the multilateral institutions.

In spite of the significant efforts to adjust made by most of these countries—and of the costs incurred in the process—the magnitude of their trade surpluses has systematically fallen short of their interest payments. In Latin America, for example, in 1986 the interest bill amounted to 5.3 percent of GDP while the trade surplus reached 2.3 percent of GDP. In most countries up to now this financing gap has been closed, usually after long and protracted negotiations, by packages of funds provided by the banks and the multilateral institutions. It is important to notice, however, that the banks have been able to significantly reduce their exposure to the major debtors in spite of the fact that they have made some contributions to financing these funds shortfalls (see IMF 1987).

Up to now banks have relied on the policing activities of the multilateral institutions, and in particular of the IMF, for determining whether a particular country is making a "sufficient" effort to adjust. A question that is still unresolved is whether the banks will make a serious commitment to providing additional financing to the indebted countries in the next few years.

A number of studies have suggested that for the great majority of the highly indebted countries it would not be possible to generate in the short run trade surpluses of a magnitude sufficient to cover interest payments without further decreasing the level of real consumption. Selowsky and van der Tak (1986), for example, have estimated that a "typical" major debtor would need additional financing for approximately five years in order to experience some recovery in real consumption (2 percent per year) and in real income (4 percent per year). Under these assumptions, since the rate of growth of income exceeds that of consumption, domestic savings rise continuously. According to this simulation exercise after five years "the typical" major debtor would start to amortize its debt. After six more years the debt would have been reduced to "normal" levels, and the country would again be "creditworthy." Cline (1987) has recently argued, along similar lines, that banks could and should indeed increase the amount of funds being intermediated to those countries that show progress in their adjustment efforts.

4.2.3   Crisis Adjustment and Traditional Stabilization Programs

The above discussion shows that, in spite of the active involvement of the International Monetary Fund, the programs followed by most of the major debtors between 1982 and 1986 differed in a number of key respects from the typical IMF sponsored program of the pre-1982 era. These differences mainly involve the selection of policy packages, as well as the availability of additional financing. Also, the behavior of the exogenous variables, including the international environment, has tended to differ from the historical experiences.

According to Khan and Knight (1985) we can distinguish a macroeconomic and a structural adjustment component in the typical IMF program. The macro or demand management package is mainly based on restrictive monetary, fiscal, and domestic credit policies, aimed at eliminating the disequilibrium between aggregate demand and aggregate supply, improving the current account, and reducing inflation. Special emphasis is usually placed on the control of fiscal deficits. The structural adjustment or resource reallocation package, on the other hand, usually includes three main policy blocks: (1) trade liberalization, (2) financial reform, and (3) major devaluation including exchange rate unification in the case of multiple rates. [17]

The objectives of the structural adjustment component of conventional programs are to increase efficiency, raise investment, and enhance growth opportunities. Historically, for most countries the implementation of IMF sponsored programs has not taken place at the same time that a gigantic foreign debt is being serviced. Quite the contrary, it has usually been assumed that while implementing the structural reforms, these countries can command significant additional net funds from abroad (see Khan and Knight 1985). Although this may have been the case in the past, it is very far from today's reality, when the highly indebted countries have to generate a significant net transfer of resources to the rest of the world.

In terms of outcome, an historically "successful" IMF program can be described by a reduced fiscal deficit, lower inflation, more liberalized trade, and an improvement in the current account and balance of payments. In many ways the current (1982–86) adjustment looks very different from this IMF blueprint. Generally speaking, and as is captured by tables 4.8 and 4.11, this has been an inflationary adjustment process with high and persistent fiscal deficits. Additionally there has been an escalation in the degree of distortions of the external sectors, with a profusion of QRs and multiple exchange rates.

The behavior of investment has also been very different during the current crisis adjustment period when compared to the historical episodes. In a detailed study of 39 historical episodes of structural adjustment programs between 1962 and 1982, Edwards (forthcoming) found that for the group as a whole the investment ratio did not experience a significant decline in any of the four years following the implementation of the programs. Moreover, according to this study, on average in these historical episodes it is not possible to detect, as in the current case, significant declines in real output.

To a large extent the "unorthodoxy" of these new stabilization and adjustment programs can be attributed to three main factors: (1) the magnitude of the adjustment required, (2) the urgency with which it had to be implemented, and (3) the global nature of the crisis. In a way, when faced with the trade-offs between current account corrections, efficiency of the adjustment, and inflation, these countries opted— or were forced to opt—for the current account improvements placing, at least during the initial phases of the process, little priority on inflation, efficiency, or costs. Implicitly the IMF endorsed or encouraged these adjustment programs, in spite of the fact that they departed from its traditional view. Now, however, as things are somewhat under control, more emphasis is indeed being placed on efficiency, growth, and other social costs. These issues are discussed in more detail in section 4.3.

4.3 Trade Liberalization and Adjustment with Growth

The emergency packages implemented until now have succeeded in averting what some considered to be an almost sure collapse of the world financial system. This has been achieved, however, at a significant cost for the major debtors in terms of decline in employment, income, and standard of living. The key question now is how to move from the current situation towards what we can call phase 2 of the adjustment process, a phase characterized by adjustment *with* growth. At a more concrete level, the Baker and the Bradley plans, among other initiatives, clearly reflect the preoccupation of politicians with this issue.

A number of authors—and indeed the supporters of the Baker plan, as well as the IMF—believe that a rapid trade liberalization, coupled with devaluation, privatization, and financial reform, is the most reasonable strategy to achieve these objectives.[18] For example, Balassa et al. (1986, 88) have recommended that, among other things, the developing nations should eliminate all QRs and reduce, in a period of five years, imports tariffs to a uniform 15 to 20 percent; these tariff reforms should be coupled with significant devaluations in order not to "deprotect" the tradable goods sectors.[19] To a large extent these recommendations are very similar to what many economists have been advocating for many years for the developing countries. However, these new proposals are more drastic, in the sense of arguing for a bolder movement towards free trade. The current proposals on significant trade liberalizations have not involved a detailed discussion of the important issues related to strategy, including the appropriate speed and sequencing of reform. Also, there has been little consideration on the possible short-run trade-offs between these liberalization reforms aimed at improving efficiency and other objectives of the overall programs.

Most of the traditional literature on trade liberalization has assumed that these reforms take place in the absence of a foreign debt overhang problem. Moreover, many writers have assumed that during the trade reform process countries will be able to attract substantial voluntary lending. McKinnon (1973, 1982), for example, has forcefully warned us of the dangers related to excessive capital *inflows* during a trade liberalization episode. However, it is clear that at the present time, in the vast majority of LDCs there is very little danger of trade liberalization attracting excessive (or indeed any) voluntary capital inflows. Today, the problem is quite the opposite: Countries have to generate a positive resource transfer *to* the rest of the world.

The purpose of this section is to analyze some specific issues related to trade reforms. I first discuss the relation between outward orientation, trade liberalization, and export promotion. I then analyze issues related to the order and speed of reforms, focusing on the relation between stabilization policies and trade reforms and on the unemployment effects of liberalization. Finally I deal with the role of devaluation and of credibility during a structural adjustment process.

4.3.1   Outward Orientation, Export Promotion, and Trade Liberalization

There is by now an impressive amount of empirical evidence suggesting that countries that have adopted outward-oriented development policies, which emphasize export promotion, have outperformed those countries that have followed inward-oriented strategies based on import substitution. Even CEPAL—not exactly known for its endorsement of outward policies—has recently recognized that the excesses of import substitution have been very costly for Latin America; some of its senior staff members have recommended that in the future export promotion should play a more central role in that region's development policies.[20]

There seems to be relatively less agreement, however, on whether "trade liberalization" packages have played an important role in the performance of the outward-oriented economies. For example, in a recent paper Sachs (1987) questioned the idea that trade liberalizations are indeed a required component of successful outward-oriented strategies. Making reference to the experiences of the East-Asian countries—Japan, Korea, Singapore, Taiwan, and Hong Kong—Sachs argues that the success of these countries was to a large extent due to an active role of government in promoting exports in an environment where imports had not yet been fully liberalized, and where macroeconomic (and especially fiscal) equilibrium was fostered. Whether one agrees with Sachs depends on how outward orientation, export promotion, and trade liberalization are defined. Recently some confusion has emerged regarding these concepts, and it is not exactly clear what people mean by them.

In the more traditional policy literature of the 1960s and 1970s trade liberalization was defined in a very general way: What economists usually meant was *some* relaxation of trade and exchange controls. In fact, in the by now classic NBER study on trade regimes directed by Bhagwati and Krueger, a liberalization episode was defined as a more extensive use of the price mechanism that would reduce the anti-export bias of the trade regime.[21] In her 1986 review article on the problems of liberalization, Krueger went as far as saying that even a (real) devaluation in the presence of QRs constituted a liberalization episode. These are indeed very mild definitions of liberalization. In fact today very few people will raise an eyebrow about them. Only recently has "trade liberalization" acquired a more drastic connotation, meaning (for many people) an elimination of QRs coupled with a severe reduction of import tariffs to a uniform level of around 10 percent. Moreover, recently trade liberalization has, in many ways, become synonymous with free-market policies involving minimum or *no government intervention* at any level.[22]

The difference between the old and new definitions of trade liberalization is, to a large extent, one of degree or intensity. While a devaluation in the presence of QRs, or the replacement of QRs by (quasi) equivalent tariffs is a mild form of liberalization, the reduction of tariffs (with no QRs) to a uniform 10 percent or, for that matter, the complete elimination of tariffs is a very drastic liberalization. In order to clearly understand the different issues involved in policy discussions it is, crucial to specify the *intensity* of liberalization we are referring to.

Unfortunately this is not always done; the policy literature on the subject is plagued with imprecisions and ambiguities.

There is little doubt that a successful export promotion policy requires *some* kind of trade liberalization. In fact, the historical evidence clearly shows that those countries that have successfully embarked on that kind of strategy have had a more "liberal" trade regime than those countries following indiscriminatory import substitution. The successful outward-oriented countries have generally had lower coverage of prior license systems, lower average tariffs, less dispersion in their tariffs, and less episodes of real exchange rate overvaluation.[23]

In a recent major multi-country study by the World Bank it was found that there was a clear relation between movements toward more liberal trade systems and a higher performance (Papageorgiou, Michaely, and Choksi 1986). In that regard, the case of Korea—one of, if not *the* most successful of the export-oriented countries—is very educating. In 1985, for example, 90 percent of Korean imports were subject to automatic approval (i.e., were not subject to any form of QRs) and the average tariff rate was only 26 percent. Moreover, the tariff structure was characterized by higher tariffs concentrated on final goods, with capital equipment and intermediate inputs having relatively low degrees of protection.[24] This extent of import protection was significantly below that of most of the developing nations and also below the degree of Korean protection in 1965, before the outward-oriented policy was embraced. The Korean experience of export promotion coupled with trade liberalization can be contrasted with the Chilean case. Between 1975 and 1979 a drastic trade liberalization that eliminated all QRs, and reduced tariffs to a uniform 10 percent in four years was implemented in Chile; in addition, as part of a massive move towards free market orientation, this period's policies almost completely eliminated the government's role in defining external sector strategies. By allowing the real exchange rate to slip by approximately 30 percent between 1979 and 1982, the Chilean experience of that period became one of ultra trade liberalization *without* export promotion (see Edwards and Cox-Edwards, 1987).

Within the Latin American context Colombia after 1967 provides another educating example of successful export promotion with some trade liberalization. Until that year the Colombian external sector was highly distorted and had been subject to deep and recurrent crises; coffee exports provided most foreign exchange, and the Colombian economy was subject to the vagaries of the world coffee market. In 1967 three major measures were taken. First, any attempt to fix the exchange rate was abandoned, and a crawling peg system aimed at avoiding real exchange rate overvaluation was adopted. Second, an aggressive export promotion program was enacted. Here a subsidies scheme—the so-called CATs—and the government export promotion office (Proexpo) played an important role. And third, imports were greatly liberalized; in 1983 the average tariff in Colombia was only 29 percent, while the proportion of imports subject to QRs had greatly declined since 1967. As a consequence of these policies the Colombian noncoffee exports sector has performed in an efficient way, helping Colombia sustain a vigorous growth rate during the last 20 years.[25] In fact, today Colombia stands alone among the Latin American nations as a country that escaped the traumatic debt experience of the crisis while being able to maintain a reasonable rate of growth.

Although the evidence supporting the merits of outward orientation is abundant, there is no well-developed theoretical model—or empirical evidence for that matter—linking very low (or zero) import tariffs to higher *growth*.[26] Nor is there evidence suggesting that a completely "hands-off" policy on behalf of the government is the most desirable alternative. In fact, the success of the East Asian countries with export-led growth suggests that some selectively determined degree of intervention specially aimed at supporting exports, played a key role.[27] In this section no attempt will be made to solve the difficult and very important question of the optimal degree of government intervention, or of the optimal level and structure of import tariffs. This is indeed one of the most difficult question of economic policy, whose answer (even at the purely abstract and theoretical level) will depend on the existence of other distortions, the completeness of markets, and the availability of other policy tools, among other things. Instead we will proceed under the assumption that in most of the highly indebted countries the current structure of import protection is higher than the (unknown) optimal level and that, in the long run, these countries will gain from engaging in *some* trade liberalization that is aimed at reducing import tariffs and making them uniform. Under these (very plausible) assumptions, in the rest of this section we will discuss specific issues dealing with the appropriate speed and sequencing of the trade liberalization component of an outward-oriented strategy.

4.3.2 Trade Liberalization with a Government Budget Constraint

An important policy question is whether the trade liberalization component of an outward-oriented strategy should be attempted at the same time as a country is embarked on a severe stabilization and anti-inflationary program. Not surprisingly, the answer depends on the intensity of the trade reform and of the ongoing inflation.

Historically, there has been a close link between *mild* trade liberalizations and stabilization programs.[28] Consider the following typical scenario leading to a stabilization program coupled with a mild to medium trade liberalization effort:[29] At some point in time the authorities of a particular country decide to pursue a fiscal policy that is inconsistent with the chosen nominal exchange rate regime, usually a pegged rate. Given the underdeveloped nature of the domestic capital market, the fiscal expansion is basically financed with domestic credit creation. As a result, there will be a loss of international reserves; domestic inflation will exceed world inflation, and the real exchange rate will become increasingly overvalued. In an effort to stop the drainage of reserves the authorities will usually respond by imposing exchange controls and by increasing the degree of restrictiveness of the existing trade impediments: tariffs will be hiked and QRs will be imposed. Naturally, as long as the ultimate causes of the macroeconomic disequilibrium—that is, the inconsistent credit and fiscal policies—are not tackled, all the authorities will gain by imposing new trade restrictions is a delay in the need for corrective macroeconomic measures. The real exchange rate will become more overvalued, international reserves will continue to decline, and a black market for foreign exchange will emerge. At some point this disequilibrium situation will become unsustainable, and a stabilization program, usually under the aegis of the IMF, will be enacted. This program will usually consist of a significant nominal devaluation geared at correcting the overvaluation developed in the previous period, of a contractionary macroeconomic policy, and of a liberalization of trade restrictions aimed at dismantling those controls imposed during the expansionary phase of the process. These types of trade liberalizations have historically been mild and have seldom consisted of complete elimination of QRs and major tariff reductions of the kind now recommended for the indebted countries.[30]

Table 4.13 contains a summary on the evolution of trade exchange and capital controls in the period immediately following the adoption of 14 major Latin American stabilization episodes. In determining the timing of these programs, the implementation of the major nominal devaluation was taken as defining the beginning of the program. As may be seen, in many countries there were mild, and sometimes short-lived liberalizations; out of these 14 episodes we do not find a single major liberalization attempt.

Perhaps Chile during 1975–81 constitutes the most notable case of a major liberalization undertaken in conjunction with a major stabilization effort. The trade liberalization that eventually eliminated all QRs and reduced tariffs to a uniform 10 percent level was pursued at the same time as inflation was being reduced from 400 percent to 10 percent.[31] The Chilean episode illustrates very vividly one of the most serious trade-offs that emerges when a major liberalization is undertaken at the same time as a major anti-inflation program. As in most successful stabilization programs, in the last phase of the Chilean

Table 4.13   **Summary of Evolution of Exchange Controls and Trade Restrictions after Enactment of Stabilization Programs in Selected Latin American Countries**

Country	Year	Payments Restrictions on Current Transactions	Tariffs, Duties, and Cost-Related Measures	Restrictions on Capital Transactions
Argentina	1970	Decreasing restrictions for one year. Then highly restrictive	Short run liberalization; abrupt increase in tariffs 6 months after devaluation	Increased restrictiveness
Bolivia	1972	No significant changes	No change for 1 year. Rapid increase in tariffs 1 year after	No change
Bolivia	1979	No significant changes	Mild liberalization	Slight liberalization of capital movement ceilings
Chile	1982	No changes for 2 years	Slight increase in tariffs; no advanced deposits.	Slight reduction and then increase in restrictions
Colombia	1962	Decreasing	Liberalization of advanced deposits	No change
Colombia	1965	Short-lived liberalization	Short-lived liberalization of advanced deposits	After 14 months restrictions greatly hiked
Colombia	1967	Slow liberalization	Slow liberalization	Mild liberalization
Costa Rica	1974	Very short run liberalization	Short run liberalization tariffs were later raised	Restrictions on capital flows introduced
Ecuador	1961	No clear pattern	No change in tariffs; increase in advanced deposits rates	No change
Ecuador	1970	Slight liberalization	Mild reduction in tariffs; important liberalization of advanced deposits	Mild liberalization of capital movement restrictions

Table 4.13   (continued)

Country	Year	Payments Restrictions on Current Transactions	Tariffs, Duties, and Cost-Related Measures	Restrictions on Capital Transactions
Nicaragua	1979	Very slight liberalization	No changes	Very sharp increase in degree of restrictions
Peru	1967	Increased restrictiveness	Tariffs raised	Sharp increase in restrictions
Peru	1975	No significant change	Increase in tariffs levels	Slight liberalization
Venezuela	1964	Slight increase in restrictiveness	No change	No change

Source: Constructed from information obtained from various issues of the IMF's *Annual Report on Exchange Arrangements and Exchange Restrictions* and from various issues of *Pick's Yearbook* and *World Currencies Yearbook.*

stabilization effort when inflation was reduced from 40 percent to 9 percent per annum, there was a significant real exchange rate appreciation that reduced the degree of competitiveness of the tradables sector at a time when, because of the trade reform among other factors, the *equilibrium* real exchange rate had significantly depreciated. In the Chilean case this real appreciation was partially the result of the active use of exchange rate management to bring down inflation; in mid-1979 the nominal exchange rate was fixed relative to the dollar. As is well known by now this real appreciation played an important role in the disappointing outcome of the Chilean episode; it seriously deprotected the tradables sector, it generated perverse expectations of devaluation and, ultimately, it conspired with the high real interest rates to provoke the worst financial debacle of Chilean history (Edwards and Cox-Edwards 1987).

A crucial objective of any stabilization program and, as pointed out in section 4.2, indeed of those undertaken by the major debtors, is to reduce the magnitude of the fiscal deficit. Many times there will be an important trade-off between a trade liberalization that reduces import tariffs and the achievement of this fiscal objective. Surprisingly, the policy and theoretical literatures on trade liberalization policies have most times tended to ignore the fiscal role of tariffs in the developing nations. Most theoretical and policy discussions on trade liberalization assume, along the lines of traditional trade theory, that tariff proceeds are handed back to the public. In reality, however, things are very different, with governments using tariff proceeds to finance their expenditure. This is particularly the case in many of the poorer developing countries where for different institutional reasons taxes on international trade represent a high percentage of government revenue. Table 4.14, for example, contains data on the fiscal importance of taxes on international trade for eight countries. As may be seen, taxes on trade are as high as one-third of the total revenue of the central government.

As long as tariff rates are below the maximum revenue tariff, there will be a trade-off between trade liberalization and the generation of the government surplus required to finance debt servicing. While the reduction of tariffs will generally reduce distortions, it will also have a negative effect on government finances. What is required, then, is to replace trade restrictions by less distortive taxes that can generate the same (or a higher) amount of revenue. This, of course, means that major reforms of the tax system would be required in most countries. As long as this tax reform effort also focuses on efficiency aspects, it will tend to be concentrated on the imposition of a value-added tax (VAT), among other taxes. This is not easy and takes time, as a number of efforts to implement sweeping tax reforms have recently shown. Tax reforms are not only politically difficult to have approved, but from an administrative perspective it is many times very difficult to get them going. This is particularly the case in the poorer countries where the preexisting tax system is extremely rudimentary. Indeed the recent Indonesian tax reform has very clearly shown the difficulties involved in these types of efforts. (See Conrad and Gillis 1984). However, in middle income countries where there is an operating tax system of some sophistication, a major tax reform can be implemented with some speed. The Chilean tax reform of 1975 is, in that sense, a good example;

Table 4.14   **Taxes on International Trade as a Percentage of Government Revenue: Selected Developing Countries, 1984**

	$\left(\dfrac{\text{Import Tariffs}}{\text{Total Tax Revenue}}\right)^{a}$	$\left(\dfrac{\text{Taxes on Trade}}{\text{Total Revenue}}\right)^{a}$
Argentina	4.9%	13.3%
Bolivia	25.6	30.0
Chile	13.4	10.8
Indonesia	3.5	3.3
Korea	16.1	14.0
Mexico	3.0	2.7
Peru	10.2	n.a.
Philippines	22.1	23.7

Source: Constructed from raw data from the International Monetary Fund's *Government Finances Statistics Yearbook.*

[a]Refers to central government.

n.a. = not available.

in little over a year a major tax overhaul that introduced a VAT, full indexation, and unification of corporate and noncorporate tax rates was successfully implemented (Corbo, de Melo, and Tybout 1986).

Although in most cases the implementation of a major tax reform will take a substantial amount of time, there are some policies conducive both towards improved efficiency and higher revenues in the short run. The most obvious one is the replacement of QRs, (i.e., licenses, prohibitions, and so on) by import tariffs. A well-known feature of QRs is that unless they are auctioned, the government misses the revenue associated with the trade restriction. By replacing the QR by a tariff it is possible for the government to recapture this revenue.

The replacement of QRs by tariffs has two other potentially desireable effects. First, there is a potential for a positive effect on income distribution. This is be cause in most cases large (or even multinational) firms or large established merchants get the import licenses and, thus, the rents. By replacing the QRs by tariffs these rents are passed on to the government, allowing it to reduce other taxes, or even increase expenditures on social programs. Second, the replacement of tariffs by QRs will generally increase the effectiveness of devaluations. The reason is that the effects of devaluations are significantly different under quantity rationing (i.e., import quotas or licenses) than under import tariffs. In the latter case a (real) devaluation will result in a higher price of both importables and exportables relative to nontradables. Under QRs, however, while the domestic price of exportables will still increase, that of importables will usually not be affected. All the devaluation will do is reduce the rents received by the party that got the license.

A potential problem with the replacement of QRs by tariffs is that it is not easy to decide on the tariff level that should be imposed instead of the QR, since under a number of plausible conditions (domestic monopoly being perhaps the most common) tariffs and quotas will not be equivalent. In this case there is *no* tariff that will exactly replicate both the domestic price and quantity resulting from the QR. One possible alternative policy that has been used with some success in a few countries is to auction the quotas rather than allocate them in an arbitrary way.[32] Among the attractive features of this option is the fact that it is possible to maintain certainty on the volume imported, while at the same time the government captures back the rent associated with the quota allocation.

To sum up, in many countries, and in particular in the poorer ones with rudimentary tax systems, taxes on trade are a very important source of government revenue. This introduces an important trade-off between trade liberalization reforms and the maintenance (or achievement) of fiscal balance. In terms of the sequencing of reform, then, an important principle is to make sure that tariff reduction reforms should only be undertaken once the fiscal sector has been reformed and other sources of revenue have been found.[33] Replacing QRs by tariffs or devising a QRs-auctioning system are measures that can be implemented without producing fiscal costs, while at the same time they improve efficiency. Also, by solving the fiscal imbalance first, the possibility of real exchange rate overvaluation is reduced.

4.3.3   Tariff Reform and Unemployment

The effects of trade reform on employment are a key consideration when evaluating the short-run effects of these policies. This is particularly the case under the current conditions, where countries are already experiencing very high levels of unemployment. Moreover, from a political economy perspective the unemployment effects of any policy are crucial; democratic governments—and even those not so democratic, but in a weakened position—will try not to generate massive unemployment: The costs of unemployment are recognized in the short run, while the benefits of the structural policies that provoked it usually are reaped in the medium run, when a different government is in office.

According to the simplest textbook approach, in a small developing economy with capital-intensive imports, fully mobile factors of production, and flexible prices, the reduction of import tariffs will have no effect on total employment even in the short run. In this simple setup the only labor market effects of trade liberalization will be a reallocation of labor out of importables and an increase in the real wage rate. However, in reality there are a number of reasons why these textbook conditions do not hold, and why tariff reforms can result in a decline of employment in the short run.

The Ricardo-Viner model with downward real wages inflexibility provides the simplest model for illustrating the possible short-run unemployment effects of a tariff reform. In this model capital is, in the short run, fixed to its sector of origin; only slowly through time (and possibly via investment) can capital be reallocated. Contrary to the more traditional textbook case with full flexibility of price and resource movements, in this more realistic model a tariff reduction can result in a reduction of the *equilibrium* real wage rate required to maintain full employment.[34] However, if for some reason such as government imposed minimum wages, indexation, or staggered contracts there is downward inflexibility of real wages, the required reduction in the wage rate will not take place, and unemployment will result. (See Edwards 1988a for a formal exposition on how this model works in a world with importables, exportables, and nontradables.) This unemployment, however, will only be of a short-run nature. As capital moves out of the importables sector and into the exportables and nontradables sectors, there will be forces working for the equilibrium real wage to increase, and those workers previously laid off will be rehired. A requirement for real wages to increase and for unemployment to disappear in the longer run is that capital is indeed reallocated. However, if the reform lacks credibility as has been the case very often with liberalization episodes capital will not be reallocated and unemployment will persist (Edwards 1986).

A shortcoming of the version of the Ricardo-Viner model discussed above is that it assumes economy-wide real wage inflexibility and no initial unemployment. In fact, in most developing countries minimum or inflexible wages do not cover all sectors, and usually apply to the urban sector only. In that regard, a more satisfactory model can be built using a three-goods open economy version of the well known Harris-Todaro model with short-run sector-specific capital. (Throughout we maintain the very realistic assumption that importables are the most capital intensive, while nontradables are the most labor intensive goods.) Assume that while the importables (i.e., manufacturing) sector is subject to a minimum wage (in real terms), in the exportables and nontradables sectors there is wage flexibility. Initial equilibrium will be characterized by a positive amount of unemployment that will generate an equalization between the real wage in the exportables and nontradables sectors and the *expected* real wage in the importables (manufacturing) sector covered by the minimum wage. Under our assumptions the post-tariff reform short-run equilibrium (with capital still fixed to its sector of origin) will be characterized by (1) lower employment in the sector covered by the minimum wage (importables); (2) lower wages in the uncovered sector, expressed in terms of exportables; (3) either higher or lower equilibrium unemployment; (4) either lower or higher employment in nontradables; (5) higher employment and production of exportables. (see Edwards 1988a for a detailed analysis).

Not surprisingly this case of partial minimum wage coverage generates very different results from the case of an economy-wide minimum wage discussed above. First, we now have an increase in production and employment in exportables. Second, it is possible that in our partial-coverage case employment in nontradables will also increase. Also, in this case a tariff reduction reform may generate smaller unemployment in the short run, whereas in the case of an economy-wide minimum wage greater unemployment always resulted in the short run as a consequence of a decline in the tariff (see Edwards 1988a for a detailed discussion).

These models suggest that, contrary to the simplistic textbook view, as long as it takes time to reallocate capital from one sector to the other and (real) wages are inflexible, a tariff reduction reform may very well result in unemployment. A first-best solution to this problem is to (fully) eliminate the sources of real wage rigidity; with complete flexibility wages will, in the short run, go down until all the labor force is absorbed. However, if for political or other reasons real wages cannot fall sufficiently, a second-best solution is to proceed slowly with the trade reform; tariffs should be reduced gradually in a preannounced fashion. In theory, in this way capital owners will have time to reallocate capital, avoiding the unemployment effects of the trade reform (see Edwards 1988a). Once again, for this solution to work, capital allocation should, in fact, respond to the *announcement* of reform; that is, the reform should be *credible*.[35] (See section 4.3.5 below.)

The NBER multicountry study on trade regimes and employment directed by Anne Krueger (1983) has provided ample evidence suggesting that countries that have followed outward-oriented policies have generally had a better employment record, both in terms of employment creation and lower unemployment rates over the long run, than those nations that have adopted import substitution industrialization strategies. This study, however, refers to the long-run characteristics and performance of the labor markets and does not say much about the aggregate employment effects during the transition immediately following a tariff reform.

The limited existing evidence on the short-run aggregate employment consequences of trade liberalization indicates that in the case of mild reforms there have not been significant aggregate unemployment effects. This, indeed, would seem to be one of the preliminary conclusions of the exhaustive cross-country study undertaken at the World Bank and directed by Papageorgiou, Michaely, and Choksi (1986). It is, however, somewhat difficult to interpret the evidence from this massive investigation. For example, the episodes analyzed many times refer to exceedingly mild liberalizations; for example, the 1970 Turkish devaluation, included in the study, would barely qualify as even a very timid liberalization. Also, from these studies, it is not possible to know in a precise way whether specific changes in aggregate employment respond to the trade reform, or if they are the result of other policies. This is the case, for example, of the slight increases in aggregate unemployment observed after a number of trade reforms, including the Turkish liberalization of 1980, the Korean reform of 1979–80, the Philippines' liberalization of 1981, and the Israeli reform of 1972–77.

Once again the Chilean experience, with its textbook-type policies is educational. As already mentioned, between 1974 and 1979 Chile underwent one of the most, if not the most, ambitious trade liberalization of modern times: Quantitative restrictions were fully eliminated, a multiple exchange rate system consisting of up to 15 different exchange rates was unified, and tariffs were slashed to a uniform 10 percent. During this same period unemployment in Chile was very high, reaching more than 20 percent in 1975 and never falling below 15 percent. A subject extensively debated in Chile's popular media, as well as in the specialized press, is the extent to which the process of tariff reduction "contributed" to the unemployment problem. There is little doubt that as a result of the tariff reform a number of contracting, and even disappearing manufacturing firms laid off large numbers of workers. On the other hand, expanding firms from the exporting sectors increased employment, partially offsetting the negative effect. The net result, however, was an increase in unemployment generated by the trade reform. This negative effect was particularly marked in manufacturing where firms worked their way out of the difficult situation created by increased foreign competition by trimming their payrolls and increasing productivity (Edwards and Cox-Edwards 1987).

There were two main ways in which the tariff liberalization generated short-run unemployment in Chile. First, there was a natural adjustment period where laid-off workers took time to start searching for work in a different, expanding sector. Second, the fact that in reality—contrary to the simplest textbook case—physical capital is fixed in its sector of origin made the expansion of production in a number of the exporting sectors somewhat sluggish at first. Only as additional investment took place through time was it possible to fully increase production and employment in these expanding sectors. However, the existence of wage rigidity and in particular of a minimum wage in real terms made the absorption of labor by the expanding industries more difficult.[36] It is argued in Edwards (1985) that a slower reform would have resulted in a reduced unemployment effect. The proportion of *total* unemployment that can be attributed to the tariff reform is, however, relatively small when compared to the magnitude of the overall unemployment problem. Edwards (1985), for example, calculated that an upper bound for the unemployment effects of the trade reform was 3.5 percentage points of the labor force, or 129,000 people, with the bulk of this unemployment located in the food, beverages, tobacco, textiles, and leather products subsectors (57,000 people). More recently, de la Cuadra and Hachette (1986) have calculated that the trade reform generated a reduction of employment in the manufacturing sector of approximately 50,000 workers. Even though these are not negligible numbers, they clearly indicate that an explanation for the bulk of the Chilean unemployment should be sought elsewhere.

The above discussion has concentrated on the possible beneficial effects of a gradual trade reform on employment. However, there are other channels, mainly via an intertemporal effect on expenditure, through which a gradual tariff reform can have positive effects on the economy. For example, a slow reduction of tariffs will generally have a positive impact on the savings rate and on the current account. To the extent that the gradual trade liberalization process is a credible proposition, it will have a nontrivial effect towards reducing the consumption rate of interest. As the public expects tariffs, and thus the domestic price of importables, to be lower in the future it will postpone current consumption. Consequently savings will increase and the current account will improve.

In sum, a gradual lowering of tariffs offers a number of attractive features for economies such as those in the debt-ridden countries. First, this strategy is likely to reduce the short-run unemployment consequences of the trade reform. Second, there will likely be positive effects on savings, helping growth prospects. Third, it will tend to improve the current account. And finally, a gradual reduction of tariffs will have positive effects on the government budget. On the negative side a gradual trade reform may lack credibility, in which case it may even induce perverse responses (see section 4.3.5).

4.3.4   Structural Adjustment and Devaluation

Nominal devaluations are an important component of most stabilization programs, and as discussed in section 4.2 they have played a central role in the adjustment efforts following the debt crisis. The purpose of these nominal devaluations is to generate a *real* exchange rate adjustment, that would reverse the real appreciation that most times precedes the balance of payments crisis. In turn, by improving the degree of domestic competitiveness and raising the domestic price of tradables the real devaluations are supposed to improve the external sector accounts of the country in question. Historically, however, when implementing stepwise discrete nominal devaluations, many developing nations have found it difficult to sustain the real devaluations for a long period. In a large number of cases after some time, usually ranging from one to two years, the real exchange rate effect of the nominal discrete devaluation has been fully eroded. In almost every instance this erosion can be traced back to the failure to implement consistent macroeconomic policies alongside the devaluations (see Edwards, forthcoming).

Devaluations have also played a key role in the trade reform component of structural adjustment programs. It is generally accepted in policy circles that in order for a tariff reform to be successful, it has to be accompanied—if not preceded—by a real devaluation (see, however, Edwards forthcoming for a critical evaluation of this proposition). The argument usually given is based on a partial equilibrium interpretation of the elasticities approach to exchange rate determination, and runs along the following lines: A lower tariff will reduce the domestic price of importables, and consequently increase the demand for imports. This, in turn, will generate an external imbalance (i.e., a trade account deficit), which assuming that the Marshall-Lerner condition holds, will require a (real) devaluation to restore equilibrium. This view is clearly captured by the following quotation from Balassa (1982, 16): "[E]liminating protective measures would necessitate a devaluation in order to offset the resulting deficit in the balance of payments." It is along these lines, then, that the proponents of major liberalizations by the debt-ridden countries have insisted that these tariff reductions should be accompanied by significant nominal devaluations (Balassa, Kuezynski, and Simeonsen 1986).

The "required" amount of devaluation will depend on a number of factors, including the initial conditions, the extent of the trade reform, the magnitude of the disequilibrium gap to be closed, and the accompanying macroeconomic policies.[37] In addition, and perhaps more importantly, the required devaluation will also depend on the speed at which the trade reform is implemented. Since, for a number of reasons including the short-run fixity of capital, short-run supply elasticities are much lower than long-run elasticities, under most circumstances a rapid trade reform will necessitate a higher real devaluation to maintain external equilibrium.[38]

Until quite recently most traditional structural adjustment programs in the developing nations have contemplated discreet nominal devaluations where the official nominal exchange rate is abruptly adjusted by a fairly large percentage. More recently, however, more and more countries are opting for the adoption of some sort of crawling peg after the devaluation. In a recent study on 18 devaluation episodes in Latin America, Edwards (1988b) found that those countries that had adopted a crawling peg had been significantly more successful in sustaining a real depreciation than the discrete devaluers. This, of course, is not in itself surprising, since the crawlers maintained their real devaluation targets by "fighting off" the real exchange rate erosion with additional nominal devaluations in the following years. Typically, under this type of regime, after the initial exchange rate adjustment the authorities further devalue the currency in magnitudes approximately equal to the domestic rate of inflation. Of course, a potential problem with this policy is that it can lead to an explosive (nonconvergent) process, where the devaluation generates inflation, which partially erodes the real effect of the devaluation; this leads to a higher devaluation and even higher inflation and so on, *ad infinitum*. This possible unstable path could happen in those countries where the structural macroeconomic disequilibrium, and in particular the fiscal deficit, have not been corrected to a significant extent. An alternative scenario is one where macroeconomic equilibrium is attained and the process is stabilized at some mild rate of inflation, as in Chile in the recent period and in Colombia since 1967. The cited study by Edwards indicates that among the Latin American crawlers in Bolivia (1982), Peru (1975), and Mexico (1982), the higher real exchange rate was sustained at the cost of a substantial permanent increase in the rate of inflation.

In spite of the prominent role of devaluations in conventional adjustment programs, very little work has investigated empirically the effects of devaluations on the real level of economic activity or on income distribution. A recently revived strand of literature has argued that although devaluations may have a positive effect on the external accounts, they will achieve this at the cost of significant reductions in real activity. This is the so-called contractionary devaluation hypothesis. Edwards (forthcoming), has analyzed in detail the behavior of a large number of key economic variables during 39 devaluation episodes in developing countries. In this study the evolution of some key variables during the period going from three years prior to the devaluation to three years after the devaluation was analyzed and compared to the behavior of the same variables for a control group of 24 nondevaluing countries. Table 4.15 provides a summary of the distribution of the rate of growth of real GDP for the devaluing countries and the control group. Notice that three years prior to the devaluation this distribution is very similar to that of the control group. In fact, using a chi-square test for homogeneity we are unable to reject the null hypothesis that these data come from the same distribution ($\chi^2(2) = 0.046$).

Things, however, are very different as we approach the devaluation. Already during the two years prior to the devaluation we can see a significant difference between the devaluing and control groups, with the former exhibiting substantially lower levels of growth in every quartile. The chi-square test strongly rejects the null hypothesis of

Table 4.15   **Growth of Real GDP in Devaluing and Nondevaluing Countries (in percent)**

	First Quartile	Median	Third Quartile
A. 39 Devaluing Countries			
3 years before	7.4	6.0	4.7
2 years before	8.4	6.1	3.6
1 year before	7.3	5.4	2.3
Year of devaluation	6.1	4.2	1.2
1 year after	6.4	4.7	3.1
2 years after	6.4	4.7	3.1
3 years after	9.2	5.8	3.2
B. Control Group of 29 Nondevaluing Countries			
	7.4	6.4	4.5

Source: Edwards (forthcoming).

homogeneity for the year of the devaluation ($\chi^2(2) = 7.02$) and all three years following devaluation. Notice, however, that the years following devaluation a fairly fast recovery in the rate of growth of real GDP is detected. Although the information presented in this table is quite revealing, it does not allow us to know whether this behavior of real GDP growth is caused by devaluation or if it is the result of some of the policies preceding the devaluation. This problem can be partially avoided by using regression analysis. The following result was obtained using instrumental variables on a variance component model of 12 countries for 1965–80:

$$\log y_{tm} = 0.102 \, [\Delta \log M_t - \Delta \log M_t^*] + 0.210$$
$$\qquad (1.146) \qquad\qquad\qquad\qquad (2.331)$$
$$\qquad\qquad\qquad\qquad\qquad [\Delta \log M_{t-1} - \Delta \log M_{t1}^*]$$

$$+ \, 0.112 \log(GE/Y)_t - 0.083 \log e_t + 0.069 \log e_{t-1}$$
$$\quad (3.023) \qquad\qquad (2.103) \qquad\qquad (2.086)$$

$$+ \, 0.044 \log \tau_t - 0.008 \log \tau_{t-1} \qquad \bar{R}^2 = 0.998$$
$$\quad (1.431) \qquad\quad (-0.265) \qquad\qquad SEE = 0.038$$

where y is real output, $[\Delta \log M - \Delta \log M^*]$ is the unexpected rate of growth of money, (GE/Y) is the ratio of government expenditure to GNP, e is the real exchange rate, and τ is the terms of trade. According to these results then, in the short run devaluations have led to a slight fall in output: A 10 percent depreciation leads to a one-time loss of almost 1 percent of GNP. In the second year, the economy returns to trend.[39]

Income distribution data are very scarce in the developing countries. This undoubtedly explains, at least partially, why there have been practically no studies on the effects of devaluations on income distribution. However, there is little doubt that income and wealth distribution considerations enter heavily in the decisions of what kind of policies to implement. In table 4.16 I present, as an illustration, some very preliminary data on devaluation and income distribution in 23 developing nations. This table contains the ratio of labor compensations to GDP for a period that goes from four years prior to a major devaluation to three years after the devaluations. The first column in the table provides information on the year of the devaluation. Although the ratio of workers' compensations is a very rudimentary measure of income distribution, and this type of "before" and "after" methodology has well-known shortcomings, the data are quite revealing. They confirm that in *some* instances devaluations have been followed by major worsenings in income distribution (i.e., Peru 1975). This trend, however, cannot be found in all cases, and not even in the majority of episodes. In

Table 4.16   **Devaluations and Income Distribution (percentage of compensation to employees with respect to GDP)**

	Year of Devaluation	−4	−3	−2	−1	Devaluation Year 0	+1	+2	+3
Argentina	1970	40	41	40	40	41	42	39	43
Bolivia	1971	37	37	34	36	35	32	30	33
	1979	33	34	35	35	36	36	n.a.	n.a.
	1982	35	36	36	n.a.	n.a.	36	n.a.	n.a.
Chile	1982	39	36	38	40	n.a.	n.a.	n.a.	n.a.
Colombia	1962	n.a.	n.a.	34	36	38	38	36	37
	1964	34	36	38	38	36	37	36	37
	1965	36	38	38	36	37	36	37	36
	1967	38	36	37	36	37	36	38	38
Costa Rica	1974	47	48	48	45	45	46	47	45
Cyprus[a]	1967	87	87	88	87	88	88	88	88
Ecuador	1961	n.a.	n.a.	n.a.	28	29	29	29	28
	1970	27	27	28	28	29	30	28	26
	1982	28	28	32	30	29	n.a.	n.a.	n.a.
Egypt[b]	1962	n.a.	n.a.	39	41	42	42	40	41
	1979	46	39	38	37	33	34	n.a.	n.a.
Guyana	1967	47	47	48	49	49	49	48	49
India	1966	73	72	74	72	74	77	75	74

Country	Year								
Indonesia[a]	1978	89	89	89	89	89	89	90	90
Israel	1962	n.a.	n.a.	44	44	44	44	45	48
	1967	44	45	48	50	50	46	44	47
	1971	50	46	44	47	46	43	45	43
Jamaica	1967	50	50	50	46	47	48	49	50
	1978	54	56	57	56	52	51	51	53
Kenya	1981	32	34	35	35	n.a.	n.a.	n.a.	n.a.
Korea	1980	32	33	37	36	37	35	38	n.a.
Malta	1967	49	50	49	47	47	47	47	50
Mexico	1976	37	36	37	38	40	39	38	38
	1982	38	38	36	37	36	n.a.	n.a.	n.a.
Nicaragua	1979	54	55	54	56	n.a.	n.a.	n.a.	n.a.
Pakistan[a]	1972	87	81	84	85	85	86	88	86
	1982	86	84	83	84	84	n.a.	n.a.	n.a.
Peru	1975	36	38	39	37	37	37	37	32
Philippines[a]	1962	n.a.	n.a.	88	87	87	86	86	86
	1970	86	86	86	86	84	83	83	82
Sri Lanka	1967	45	41	43	42	41	41	39	36
Venezuela	1964	45	45	42	43	43	43	44	45

Source: United Nations, *Yearbook of National Accounts Statistics.*

[a](Compensation to employees + operating surplus)/GDP.

[b]Year beginning July 1.

n.a. = not available.

fact, in a number of them the ratio of labor compensation increased following the devaluation. More than anything, however, these data indicate that in order to have a full understanding of the income distribution consequences of devaluations, it is necessary to look at more detailed data and at alternative categories, including the effect of devaluations on the rural/urban distribution of income.

To sum up then, the discussion in this section reveals once again the existence of important trade-offs associated with the different goals of the adjustment program. While devaluation will generally have a positive effect on the external sector, helping generate the necessary excess supply for tradables, and easing the transition following a trade liberalization, it will have a negative impact on the cost of foreign exchange to the government and on real GDP growth. In addition, devaluation will usually have important effects on income distribution and on inflation. Since the magnitude of "required" (real) devaluations will be closely related to the speed at which structural reforms are implemented, this discussion points out, once more, the desirability of proceeding gradually both with respect to debt payment and to structural reforms.

4.3.5 Credibility, Sustainability, and Reversibility of Trade Reforms

Credibility is a fundamental ingredient of successful structural reforms. If the public attaches a nontrivial probability to policy reversal, it will try to anticipate this event, generally introducing strong destabilizing forces into the structural adjustment process.

Latin America's history is replete with frustrated economic reforms that have failed because of their lack of credibility. In that respect, the frustrated Argentine trade reform during the Martinez de Hoz period is very educational. Because of lack of credibility on the future of the preannounced trade reform, firms used foreign funds in order to survive in the short run. As Carlos Rodriguez (1983, 28) has put it in his evaluation of the Argentine experience of 1978–82: "As a consequence of the *lack of credibility* on the continuity of the economic program, many firms—which would have disappeared due to the tariff reductions—decided to get into debt in order to remain operating while waiting for a change in the economic strategy"[emphasis added].

A fundamental aspect of establishing credibility is related to the perception the public has of the internal consistency of the policies being pursued. In that respect, for example, the inconsistency of the Argentine fiscal policy, which maintained a very large deficit, and the preannounced exchange rate policy severely undermined the degree of credibility of the reform process. In the case of Chile the markedly overvalued currency in 1981 was seen by large segments of the public as inconsistent with the long-run viability of the liberalized economy. In general, if the real exchange rate experiences an unprecedented real appreciation, the public will think that exports will not be able to develop and that there is a nontrivial probability of the reform's being reversed in the future. Under these circumstances it will be optimal for consumers to get into debt today in order to acquire "cheap" importables.

The inability to establish consistency between fiscal and exchange rate policies has many times been at the heart of the trade reform credibility crises in Latin America. For example, in most cases where (mild) trade reforms have been reversed, the public early on perceived that the inflation tax required to finance the fiscal dificit was inconsistent with maintaining a predetermined nominal exchange rate. Under these circumstances expectations of overvaluation, speculative attacks, exchange controls, and future devaluations developed. In trying to anticipate these events the optimizing private sector will usually take steps—such as diversifying its portfolio internationally (i.e., "capital flight")—that will sometimes move the economy in the opposite direction from that intended by the reform. Edwards (1988c) has found that more than 80 percent of reversals of trade liberalizations in Latin America can be traced to inconsistent fiscal policies.

An important question is whether a gradual (i.e., slow) trade reform will be less or more credible than an abrupt one. Theoretical models of credibility of economic policy are only now being developed, and have not yet reached a level that enables us to answer this question with enough precision.[40] In principle, it is possible to argue that gradualism has characteristics that work in both directions, at the same time enhancing and compromising credibility. On the one hand, by reducing the unemployment effect, and by allowing for a firmer fiscal equilibrium, a gradual trade reform will tend to be more credible; on the other hand a slow reform will allow those groups negatively affected by it (i.e., the import substitution manufacturing sector) to organize and lobby against the policies. At the end, as is so often the case in economics, whether gradualism will enhance credibility will depend on factors specific to each country. What is clear, however, is that policymakers should always pay special attention on the establishment of credibility when persuing important long-term structural changes.

Although at this point, given our knowledge of the policymaking process and its interaction with the private sector, it is not possible to derive a precise theorem, the arguments presented in this section—including unemployment, fiscal, and other considerations—suggest that, in general, it would be more prudent to implement the trade reform component of an outward-orientated policy in a gradual way.

4.4 Concluding Remarks and Summary

The adjustment packages of 1982–87 sought "effectiveness." On some grounds, and especially in terms of the turnarounds of the current accounts, the results have been quite impressive. The costs, however, have been high. Not only did real income decline, as illustrated in table 4.2, but real wages declined in most countries, and unemployment soared. There is little doubt that this is not a sustainable adjustment path. A successful adjustment means that debtor countries will have to bring down their debt-to-GDP ratios to a level consistent with the reestablishment of creditworthiness, while recovering their growth of output and consumption. The first objective means that the country has to transfer a given discounted value of resources to the rest of the world. The second means that the country has to increase its rate of capital formation and the efficiency of resource use. The problem faced by the highly indebted nations can be posed as follows: how to minimize the present value of the foregone consumption from making a transfer of a specific discounted value. The problem then has two dimensions: how to minimize the cost of the transfer at each moment of time, including its distributive aspect, and what should be the flow of transfers over time consistent with a given present value of the flow.

The speed with which the transfer to the rest of the world is made will affect the (discounted value of the) cost of achieving creditworthiness. A very fast increase in the trade surplus can only be obtained at a very high cost in terms of nontraded goods and losses in employment, both because it takes time for factors to be retrained and to move, and because of wage inflexibility in the short run. It also takes time to implement efficient fiscal instruments to generate the fiscal surplus, particularly if one wants to eliminate the present reliance of taxes on trade and the inflationary finance of the deficit. Finally, improving the allocation of investment and promoting the return of capital flight may involve liberalizing financial markets, which will increase the fiscal cost of servicing internal debt. Thus, improved efficiency and capital accumulation will require important increases in nondistortive taxes and cuts in public expenditures: but this takes time. In sum, there are important trade-offs between effecting the transfer rapidly and minimizing its cost at one moment of time. Instruments that help generate the trade surplus quickly—like quantitative restrictions—increase the resource cost of achieving the transfer. Instruments that solve the fiscal problem quickly—like using tariffs or QRs instead of a devaluation— also increase that cost.

A slower speed of adjustment can only be achieved if the magnitude of the transfer countries have to make is reduced during the initial years. One way of achieving this is by providing these countries with additional lending during the transition. In principle this will allow the implementation of slower expenditure-switching policies and the implementation of more efficient fiscal instruments to raise public resources. Most importantly, it will allow the investment rates to be kept up without unduly sacrificing consumption. Thus there is a complementarity between extra lending during the transition and the recovery of growth while transferring abroad a given present value of resources.

A longer-run solution of the debt crisis will clearly require the adoption of policies that rely more heavily than in the past on export growth. Even ECLA/CEPAL, the former champion of import substitution development, has recommended outward-oriented policies. Export promotion requires some kind of trade liberalization and tariff reduction, especially of imported inputs and capital goods. Indeed, the historical evidence clearly shows that those countries that have successfully pursued export promotion (i.e., the East Asian nations), have had a trade regime substantially more liberal than those countries that have followed indiscriminate import substitution based on protectionism. A crucial question, however, is how much trade liberalization is needed. It is argued in the chapter that although outward orientation requires *some* trade liberalization, there are no reasons, either theoretical or empirical, that suggest that the "optimal" degree of liberalization implies zero, or even very low, tariffs coupled with no government intervention in any sphere of the development process. The successful experiences with export-led growth in the East Asian countries support this view; although in these countries the trade regime has been significantly liberal, government intervention has been important and tariffs have never been anything close to zero or a very low (i.e., 10–15 percent) uniform level.

An important policy question is whether the trade liberalization component of an outward-oriented strategy should be attempted at the same time that a country is embarked on a severe stabilization program. It is argued in the chapter that, in general, it is not recommended to undertake substantial trade reforms at the same time that a major anti-inflationary program is underway. This is both for fiscal and real exchange rate reasons. However, there are some measures, such as the replacement of quotas for tariffs, that can help both the anti-inflation drive as well as the quest for improvement of efficiency.

Under the most plausible circumstances a fast trade liberalization will generate short-run unemployment effects. Indeed, the empirical evidence from the Southern Cone tends to confirm this presumption. This suggests that trade liberalization should be a gradual and pre-announced process. This, however, brings up serious credibility issues. Only if the announced gradual trade reform is "credible" will economic agents react as expected by the authorities. The analysis of devaluations presented in section 4.3 clearly suggests that under many circumstances abrupt devaluations can generate nontrivial short-run costs in the form of output reductions and unemployment. It is argued that gradual liberalizations will require smaller devaluations, possibly reducing the associated costs.

A sustained increase in the indebted countries' exports—which is, of course, a prerequisite for a long-term solution to the crisis—will not only require an efficient tradables sector and a "realistic" real exchange rate but, more important, that the current protectionist trend in the industrial countries and in particular in the United States be reversed. Data presented by Edwards (1987a) indicate that at this time the extent of nontariff barriers, as a form of protection in the industrial countries, is very significant. Moreover, the data show that these trade impediments are particularly important for goods originating in the developing nations, and that their tariff equivalents are in many cases very significant. Asking the highly indebted developing countries to pay their debts while impeding their exports from reaching the industrialized markets is not only unfair, but also politically unwise.

Notes

1. It should be noticed, however, that most experts now agree that in some of the poorer countries it would be highly implausible to reduce the debt-export ratio to the levels required for access to new voluntary financing. In these cases some innovative and less orthodox solutions, including debt forgiveness, may be the most efficient way out.
2. See, for example, Balassa et. al. (1986) and Krueger (1987).
3. The IMF's 15 highly indebted countries are: Argentina, Bolivia, Brazil, Chile, Colombia, Ivory Coast, Ecuador, Mexico, Morocco, Nigeria, Peru, Philippines, Uruguay, Venezuela, and Yugoslavia.
4. On the Brazilian experience see Cardoso and Fishlow (1987); on Mexico see Buffie and Sangines (1987); Celâsun and Rodrik (1987) deal with Turkey. These papers are published in the country studies volumes of this project. On Chile see Edwards and Cox-Edwards (1987).
5. See Dornbusch (chap. 8 in this volume) for discussion of the role of the developed countries' macropolicies on the development of the crisis.
6. See Bianchi, Devlin, and Ramos (1987).
7. Notice, however, that it is not completely rigorous to talk about overvalued real exchange rates without first analyzing the way in which the equilibrium real exchange rate has evolved (see Edwards, forthcoming). In the case of the debtor countries, however, the existing evidence clearly suggests that significant overvaluations developed.
8. On the Chilean experience see Edwards (1985) and Edwards and Cox-Edwards (1987).
9. On Argentina see Calvo (1986a) and Corbo, de Melo, and Tybout (1986).
10. On Colombia see Thomas (1986). See Collins and Park (1987) on Korea and Woo and Nasution (1987) on Indonesia.

11. The exact time periods are Argentina, 1982–85; Ecuador, 1982–83; Mexico, 1983–84; Uruguay, 1982–84; and Venezuela, 1982–83.

12. Computed from raw data published in IMF, *Government Finance Statistics Yearbook*, 1986.

13. See Edwards and Cox-Edwards (1987).

14. Although real devaluations will increase the servicing of public debts in real domestic currency, they can have some other positive effects on the public sector's budget. This will be the case in those countries where the main exporting firms are government owned.

15. On the Argentine exchange rate guarantees scheme, see Calvo (1986a); on Chile see Edwards (1985).

16. For a detailed analysis on the nonequivalence between quotas and tariffs see Bhagwati (1978). See also Hillman, Tower, and Fishelson (1980).

17. Note, however, that in spite of Khan and Knight's description in the past not every Fund sponsored program included exchange rate actions. It is in fact important to recognize that historically the IMF has exhibited significantly more flexibility than its critics have given it credit for. There has been, to some extent, a case-by-case approach. From the record it seems, however, that the Fund staff considers that the vast majority of the cases are quite similar.

18. Balassa et al. (1986) and Krueger (1987) are good representatives of this view. See also Fischer (1986).

19. The other policies advocated by Balassa et al. (1986) include financial reform, stable real exchange rates, and a much reduced role for the government.

20. On the evidence on the performance of outward- vs. inward-oriented strategies see, for example, the World Book, *World Development Report 1987* and the literature cited therein. On CEPAL see, for example, Bianchi, Devlin, and Ramos (1987).

21. See Krueger (1978) and Bhagwati (1978). On earlier discussions on liberalization see Little, Scitovsky, and Scott (1971). For a recent treatment of many of these issues see the volume edited by Choksi and Papageorgiou (1986).

22. This was indeed the meaning given by some to the concept during the Southern Cone experiences with market-oriented policies in the late 1970s and early 1980s. In a recent paper Bhagwati (1986) has made an effort to define in a precise way export promotion, import substitution, and ultra trade-promoting trade policies. In the rest of this paper we will stick to trade and commercial policies when referring to trade liberalization.

23. See, for example, Bhagwati's (1986) splendid paper on outward orientation. To date the most impressive accumulation of empirical evidence supporting the better performance of outward orientation has been compiled in the 1987 *World Development Report*. See also Bhagwati and Srinivasan (1978).

24. See, for example, World Bank (1986).

25. On Colombia see Thomas (1986).

26. Naturally, the welfare effects of trade liberalizations fall within the realm of second-best economics. Rigorously speaking if there are other distortions, as invariably there are in the real world, it is not possible to know a priori if a partial trade liberalization will be welfare improving. If there are no other distortions, it is possible to establish a positive relation between the level of tariffs and the level of *income*. Still however, no traditional growth model will link no tariffs to higher growth (see Lucas 1985).

27. Notice, however, that even the Koreans made mistakes when they pushed the government role too far. In that respect, the fiasco of 1974–79 when the government picked the wrong "winners" is well known. See World Bank (1986).

28. See, for example, Krueger (1981) and Little (1982).

29. See, for example, Edwards (1988b) for a detailed analysis of 18 stabilization with mild liberalization episodes in Latin America.

30. Naturally, although very common, this is not the only scenario leading to a stabilization with structural adjustment program. In an alternative scenario that fits some country's experiences during the period leading to the debt crisis, the fiscal expansion is financed with foreign borrowing instead of money creation. In this case the path leading to the need to adjust in not necessarily characterized by a piling up of trade and exchange controls.

31. The recent Bolivian experience is also characterized by a tremendous trade liberalization. However, the fact that this was part of a package to defeat *hyperinflation* sets the Bolivian case apart.

32. While a number of countries have successfully used foreign exchange auctions—Jamaica, Sierra Leone, Uganda—only a few have implemented generalized auctions for imports of goods. See Krumm (1985) for a discussion on different experiences with exchange auctions.

33. Notice, however, that from a welfare perspective this is by no means a trivial proposition. Indeed, from a purely theoretical point of view it is not clear that reducing tariffs and increasing other taxes will be welfare improving. Moreover, at least at the theoretical level, it is not clear that welfare will increase if, as liberalization advocates have sometimes proposed, consumption taxes are raised as tariffs are reduced. This, of course, is a simple application of the second-best theorem.

34. Whether this reduction in the equilibrium real wage will actually take place will depend on the weight of exportables in the price level relevant for determining real wages. If, as in a large number of developing countries, exportables (i.e., foodstuffs) have a large weight in the consumer price index the equilibrium real wage will indeed decline (see Edwards 1988a).

35. On theoretical models of the labor market effects of trade reforms see Edwards (1986; 1988a) and the references cited therein.

36. See chapter 6 of Edwards and Cox-Edwards (1987) for a detailed discussion of the evolution of wages in Chile.

37. We are referring to the extent of *real* devaluation. However, since the real exchange rate is not a policy tool, economic authorities face the additional difficulty of deciding by how much to adjust the *nominal* exchange rate in order to generate a given real devaluation.

38. This statement assumes that a tariff reduction will result in an equilibrium real exchange rate depreciation. Although this is the more plausible case, theoretically it is not the only possible result (see Edwards 1987b).

39. The countries included in this regression are: Brazil, Colombia, El Salvador, Greece, India, Israel, Malaysia, Philippines, South Africa, Sri Lanka, Thailand, and Yugoslavia. The equation was estimated using a fixed effect instrumental variables procedure, where country-specific dummy variables were included. The following instruments were used: all the exogenous variables, twice-lagged money surprises, twice-lagged terms of trade, twice-lagged real exchange rates, contemporary, lagged and twice-lagged growth of domestic credit (for details, see Edwards 1986).

40. Guillermo Calvo, however, has recently made important contributions to this key area of the theory of economic policy (see Calvo 1986b; 1987).

References

Balassa, B. 1982. *Development strategies in semi-industrial countries.* Oxford: Oxford University Press.

Balassa, B., G. M. Bueno, P. P. Kuczynski, and M. H. Simeonsen. 1986. *Toward renewed economic growth in Latin America.* Washington, D.C.: Institute of International Economics.

Bhagwati, J. 1978. *Anatomy and consequences of exchange control regimes.* Cambridge, Mass.: Ballinger Publishing Co.

———. 1986. Export-promoting trade strategies: Issues and evidence. World Bank Discussion Paper UPERS7. Washington, D.C.: World Bank.

Bhagwati, J., and T. N. Srinivasan, 1978. Trade policy and development. In *International economic policy: Theory and evidence*, ed. R. Dornbusch and J. Frenkel. Baltimore, Md.: Johns Hopkins University Press.

Bianchi, A., R. Devlin, and J. Ramos. 1987. The adjustment process in Latin America, 1981–1986. Paper presented at World Bank–IMF symposium, Growth-Oriented Adjustment Programs in Washington, D.C.

Buffie, E., and A. Sangines. 1987. Economic policy and foreign debt in Mexico. Unpublished NBER ms. In *Developing country debt and economic performance, vol. 2: Country studies*, ed. J. Sachs. Chicago: University of Chicago Press, forthcoming.

Calvo, G. 1986a. Fractured liberalism: Argentina under Martinez de Hoz. *Economic Development and Cultural Change* 34(3): 511–34.

———. 1986b. Temporary stabilization predetermined exchange rates. *Journal of Political Economy* 94(6): 1319–29.

———. 1987. Reform, distortions and credibility. Working Paper, University of Pennsylvania.

Cardoso, E., and A. Fishlow. 1987. The macroeconomics of the Brazilian external debt. Unpublished NBER ms. In *Developing country debt and economic performance, vol. 2: Country studies*, ed. J. Sachs. Chicago: University of Chicago Press, forthcoming.

Celasun, M., and D. Rodrik. 1987. Debt, adjustment growth: Turkey 1970–85. Unpublished NBER ms. In *Developing country dept and economic performance, vol. 3: Country studies*, ed. J. Sachs. Chicago: University of Chicago Press, forthcoming.

CEPAL. 1985. *Anuario Estadístico de América Latina y el Caribe.* Santiago, Chile: CEPAL.

———. 1986a. *Panorama económico de América Latina 1986.* Santiago, Chile: CEPAL.

———. 1986b. *Balance preliminar de la economía Latino americana 1986.* Santiago, Chile: CEPAL.

Choski, A., and D. Papageorgiou, eds. 1986. *Economic liberalization in developing countries.* Oxford: Blackwell.

Cline, William. 1987. Mobilizing bank lending to debt countries. Washington, D. C.: Center for International Economics.

Collins, S. and W. A. Park. 1987. External debt and macroeconomic performance in Korea. Unpublished NBER ms. In *Developing country debt and economic performance, vol. 3: Country studies*, ed. J. Sachs. Chicago: University of Chicago Press, forthcoming.

Conrad, R., and M. Gillis. 1984. The Indonesian tax reform of 1983. Harvard Institute for International Development, Discussion Paper no. 162. Cambridge: Harvard University.

Corbo, V., J. de Melo and J. Tybout. 1986. What went wrong in the southern cone. *Economic Development and Cultural Change* 34(3): 607–40.

Cuddington, J. 1986. *Capital flight: Estimates, issues and explanations*. Princeton, N.J.: Princeton Studies in International Finance.

Cumby, R., and R. Levich. 1987. On the definition and magnitude of recent capital flight. NBER Working Paper no. 2275. Cambridge, Mass.: National Bureau of Economic Research.

de la Cuadra, S., and D. Hachette. 1986. The timing and sequencing of trade liberalization policy: The case of Chile. Unpublished ms. Catholic University of Chile.

Díaz-Alejandro, C. 1963. *Devaluation in a semi-industrial country*. Cambridge: MIT Press.

———. 1985. Good-bye financial repression, hello financial crash. *Journal of Development Economics* 19(½): 1–24.

Dornbusch, Rudiger. 1988. Our LDC Debts. In *The U.S. in the world economy*. ed. M. Feldstein. Chicago: University of Chicago Press.

Edwards, S. 1985. Stabilization with liberalization: An evaluation of the years of Chile's experience with free market policies, 1973–1983. *Economic Development and Cultural Change* 33(2): 223–54.

———. 1986. Are devaluations contractionary? *Review of Economics and Statistics* 68(3): 501–8.

———. 1987a. *Exchange rate misalignment in developing countries*. UCLA, Department of Economics Working Paper no. 432. Also published by Johns Hopkins Univ. Press, 1988.

———. 1987b. Tariffs, terms of trade, and real exchange rate in an intertemporal model of the current account. NBER Working Paper no. 2481. Cambridge, Mass.: National Bureau of Economic Research.

———. 1987c. The U.S. and foreign competition in Latin America. NBER Working Paper no. 2544. Also *The U.S. in the World Economy*. ed. M. Feldstein. Chicago: University of Chicago Press. 1988.

———.1988a. Terms of trade, exchange rates, and labor market adjustments in developing countries. NBER Working Paper no. 2481, forthcoming in *The World Bank Economic Review* 2(2): 165–85.

———. 1988b. Exchange controls, devaluations, and real exchange rates: The Latin American experience. *Economic Development and Cultural Change*, forthcoming

———. 1988c. *Real exchange rates, devaluations, and adjustment*. Cambridge: MIT Press, forthcoming.

Edwards, S., and A. Cox-Edwards. 1987. *Monetarism and liberalization: The Chilean experiment*. Cambridge, Mass.: Ballinger Publishing Co.

Fischer, S. 1986. Issues in medium-term macroeconomic adjustment. *World Bank Research Observer* 1(2): 163–82.

Hillman A., E. Tower, and F. Fishelson. 1980. On water in the quota. *Canadian Journal of Economics* 13(2):310–16.

International Monetary Fund. 1986. *Government finance statistics yearbook*. Washington, D.C.: IMF

———. 1987. *World Economic Outlook* (April).

———. *Annual report on exchange arrangements and exchange restrictions*, various issues. Washington, D.C.: IMF.

———. *International financial statistics*, various issues. Washington, D.C.: IMF.

Khan, M., and M. Knight. 1985. *Fund supported adjustment programs and economic growth*. IMF Occasional Paper no. 41. Washington, D.C.: IMF.

Krueger, A. O. 1978. *Foreign trade regimes and economic development: Liberalization attempts and consequences.* Cambridge, Mass.: Ballinger Publishing Co.

———. 1981. Interaction between inflation and trade regime objectives in stabilization programs. In *Economic Stabilization in Developing countries*, ed. W. Cline and S. Weintraub. Washington, D.C.: Brookings Institution.

———. 1983. *Trade and employment in developing countries: Synthesis and conclusions.* Chicago: University of Chicago Press.

———. 1986. Problems of liberalization. In *Economic liberalization in developing countries,* ed. A. Choksi and D. Papageorgiou. Oxford: Blackwell.

———. 1987. The problems of LDC debt. Paper presented at the NBER conference, The U.S. in the World Economy, at West Palm Beach, Fla.

Krumm, K. 1985. Experiences with foreign exchange rate auctions. CPO Working Paper. Washington D.C.: World Bank.

Little, I. M. D. 1982. *Economic development.* New York: Basic Books.

Little, I. M. D., T. Scitovsky, and M. Scott. 1970. *Industry and trade in some developing countries.* Oxford: Oxford University Press.

Lucas, R. E. 1985. Economic growth and development. Unpublished ms. University of Chicago.

McKinnon, J. 1973. *Money and capital in economic development.* Washington, D.C.: The Brookings Institution.

———. 1982. The order of economic liberalization: Lessons from Chile and Argentina. In *Economic policy in a world of change*, ed. K. Brunner and A. Meltzer. Amsterdam: North-Holland.

Neary, P. 1978. Dynamic stability and the theory of factor-market distortions. *American Economic Review* 68(4): 671–682.

Papageorgiou, D., M. Michaely, and A. Choksi. 1986. The phasing of a trade liberalization policy: Preliminary evidence. Paper presented at AEA meeting in New Orleans.

Pick's Yearbook. Various issues. London.

Ramos, J. 1986. *Neoconservative economics in the Southern Cone of South America.* Baltimore, Md.: Johns Hopkins University Press.

Rodriguez, C. A. 1983. Políticas de estabilización en la economía Argentina, 1978–1982. *Cuadernos de Economía* 20(59): 21–42.

Sachs, J. 1986. Managing the LDC debt crisis. *Brookings papers on economic activity* 2: 397–432.

———. 1987. Trade and exchange-rate policies in growth-oriented adjustment programs. NBER Working Paper no. 2226. Cambridge, Mass.: National Bureau of Economic Research.

Selowski, M., and H. van der Tak. 1986. The debt problem and growth. *World Development* 14(9): 1107–24.

Thomas, V. 1986. *Linking macroeconomic and agricultural policies for adjustment with growth.* Baltimore, Md.: Johns Hopkins University Press.

United Nations. *Yearbook of National Accounts Statistics.* Various years.

Woo, W. T., and A. Nasution. 1987. Indonesian economic policies and their relation to external debt management. Unpublished NBER ms.

World Bank. 1986. *Korea: Managing the industrial transition.* Washington, D.C.: World Bank.

———. 1987. *World development report 1987.* Oxford: Oxford University Press.

World Currencies Yearbook. Various issues. London.

5 The Politics of Stabilization and Structural Adjustment

Stephan Haggard and Robert Kaufman

5.1 Introduction: Politics and Debt

A major theme of the country studies for this project is the relationship between policy choice and economic performance. What policies contributed to national debt crises in the first place and what corrective measures have been most successful in managing them? This chapter, by contrast, examines the way political processes and institutions influence developing country stabilization and adjustment efforts. Rather than treating policy choice as exogenous, we attempt to explain why countries pursue the mix of policies they do and why they vary in their success at implementing them.

Of course, economic circumstance defines the policy agenda and is a powerful constraint on the range of options available. But states that are similarly situated in economic terms have adopted quite different adjustment strategies and external bargaining positions because of domestic political constraints. Programs that succeed in one context prove difficult to implement in others. Political analysis is important, therefore, not only to understanding the past, but for generating realistic and sustainable programs in the future.

The politics of the debt crisis has unfolded on two intersecting planes, one international, the other domestic. Debtor governments play a Janus-faced role in these conflicts. Where possible, they attempt to reduce the costs of adjustment through bargaining with commercial banks, multilateral institutions, and creditor governments. In the first half of

Stephan Haggard is an associate professor of government and an associate at the Center for International Affairs, Harvard University. Robert Kaufman is a professor of political science, at Rutgers University.

We have benefitted from comments by Werner Baer, Jeff Frieden, Howard Handleman, Joan Nelson, and Jeffrey Sachs.

the paper, we examine the determinants of international bargaining positions and outcomes.

Since no debtor government can deflect all of the costs of adjustment, however, each must also bargain with domestic actors over how to allocate burdens on the home front. The central political dilemma is that stabilization and adjustment policies, no matter how beneficial they may be for the country as a whole, entail the imposition of short-term costs and have distributional implications. The second half of the paper examines a number of hypotheses on why governments choose the policy packages they do and the political conditions under which they will be sustained. While our primary emphasis is on short- and medium-term adjustment, we also address the question of the institutional and political foundations of longer-term growth strategies. The outward-oriented pattern of growth characteristic of the East Asian newly in-dustrializing countries (NICs) receives particular attention, since it has been advanced as a model for other developing countries.

A word should be said about method. In recent years, theories of rational and public choice have gained ground among political scien-tists, as has the application of econometric techniques to the study of political phenomena (Alt and Chrystal 1983; Ordeshook 1986). While we have drawn on this literature, we do not model our arguments in a formal way or offer rigorous tests. We have opted, rather, to review a range of different hypotheses and to build some contingent generali-zations around the countries included in this project and others that have been analyzed by political scientists and economists.

5.2 The International Politics of the Debt Crisis

5.2.1 The Bargaining Structure and the Political Resources of the Debtors

One of the most notable features of the crisis period that began in August 1982 with the emergency rescheduling of the Mexican debt has been the politicization of international credit issues. International po-litical factors certainly played some role in developing country bor-rowing prior to the crisis. Creditor governments competed with one another through their export credit schemes (Wellons 1987) and Ger-many and Japan were able to coordinate commercial bank lending to further foreign policy goals in some cases (Spindler 1984). On the whole, however, loan negotiations were typical of those characterizing any market transaction.

Although the Reagan administration initially hoped to maintain a distance from the negotiations between debtors, banks, and the IMF that has characterized the post-crisis period, concerns about the stability of the international financial system impelled treasury and central bank officials from all of the creditor countries to become actively involved. In the case of certain strategically important countries, such as Mexico, Turkey, the Philippines, Egypt, and, in a different way, Poland, traditional foreign policy concerns also came into play, just as they had in previous international financial crises (Fishlow 1986; Lindert and Morton, chap. 2 this volume; Eichengreen, chap. 3 this volume).

Notwithstanding calls for more comprehensive solutions, rescheduling remained the central mechanism for managing the debt crisis through 1987. International credit flows to developing countries could therefore be analyzed in a bargaining framework (Krugman, chap. 7 this volume). Despite some marginal innovations, three features of the international bargaining structure remained more or less constant. First was the assumption—or the fiction—that all obligations would be met in full. Relief was not on the agenda, despite the development of a secondary market in which developing country debt traded at fairly deep discounts. Second was the assumption that the burden of policy changes should fall primarily on the debtors rather than the creditors. Developing countries failed in their political efforts to link the debt issue with developed country fiscal and trade policies, interest-rate management, or the reform of international commodity trade, and had very uneven success in securing additional concessional aid flows. Finally, all negotiations were handled on a case-by-case basis. Each debtor confronted its creditors alone, rather than in collaboration with other debtor countries facing similar problems. Whatever practical arguments could be advanced in favor of this system over a more comprehensive one—and there were many (Cooper 1986)—it was clearly a bargaining structure that tended *eo ipso* to favor the creditors.

Within this structure, debtor governments have had three sets of resources they could draw on to improve the terms of their negotiations with creditors: size, political significance for creditor security calculations, and access to nonconditional resources.

Size

Following Keynes's familiar adage that big debts become the creditor's problem, we would expect large debtors to have more leverage than smaller ones. Throughout the 1980s, the two countries with the largest debt, Brazil and Mexico, have been in a position to threaten widespread disruption of the financial system. Size of the economy also matters. Compared to small open economies, the governments of large countries may perceive themselves to be in a better position to ride out the shock of credit disruption by adopting more autarkic policies. Countries such as Brazil have long domestic traditions of economic thinking based on such a nationalist logic; during times of economic crisis, they are likely to gain in intellectual currency.

To date, big debtors have received concessions on conditionality and restructuring terms that are unavailable to smaller debtors. A study of commercial reschedulings with Latin American countries by Bogdanowicz-Bindert (1985) found rescheduling packages for smaller debtors offered shorter grace and repayment periods and higher spreads and fees than those extended to Argentina, Brazil, Mexico, and Venezuela. In a study of small countries' relations with the IMF, John Williamson (1985) found evidence of some, but not marked, discrimination in standbys and Extended Fund Facility (EFF) agreements from 1977 through 1984. Williamson concluded that small countries were less likely to borrow under the EFF, were less likely to be given multi-year arrangements, and were likely to receive loans that were smaller relative to quota. On the other hand, the formula for calculating quota includes a measure of foreign trade relative to GNP and thus allows for the fact that small countries are subject to greater external vulnerability.

Larger debtors have also pioneered more unorthodox rescheduling agreements and adjustment packages. In 1985, Argentina was able to win IMF acceptance of the unorthodox price freeze and currency plan known as the Plan Austral. Mexico was the first country to receive a multi-year rescheduling agreement (MYRA) and in 1986–87 negotiated an even more unprecedented series of agreements which tied external financing to fluctuations in oil prices and growth and included an unusually low interest-rate spread over LIBOR (London interbank offer rate for dollar deposits). Both deals were concluded only after significant pressure from U.S. authorities.

A broader picture of the influence of size is provided by table 5.1, which summarizes the terms of agreements for the rescheduling of medium- and long-term bank debt reached between 1978 and September 1986. Small debtors fared worst in terms of the length of the grace period, the tenure of the loan agreement, and interest rates. The largest debtors, conversely received the best interest rates and longest loan tenures, and were second to the medium-sized debtors only in length of grace periods.[1]

Large debtors have also been more successful in securing additional forms of relief, including bridging loans, cofinancing agreements and the maintenance of trade credits. Sachs and Huizinga (1987) have found that large debtors have also been more likely to secure concerted lending agreements. Between 1983 and the third quarter of 1986, three of the four large debtors (Mexico, Argentina, and Brazil) and four of five

Table 5.1   **Average Terms of Bank Debt Reschedulings, by Group of Countries (1978–June 1985)**

	Grace Period	Maturity	Interest Rates (spread over LIBOR)
Large debtors (> $25 billion, 1 Jan. 1985)	3.25 years	11.31 years	1.41%
Medium-sized debtors ($10 to $25 billion)	4.36 years	8.28 years	1.69%
Small debtors (< $10 billion)	2.61 years	7.26 years	1.82%

Source: Watson et al. (1986).

Note: Average terms for rescheduling of medium- and long-term bank debt, both public and private. Excludes restructuring of short-term debt, arears, and terms of trade facilities. Debtors are classified on the basis of total external liabilities of banks and nonbanks to banks end-December 1985. "Large" debtors are Brazil, Mexico, Argentina, and Venezuela; "medium-sized" debtors reaching rescheduling agreements during the period are Chile, the Philippines, Yugoslavia, and Poland. LIBOR = London interbank offer rate for dollar deposits.

medium-sized debtors (Chile, the Philippines, Poland, and Yugoslavia) won concerted lending agreements. Only 7 of the 26 small debtors rescheduling during this period secured concerted lending. Agreements signed between debtors and commercial banks in 1985 and 1986 showed the continuing importance of size (World Bank 1987). Agreements were signed with 23 countries during these two years. Nine countries received new money from the commercial banks: two of the three large debtors signing agreements (Argentina and Mexico); two of the four medium-sized debtors rescheduling (the Philippines and Chile); but only five of the remaining eighteen small debtors—Costa Rica, Ivory Coast, Ecuador, Nigeria, and Panama. While Brazil did not receive new money in its agreement of July 1986, it did secure a large bridge loan that accounted for nearly one-third of all the relief granted to it. Only two other states received bridging loans, Mexico and Guyana. Larger debtors were also more successful in securing agreements for the maintenance of short-term credit. Seven countries secured such agreements in 1985 and 1986: Argentina, Brazil and the Philippines, and four of eighteen small debtors, Cuba, Ecuador, Morocco, and Panama.

The Political and Strategic Importance of Debtor Countries

Size is not the only resource that debtor governments can bring to the bargaining table. Small countries can also seek to extract concessions by exploiting the political concerns of their patrons about national or regional security. Thomas Callaghy (1984; 1987) has shown how

Zaire's President Mobutu has deftly exploited U.S. concern with Soviet gains in central and southern Africa to extract concessional aid. A related fear is that the imposition of austerity associated with stabilization might create domestic political instability which in turn would have strategic implications. As the Senate Foreign Relations Committee staff has written, America "has important security interests in other debtor countries. . . . It can hardly afford to stand by and watch the economies of these countries collapse, or to have their governments undermined politically by financial difficulties" (cited in Cohen 1986a, 131). A third, somewhat different argument is that stabilization episodes tend to be associated with political instability, repression, or the rise of authoritarian governments (Skidmore 1977; Frenkel and O'Donnell 1979; Sheahan 1980; Díaz-Alejandro 1981; Pion-Berlin 1983). New and fragile democracies, such as the Philippines, have argued that additional support is warranted on these grounds.

It is clear that policy actions associated with stabilization and structural adjustment have lead to political violence and instability in particular cases. The policies most likely to generate spontaneous political protest are those that result in sharp changes in the prices of basic goods and services: devaluation, increases in oil prices leading to increased power and urban transportation costs, and the lifting of food subsidies. Poorly managed and ill-timed elimination of subsidies have been responsible for urban rioting in Egypt, Peru, the Dominican Republic, Morocco, Zambia, and a number of other countries. Nonetheless, it is difficult to establish any unambiguous causal relationship between stabilization and political instability, since these programs are launched in response to a variety of economic difficulties that may also plausibly be linked with political unrest (Sidell 1987). As Bienen and Gersovitz (1985) point out, food subsidies have been lifted in a number of other cases without destabilizing political protest.

A general relationship between stabilization and the emergence of authoritarian or repressive rule is difficult to establish as well, even though they appear to be linked in several specific cases, including Turkey in 1958–60, 1970–71, and 1980. A number of Latin American countries have undergone dramatic moves toward democratic rule, however, in part because the economic crisis has delegitimated military governance. The economic conditions leading to political instability and change need to be carefully specified. Is it the austerity of stabilization programs that leads to political instability and repressive solutions or, as Wallerstein (1980) argues convincingly for Brazil prior to the 1964 coup, the class conflict and polarization resulting from inflation? It is important to pose the historical counterfactual: What political difficulties are likely to arise in the *absence* of corrective measures?

Sheahan (1980) argues that those countries in Latin America *failing* to stabilize early in the postwar period were more rather than less likely to get authoritarian regimes.

The precise relationship between economic and political change may be difficult to specify, but strategic and political concerns have nonetheless led creditor governments to use their influence on the boards of the IMF and the World Bank to press for greater leniency and to lobby bank advisory groups for expeditious settlement of rescheduling negotiations (Cohen 1986b). Central banks of the Group of Five have played an important role in managing particular crises through the organization of rescue packages and the provision of bridging loans. Informal conventions have divided these international lender of last resort responsibilities along lines of regional and political influence and interest. Germany has played a leading role in Turkey and Poland, the United States in Mexico, France in Francophone Africa (Wellons 1987, chap. 7). This decentralized pattern of leadership includes the provision and orchestration of concessional assistance, which also follows lines of political interest (OECD 1987). In 1983–84, 27 percent of all U.S. official development assistance (ODA) went to Egypt and Israel. Among the other top ten recipients of American bilateral assistance were El Salvador, Costa Rica, Turkey, the Philippines, and Sudan. The top ten recipients of British and French bilateral assistance are all former colonies. Nine of the top ten recipients of Japanese ODA are in Asia, and four of the top five in the Association of Southeast Asian Nations, with which Japan maintains extensive trade and investment relations.

Turkey provides an example of how geo-strategic concerns influence official assistance. Positioned on NATO's southern flank, Turkey's political significance to the Western alliance grew in the wake of the Iranian revolution. Domestic political violence in the late seventies enhanced Western concern. Between mid-1977 and 1982, Turkey was effectively cut off from international capital markets. Celasun and Rodrik (see the country studies for this project) show that the net transfers to Turkey in the period following her debt crisis were much more substantial than were the corresponding transfers to the other debtors after 1982, however. Of $9.8 billion of debt that Turkey has restructured since 1978, $5.5 billion has been negotiated through a consortium of OECD governments. Although the OECD did link its 1979 offer of concessional finance to acceptance of an IMF program, the amount of additional assistance totaled $3 billion over the next three years. The OECD commitments were followed by unusual levels of assistance from the World Bank and the IMF. These included five consecutive structural adjustment loans totaling $1.6 billion, the largest number of such loans ever made to a single country, and a three-year standby agreement in 1980 that, together with previous purchases, brought total IMF commitments to 870 percent of quota, the largest multiple awarded to any country up until that time.

In the case of Mexico, it is difficult to disentangle the effects of size and political significance. Nonetheless, the U.S. response to Mexico's difficulties was more rapid and comprehensive than its response to the problems of other large debtors, and was linked to concerns about security and Mexico's political stability (Leeds and Thompson 1987). Within a 48-hour period, the United States pieced together a rescue package that included prepayment of $1 billion for Mexican oil sales to the Strategic Petroleum Reserve and a peso-dollar swap arranged through the U.S. Department of Agriculture. U.S. Federal Reserve officials persuaded the central banks of other creditor countries to provide a bridge loan under the auspices of the Bank for International Settlements and acted as a third party in facilitating the negotiations between Mexico and the IMF and its commercial bank creditors (Kraft 1984).

Creditor government involvement in rescheduling has been even more direct with the low-income countries who rely heavily on concessional finance and official borrowing. While the debt crisis is generally associated with commercial bank debt, twice as many LDCs classified as "official borrowers" as "market borrowers" have experienced debt servicing difficulties (IMF 1987).[2] Of 185 multilateral debt agreements signed between 1980 and 1986, 97 were with commercial banks and 88, or 48 percent were with official creditors. In 1985 and 1986, by contrast, 39 of 68 agreements signed, or 57 percent, were with official creditors (World Bank 1987, appendix 2). As a result, Paris Club members are under increasing pressure to consider official relief for low-income aid recipients, many of which are concentrated in Africa.

Temptation: The Availability of Nonconditional Resources

Since the bargaining power of the creditors rests on the debtor's need for continued funding, access to alternative sources of finance will tilt the balance of bargaining power toward the debtor. The availability of additional resources will make a country less willing to accept IMF conditionality and more likely to experiment with heterodox policy alternatives. In general, such windfalls have proved mixed blessings (Amuzegar 1982; 1983). The reasons are not only economic, but have to do with the political correlate to the Dutch disease that might be called the "Nigerian disease." This phenomenon helps explain the problems of the capital-importing oil exporters Venezuela, Nigeria, Ecuador, Mexico, and Indonesia prior to the Pertamina crisis.

The stylized facts are as follows. Commodity booms make governments more dependent on commodity-based revenue because of the relative political ease of taxing commodity exports as opposed to income, particularly in cases, such as oil, where the commodity is directly controlled by the government. In addition, the income from commodity exports provides the basis for additional foreign borrowing. This double windfall has three political consequences. First, it reduces the political incentives to undertake any adjustments that have distributional consequences; difficult decisions are deferred. Second, it increases the range of political claims on state-controlled resources, not only from rent- and revenue-seeking groups in society, but from spending and planning constituencies within the government itself. Finally, the windfalls provide governments with resources that can be used for political ends, whether through corruption and the "financing" of elections, through pork-barrel projects that cement geographically defined bases of support, or through the expansion of subsidies and entitlements.

It is thus common to see increased government revenues from commodity booms mark the beginning of a cycle of increased borrowing, widening fiscal deficits and, ultimately, a return of balance of payments crises. Mexico provides an example. In 1978 when the country began to experience a boom as the result of increased oil revenues, it repaid its obligations to the IMF and abandoned the terms of a standby agreement reached in 1976. A new cycle of borrowing began, purportedly to finance investment in the oil sector itself. Voices within the government and the international financial community were urging caution by early 1982, and even before. Yet as Angel Gurría, the Mexican Finance Ministry's director of external borrowing admitted, "there was a political decision not to stop the country's growth in the middle of the year" prior to elections (*Miami Herald* 30 July 1982). Central to the fiscal problems the country faced was a rapid expansion of subsidies to food and domestic energy consumption designed to increase ruling party support among the urban working and middle classes. The Lopez Portillo administration also witnessed a dramatic growth of corruption at all levels of government.

5.2.2 Anti-systemic Options: Debtor Cartels and Repudiation

In addition to the possibility of exploiting available resources within the prevailing case-by-case bargaining regime, debtors may conceivably seek to alter the rules of the game through cooperative behavior or unilateral attempts to reduce their debt burden. What are the conditions under which such anti-systemic options might be exercised?

A number of institutional features make the barriers to collective action among the banks less formidable than those facing debtor countries, including the dominance of a relatively small group of money-center banks with large exposures and extensive correspondent relations with smaller banks (Lipson 1985). These features, as well as the bargaining structure outlined above, have made it easier for the banks to discourage a debtors' cartel by isolating and punishing recalcitrant debtors (eg., Argentina in 1983–84 or Brazil in 1987), while rewarding others, such as Mexico, for "good behavior." Given these circumstances, the debtors with real power—Brazil, Mexico, Argentina—have preferred the advantages of striking their own separate deals to the risks involved in assuming cartel leadership.

This behavior reflects a collective action dilemma. The adoption of a common front of "tough" bargaining postures among the debtors would bring relief or better terms, but this public good is likely to be underprovided because of free riding. Despite the failures of the Cartagena group of debtors to reach a collective position, the barriers to collective action among debtors should not be overestimated. First, though LDC debt is highly concentrated among a relatively few lenders, it is even more concentrated on the borrower side. The defection of one large debtor would be enough to change the system substantially, even with the assumption of free riding. There can be little doubt that the negotiations surrounding Brazil's February 1987 suspension of interest payments will have a profound effect on future reschedulings. Second, learning among debtor governments allows the concessions granted in one case to become the basis for demands by other countries even in the absence of overt collaboration. When Mexico negotiated an innovative and relatively lenient restructuring in the fall of 1986, the banks claimed that the deal was sui generis. When similar interest-rate terms—13/16% over LIBOR—were extended to Argentina in the spring of 1987, the Philippines threatened to reopen negotiations to secure these terms as well. Though the banks insisted that it would not reopen talks with the Philippines, and the quest was eventually dropped, fear of such contagion is one reason why there has been a general reluctance on the part of the banks to discuss forgiveness or interest-rate capitalization.

Until recently, the threat of exclusion from access to future financing, including not only long-term lending but short-term trade credits, was held to be a powerful deterrent against repudiation by individual debtors (Eaton and Gersovitz 1981; Eaton and Taylor 1986, 221–28). A growing number of countries have unilaterally suspended debt payments or announced ceilings on repayments, however, often linked to overall export earnings.

There are a number of reasons why countries may repudiate. In some cases, "repudiation" occurs gradually, growing out of the accumulation of arrearages that become so large they are difficult to cover up through "new" lending. In some cases, the provision of "new" money through concerted lending agreements is foreclosed by banking regulations that force banks to write down nonperforming debt; this has been the case for Bolivia.

Domestic political pressures can play a role in the decision to repudiate, or can at least help explain the economic conditions making such a decision more likely. Alan García's decision to limit Peru's debt service in 1985 provides the clearest case of a repudiation with domestic political roots. García had used economic policy and relations with the IMF to mobilize left opposition to the conservative Belaúnde regime prior to his election. When announcing Zaire's decision in October 1986 to limit its debt service, Mobutu noted that several other African countries had obtained softer terms after outbreaks of domestic unrest, while in Zaire, "where the people are disciplined and follow their leader in whom they have full confidence, our partners try to tighten the screw more and more" (Callaghy 1987, 18). In the case of Brazil, politically motivated policy created the conditions leading to suspension of payments. Sarney came to office as the head of a new democratic government with the advantage of large international reserves built up by his predecessor. These allowed him to pursue expansionist policies and to oversee dramatic increases in consumption and wages. These policies ultimately contributed to new payments difficulties.

Yet repudiation still presents a puzzle. If a country is capable of repudiating, it should have a threat credible enough to secure its desired level of repayment *within* the normal restructuring process. Banks should be willing to make up the difference between what a country is willing to repay and the total debt service with "new" money that will cover interest payments and thus keep the loan on the books at full face value. This outcome is also superior for the country, even if politics are taken into account, since it would result in a higher level of welfare than with repudiation and reduced access to lending. It is possible that the threat of repudiation was not held to be credible by the banks and that repudiation can thus be seen as the result of failed communication. Repudiation might also simply be a move in a more extended bargaining game rather than a final outcome. President Sarney, for example, coupled his announcement of Brazil's open-ended suspension of interest payments with conciliatory signals that the government was not adopting "an attitude of confrontation" but rather sought a comprehensive solution (*New York Times,* 21 February 1987). President Mobutu of Zaire quickly followed his announcement with a trip to Washington seeking additional concessional aid.

A final reason for repudiation, however, has to do with size, and reverses the Keynsian adage that the large debtor holds the bargaining advantage, at least if exercising the option of repudiation is seen as an advantage. While Brazil's suspension of interest payments in February 1987 provides the most dramatic example of effective repudiation, the large countries have more typically exercised the tacit *threat* of withdrawal. It has been the smaller and weaker countries that have actually exercised the option: Bolivia, Peru, Ecuador, Costa Rica, the

Dominican Republic, Honduras, the Ivory Coast, Zaire, and Zambia. Small debtors may be more tempted to "free ride," particularly in a setting where increasing numbers of other countries are doing so. Reputational reasons on the part of the banks are also a factor, however. It is less costly for banks to let small countries go into default than to capitulate to their demands for additional credits if such demands establish a precedent.

5.3   The Domestic Politics of Stabilization and Adjustment

In the international bargaining arena, where the balance of power is weighted primarily on the creditor side, the central issue has been the terms of debt service; it is assumed that repayment hinges on a range of domestic macroeconomic and structural adjustment measures. At the domestic level, the emphasis is typically reversed. External bargaining positions have been politicized, but this is because stabilization and adjustment have distributional consequences for various social groups and thus political consequences for governments in power. In this section we seek to explain the conditions under which governments will adopt orthodox stabilization measures—particularly fiscal and monetary restraint and devaluation—as opposed to some heterodox alternative, or simply no coherent program at all. This is the problem of program *design*. Second, we seek to identify the most likely constraints governments face in carrying out their intentions, the question of program *implementation* or "sustainability" (Nelson 1984a).

Since these choices have distributional implications, we begin with a consideration of the way policy decisions are influenced by the relative power of competing social groups. Widely different intellectual traditions, including Marxist, pluralist, and neoclassical political economy, all converge on the importance of interest conflicts in the formation of public policy, even if they differ on the types of groups they consider politically relevant. Such "societal" explanations, however, often ignore the institutional setting in which policy is formulated and implemented. We therefore examine three institutional variables: the type of regime, political-electoral cycles, and the strength of the administrative apparatus.

5.3.1   Economic Interests and their Representation

To simplify, interest-based explanations assume that policies are the result of exchanges between politicians and their constituents. Politicians respond to constituent demands in order to advance their personal, electoral, and ideological goals. Interest groups deploy resources in order to gain particularistic benefits, whether through lobbying, threats, the donation of funds, or the promise of votes (Olson 1982). Studies of economic policies generally define the range of relevant interests in terms of factor of production (labor vs. capital) or by sector (urban vs. rural, export-oriented vs. domestic, etc.), and deduce actor preferences from the income and distributional consequences of different policy outcomes (Bhagwati 1982). Policy choice is then explained by reference to the balance of power among competing groups or by reference to the composition or support base of the ruling coalition or party in power.

There are a number of problems in applying this approach, including how to identify the "dominant coalition" in authoritarian settings where electoral politics is not central to the design of policy. Additional complexities are created by the fact that the distributional consequences of individual policies are not always clear, can vary between the short and long run, and are usually combined in policy packages. The influence of particular measures is often difficult to gauge, even for the actors themselves. As a point of departure, however, it is useful to examine the political role of business, labor, and agriculture in the adjustment process, though as we argue, none of these sectors represent undifferentiated sets of interests.

Business-Government Relations and the Politics of Adjustment

The central problem confronting any government in its relation with the private sector is establishing a credible and predictable policy environment. Confidence in government policy is a major factor in determining time horizons and willingness to take risk, and thus affects levels of investment and capital flight. In turn, the ability of business to withhold investment provides it with a potent lever for bargaining with political authorities over economic policy. The pressure to improve the business climate will pose particular problems for leftist governments, since business demands for "reassurance" place them in an awkward position vis-à-vis their core constituencies. Leftist governments, and parties with a history of attacking business and property rights, will have difficulty in establishing credibility even if announced intentions are conciliatory.

Argentina and Korea present a sharp contrast in the ability to inspire private-sector confidence. During the 1950s and early 1960s, recurrent balance of payments pressures impelled a succession of Argentine governments, including Perón himself in 1951–52 and the popularly-elected Arturo Frondizi in 1959–60, to adopt exceptionally severe wage and credit restrictions and devaluations. These actions took place in a context of deep political divisions dating to the period of Perón's populist rule. Orthodox policy measures could reduce imports, but were unsuccessful in generating new investment in the agro-export sector, which stagnated over the 1950s and 1960s. The prices of food exports showed a rising secular trend over the period, but the standard deviation of annual fluctuation was over twice as great as the average yearly rate of improvement, reflecting turbulent political cycles (Mallon and Sourrouille 1975).

Korea's political history is not without periods of turbulence and political protest. Nonetheless, during 18 years of uninterrupted rule, Park Chung Hee constructed a political system based on close working relations with, and support for, large domestic manufacturers. Labor wielded little influence. Even during the period of democratic rule (1964–72), opposition parties were weak, and overtly leftist groups precluded from politics. Investment's share of GNP rose steadily during Park's rule, influenced by a coherent indicative planning framework that ensured large firms adequate financing for approved projects (Collins and Park, see the country studies for this project). Korean economic policy under Park was flexible and responsive to changes in the economic environment, but enjoyed a high degree of credibility among business, particularly when compared with the Rhee regime of the fifties (Jones and Sakong 1980, 137).

Though leftist governments will, in general, have more difficulty in establishing the credibility of their economic policies than rightist governments, it is not necessarily true that all segments of business will favor orthodoxy. Much depends on sectoral position and the nature of international trade and financial links. Liquid asset holders, export-oriented industries, financial interests, and larger industrial and commercial firms with access to external credit markets are more likely to benefit from traditional stabilization and structural adjustment measures. Even where they are not politically organized, liquid asset holders can exert pressure on decision makers through the threat of capital flight.

Firms with investments in specific assets, import-substituting industries, (ISIs), and companies dependent on government contracts and credit are more likely to be threatened by devaluation, budget cuts, restrictions on domestic credit, and reforms that reduce protection and government support. Where they are weak politically, firms of this sort will adjust economically or fail. In countries where such firms are prominent and can mobilize political resources through peak organizations, parties, and the media, they will challenge the imposition of fiscal and monetary austerity. Unable to flee or circumvent the adverse consequences of stabilization, they stay and fight.

Though it is empirically difficult to disentangle these conflicting sets of business interests, the responses of Argentina, Mexico, and Brazil to the stabilization issues of the 1980s are suggestive of their significance (Frieden, forthcoming). In Argentina under the ultraorthodox military governments of the 1970s, deregulation of financial markets induced large firms in the industrial sector to invest in financial activities. The legacy was highly volatile financial and foreign exchange markets that operated as a major constraint on the heterodox leanings of the Alfonsín government, encouraging a cautious approach to fiscal and monetary policy after 1985 (Kaufman 1987). In Mexico, larger industrial groups in Monterrey, Puebla, and Guadalajara, commercial enterprises and new financial institutions played a similar role to the liquid asset holders in Argentina (Maxfield 1986). Although during the 1970s, the government encouraged the growth of industrial groups with close links to the state-owned enterprise sector, the stabilization of the De la Madrid government after 1982 reflected strong pressures from more economically liberal segments of the business class, whose resources held abroad have been estimated to equal over 40 percent of the country's total external debt (Garrido and Quintana 1986, 117).

In Brazil, the São Paulo industrial elite has been a force pushing government policy in a different direction, emphasizing more expansionary credit and fiscal policies. As early as the 1950s, the São Paulo Industrial Association played a role in scuttling a series of orthodox stabilization programs. And although they grudgingly accepted the austerity program under the military government in 1964–67, they lobbied intensively for the more expansionary industrialization programs adopted after the late 1960s. In 1981–83, when balance of payments pressures again forced the military to adopt tight money policies, the industrial elite stepped up its opposition to the regime itself, helping to tip the political balance toward a transition to civilian government in 1985 (Frieden 1987). Since that time, the São Paulo elite generally backed the expansionary aspect of the government's economic policy—especially the strong impetus its Cruzado program gave to domestic demand—while clamoring strongly after 1986 for a relaxation of the anti-inflationary price freeze and resisting governmental efforts to raise interest rates and reduce the size of the growing federal deficit (Kaufman 1987). While exchange rate policy is obviously the critical variable, it is noteworthy that Brazil's capital flight between 1976 and 1985 was substantially less than that from Argentina, Mexico, and Venezuela. (Watson et. al. 1986, 142)

Support for structural adjustment measures will also vary by sector. The stance of import-substituting manufacturing interests towards export-oriented policies, for example, is likely to be ambivalent. On the one hand, industries with inherent cost advantages will benefit from new incentives. These potential beneficiaries are unlikely to be aware of their competitiveness, however, because of long-standing distortions in the system of incentives, and are thus unlikely to provide the political impetus to such reforms. Because of the import-substituting policy regime, information on market conditions and knowledge on the mechanics of production for export is likely to be scarce. In Taiwan in the late fifties, local firms responded to the slowdown in ISI by calling for the cartelization of the domestic market (Lin 1973). The political efforts of organized business in Korea in the early sixties centered on securing government support for large import-substituting projects and increased access to foreign loans (Haggard, Kim, and Moon 1987). In both cases, import-substituting firms demanded and received assistance in making the transition to production for international markets.

The longer an import-substituting policy regime is in place, the more politically difficult the transition becomes. Import-substituting policies generally begin by protecting final consumer goods, while allowing the relatively free import of capital goods. As ISI continues, however, protection is extended upstream into intermediate and capital goods industries. This broadens the coalition of industries supporting protective policies, not only by creating new protected industries but by disadvantaging producers of consumer goods forced to rely on higher-cost domestic inputs. The relevant comparison is between the industrial policies of the East Asian and Latin American newly industrializing countries. Korea and Taiwan experienced relatively short periods of import-substitution before emphasizing exports and had not committed substantial investment to intermediate and capital goods industries. Brazil and Mexico, by contrast, sought to diversify their exports only after decades of ISI policies. Such a pattern of industrial development produces strong protectionist interests, as the heated debate over Mexico's entry into the GATT in 1979 showed. The diversification of exports is therefore even more likely to be characterized by subsidies and administrative measures designed to "push out" exports by offsetting previous biases.[3] A major point of interest is whether the economic crisis of the early eighties will lead to a rearrangement of basic coalitional patterns in Latin America, as the necessity to export creates new trade-related interests.

The Role of Labor

Labor plays a critical role in stabilization and adjustment episodes, even in situations where it is the dog that does not bark. As in the case of business groups, sectoral distinctions must be taken into account since they will determine both the ability of labor to organize and its likely policy preferences. The urban informal sector has constituted a powerful constraint on policy reform in a number of countries because of the threat of rioting, but in general, those segments of the labor force that are presumed to benefit most from structural adjustment measures, including rural workers and smallholders and underemployed informal sector workers, are difficult to mobilize politically. By contrast, unionized workers in both the public and private sectors are better positioned to oppose devaluation and fiscal restraint, with their anticipated consequences for real wages and employment. These workers are also likely to be concentrated in protected industries, and oppose import liberalization or an emphasis on exports that demands more realistic wage rates. They are also likely to constitute a barrier to the privatization or rationalization of state-owned enterprises.

One might therefore expect that the level of unionization and the likelihood of adopting and sustaining orthodox stabilization and structural adjustment measures will be inversely correlated, other things being equal. It might also be expected that populist or leftist governments that rely heavily on working class support are more likely to tolerate inflation (Hibbs 1977), experiment with heterodox programs, and adopt "tough" bargaining postures, since the costs of stabilization and continued repayment are more likely to fall on their core constituents (Korpi 1983).

A growing literature on the advanced industrial states has questioned the logic underlying these presumptions, particularly the inattention to the institutional setting in which labor demands are formulated (Katzenstein 1986; Crouch 1985; Cameron 1984) and the relationship between leftist parties and unions (Jackman 1987). Cameron, for example, finds that "nations with frequent leftist governments tended to experience low unemployment and strike activity and modest increases in earnings and prices, relative to the levels and rates found in nations dominated by nonleftist governing parties" (1984, 159–60) Indeed, it has become almost a new conventional wisdom that leftist governments working closely through corporatist structures with encompassing peak labor organizations are better positioned to secure wage moderation by negotiating compensatory agreements concerning job security, retraining, or unemployment compensation. Nelson (1984a, 1984b, 1985, 1987) has shown that such compensatory packages are crucial to the success of a number of stabilization and adjustment measures in the developing world, such as the lifting of food subsidies.

Holding the economic variables likely to affect labor behavior constant, particularly levels of unemployment, we hypothesize a nonmonotonic relation between the political strength of organized labor and the challenges they are likely to pose to stabilization and adjustment initiatives. Where strategic labor sectors are weak and penetrated, the burdens of stabilization policies are easy to impose, although the economic program, and the government itself, may encounter long-term costs in terms of losses of legitimacy. Controls on wages and limits on the ability of labor to organize were features of the stabilization programs of the "bureaucratic authoritarian" governments of Brazil, Argentina, Uruguay, and Chile over the sixties and seventies (Kaufman

1979) and were components of the Turkish and Korean programs of the early eighties.

On the other hand, labor may acquiesce to restraint within the context of a stabilization program in situations where it is represented by powerful peak associations with secure positions in the political process. There are few, if any, developing countries that can match the social-corporatist arrangements of Western Europe. Nevertheless, in Mexico and Venezuela the integration of unions as components of dominant multiclass parties has mitigated labor opposition by offering labor leaders the opportunity to negotiate short-term compensation and to exercise some influence over longer-run policies.

The most immediate political challenges to stabilization are likely to emerge in intermediate situations, where unions or informal sector workers possess sufficient resources for defensive mobilization but are still vulnerable to periodic repression and lack secure access to decision making or clear rights to organize. Many populist movements in Latin America fall into this category, including those recently resurfacing in Argentina, Brazil, and Uruguay after years of military exclusion. Turkish labor activity during the seventies, Bolivian labor demands in 1984–85 and recent strikes in Korea reveal a similar pattern. One widely suggested strategy for limiting conflict with such groups during periods of attempted stabilization has been the negotiation of comprehensive social pacts, including understandings concerning wage and price policy and other issues of macroeconomic policy. Social pacts, however, have been and are likely to be difficult to conclude or sustain with movements that are decentralized, divided by internal rivalries and concerned with restoring living standards and political rights (Kaufman 1985; Bianchi 1984). Nor is it clear that relatively weak governments can deliver the necessary quid-pro-quos.

An alternative means of containing conflict, recently explored in Argentina, has been to strike agreements with workers in key industrial sectors and to live with strong criticism and opposition from other groups within the labor movement. Such opposition, of course, can be considered a normal part of political life and need not in itself jeopardize the sustainability of stabilization and adjustment policies, assuming that a democratic politics has been institutionalized and labor is willing to accept the role of a loyal opposition. The still unresolved question among the new Latin American democracies is whether the military and right-wing groups will tolerate "legitimate" labor opposition, or conversely, whether labor leaders can hold rank-and-file opposition within "tolerable" bounds.

If labor organization affects the design and implementation of stabilization programs, it is also crucial in efforts to adopt more outward-looking policies. In a series of comparative studies, Gary Fields (1984; 1985; Fields and Wan 1986) has argued that wage-setting institutions in the East Asian newly industrializing countries—Korea, Taiwan, Singapore, and Hong Kong—have favored market determination of wages, while those in a number of other small open economies, including Costa Rica, Jamaica, and Panama, have been subject to institutionalized wage setting. These institutional arrangements limit the downward flexibility of wages, with consequences for relative economic performance. The advantages of market-clearing wage rates in the developing country context are well known: the avoidance of economic inefficiencies in the allocation of labor; fuller labor utilization and lower levels of unemployment; greater equity both within the urban working class and between the urban and rural sectors; and greater ease in attracting foreign investment.

What has not been adequately underlined is that the labor movements in the East Asian success stories have been politically weak, even by developing country standards (Deyo 1987; Deyo, Haggard, and Koo 1986). Labor in Hong Kong has been weakened by waves of migration from the mainland, by splits between rival federations—one supporting the mainland, one neutral, one supporting the Kuomintang on Taiwan—and by a liberal policy governing union formation and registration that has led to the proliferation of small unions. In Singapore, a powerful labor movement and the leftist party with which it was linked were politically outmaneuvered by Lee Kuan Yew's People's Action Party (PAP) in the early sixties. PAP-affiliated unions were brought under quasi-corporatist control. Labor unions in Taiwan developed under the auspices of the ruling Kuomintang Party in the early postwar period, and are thoroughly penetrated by party cadre. Korea has had the most conflictual and openly repressive labor system of the four Asian NICs. Labor relations were liberalized following the return to democratic rule in 1964, but over the late sixties a number of economically motivated restrictions were placed on labor organization, beginning with workers in foreign-invested companies. Control of labor became more marked after the turn to authoritarian rule in 1973, and has been particularly harsh under the government of Chun Doo Hwan when a number of labor leaders have been arrested.

With the exception of Singapore, there is no evidence that controls on labor activity were instituted for the *purpose* of launching export-oriented growth. It is plausible, however, that the political weakness of the labor movements in these four countries facilitated market-oriented wage setting systems, managerial flexibility, and the maintenance of industrial peace which in turn were central to the success of export-led growth.

Agriculture and the Rural Sector

Markos Mamalakis (1969; 1971) and Michael Lipton (1977) have argued that the sectoral clashes between agriculture and industry and between countryside and city are likely to be of greater political salience in the process of economic development than the class conflict between labor and capital. This sectoral clash is of importance in the determination of trade and exchange rate policies, agricultural pricing policies, and subsidies to food consumption. The distributional consequences of these various policies are complex, but it is now clear that the policies associated with import-substitution—an overvalued exchange rate, high levels of protection to the manufacturing sector, and low or negative rates of protection to agriculture—shift income away from agriculture and mining toward services and industry, activities which, in turn, tend to be located in the cities. This observation has lead to several hypotheses about why these policies come about and are sustained. The most obvious concerns the overall balance between rural and urban interests. First developed by Michael Lipton (1977), this view is stated concisely by Sachs (1985) in a recent comparison of Latin American and East Asian growth strategies:

> The Latin American governments—whether civilian or military, right-wing or left-wing—find their most important constituents among urban workers and capitalists. For decades, the agricultural sector has been relatively weak, though certainly not powerless, almost everywhere in Latin America, with peasants only loosely organized and, with some exceptions, large-scale agricultural interests unable to hold decisive sway. Moreover, political unrest is most dangerous in the cities, so that urban interests must be bought off first in difficult periods. Interestingly, the opposite seems to be true in most of East Asia. Governments there, whether Japanese colonial rulers before World War II or nationalist governments, have felt the pressing need to win support of, or at least to appease, the rural sector (p. 550).

Sachs suggests several proxies for the balance between urban and rural interests in East Asia, including the degree of urbanization. He finds that levels of urbanization are much higher in Latin America than in East Asia, where policies have tended to be more favorable to agriculture.

A second, related argument has been developed by Gustav Ranis (1987) in drawing the same regional contrast. Ranis gives attention to the absence of large rents accruing from agriculture and natural resource exports in Korea and Taiwan when compared to the Latin American NICs. Natural resource exports allowed the Latin American NICs to maintain import-substitution longer than would otherwise be desirable. Once urban groups gained political control over these rents, they became powerful advocates of continuing ISI at the expense of agricultural and mining. Abundance of natural resources had the additional effect of making the Latin American countries vulnerable to fluctuations in their terms of trade. Thus liberalization episodes were subject to backsliding in response to changes in export earnings. The result is a stop-go pattern of liberalization in response to external shocks. In Taiwan and Korea, by contrast, there were no such rents available to finance continued ISI and thus when U.S. aid began to decline in the late fifties and early sixties, it was necessary to shift toward nontraditional exports. The absence of surpluses from agricultural exports meant that the rent-seeking aspects of economic policy that characterized the Latin American model were partly mitigated, and thus the degree of resistance to market-oriented economic policies was less.

While these arguments are broadly plausible, it is useful to introduce some caveats that draw closer attention to how agricultural interests are actually represented in the political process. As with business and labor, it is first important to draw some rough distinctions within the agicultural sector between large landholders on the one hand—whether traditional latifundia, plantations, or commercial farms—and smallholders, tenants, and landless agricultural labor on the other. In general, the second group of agricultural interests are difficult to organize, since they are poor, small, and geographically dispersed. Where they are organized, it is likely to be through the efforts of the government itself, which can exercise control through its power over credit, inputs, and marketing. Thus the degree of urbanization is not necessarily a good proxy for the power of urban as opposed to rural interests, as table 5.2 suggests. A relatively large unorganized rural sector can be politically offset by a highly organized or volatile urban popular sector, particularly where governments are weak. Levels of urbanization in African countries are quite low, comparable to those in Indonesia today or in Korea at the time of its shift toward manufactured exports, even though many of these countries have pursued policies that are strongly biased against agriculture (Bates 1981).

Conversely, it is not accurate to argue that "rural interests" are politically weak in Latin America simply because the level of urbanization is high. While it is true that agricultural producers as a whole have been disadvantaged by macroeconomic policies, large landholders have been able to use their political influence at both the local and national levels to capture particularlistic benefits for themselves, such as credit, access to inputs, irrigation, and infrastructure investments (de Janvry 1981; Grindle 1986). The political conflicts that have wracked Argentina in its postwar history have been closely related to a sectoral stalemate, even though only a very small share of the country's population is involved in agriculture. During periods of balance of payments difficulties, the need to expand exports gives export-oriented agriculture renewed power.

Table 5.2   Indicators of the Rural/Urban Balance

	Urban Population as Percentage of Total		Share of Labor Force in Agriculture (%)	
	1965	1984	1965	1980
Argentina	76	84	18	13
Bolivia	40	43	54	46
Brazil	51	72	48	31
Mexico	55	69	50	37
Indonesia	16	25	71	57
Korea	32	64	56	36
Philippines	32	39	58	52
Turkey	32	46	75	58
Low-income sub-Saharan Africa	11	21	75	58
Middle-income sub-Saharan Africa	16	28	52	50

Source: World Bank, World Development Report 1986, tables 30 and 31.

Despite the rapid growth of nontraditional exports in the Latin American NICs, in 1983 fuels, minerals and other primary commodities accounted for 59 percent of total exports in Brazil, 73 percent in Mexico, and 84 percent in Argentina.

One key political variable in determining the orientation of government policy is the extent to which smallholders, tenants, and landless labor are available for mobilization by revolutionary or opposition parties, a point made clearly in the country study on Indonesia. According to Woo and Nasution (see the country studies), Soeharto's attitude toward the exchange rate was heavily influenced by fears of the resuscitation of the Communist Party of Indonesia (Partai Kommunis Indonesia, PKI). In 1965, the PKI had more than two million members, largely landless peasants in Central and East Java where rice production had virtually stagnated for over a decade. The conflict between the government and the PKI following a failed coup in September 1965 left at least 500,000 people dead. The economic policies that followed, including a sharp devaluation, showed greater attention to the countryside than had been the case under Sukarno, even if they fell short of the redistributionist aims of the Communists. The turn to democracy in Turkey in 1950 allowed the opposition Democratic Party to mobilize support through appeals to rural interests. Democratic Party governments over the fifties sought to reverse the bias toward industrialization that had characterized economic strategy during the 1930s and 1940s. Concerns about the growth of rural insurgency have also colored the economic policy pronouncements of the Aquino administration in the Philippines.

Balance of payments constraints rather than concern with the agricultural sector appear to be the critical variable in explaining the transition to export-led growth in Korea and Taiwan. In Korea, *reducing* government credit and subsidies to agriculture was a crucial step in the stabilization required to make the transition (Haggard, Kim, and Moon 1987). Land reforms in both countries sprang from fears of rural-based insurgency, however. The Kuomintang (KMT) lost the Chinese civil war to a revolutionary communist party that built its base of support in the countryside. While no such threat was present in Taiwan, KMT leaders were heavily influenced by their experience on the mainland in the design of their development policies. The South Korean government faced rural insurgency up until the eve of the Korean War and was powerfully influenced in its land reform efforts by the sweeping reforms undertaken in North Korea.

The absence of a powerful agricultural elite may mitigate the sectoral conflict that often surrounds devaluation, but for reasons somewhat different than those suggested by Ranis. In countries otherwise as diverse as Argentina and Costa Rica, devaluation has been politically controversial precisely because it so clearly favors large landholding elites. The distributional conflict is particularly acute in Argentina, since the country's two main agricultural exports, wheat and beef, are also wage goods. Hong Kong and Singapore, of course, have no rural sectors to speak of. In Korea and Taiwan, land reform eliminated this divisive political cleavage and thus changed the politics of devaluation and agricultural pricing policies. It should be noted that both Korea and Taiwan have now followed a trajectory that is common to Japan and a number of European countries. As comparative advantage has shifted out of agriculture, the continuing political concern with rural support has led to highly protective policies.

Finally, it is not clear that the turn to import-substitution policies in Latin America was the result of the rise of urban political forces alone, even though the adoption of such policies created its own constituency over time (Kaufman 1979). Prior to the Great Depression, white-collar urban workers and industrialists identified their welfare with the expansion of the export-economy. With the exception of Mexico, there was never a serious challenge to the property of traditional elites or to their control of the agrarian and export sectors. A key factor was the Depression and World War II which resulted in dissatisfaction with the prevailing export model. But overtly "nationalist-populist" coalitions rose to power relatively infrequently in the thirties and forties. While "populist," the Cárdenas government of the thirties in Mexico depended to a much greater extent on the mobilization of rural support. The post-Depression industrialization process began under the aegis of regimes strongly influenced by the agro-export oligarchies in both Argentina and Chile. And in post-Cárdenas Mexico and the Brazilian Estado Novo (1937–45), manufacturing expanded under governments that, like the authoritarian regimes of the sixties and seventies, placed strict restrictions on the political activities of the urban popular sector.

This historical digression suggests two further observations. First, in the past, external shocks have increased returns to capital and labor in the modern manufacturing sector resulting in "natural" import substitution. Latin American ISI moved forward by a series of shocks, beginning with World War I and lasting through the supply interruptions associated with World War II. The Depression played a critical role in the evolution of Turkey's industrial policy and in Korea, Indonesia, and the Philippines, postwar balance of payments crises set the stage for the adoption of import-substituting policies. The current crisis may push countries in the opposite direction because of the need to generate exports to service their debt. On the other hand, the rise in protectionism and the general slowdown in world economic growth constitute less auspicious conditions for the launching of export-oriented policies than those facing Japan and the East Asian NICs in the fifties and sixties.

Second, caution has to be exercised in drawing too sharp a line between "rural" and "urban," or "agricultural" and "industrial" interests. In the Philippines, landed elites have integrated into financial and manufacturing activities, giving them a somewhat ambivalent set of interests vis-à-vis trade and exchange rate policy. This might help explain why the Philippines, with a relatively low level of urbanization, has pursued a development strategy more similar to the Latin American pattern.

5.3.2   The Influence of Representative Institutions and Regime Type

Identifying the interests of major actors is obviously important in understanding the politics of stabilization and structural adjustment, but as we have argued, the institutional setting can determine which interests matter politically. The major debate in the political science literature on stabilization in the last ten years has centered less on the role of competing interest groups than on the nature of the overall political regime, and in particular, the question of whether "successful" economic stabilization requires authoritarian governments or repression (Skidmore 1977; Díaz-Alejandro 1981, 1983; Pion-Berlin 1983; Kaufman 1979, 1985; Haggard 1986; Bienen and Gersovitz 1985; Remmer 1986; Sidell 1987).

There is no clear evidence that authoritarian regimes in general do any better than democracies in imposing conventional fiscal and monetary restraint. During the 1960s and 1970s, exclusionary military governments in Brazil, Argentina, and Chile did carry out extremely harsh shock packages that would not have been sustainable in less repressive systems (Kaufman 1979). But during the crisis of the 1980s, Mexico's milder one-party civilian government imposed comparable shocks and competitive electoral regimes in Costa Rica and Argentina carried out tough, if more moderate, fiscal and monetary restrictions. In addition, a number of "authoritarian" regimes, such as Haiti and Zaire, have done poorly. The few cross-national political comparisons of IMF programs that do exist, such as Remmer's (1986) study of Latin American programs and Haggard's (1986) analysis of Extended Fund Facility agreements reveal no systematic association between either democracy or dictatorship and the ability to stabilize. Broader studies that have attempted to measure the influence of democracy and authoritarianism on growth have yielded conflicting results (Marsh 1979; Dick 1974; Weede 1983; Kohli 1986).

Despite the lack of a clear empirical pattern, however, it remains plausible that the rules governing public participation and representation are important, quite apart from the nature of the coalition in power. The problem lies in the fact that the "democratic" and "authoritarian" categories are too broad to be of analytic use. Finer distinctions are required to differentiate between types of democratic and authoritarian rule and to link them more convincingly to economic outcomes.

Variation in Democratic Institutions: Plebiscitary vs.
Consultative Democracy

A number of variations in democratic institutions can influence the making of economic policy, including the strength of political parties and the differences between presidential and parliamentary rule (Rogowski 1987; Jackman 1987). As noted above in the discussion of labor, Katzenstein (1986) and others (e.g., Goldthorpe 1984) argue that adjustment in the advanced industrial states is facilitated by social-corporatist forms of interest representation in which economic policies are framed through institutionalized bargaining among state officials and centralized peak associations of business and labor. Democratic governments with more pluralistic and decentralized modes of decision making typically had greater problems in this regard.

A slightly different distinction might be made in the developing country context between "plebiscitary" and "consultative" democracies. In plebiscitary democracies, such as Peru or the Philippines, elites rely primarily on diffuse populist appeals to legitimate their authority. Policy is framed through closed-door deliberations among technocrats and other interests within the "inner circle," and while individual political leaders may develop systems of consultation with affected interest groups, they are not constrained to do so. Parties tend to be weak, vehicles for electoral mobilization rather than for the ongoing representation of interests. Although economic stabilization initiatives may have momentary success in such a framework, particularly as such a system is likely to imply a greater degree of executive discretion, they may be more difficult to sustain. On the other hand, we might expect better performance in systems that manage to strike a balance between coherent executive decision-making authority and institutionalized channels through which organized groups can articulate their interests.

An interesting example is provided by Argentina's Austral Plan of 1985–87, a relatively successful combination of orthodox fiscal and monetary restraint with more experimental attempts to control prices and institute a currency reform (Kaufman 1987). The comparatively heterodox aspects of this package reflected strong political pressures for a socially acceptable alternative to the orthodox shocks that had been a feature of military rule. At the same time, during 1986 and 1987, after several years of unsuccessful negotiations with the central leadership of the Peronist unions over a "social pact," the government adopted a new bargaining strategy that centered on negotiated wage agreements with individual Peronist unions representing key economic sectors. While the heads of the central union confederation continued to criticize and demonstrate against government measures, the new bargaining framework did much to deflect opposition to the more orthodox fiscal and monetary components of government policy. In contrast, in Brazil—which corresponds more closely to the plebiscitary pattern—a parallel program, the Plan Cruzado, collapsed in early 1987 when the government was unable or unwilling to build a broad coalition of party and union interests behind necessary demand restraint measures.

Although the Argentine story is particularly dramatic because of the country's long history of instability and zero-sum politics, it is not the only instance of effective democratic response to stabilization. In Costa Rica, a tradition of informal consultation with business and labor unions facilitated acceptance of a comparatively successful orthodox IMF program in 1982–83 (Nelson 1987). While devaluing and sharply raising taxes and public utility and state-owned oil-refinery rates, the government managed and preempted popular discontent with a combination of selective wage concessions to low-income workers and a temporary food aid program. As a class, these democratic governments may well be more effective than many authoritarian regimes, as well as "plebiscitary democracies.'' At the very least, they place some limits on the kind of policy adventurism designed for populist appeal; at best, consultation provides opportunities for persuasion, obtaining feedback and negotiating compensating agreements.

The Variety of Authoritarian Institutions: Weak vs. Strong Authoritarian States

As a first cut at classification of single-party and military authoritarian governments, it is useful to note some broad characteristics of what might be termed "strong" and "weak" authoritarian regimes, even though these characterizations lump together a number of different variables. The typical "strong" authoritarian regime would have the following features:

1. Continuity in leadership and/or relatively clear rules governing succession.
2. A political structure that insulates technocrats and economic decision-makers from societal pressures, as well as from the demands of political elites themselves. The mechanisms may be through the dominance of a single party, as in Mexico, Taiwan, and Singapore, or through military rule, as in Korea, but rests ultimately on the decision by political elites to allow technocrats the political space to operate.
3. An economic policy machinery with a minimum of capture by social groups.
4. "Corporatist" organization of interests through state-sanctioned and-controlled associations. These permit official supervision of key social groups and give government officials the capacity to control the agenda of demands.
5. A military, police, or domestic intelligence network capable of penetrating strategic social insitutions and deploying violence where "necessary."

A "weak" authoritarian state may share many of the formal characteristics of a strong one, such as prohibitions on independent political organization, and repressive or one-party or military rule. But weak systems also have these charcteristics:

1. Frequent changes in leadership through "palace coups" or factional rivalry within the ruling political elite.
2. A low degree of insulation for technocrats from the political demands of powerful social groups and the executive itself.
3. A dualistic decision-making structure in which technocrats control only a limited range of policy instruments and compete with political elites who deploy other public resources for both political and private purposes.

4. Extensive networks of patron-client, personalistic, and familial relations within the formal government structure, sustained by corruption, rent-granting, nepotism, and the discretionary allocation of governmental resources.
5. Predatory behavior by military and domestic security forces and the lack of independent, nonpenetrated organizations of social control.

"Strong" authoritarian regimes may differ as much from weak ones as from democracies in the way they implement stabilization policy. In fact, there is probably greater variation in the performance of developing authoritarian regimes than among developing country democracies, since weak authoritarian regimes are less capable or interested in controlling rent-seeking behavior than either strong authoritarian regimes or democracies.

Korea is illustrative of how the institutional capabilities of "strong" authoritarian regimes help explain the coherence of adjustment policy and the speed of its implementation (Haggard and Moon 1986). The need for stabilization and structural adjustment was recognized among an alliance of monetarist technocrats prior to Park Chung Hee's assassination in October 1979, but reform was delayed by the transition to a new government under Chun Doo Hwan. The constitution of the new Fifth Republic, designed by the military coup leaders, exhibited continuity with its predecessor: a strong executive; a weak legislature controlled by the ruling party; forceful executive support for technocratic initiatives; and various limits on the freedom of the press, assembly, and opposition activity. Seeking to distance himself from the economic difficulties that had plagued Park's last years, Chun threw his support behind the stabilization plans of the monetarists. The executive's tight control of the budgetary process allowed a dramatic reversal in the rate of increase of government spending. While expenditure grew 21.9 percent in 1981, it was zero in 1984. The high level of the budget devoted to military expenditures makes the Korean fiscal structure quite rigid. Nonetheless, the government acted against the interests of groups usually able to organize against the imposition of austerities. Food price supports were cut dramatically, various special funds used to target supports to industry were consolidated or eliminated and even the government administration itself was streamlined through the laying off of over 15,000 employees, an action unthinkable in most developing countries. The Korean government never intervened extensively in wage setting prior to the eighties. After 1981, the government relied on new and established institutional controls, including its informal penetration of the union movement, arrest of labor leaders, and restrictive trade union and new dispute settlement laws to curb labor demands.

A second example of the significance of military-imposed institutions is provided by the Turkish case (Pevsner 1984; Okyar 1983). In January 1980, the civilian government of Suleyman Demirel moved belatedly to develop a stabilization and structural adjustment plan. Efforts at implementation took place against a backdrop of parliamentary stalemate, politically-mobilized labor opposition, and escalating violence. In September, the military intervened and enjoyed a high level of public confidence because of its ability to control violence and its reputation, from previous interventions, of disinterest in long rule. Parliament was dissolved and, in general, the military moved to depoliticize society through large-scale arrests and limits on the press and the freedom of interest-group and political organization. Rather than turning to a new economic team, the military retained Turgut Ozal, the principal architect of stabilization under the civilian Demirel government, and gave him new freedom to act. The military took major actions in the area of fiscal policy, including a reversal of politically motivated decisions on agricultural price supports, and developed a new set of institutions for wage settlement that significantly weakened labor's power. Strikes were banned, the major left-wing labor federation was disbanded and collective bargaining suspended. Nominal wage increases that were running in the 60 to 70 percent range prior to military intervention dropped to around 25 percent for 1981. As in Korea, the government's actions were not limited to control of labor. Other politically sensitive moves included the beginnings of reform of the tax system and the state-owned enterprise sector, the liberalization of imports and, in general, the adoption of more liberal and outward-oriented policies that had been the subject of political controversey between the parties during the 1970s.

The Philippines in the late Marcos years represents an intermediate, or "dualistic," type of government that mixed features of "strong" authoritarian rule, such as a powerful executive, weak legislature, and the insulation of economic policy making from electoral pressures, with extensive corruption and political interference by the president. The assassination of Benigno Aquino in August 1983 triggered a reassessment of the Philippines by external creditors. Following a foreign exchange crisis and the declaration of a moratorium on debt payments in October, the government came under intense pressures from the private sector, foreign banks, multilateral agencies, and the United States to initiate stabilization and structural adjustment measures. Despite this pressure, the government continued to balk at stabilization through the first half of 1984, extending large credits to financially troubled "crony" companies and borrowing heavily to "finance" the parliamentary elections of May 1984.

As the pressure on Marcos grew from the IMF and external creditors, the technocrats were granted the leeway to pursue policies destined to have a high political cost, particularly the dramatic stabilization program based on the issue of high-yielding treasury bills. On the other hand, a number of structural adjustment measures were actively resisted. The most important of these was the restoration of market forces in the sugar, coconut, and grains sectors. Though the mechanisms differed slightly in each case, all three industries had come under state or state-sanctioned monopoly control. These monopolies, in turn, were in the hands of close political allies of Marcos who provided political funds and organized regional and sectoral bases of support (Hawes 1987). The failure to move forward with reform of this sector was the critical factor leading to the suspension of IMF drawings in October 1985. The study of Indonesia by Woo and Nasution (see the country studies) suggests a broadly similar political structure, combining islands of technocratic rationality and administrative competence with clientelism, executive intervention, and institutionalized corruption.

For a number of small, poor developing countries, the nature of "authoritarianism" is in no way conducive to implementing stabilization and adjustment measures; indeed, the question must be seriously entertained whether such countries are capable of formulating, implementing, and sustaining *any* coherent economic strategy. In poor, ethnically fragmented societies, such as many of the small sub-Saharan states, political authority is maintained by patron-client relations. The highly personalistic, even familial autocracies such as those in Zaire (Callaghy 1984) or Haiti under the Duvaliers are the clearest examples, but the class of such cases is more extensive. While Bolivia saw an alternation of constitutional and military rule between 1978 and 1982, these formal features of governance were less important than the endemic instability of ruling coalitions and the dense networks of patronage that linked political elites, the bureaucracy, and state-owned enterprises and client groups. As Malloy argues, legal and political institutions were "seen not as ways of doing things but as obstructions to any action" (Malloy and Gamarra 1987, 117). Such countries have histories of failed IMF programs that founder on the inability of outside agencies to induce a rationalization of central government finances, even, in the case of Zaire, where recourse was had to the 19th century solution of installing expatriate teams in strategic economic policy posts (Callaghy 1984). Since the maintenance of political power in such systems rests on discretionary access to state funds and instrumental ties with key regional, bureaucratic, or ethnic elites, the rationalization of public finances is immediately irrational in a political sense.

The problem is not simply one of "corruption"; many countries, including Korea, have grown rapidly with some corruption, though the levels do not approach the drain on resources visible in Zaire, Haiti, or the Philippines under Marcos. The problem is the deeper one of lack of political institutions capable of channeling and containing demands and weak administrative capacity. Under extreme external pressure or absolutely forcing domestic economic developments, such countries may institute surprising reforms, such as Zaire's dramatic devaluation of 1982. Nonetheless, in the absence of political and administrative development, the ability to sustain such reforms or to implement the type of structural adjustment required to get on a higher growth path is open to serious doubt.

5.3.3 Political Cycles

The analysis of the overall balance of interest groups and the nature of the political regime are useful for underlining some broad cross-national variations in policy patterns. Within nations, however, policies are affected by short-term shifts in the political context that condition the expectations of key actors and shape opportunities for mobilizing support for new policy initiatives. A large literature on the political business cycle has argued that regardless of the party in power, economic policy will change over the electoral cycle (Nordhaus 1975; Lindbeck 1976; Tufte 1978). While these arguments have been criticized on both empirical and theoretical grounds, they focus attention on a critical variable: the time horizons of governments. It seems plausible that incumbent governments will grow increasingly reluctant to impose unpopular measures as their tenure in office becomes shorter and/or less secure. Conversely, they will be more prone to take short-term political risks if they perceive they will be around to reap the projected political gains later on.

To make such arguments relevant to developing countries, however, it is necessary to consider not only changes of elected governments but noninstitutional changes of regime. Military intervention or the transition to authoritarian one-party rule has occured in the postwar period in all of the cases included in this project except Mexico (see table 5.3). During the 1980s, this trend was reversed: Argentina, Brazil, Bolivia, the Philippines, Turkey, and Korea have made, or are making, transitions to democratic rule. We thus explore the political cycle hypothesis in two developing country contexts: in those where constitutional changes of government have been comparatively routine and stable, and those where the security of incumbents is less securely institutionalized.

Electoral Cycles in Constitutional Systems

There are several variants of the political business cycle model, but all rest on several basic assumptions: that governments seek to maximize their electoral chances; that voting behavior is driven by short-run economic conditions, particularly levels of unemployment; and that

Table 5.3   **Changes in Government, 1970 to Present, Select Countries**

Country/Date	Head of Government	Form of Government
Argentina		
6/1966–6/1970	Juan Carlos Onganía (deposed)	Military
6/1970–3/1971	Roberto Levingston (deposed)	Military
3/1971–5/1973	Alejandro Lanosse	Military (transitional)
5/1973–8/1973	Héctor Cámpora	Directly elected
8/1973–7/1974	Juan Perón	Directly elected
7/1974–3/1976	Isabel Perón (deposed)	Succeeded Juan Perón on his death
3/1976–3/1981	Jorge A. Videla	Military
3/1981–12/1981	Roberto Viola	Military
12/1981–12/1983	Reynaldo Bignone	Military (transitional)
12/1983–	Raúl Alfonsín	Directly elected
Bolivia		
9/1969–10/1970	Ovando Candia (deposed)	Military
10/1970–8/1971	Juan José Torres (deposed)	Military
8/1971–7/1978	Hugo Bánzer Suárez	Military-civilian (1971–1973); military (1973–1978)
7/1978–11/1978	Juan Pereda Asbún (deposed)	Directly elected
11/1978–8/1979	David Padilla	Military (transitional)
8/1979–11/1979	Wálter Guevara Arze (deposed)	Civilian-interim
11/1979	Natusch Busch	Military
11/1979–6/1980	Lydia Gueiler (deposed)	Civilian-interim
6/1980–8/1981	Luis García Mesa (deposed)	Military
8/1981–9/1981		Military junta
9/1981–7/1982	Celso Torrelio Villa (deposed)	Military
7/1982–10/1982	Guido Vildoso Calderon	Military (transitional)
10/1982–8/1985	Hernán Siles Zuazo	Indirectly elected
8/1985–	Paz Estenssoro	Directly elected
Brazil		
10/1969–3/1974	Emilio Garrastazu Medici	Military
3/1974–3/1979	Ernesto Geisel	Military
3/1979–3/1985	João Baptista Figueiredo	Military
3/1985	José Sarney	Indirectly elected[a]
Mexico		
12/1970–12/1976	Luis Echeverría	Directly elected, dominant party system
12/1976–12/1982	José Lopez Portillo	Directly elected
12/1982–	Miguel De la Madrid	Directly elected
Indonesia		
3/1966–	General Soeharto	Dominant party system

Table 5.3   (continued)

Country/Date	Head of Government	Form of Government
Korea		
1964–10/1972	Park Chung Hee	Directly elected
10/1972–10/1979	Park Chung Hee	Authoritarian
10/1979–5/1980	Choi Kyu Hah	Civilian-interim
5/1980–2/1981	Chun Doo Hwan	Military
2/1981–	Chun Doo Hwan	Indirectly elected, authoritarian
Philippines		
9/1972–1/1981	Ferdinand Marcos	Martial law rule
1/1981–2/1986	Ferdinand Marcos	Directly elected, dominant party system
2/1986–	Corazon Aquino	Directly elected, took office following revolution
Turkey		
10/1969–3/1971	Suleyman Demirel	Directly elected
3/1971–7/1974		Military-civilian interim governments
7/1974–9/1974	Bulent Ecevit	Directly elected
9/1974–4/1975	Sadi Irmak	Civilian interim
4/1975–1/1978	Suleyman Demirel	Directly elected
1/1978–10/1979	Bulent Ecevit	Directly elected
10/1979–9/1980	Suleyman Demirel	Directly elected
9/1980–11/1983	Kenan Evren	Military
11/1983–	Turgut Ozal	Directly elected

[a]Sarney was chosen vice-president, and assumed the presidency on the death of the presidential candidate, Tancredo Neves.

governments can manipulate the economy to enhance their electoral chances. According to the model developed by Nordhaus (1975), for example, governments will choose combinations of inflation and unemployment on the short-run Phillips curve that are optimal with reference to the popular vote function, even if they involve a heavy discount for future inflation. In the context of stabilization episodes, governments facing electoral contests would therefore be more likely to resist orthodox measures and to seek heterodox alternatives.

The empirical evidence for a political business cycle is extremely weak for the advanced industrial states (Alt and Chrystal 1983, chap. 5). Brian Barry has also forcefully challenged the analytic underpinnings of the model, arguing it assumes "a collection of rogues competing for the favors of a larger collection of dupes" (Barry 1985, 300). Many of the political and institutional characteristics of the advanced industrial states that mitigate the political business cycle are absent in the developing country context, however. These include, among other things, more informed publics, more independent media coverage of economic policy, more institutionalized forms of consultation which lengthen the time horizons of affected social groups, and extensive welfare systems that cushion the costs of unemployment. Given generally lower levels of income and extensive poverty, electoral support in the developing world might plausibly be linked to the government's ability to deliver short-term material benefits.

These hypotheses can be explored in two ways. One is to focus directly on the politics of stabilization. The political business cycle hypothesis would lead one to expect strong pressures on decision makers from members of the party in power facing electoral contests. Regardless of initial ideological predilections, this has the effect of splitting governments into pro- and antistabilization factions. In Jamaica under the leftist Manley, where there was little faith in IMF programs in the first place, there is evidence that populist factions within the government party sought to advance their agenda by aggressively politicizing the IMF issue (Stephens and Stephens 1986). In Sri Lanka, by contrast, where a conservative government under J. R. Jayardene launched wide-ranging reforms after 1977, battles between the party in parliament and the more conservative Finance Ministry are also visible (Haggard 1986). Similarly, as Korea has moved toward electoral politics, government party legislators have been forced to respond to the opposition by taking positions critical of unpopular government initiatives, such as import-liberalization (Haggard and Moon 1986).

The electoral cycle hypothesis can also be analyzed by observing the government's macroeconomic policy behavior. Barry Ames's (1987) research on Latin American fiscal policy from 1945 to 1980 finds strong evidence of electoral cycles. When an election approached, expenditures rose as a way of reassuring followers and attracting new ones. When the election passed, expenditures continued to rise if a new leader or party was elected.

The Mexican experience over the last twenty years provides the clearest example of a political business cycle. Despite the continuity of one-party rule, elections are seen by Mexican political officials as playing an important function in legitimating the political system. In each of the last three changes of administration (1970, 1976, and 1982), expansionary fiscal and monetary policies coinciding with elections generated subsequent inflationary and balance of payments pressures. Stabilization initiatives followed during the initial years of each new administrative term, generally leading to reductions in inflation rates and current account deficits, that were then followed in 1975–76 and 1981–83 by a new round of inflationary and balance of payments pressures. The balance of payments crisis of 1970 in the Philippines has also been attributed to election year spending (Dohner and Intal, see the country studies).

If the period prior to elections is likely to be characterized by expansionary policies and resistance to stabilization, the periods following elections will allow governments more leeway to introduce reforms. Certain factors are likely to expand the room for maneuver of newly elected governments beyond the temporary deliverance from the pressure of electoral contest. First, is the nature of the previous government's policies. The greater the perception and reality of failure, the greater the space for innovation and reform. This helps explain the dramatic initiatives undertaken in Bolivia under the Paz Estenssoro government in September 1985. Second, the government gains where electoral opposition is weak and divided. This is not only true because it provides the legislative space to launch initiatives, but because it is likely to be correlated with a weak ability of the opposition to galvanize action outside of the legislature, such as through strikes, that would undermine stabilization and adjustment efforts.

Unstable Democracies and Transitions to and from Authoritarian Rule

As table 5.3 suggests, the majority of stabilization efforts have come in situations where the tenure of incumbent governments, whether authoritarian or democratic, is highly uncertain. This uncertainty surrounding the fundamental rules of the political game affects politicians' time horizons and policy choices.

The principal challenge facing the leaders of new governments in unconsolidated democracies is typically to sustain the mass support that had previously been built up during the challenge to the outgoing dictatorships. Since the shift from authoritarianism to democracy raises hopes for an improvement in welfare as well as political freedom, newly elected leaders face expectations that are not conducive to the imposition of austerity. On the contrary, whereas new administrations in stable electoral systems may choose to pay the short-term costs of stabilization early in their terms, the leaders of unconsolidated democracies may turn to economic populism as a means of cementing both electoral support and, where there is a lingering threat from antidemocratic forces, broader societal support for the democratic project itself. The new administrations of Alfonsín in Argentina, Sarney in Brazil, and the succession of civilian governments in Turkey after the return to democracy in 1973, and again after 1983, behaved in precisely this way. The return to democracy in Bolivia under the Siles government in 1982 was not followed by large increases in public spending, but as Morales and Sachs (see the country studies) point out, the new-left coalition government was unable to reduce the deficits it inherited from earlier governments. This pattern holds for earlier periods as well.

In Argentina, for example, Frondizi (in 1958), Illia (in 1964), and the Peronists themselves (in 1973), all entered office after periods of military dictatorship with wage increases and expansionist economic programs aimed at accelerating growth.

A new phase in the cycle is reached as such projects encounter constraints and governments are forced to turn toward orthodoxy. During the 1950s Perón and Frondizi imposed two of the harshest and most orthodox stabilization programs in Argentine history. Menderes formulated a wide-ranging stabilization program in Turkey in 1958 after years of expansionist policies. Alfonsín began to change policy course late in 1984, while the populist Bernardo Grinspun was still finance minister. The Austral package of 1985, despite its heterodox price control features, continued in quite conservative fiscal and monetary directions throughout most of 1986–87. In early 1987, after several years of rapid economic expansion, the Sarney government faced similar external accounts pressures, and although one component of the response was a moratorium on external debt payments, the government also appeared to be preparing to adopt a tougher stabilization package at home under the leadership of a new finance minister, Bresser Pereira. These episodes suggest the following stylized cyclical pattern for new democracies: expansion, followed by balance of payments problems, followed by attempts to impose relatively orthodox stabilization packages.

New authoritarian regimes appear to follow the opposite path. There are examples of populist military governments: Bolivia in 1970–71, the Peruvian experiment of the early seventies, and the first year of Korea's military rule in 1961–62. Typically, however, the military seizes power in the midst of political crises that have economic correlates, and the policies pursued in the initial years in office reflect commitments to impose "discipline" and "rationalize" the economic system, in part by politically limiting the demands of leftist and labor groups. This was the general pattern, through under different constraints, in Brazil (1964), Argentina (1966 and 1976), Turkey (1971 and 1980), Indonesia (1966), Bolivia (1971), and Korea (1980–81), as well as in Chile and Uruguay in the mid-1970s. As the initial crisis is brought under control, however, authoritarian regimes begin to face new problems of political consolidation or transition (Ames 1987, chap. 5). At this point, they come under strong pressure to pursue more growth-oriented policies, if not to build support, then at least to fend off or moderate the militancy of the opposition. Brazil's externally financed industrial expansion of the 1970s provides one striking example. The decisions to pursue high-growth policies through the oil shocks coincided almost exactly with decisions taken by the military regime concerning the "decompression" of the political system by gradually expanding opportunities for electoral competition and pluralistic politics. The transition from martial law in the Philippines (announced in December 1981) was followed by local and parliamentary elections in 1982 and 1984 that were accompanied by sharp expansions in the money supply. The military regimes exiting from Argentina in 1970–73 and 1980–83 did so under much more chaotic and unplanned circumstances. Yet both felt it imperative to step away from the economic orthodoxy of the early years of the regime and to adopt policies considered more favorable to the Peronist unions and local manufacturing groups. Thus, while governments in unconsolidated democracies expand then stabilize, their authoritarian counterparts stabilize then expand. In the aggregate, economic performance may look similar for democratic and authoritarian regimes, as Remmer (1986) argues, but these averages conceal differences in the underlying dynamics and timing of policy choices.

5.3.4 The Bureaucracy: Adminstrative Capacity and the State as Interest Group

The foregoing discussion has focused on political competition among interest groups, politicians, and parties. It is clear, however, that characteristics of the bureaucracy and bureaucratic politics are also important for understanding the ability of governments to manage stabilization crises. This is true for two reasons. First, the administrative capacity of the government affects its ability to carry out coherent economic policy. This is particularly true of those structural adjustment measures which demand complex organizational support to be effective. The attention given to "policy reform" among economists is rarely matched by adequate attention to the administrative requirements of successful policy implementation. But the bureaucracy is important for a second reason. In many developing countries, whether democratic or authoritarian, public employees constitute an extremely powerful political force. In a number of low-income developing countries, they *are* the "urban interest." A number of policies associated with stabilization and structural adjustment, including fiscal and wage restraint and the privatization of state-owned enterprises, pose direct challenges to the interests of public employees.

Administrative capacity is affected by several interrelated aspects of staffing and organization. The most basic factor is the existence of institutional mechanisms for training technocratic personnel and recruiting them into pivotal decision-making positions. Such mechanisms are well developed in Korea, where technocratic teams with fairly unified economic ideologies have controlled a highly centralized economic decision-making apparatus over a long period of time. They are less developed in countries like Bolivia, Haiti, and a number of low-income African and Caribbean states where the level of technical expertise is generally low or where trained technicians face overwhelming political constraints in their efforts to influence the policy agenda. In between lie a number of cases where the overall level of technical expertise is high, but where economic decision-making authority is fragmented among ministries representing competing ideological visions or political constituents. This was true for the Lopez Portillo administration in Mexico, under Soeharto in Indonesia, and in Turkey over the late 1970s. Elsewhere, technocrats have been circumvented by interventionist executives, as was true in the late Marcos years in the Philippines. While it is very difficult to generalize about these intrabureaucratic conflicts, it is a truism to say that they have a powerful influence on the design and implementation of economic programs. The politics of stabilization and structural adjustment is also a form of bureaucratic politics.

Procedures for monitoring economic variables, including the accumulation of debt itself, are one revealing indicator of the administrative capacity of developing country bureaucracies. The studies for the project suggest repeatedly that even in relatively developed countries, major gaps existed prior to the debt crisis in governments' knowledge of the extent of debt accumulation. In Mexico, there was a sophisticated system for monitoring public, but not private, debt and in Argentina the crisis was clearly exacerbated by lack of clear information.

States also vary in the organizational resources and range of policy instruments available to implement the more selective forms of economic intervention associated with some structural adjustment measures. These include promoting technological research, facilitating adjustments in labor supply or shifting resources expeditiously into the export sector. Korea's transition to export-led growth provides an important, and often misunderstood, example (Haggard, Kim, and Moon 1987). The dominant neoclassical explanation of this transition holds that it was the result of reforms in the structure of incentives, including primarily a liberalization of imports and a devaluation of the exchange rate. While these reforms were no doubt important, they were accompanied by a range of supportive interventions, including highly subsidized credit from the state-owned banking sector. But the government also developed a sophisticated *organization* for providing market information, assisting firms in developing new products, forging links with foreign buyers, and monitoring export behavior, in some cases down to the level of the individual firm. In addition, the transition to export-led growth was preceded by fundamental institutional changes in the structure of economic decision making. Under President Syngman Rhee (1948–61), business-government relations were characterized by pervasive rent seeking and corruption, with the result that reformist technocrats within the burearcracy were politically marginalized. Under military rule (1961–63), old networks of political influence were broken and new power invested in a highly centralized and autonomous Economic Planning Board. Technocrats gained new access to political elites. New organizations were also developed to allow business to communicate with government over their policy needs, such as monthly export meetings attended by the president himself. In sum, the transition entailed not only policy reforms but institutional innovation as well.

The issue is not simply whether the state has appropriate information and policy instruments at its disposal. The bureaucracy must also be seen as a political actor. The case studies show repeatedly that individual government units and corporations made foreign exchange commitments without the approval of ministers of finance or central banks, even though such commitments became central government liabilities. The behavior of the state-owned enterprise sector was crucial to understanding the debt crises in all the countries included in this project. Some of these enterprises, such as Mexico's PEMEX or Indonesia's Pertamina, represent political constituents in their own right; the managers who head them are more powerful than the ministers who are nominally responsible for overseeing their behavior. As is now well known, state-owned enterprises have assumed a host of political functions, including the transfer of subsidies to consumers, the provision of employment, and in Indonesia, the generation of revenue to finance the military. Over time, domestic suppliers and purchasers of the outputs of state-owned enterprises also develop strong interests in their procurement, and pricing policies can be used to favor selected client groups. Where public sector workers are unionized, they place additional constraints on the government's freedom of maneuver. New studies suggest that the main political barriers to privatization are likely to reside within the state apparatus itself (Vernon, forthcoming).

While it should be clear that bureaucratic capabilities matter, two somewhat contradictory caveats are required. First, the ability of bureaucracies to act, even highly competent ones, is dependent on the larger balance of forces within the political system as a whole. In Mexico during recent decades the technocratic influence of the treasury and central bank has changed directly with the broader political strategy of successive presidential terms. The treasury and central bank dominated economic policy making in the 1950s and 1960s, but their power declined dramatically under Luis Echeverría (1970–76), and to some extent, under Lopez Portillo (1976–82) before being restored to a pivotal decision-making role under De la Madrid (1982–88). Similar stories could be told about Indonesia and the Philippines, where the freedom of the technocrats to act independently was ultimately determined by powerful presidents.

The second, partially contradictory caveat concerns the possibility of "overcapacity"—rigidities that result from the persistence of organizational routines that impede, rather than facilitate adjustment. The dogmatic course pursued by entrenched laisser-faire technocrats in Argentina and Chile provides one possible example of this in the late 1970s. The central policy debate in Korea, Taiwan, and Singapore in the early eighties has been over the degree to which government should continue to guide the process of industrial innovation (Cheng and Haggard 1987). All three possess strong dirigiste traditions, some elements of which may now present barriers to more rapid growth.

5.4 Conclusion: Politics and Policy

Before suggesting some conclusions, it is important to underline an important limitation on political analysis. Prescriptive policy analysis has as its purpose the identification of policies that are optimal given some criteria such as efficiency or growth. Positive political analysis, by contrast, often takes the form of suggesting why certain economically optimal policies are unlikely to be adopted, or are likely to be distorted in implementation. If economists often tend toward voluntarism, in which political contraints are explained by lack of "will," political scientists can be overly deterministic. The challenge for a prescriptive policy analysis that incorporates political variables is to identify those variables which are manipulable and those which are not. This task is by no means easy; what constitutes a constraint in one political system may be overcome through astute political leadership and persuasion in another.

It may appear that the most unmanipulable variable in the policy equation is the overall balance of interest groups. We suggested some conditions under which the interests of business, labor, and urban groups were likely to cut against orthodox stabilization measures, or even to undermine the integrity of more heterodox ones. But interests are not, in fact, fixed. Actors are not necessarily aware of their interests in a particular policy issue, and may be myopic with reference to the longer-term consequences of their own preferences. Some policies, such as taxation, are immediately visible in their effects. The distributional consequences of others, such as exchange rate management or trade policy, are less visible. If we begin with the critical assumption that stabilization and adjustment are not just technical exercises, but demand the building of coalitions of support, it is crucial that potential beneficiaries be identified and persuaded of their interest in the success of the programs. This is true regardless of the substantive design of the program. Research on the distributional consequences of stabilization programs is not only important to identify who gains and loses economically, but to identify relevant political actors.

Regime type also seems a variable that is not manipulable. Within the broad categories of "democratic" and "authoritarian" regimes, we have suggested that consultative mechanisms may assist in reaching consensus on program goals, but studies by political scientists have shown that the nature of these mechanisms—who is included and excluded and on what terms—can themselves be the source of intense political fights (Bianchi 1984). Administrative development is, at least over the longer run, a variable which is subject to manipulation, including by outside actors. In general, it seems that the multilateral institutions have focused too much attention on discrete policy reforms, and not enough on designing the institutions and training the personnel that will be able to implement them over the longer run. Exercising outside influence demands strengthening the hands of reformers within the government.

It is not clear, however, how far outside agents can, or should go in urging changes in the political and administrative structures of target countries. If the charge of interference in economic policy is a common stumbling block to effective programs, the charge of interference in domestic politics is likely to be even more damning. A second reservation is that dissimilar political systems will require different types of policy advice; this necessarily complicates program design. In systems with a "critical mass" of technocratic expertise and with relatively well-developed administrative routines and capacities, consultative mechanisms that enhance the capability of the administration are likely to be a good. In countries where the bureaucracy is penetrated by outside political forces and the level of technical expertise is low, it may be better to advise market-oriented policies and a reduction of the state's role, not only on the grounds of economic efficiency, but on the grounds that such policies reduce opportunities for rent-seeking behavior. It is not enough, however, simply to assume that all developing countries fall in the latter category.

The greatest degree of planning freedom appears to come with reference to the timing of outside advice. We have suggested some fairly obvious generalizations about when programs are likely to succeed and fail as a result of political cycles. This suggests that in some circumstances, no program may be superior to one that is likely to raise expectations and fail. In the end, however, there is no substitute for a nuanced understanding of the particular political setting into which economic programs are introduced.

Notes

1. This was the result of two agreements, one with Mexico, one with Venezuela, which provided long maturities but no grace periods.

2. "Market borrowers" are those obtaining at least two-thirds of their external financing from commercial sources from 1978 to 1982; "official borrowers" are those obtaining less than two-thirds of their external financing from commercial sources (Watson et al. 1986).

3. An alternative solution is the creation of an export enclave, such as that along Mexico's border with the United States, which is only weakly integrated with the rest of the economy.

References

In addition to the references cited here, we have also drawn on the country studies done for this project: Juan Antonio Morales and Jeffrey Sachs, Bolivia; Eliana Cardoso and Albert Fishlow, Brazil; Rudiger Dornbusch and Juan Carlos de Pablo, Argentina; Edward Buffie, with the assistance of Allen Sangines Krause, Mexico; Wing Thye Woo and Anwar Nasution, Indonesia; Susan Collins and Won-Am Park, Korea; Merih Celâsun and Dani Rodrik, Turkey; Robert Dohner and Ponciano Intal, Jr., the Philippines.

Alt, James A., and K. Alec Chrystal. 1983. *Political economics.* Berkeley: University of California Press.

Ames, Barry. 1987. *Political survival: Politicians and public policy in Latin America.* Berkeley: University of California Press.

Amuzegar, Jahangir. 1982. Oil wealth: A very mixed blessing. *Foreign Affairs* 60, no. 4:814–35.

———. 1983. Oil exporters' economic development in an interdependent world. International Monetary Fund Occasional Paper no. 18 (October). Washington, D.C.: IMF.

Barry, Brian. 1985. Does democracy cause inflation? Political ideas of some economists. In *The Politics of inflation and economic stagnation,* ed. Leon N. Lindberg and Charles S. Maier. Washington, D.C.: The Brookings Institution.

Bates, Robert. 1981. *States and markets in tropical Africa.* Berkeley: University of California Press.

Bhagwati, Jagdish, ed. 1982. *Import competition and response.* Chicago: University of Chicago Press.

Bianchi, Robert. 1984. *Interest groups and political development in Turkey.* Princeton N.J.: Princeton University Press.

Bienen, Henry S., and Mark Gersovitz. 1985. Economic stabilization, conditionality, and political stability. *International Organization* 39, no. 4:729–54.

Bogdanowicz-Bindert, Christine A. 1985. Small debtors, big problems: The quiet crisis. Overseas Development Council Policy Focus Series 1985 no. 5. Washington, D.C.: Overseas Development Council.

Callaghy, Thomas M. 1984. *The state-society struggle: Zaire in comparative perspective.* New York: Columbia University Press.

———. 1987. Restructuring Zaire's debt. Unpublished ms., Columbia University.

Cameron, David R. 1984. Social democracy, corporatism, labor quiescence, and the representation of economic interest in advanced capitalist society. In *Order and conflict in contemporary capitalism,* ed. John H. Goldthorpe. Oxford: Clarendon Press.

Cheng, Tun-jen, and Stephan Haggard. 1987. *Newly industrializing Asia in transition.* Berkeley: Institute of International Studies.

Cohen, Benjamin. 1986a. International debt and linkage strategies: Some foreign policy implications for the United States. In *The politics of international debt,* ed. Miles Kahler. Ithaca, N.Y.: Cornell University Press.

————. 1986b. *In whose interest?: International banking and American foreign policy.* New Haven: Yale University Press.

Cooper, Richard. 1986. The lingering probem of LDC debt. In *The Marcus Wallenberg papers on international finance.* Vol. 1, no. 5. Washington D.C.: International Law Institute and School of Foreign Service, Georgetown University.

Crouch, Colin. 1985. Conditions for trade union wage restraint. In *The politics of inflation and economic stagnation,* ed. Leon N. Lindberg and Charles S. Maier. Washington, D.C.: The Brookings Institution.

de Janvry, Alain. 1981. *The agrarian question and reformism in Latin America.* Baltimore, Md.: Johns Hopkins University Press.

Deyo, Frederic. 1987. State and labor: Modes of exclusion in East Asian development. In *The political economy of the new Asian industrialism,* ed. Frederic Deyo. Ithaca, N.Y.: Cornell University Press.

Deyo, Frederic, Stephan Haggard, and Hagen Koo. 1986. Labor and development strategies in the East Asian NICs. *SSRC Items* 40: 64–68.

Díaz-Alejandro, Carlos. 1981. Southern Cone stabilization plans. In *Economic stabilization in developing countries,* ed. William Cline and Sidney Weintraub. Washington, D.C.: The Brookings Institution.

————. 1983. Open economy, closed polity? In *Latin America in the world economy: New perspectives,* ed. Diana Tussie. London: Gower.

Dick, G. William. 1974. Authoritarian versus nonauthoritarian approaches to economic development. *Journal of Political Economy* 82:817–27.

Eaton, Jonathan, and Lance Taylor. 1986. Developing country finance and debt. *Journal of Development Economics* 22: 209–65.

Eaton, Jonathan, and Mark Gersovitz. 1981. Debt with potential repudiation: Theoretical and empirical analysis. *Review of Economic Studies* 48: 289–309.

Fields, Gary S. 1984. Employment, income distribution, and economic growth in seven small open economies. *Economic Journal* 94: 74–83.

————. 1985. Industrialization and employment in Hong Kong, Korea, Singapore, and Taiwan. In *Foreign trade and investment: Economic growth in the newly industrializing Asian countries,* ed. Walter Galenson. Ithaca, N.Y.: Cornell University Press.

Fields, Gary S., and Henry Wan, Jr. 1986. Wage-setting institutions and economic growth. Unpublished ms., Cornell University.

Fishlow, Albert. 1986. Lessons from the past: Capital markets during the 19th century and interwar period. In *The politics of international debt,* ed. Miles Kahler. Ithaca, N.Y.: Cornell University Press.

Frenkel, Roberto, and Guillermo O'Donnell. 1979. The "Stabilization Programs" of the IMF and their internal impacts. In *Capitalism and the state in U.S.–Latin American relations,* ed. Richard Fagen. Stanford: Stanford University Press.

Frieden, Jeffrey. 1987. The Brazilian borrowing experience. *Latin American Research Review* 22, no. 2: 95–131.

————. n.d. Debt, development, and democracy in Latin America: Classes, sectors, and the international financial relations of Mexico, Brazil, Argentina, Venezuela and Chile. *Comparative Politics,* forthcoming.

Garrido Noguera, Celso, and Enrique Quintana López. 1986. Financial relations and economic power in Mexico. In *Government and the private sector in contemporary Mexico,* ed. Sylvia Maxfield and Ricardo Anzaldúa Montoya. San Diego: University of California, Center for U.S.–Mexican Studies.

Goldthorpe, John H., ed. 1984. *Order and conflict in contemporary capitalism.* Oxford: Clarendon Press.

Grindle, Merilee. 1986. *State and countryside: Development policy and agrarian politics in Latin America.* Baltimore Md.: Johns Hopkins University Press.

Haggard, Stephan. 1986. The politics of adjustment: Lessons from the IMF's extended fund facility. In *The politics of international debt,* ed. Miles Kahler. Ithaca, N.Y.: Cornell University Press.

———. 1988. The Philippines: Picking up after Marcos. In *The promise of privatization,* ed. Raymond Vernon. New York: Council on Foreign Relations.

Haggard, Stephan, Byung-kook Kim, and Chung-in Moon. 1987. The transition to export-led growth in Korea, 1954–1966. Unpublished ms., Harvard University.

Haggard, Stephan, and Chung-in Moon. 1986. State power and industrial change: The politics of stabilization and structural adjustment in Korea. Paper presented to the American Political Science Association Conference, 27 August–1 September.

Hawes, Gary. 1987. *The Philippine state and the Marcos regime: The politics of export.* Ithaca N.Y.: Cornell University Press.

Hibbs, Douglas. 1977. Political parties and macroeconomic policy. *American Political Science Review* 71: 1467–87.

International Monetary Fund. 1987. Implementing the debt strategy: Current issues. Mimeo.

Jackman, Robert W. 1987. Elections and the democratic class struggle. *World Politics* 39, no. 1: 123–46.

Jaffee, Dwight, and Thomas Russel. 1976. Imperfect information, uncertainty, and credit rationing. *Quarterly Journal of Economics* 90: 651–66.

Jones, Leroy, and Il Sakong. 1980. *Government, business, and entrepreneurship in economic development: The Korean case.* Cambridge: Harvard University Press.

Katzenstein, Peter. 1986. *Small states in world markets.* Ithaca, N.Y.: Cornell University Press.

Kaufman, Robert R. 1979. Industrial change and authoritarian rule in Latin America: A concrete review of the bureaucratic-authoritarian model. In *The new authoritarianism in Latin America,* ed. David Collier. Princeton, N.J.: Princeton University Press.

———. 1985. Democratic and authoritarian responses to the debt issue: Argentina, Brazil and Mexico. 1986. In *The politics of international debt,* ed. Miles Kahler. Ithaca, N.Y.: Cornell University Press.

———. 1987. The Austral and Cruzado plans in Argentina and Brazil: The politics of stabilization in historical perspective. Paper presented to the American Political Science Association conference, 2–7 September in Chicago.

Kohli, Atul. 1986. Democracy and development. In *Development strategies reconsidered,* ed. John P. Lewis and Valeriana Kallab. New Brunswick, N.J.: Transaction Books.

Korpi, Walter. 1983. *The democratic class struggle.* London: Routledge and Kegan Paul.

Kraft, Joseph. 1984. *The Mexican rescue.* New York: Group of Thirty.

Leeds, Roger, and Gale Thompson. 1987. The 1982 Mexican debt negotiations: Response to a financial crisis. Washington, D.C.: Foreign Policy Institute, School of Advanced International Studies, Johns Hopkins University.

Lin, Ching-yuan. 1973. *Industrialization in Taiwan, 1946–1973.* New York: Praeger.

Lindbeck, Assar. 1976. Stabilization policy in open economies with endogenous politicians. *American Economic Review* 66 (May): 1–19.

Lindberg, Leon N., and Charles S. Maier, eds. 1985. *The politics of inflation and economic stagnation.* Washington, D.C.: The Brookings Institution.

Lipson, Charles. 1985. Bankers' dilemmas: Private cooperation in rescheduling sovereign debt. *World Politics* 38, no. 1: 205–25.

Lipton, Michael M. 1977. *Why poor people stay poor: A study of urban bias in world development.* London: Temple Smith.

Mallon, Richard D., and Juan V. Sourrouille. 1975. *Economic policy-making in a conflict society: The Argentine case.* Cambridge: Harvard University Press.

Malloy, James, and Eduardo A. Gamarra. 1987. The transition to democracy in Bolivia. In *Authoritarians and democrats: Regime transition in Latin America,* ed. James Malloy and Mitchell A. Seligson. Pittsburgh, Pa.: University of Pittsburgh Press.

Mamalakis, Markos J. 1969. The theory of sectoral clashes. *Latin American Research Review* 4: 9–47.

———. 1971. The theory of sectoral clashes and coalitions revisited. *Latin American Research Review* 6(3): 89–127.

Marsh, Robert. 1979, Does democracy hinder economic development in the latecomer developing nations? *Comparative Social Research* 2: 215–49.

Maxfield, Sylvia. 1986. The internationalization of finance and macroeconomic management: Mexico and Brazil compared. Paper presented to the American Political Science Association conference, 27 August–1 September.

Nelson, Joan. 1984a. The political economy of stabilization: Commitment, capacity, and public response. *World Development* 12, no. 10 (October): 983–1006.

———. 1984b. The politics of stabilization. In *Adjustment crisis in the Third World,* ed. Richard Feinberg and Valeriana Kallab. New Brunswick, N.J.: Transaction Books.

———. 1985. Short-run public reactions to food subsidy cuts in selected sub-Saharan and North African Countries. Report submitted to the Department of State and the Agency for International Development, 7 February.

———. 1987. Stabilization and structural adjustment in three small democracies: The Dominican Republic, Costa Rica, and Jamaica. Unpublished, Overseas Development Council, Washington, D.C.

Nordhaus, W. 1975. The political business cycle. *Review of economic studies* 42: 169–90.

OECD. 1987. *Development co-operation: 1986 report.* Paris: Organization for Economic Cooperation and Development.

Okyar, Osman. 1983. Turkey and the IMF: A review of relations, 1978–1982. In *IMF conditionality,* ed. John Williamson. Washington D.C.: Institute of International Economics.

Olson, Mancur. 1982. *The rise and decline of nations.* New Haven: Yale University Press.

Ordeshook, Peter C. 1986. *Game theory and political theory.* New York: Cambridge University Press.

Pevsner, Lucille W. 1984. *Turkey's political crisis.* New York: Praeger.

Pion-Berlin, David. 1983. Political repression and economic doctrines: The case of Argentina. *Comparative Political Studies* 16, no. 1 (April): 37–66.

Ranis, Gustav. 1987. East Asia and Latin America: Contrasts in the political economy of development policy change. Unpublished ms., Yale University.

Remmer, Karen. 1986. The politics of economic stabilization: IMF standby programs in Latin America, 1954–1984. *Comparative Politics* 19 (October): 1–25.

Rogowski, Ronald. 1987. Trade and the variety of democratic institutions. *International Organization,* 41, no. 2 (Spring): 203–224.

Sachs, Jeffrey D. 1985. External debt and macroeconomic performance in Latin America and East Asia. *Brookings Papers on Economic Activity* 2: 523–73.

Sachs, Jeffrey D., and H. Huizinga. 1987. U.S. commercial banks and the developing country debt crisis. *Brookings Papers on Economic Activity* 2: 555–601.

Sheahan, John. 1980. Market-oriented economic policies and political repression in Latin America. *Economic Development and Cultural Change* 28, no. 2: 267–91.

Sidell, Scott. 1987. *The IMF and Third World political instability.* London: Macmillan.

Skidmore, Thomas E. 1977. The politics of economic stabilization in postwar Latin America. In *Authoritarianism and corporatism in Latin America,* ed. James M. Malloy, Pittsburgh: University of Pittsburgh Press.

Spindler, J. Andrew. 1984. *The politics of international credit.* Washington D.C.: The Brookings Institution.

Stephens, John, and Evelyne Haber Stephens. 1986. *Democratic Socialism in Jamaica: The political movement and social transformation in dependent capitalism.* Princeton, N.J.: Princeton University Press.

Vernon, Raymond, ed. 1988. *The promise of privatization.* New York: Council on Foreign Relations.

Wallerstein, Michael. 1980. The collapse of democracy in Brazil: Its economic determinants. *Latin American Research Review* 15, no.3: 3–43.

Watson, Maxwell, Russell Kincaid, Caroline Atkinson, Eliot Kalter, and David Folkerts-Landau. 1986. *International capital markets: Developments and prospects.* (December.) Washington, D.C.: International Monetary Fund.

Weede, Erich. 1983. The impact of democracy on economic growth: Some evidence from cross-national analysis. *Kyklos* 36: 21–40.

Wellons, Philip. 1987. *Passing the buck: Banks, governments and Third World debt.* Boston: Harvard Business School Press.

Williamson, John. 1985. IMF conditionality in small countries. Paper presented to the Conference on External Debt of Small Latin American Countries, 9–11 December, in San José, Costa Rica.

World Bank. 1986. *World Development Report.*

———. 1987. *World debt tables, 1986.* Washington, D.C.: World Bank.

6 Conditionality, Debt Relief, and the Developing Country Debt Crisis

Jeffrey D. Sachs

6.1 Introduction

This chapter examines the role of high-conditionality lending by the International Monetary Fund and the World Bank as a part of the overall management of the debt crisis. High-conditionality lending refers to the process in which the international institutions make loans based on the promise of the borrowing countries to pursue a specified set of policies. High-conditionality lending by both institutions has played a key role in the management of the crisis since 1982, though the results of such lending have rarely lived up to the advertised hopes. One major theme of this chapter is that the role for high-conditionality lending is more restricted than generally believed, since the efficacy of conditionality is inherently limited.

A related theme is that many programs involving high-conditionality lending could be made more effective by including commercial bank debt relief as a component of such programs. I shall argue that such debt relief can be to the benefit of the creditor banks as well as the debtors, by enhancing the likelihood that the debtor governments will adhere to the conditionality terms of the IMF and World Bank loans, and thereby raise their long-term capacity to service their debts.

Almost by definition, countries in debt crisis that appeal to the Fund or the Bank for new loans have already been judged to be uncreditworthy on normal market criteria. In such treacherous circumstances, it is appropriate to ask why the IMF or the World Bank should be extending new loans. As an alternative, for example, the international institutions could allow the creditors and debtors to renegotiate new

Jeffrey D. Sachs is a professor of economics at Harvard University and a research associate of the National Bureau of Economic Research.

terms on the old loans without any official involvement. Such two-party negotiations between creditors and debtors characterized earlier debt crises, before the IMF and World Bank existed (see Lindert and Morton, chap. 2 in this volume, for a discussion of the earlier history).

In principle, continued lending by the international institutions could be justified by several nonmarket criteria: as a form of aid, as an investment by the creditor governments that finance the IMF and World Bank in political and economic stability of the debtor country (see Von Furstenberg 1985a; 1985b, for such a view), as an extension of the foreign policy interests of the major creditor governments, as a defense of the international financial system, etc. Loans are not usually defended on these grounds, though in fact such considerations are frequently important. Of course, these criteria are valid to an extent, but also extremely difficult to specify with precision as a basis for IMF–World Bank lending.

Another defense of lending, also with considerable merit in some circumstances, is that the IMF (and World Bank to a far lesser extent), can act as a "lender of last resort," analogous to a central bank in a domestic economy. The theory of the "lender of last resort" is not fully developed, though the practical importance of having a domestic lender of last resort is not much in dispute. The conceptual argument goes something as follows.

Commercial banks are at a risk of self-confirming "speculative panics" by their depositors because the banks engage in maturity transformation of their liabilities, i.e., they borrow short term and lend long term (see Diamond and Dybvig 1983 for a formal model of banking panics). If the depositors suddenly get the idea that *all other depositors* are going to withdraw their funds, it is rational for each depositor to withdraw his own funds from the bank, even if the bank would be fundamentally sound in the absence of a sudden rush of withdrawals. The depositors' collective behavior creates a *liquidity* crisis for the bank, in that a fundamentally sound intermediary cannot satisfy the sudden desire of its depositors to convert their deposits to cash. A lender of last resort, usually the central bank, can eliminate the liquidity crisis by lending freely to the bank in the short term. The banking panic is a form of market failure, that can be overcome by a lender of last resort.

The analogous argument for the IMF would hold that the private commercial bank lenders to a country might similarly panic, and all decide to withdraw their funds from the country even though the country is a fundamentally sound credit risk in the longer term (see Sachs 1984 for such a model). In this case, lending by the IMF can eliminate the liquidity squeeze on the country, and thereby help both the creditors and the debtors. As in the domestic economy, the IMF helps to overcome a well-defined market failure.

This argument was part of the basis of the original IMF intervention in the debt crisis of the early 1980s. The argument following the Mexican crisis in mid-1982 was that countries were suffering from a liquidity crisis, made acute by the simultaneous rise in world interest rates and the sudden cessation of commercial bank lending. It seemed at the time that the crisis could be quickly resolved (as argued, for example, by Cline 1984), since it represented merely a liquidity squeeze.

The liquidity arguments are no doubt true in some cases, but most observers now doubt that the developing country debt crisis represents merely a problem of liquidity. Six years after the onset of the crisis, almost no countries have returned to normal borrowing from the international capital markets, and the secondary-market value of bank loans to the debtor countries reflect very deep discounts in valuation. For many countries at least, the crisis represents more fundamental problems of solvency and longer-term willingness to pay on the part of the debtor nations.

In these circumstances, other justifications (that can be in addition to the liquidity argument) have been advanced for the large role of IMF and World Bank lending. By far the most important argument is that *strict conditionality* attached to IMF–World Bank loans can make such loans sensible on normal market terms. The assumption is that the international institutions are better than the banks at enforcing good behavior of the debtor country governments, and therefore have more scope for lending.

The importance of conditionality in justifying IMF–World Bank lending is certainly well placed. Countries in crisis are often in poor economic shape in large part because of bad policy choices in the past. IMF and World Bank policies are appropriately focused on key policy weaknesses (excessive budget deficits in the case of the IMF, and excessive inward orientation in the case of the World Bank). Moreover, the IMF and World Bank have the expertise and institutional clout to design high-conditionality programs, while the commercial banks do not.

Nonetheless, the role for high-conditionality lending is overstated, especially in the case of countries in a deep debt crisis. In practice the compliance of debtor countries with conditionality is rather weak, and this compliance problem has gotten worse in recent years, since a large stock of debt can itself be an important disincentive to "good behavior." In other words, the debt overhang itself makes it less likely that conditionality will prove successful.

The reason is straightforward. Why should a country adjust if that adjustment produces income for foreign banks rather than for its own citizenry? Since deeply indebted countries recognize that much of each extra dollar of export earnings get gobbled up in debt servicing, a very large stock of debt acts like a high marginal tax on successful adjustment. Therefore, two counterintuitive propositions could be true when a country is deeply indebted: "Good behavior" (such as a higher investment rate) can actually reduce national welfare, by increasing the transfer of income from the debtor country to creditors; and explicit debt relief by the creditors can increase the amounts of actual debt repayment, by improving the incentive of the debtor country to make the necessary adjustments.

Before turning to these arguments at greater length, we should consider one additional argument sometimes made for official lending. The argument is occasionally made that since countries are more averse to defaulting on official loans than they are on private loans, it is safe for official creditors to lend even when private creditors will not. This argument can sometimes be correct, but it is often mistaken. If official loans just raise the country's debt burden without raising its debt-servicing capacity, then repayments to the official creditors might simply crowd out repayments to its private creditors, and thereby undermine the smooth functioning of the international capital markets.

The issues of conditionality and debt relief will be discussed as follows. Section 6.2 outlines the theory of conditionality and section 6.3 focuses on the empirical record of high-conditionality lending. Section 6.4 shows the linkages between the overhang of debt and the effectiveness of conditionality, and demonstrates the potential role for debt relief in high-conditionality lending. Section 6.5 then discusses the specific problems raised by the macroeconomic situation of the heavily indebted countries: high inflation, excessive inward orientation, large budget deficits, and a prolonged economic downturn, all exacerbated by the problem of high foreign indebtedness. The recent history of stabilization has shown that few countries have been able to solve even one or two of these problems at a time, much less all of them simultaneously, and the record suggests that adjustment programs have the highest probability of success when macroeconomic stabilization precedes large-scale trade liberalization and a shift to outward orientation.

6.2 High-Conditionality Lending by the IMF and World Bank

The argument for high-conditionality lending is that the IMF and the World Bank can compel countries to undertake stabilizing actions in return for loans, thereby making the loans prudent even when the private capital markets have declared the country to be uncreditworthy. A full theory of conditionality would have to explain three things. First, if the actions being recommended to the country are really "desirable" for the country, why is it that the country must be compelled to undertake the policy? Second, if the country must indeed be compelled to undertake the actions, what types of force or sanctions could be used to guarantee compliance? And third, why is it that international institutions are better able to impose conditionality than are the private capital markets?

One solution to the conundrum of why countries must be compelled to accept conditionality is the problem of "time consistency": a debtor government accepts ex ante the need for a policy adjustment as the quid pro quo for a loan, but the government has a strong incentive to avoid the policy change once the loan is arranged. In this case, the role of conditionality is to bind the country to a course of future actions, actions which make sense today but which will look unattractive in the future. In other words, the goal of conditionality is to make the ex ante and ex post incentives for adjustment the same (where ex ante and ex post are with respect to the receipt of the loan).

In earlier papers (Sachs 1984; Cooper and Sachs 1985), I gave a simple illustration of a case in which conditionality was appropriate. I will discuss that case here, relegating the formal model to appendix A. Suppose that a government faces the problem of allocating resources between consumption and investment. The government has a very high time-discount rate (0.30 for purposes of illustration), so that current consumption is much preferred to future consumption. The investment opportunities have a return (0.20) in excess of the world interest rate (0.10), but less than the time discount rate.

The problem is the following. Once the foreign loans are obtained, and the government has to decide how to allocate over time the total pool of resources (equal to domestic resources plus foreign borrowing), the government will choose to consume rather than invest. That is because its time discount rate exceeds the rate of return on investment, so that it does not pay to sacrifice consumption expenditures in order to raise investment. For concreteness we suppose that a particular export-oriented investment project costs $100 million, and therefore yields $120 million in the future.

We assume that without investment the country will not have the resources to pay off a loan in the following period. The government is then assumed to pay off as much as it can, and to default on the rest. Under these conditions, private foreign lenders will not lend much to this country since they correctly foresee that the government will not invest the money. The situation can be depicted simply as a two-stage game between the creditors and the borrower. The creditor must first decide whether to lend; the borrower then decides whether to invest. As illustrated in figure 6.1a, once the money is received, the government's "utility" is higher by consuming today rather than investing (utility is assumed to be equal to consumption, with future consumption discounted by the rate of time preference). In particular, the country gets 100 in utility by using the loan for current consumption, and then

(a) The Loan Decision Without Conditionality

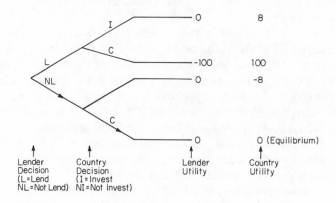

(b) The Loan Decision with Conditionality

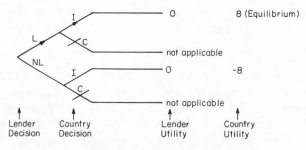

Fig. 6.1   Loan market equilibrium

defaulting on the loans, but only 8 if the loan is used for investment. Because the country's incentive to consume and then default is recognized by potential private creditors, the country is a bad credit risk. Since the loan will not in fact be made, the country's utility from the loan is of course 0.0 (the arrows indicate the equilibrium choices).

On the other hand, if the country could *commit* itself to increase investment by the amount of the foreign loans, as shown in figure 6.1b, it would result in a better outcome for the country specifically, a utility of 8 rather than 0.0. (As shown, the lender is indifferent between the two cases, because the lender just gets repaid with zero profit in the case 6.1b. In reality, the lender would presumably strictly prefer the case of lending with repayment to the case of no lending.) Since the investment opportunities have a return that is higher than the world cost of borrowing, the returns to the investment will be more than enough to pay off the loans. Moreover, since the investment is foreign financed, undertaking it does not have to reduce current consumption. Thus, if the country can commit itself to use foreign loans for investment purposes, the country will (1) maintain current consumption levels and (2) generate out of the investment project more than enough future income necessary to repay the debt. In sum, it is advantageous for the government to try to "tie its hands," and commit itself to use new foreign money for investment rather than consumption purposes.

The role for conditionality is introduced by assuming that countries cannot make credible, enforceable commitments with private lenders to use loans for one purpose or another, but that by means of conditionality agreements with the IMF or World Bank, the country can commit itself to a particular investment program. In such a case, it would be safe for the IMF or World Bank to make high conditionality loans to the country (since the loans will be used for investment purposes), while it would be imprudent for the private sector to make the same loans (since without conditionality, the government will consume the proceeds of the loan rather than invest).

The remaining problem with conditionality comes from the fact that once the IMF or World Bank lending is received, the country has the incentive to renege on its investment commitment. Given the preferences of the government, it is always better to consume than to invest once a level of foreign loans has been established. Thus, there must be some way for the country or the IMF and World Bank to guarantee that the commitment to invest is actually honored.

In practice, bargaining over conditionality almost always involves more than the debtor government's binding itself to a specific path of policies. Bargaining between a debtor country and the IMF and World Bank may also involve an implicit dispute about which objective function to use in evaluating a set of outcomes. If a program will lead to a recession next year, but a recovery over the following several years, is it desirable? The answer may well be "yes" to the Fund or the Bank (or their creditor governments, which recognize that adjustment may involve short-run pain in return for long-run benefits), but the same answer might be "no" to a precarious regime that might lose power during a period of austerity. Openness about this difference of opinion would block the signing of many agreements. In practice, neither the Fund or Bank on the one hand nor the creditor government on the other fully admit their disagreements, so that many conditionality packages are signed that have little chance of fulfillment, a point I return to below.

6.2.1 Official versus Private Lending in IMF–World Bank Packages

In the framework just described, the major role for the IMF and the World Bank is to guarantee through conditionality that the country will use a new loan for investment rather than consumption. We have discussed the issue as if the loan itself would come from the monitoring institutions, but in fact, there is no reason why there could not instead be a division of labor: The international institutions impose the conditionality; the private capital markets provide the financing. This is a well-recognized idea, that the international institutions should act mainly to provide "a seal of good housekeeping," and thereby to catalyze private lending.

Since the outbreak of the debt crisis, the IMF and World Bank have often emphasized such a catalytic role. One of the major innovations early in the crisis was the IMF's insistence to the commercial banks that any new IMF program for Mexico would require that the commercial banks commit $5 billion of additional lending to Mexico as well. Thus began the pattern of "involuntary" or "nonspontaneous" bank lending, in which the banks agreed to commit new lending to a debtor country in proportion to their existing exposures to the country, as part of an IMF stabilization package. More recently, private cofinancing with the World Bank has also been added as a condition of some package agreements (e.g., the Argentine agreement in 1986).

The details of such loan packages are beyond the scope of this chapter, and have been discussed at some length by Sachs and Huizinga (1987). Here it suffices to point out the extremely limited nature of such financing, and that the "catalytic" role of the IMF and World Bank have been vastly overstated (this may be a result of the lack of credibility of the conditionality, for reasons suggested below). Three points can be made here. First, overall net bank lending to the problem debtor countries were negative during 1982–86, not positive. That is, loan amortizations exceeded new lending, even after taking into account all of the well-publicized "concerted lending" arrangement. The concerted lending has been sporadic, and small in absolute magnitude, compared with the levels of debt amortizations in recent years. Thus, the levels of commercial bank exposure in the debtor countries actually fell after the onset of the crisis.

Second, the new lending by the commercial banks, where it has occurred, has almost always fallen far short of the debt servicing payments made by the debtor countries to the creditor banks. In this sense, the net resource transfers from the banks to the major debtor countries has been highly negative in recent years, despite the occasional application of concerted lending.

Third, and perhaps most disturbing, the IMF has not devoted much energy to getting concerted lending programs for the smaller debtor countries, but only for the larger countries (e.g., Argentina, Brazil, and Mexico). Almost no debtor country with an outstanding debt below $5 billion has been able to get any concerted lending from its commercial bank creditors, as is shown in table 6 in Sachs and Huizinga (1987). The smaller and politically weaker debtor countries have apparently had to make much larger net resource transfers than have their larger fellow debtor countries.

6.2.2   Enforcement of Conditionality Agreements: The Theory

The question of enforcement of conditionality agreements is in many ways tougher than the question of why conditionality is needed. The justification for IMF–World Bank lending rests on two propositions regarding enforcement: (1) that the enforcement of IMF–World Bank conditionality is sufficiently powerful to result in an "acceptable" rate of compliance with IMF–World Bank programs and (2) that the official institutions have an advantage over the commercial banks in enforcing conditionality. In both this section and the next, I examine the validity of these views.

6.2.3   The Strength of Conditionality

For both the international institutions and the commercial banks, the legal bases of conditionality are weak. In the domestic capital markets, bond covenants are legally binding restrictions on the behavior of debtors, which can generally be enforced with only modest transaction costs. In the international arena, particularly for loans to sovereign governments, the transaction costs for enforcing loan agreements are extremely high. As most writers have recognized recently, the main method of enforcement for lenders (whether official or private) involves the threat of cutoffs of *new* loans to misbehaving borrowers. Such a cutoff in lending can of course be extremely disruptive and costly to a borrower. Bank creditors can cut back on short-term trade credits to a country, and thereby disrupt the flow of international trade in the short term. The IMF similarly can cut back on balance-of-payments support, and by doing so, also trigger the cutoff of lending from other official sources (e.g., the World Bank, the bilateral official creditors, the multilateral development banks).

Theoretical work and empirical evidence both establish that the threat of a lending cutoff is a credible, but inherently limited sanction. Thus, conditionality, whether by the IMF and World Bank, or by the commercial banks themselves, should not on an a priori basis be expected to have the same force as a binding bond covenant in a domestic loan.

From the beginning, we should appreciate the inherent limitations of the enforcement mechanisms in conditionality on international lending.

6.2.4 The Special Problem of Negotiating with a Sovereign Borrower

Conditionality is limited in effectiveness not only because of enforcement difficulties, but also because of the complexity of negotiating with a sovereign borrower. In the case of a bond covenant, there is a clear legal responsibility on the borrower to carry out the conditions of the covenant. When a government is the debtor, however, there is likely to be a considerable diffusion of power within the government, to the extent that the individual parts of the government negotiating the conditionality agreement may well lack the authority to implement the agreement.

This problem is common with IMF agreements, though it is rarely discussed or carefully analyzed. The IMF invariably negotiates with the executive branch, and mainly with a small part of the executive branch, the finance ministry. A small group of technocrats at the ministry of finance and at the central bank will typically negotiate the IMF agreement in private, and in splendid isolation from the rest of the government. However, when the minister of finance signs the agreement with the Fund, very often there can be little assurance that the minister has the authority or political standing within the government to carry out the agreement. This is especially the case when the minister agrees to spending and tax changes that require parliamentary approval, or that require the approval of other parts of the government (independent state enterprises, regional corporations, state and municipal governments, other ministries, etc.). Often, it is the president himself that undercuts his finance minister in the execution of an adjustment program.

In this sense, most IMF and World Bank agreements start with a formal myth, that there is one unified actor in the government that can be bound by the terms of a conditionality agreement. This may be a necessary myth, and even sometimes a useful one, but uncovering the myth helps us in a simple way to account for the fact that most IMF agreements fail, a point we shall see below.

6.2.5 The Debt Overhang and the Weakness of Conditionality

What must also be appreciated is the fact that the current overhang of external debt to private creditors can greatly hinder the effectiveness of IMF conditionality, at least under the prevailing design of IMF programs. Virtually all IMF programs to date have been designed under the assumption that the debtor country can and will service its external debts in the long run on a normal market basis. The programs are constructed in the expectation of normal debt servicing. (For example, in the technical calculations in Fund programs, interest rates on the existing debt are assumed to be at market rates; the country is assumed to clear all arrears on a reasonable timetable, etc.)

It might easily be the case, however, that a country would be better off defaulting on a portion of its debts than it would be with timely debt servicing (a dozen or more countries had indeed taken such unilateral action by 1987). There simply may not exist an IMF high-conditionality program based on full debt servicing, that, if followed, would actually make the country better off than it would be without the program but with a partial suspension of debt payments. In other words, the IMF program might be too restrictive relative to the available options of the debtor government.

In such circumstances, four things could happen. One outcome would be for the IMF to design a program that is actually based on partial and explicit debt relief. So far, the IMF has avoided this rather obvious approach, partly because it has underestimated the possible efficiency gains for all parties (creditors, debtors, and the Fund) that might result. The second possibility is that the IMF and the debtor government would fail to sign a program, and the country would suspend payments on the part of its private sector debts. This has been the case with Peru during 1985–87, and Brazil in 1987. The third possibility, and indeed the typical case in recent years, is that the Fund and the country would sign a program based on full debt servicing, even though both parties fully expect that the agreement will breakdown in due course. Either the conditionality would be allowed to fall by the wayside and the country would continue to borrow from the Fund but without living up to earlier commitments, or the IMF program would eventually be suspended.

Argentina during 1987–88 provides an ideal illustration of the case in which the IMF and a debtor country signed a series of agreements in which almost no observers had any confidence, and in which the IMF simply relaxed the conditionality terms (with formal waivers) throughout the course of the agreement. Mr. David Finch, the former director of the IMF Department of Exchange and Trade Relations, writes of Argentina as a case of "renewed pressures to involve the IMF in an agreement where political solutions [in Argentina] won't allow a solution to the balance-of-payments problem. . . . [T]he IMF has been forced to continue lending [to Argentina] to maintain the facade of the debt strategy." (Finch, 1988, 127). In less diplomatic language, the U.S. government was fearful that Argentina would default to the commercial banks in the absence of new IMF money. The U.S. therefore pressured the Fund to maintain a program with Argentina despite the failure of the Argentine government to live up to earlier agreements.

A fourth possibility would be for the IMF and World Bank to approve programs with debtor countries that allow for a buildup of arrears (i.e., nonpayments) to the commercial bank creditors, in well-defined circumstances. These circumstances would include (1) a large overhang of debt that is deemed to be highly inimical to the stabilization efforts of the country and (2) the unwillingness of the commercial creditors either to grant relief or significant new financing. By allowing for the buildup of arrears to private creditors, the IMF could design more realistic programs without the need to press the private creditors for specific amounts of debt relief. The debt relief would instead emerge in the bilateral bargaining of the debtor and the creditors.

In a later section, we will explore in much greater detail the case for combining conditionality with debt relief.

6.2.6 The Strength of Official versus Private Conditionality

It remains to be asked whether the Fund and the Bank have more power than the private banks in imposing conditionality on sovereign borrowers. Here, experience will have to provide the most conclusive answers, and we discuss the historical experience in the next section. Some theoretical arguments, though, can be made as follows. First, the Fund and the Bank are ongoing institutions, while bank syndicates are ad hoc. Defaulting to the Fund or the Bank will presumably put the country at risk of rupturing the relations with these institutions, while defaulting to some private creditors in a particular syndicate might not forestall further borrowing from new lenders elsewhere.

Second, enforcement of loans raises several problems of collective action. With hundreds or even more than a thousand private creditors for a major debtor country, there is a problem in allocating the monitoring and enforcement costs of a conditionality agreement that might be reached between the country and the creditors. With the Fund or the Bank, a single actor bears the enforcement costs and reaps the rewards of enforcement. Third, it is sometimes suggested that the Fund or the Bank can dictate terms to a country while the private sector cannot because it is easier for the country to be responding to an independent political institution than it is for the country to be responding to "private capital."

Fourth, and perhaps most important, the creditor governments have made IMF conditionality the practical linchpin of all a debtor country's financial relations with the creditor governments. With few exceptions, a debtor country in crisis must have an ongoing relationship with the IMF in order to qualify for (1) a rescheduling of official bilateral (i.e., government-to-government) loans in the Paris Club; (2) new credits from official export credit agencies to the debtor government; (3) new lending from the World Bank and the multilateral development banks (even if there is no formal cross-conditionality clause between IMF and World Bank lending, there is often implicit cross-conditionality). In addition, debtor countries are often instructed by the United States to maintain good relations with the IMF in order to maintain good bilateral relations with the United States. Thus, a country's concern about foreign policy relations with the United States often strengthens the hand of the IMF.

On the other side of the ledger, the public institutions also have several disadvantages in enforcement power relative to the private sector. With respect to the first point, banks are also ongoing institutions well aware of their reputations. They have so far been extremely reluctant to ease the repayment terms for any country (for example to reschedule at below market interest rates), even for countries in dire straits, because of the demonstration effect on the dozens of other countries with which these banks are bargaining.

Second, with respect to the free-rider problems of enforcement, the banks have worked out ways to get around many of the collective action problems involved in monitoring and rescheduling. For example, small steering committees of banks are appointed to manage the negotiations with the debtor countries. A small number of banks is entrusted with most of the actual mechanics of oversight and negotiation. Syndicated loan agreements now often contain provisions for certain binding actions by the entire syndicate upon a favorable vote of some fraction of the syndicate members. This kind of procedure can help to eliminate the problem of individual banks attempting to free ride on the actions of others.

Moreover, in some cases, the presence of hundreds of small banks can actually strengthen the bargaining position of a bank syndicate. The steering committee is able to point out in some circumstances that even the small banks might ruin an agreement, so that the country must accede to better terms for these weak links in the chain. When the country is negotiating with a single creditor such as the IMF, this appeal of the creditor to the "weak" fringe members of the bargaining team cannot be made.

As to the third point, that it is easier for a government to take marching orders from the international public institutions rather than from private banks, the evidence is at best mixed. The epithet that a program is *fondo monetarista* is about as damning as possible in the Latin American political lexicon. Indeed, there are several cases in recent years in which countries have explicitly attempted private workouts with the banks, in order to avoid the opprobrium of agreeing to a Fund program.

Finally, and perhaps most importantly, the World Bank and the IMF are in a weak bargaining position for several institutional reasons. First, they are clients of the very governments to whom they are lending the money. It may be hard indeed for the IMF or World Bank to tell a member government to go away. To the credit of the Fund and the Bank, these organizations have developed several institutional levels of technical staff that intervene between the country and a final decision with respect to lending.

Because of the formal position of the multilateral agencies as clients of the member governments, there is a need for a formal equality of treatment for all member governments with regard to negotiations. It is very difficult for the Fund or the Bank to make invidious comparisons among countries concerning the likelihood that they will actually live up to commitments. If a program looks good on paper, there are great pressures for the program to be approved, even if there is widespread skepticism that the program will actually be carried out. The Fund of course keeps track of the compliance record of member governments, but it appears to be difficult to make that record a formal basis for approving or disapproving a program, assuming that the country is current in its repayments to the Fund and assuming that on paper a proposed program hangs together.

Another problem is that the Fund and the Bank have many goals other than profits, which can make them a soft touch with respect to conditionality. For the private capital markets, there is basically one bottom line: Will the loan make money? The Bank and the Fund must also worry about the political stability of the recipient country, the political interests of the creditor governments, the standard of living of individuals in the debtor countries, etc. These are admirable concerns, indeed crucial concerns. They are the raison d'être of international institutions. But these concerns do not always allow for a hard-boiled judgment about the potential success or failure of a conditionality package.

These limitations of the IMF are pointed out by Finch (1988), who cites the case of IMF relations with Egypt as an important example (we have already noted Finch's observations with regard to Argentina):

> For political reasons, Egypt had been receiving sizable support from the Western allies, much of it in the form of repayable export credits. With very limited cash aid available, servicing this credit became virtually impossible. Yet, debt relief was blocked by Paris Club rules that required that Egypt have an agreement with the IMF before the creditor countries would reschedule their loans. To maintain even a semblance of its traditional concern for timely repayment, the IMF had to insist on major changes in Egypt's economic policies.
>
> But the Egyptian government, fearing a domestic political backlash, refused to take the required action. Instead, it sought protection from other governments. The Fund was told to reach "agreement"

with Egypt without insisting on the necessary policy changes. In recompense, undoubtedly, the IMF was given assured priority over other creditors (p. 127).

In sum, the power of conditionality is certainly present in the case of IMF and World Bank lending, though conditionality will face inherent restrictions, given the limited enforcement powers at hand. The alleged superiority of the international institutions in imposing conditionality is probably correct in general but much oversold quantitatively. The private sector can indeed impose conditionality, and has done so in the past. At the same time, the conditionality emanating from the international institutions is hobbled by the nature of the relationship of those institutions to the member governments. In the last analysis, the success or failure of conditionality is an empirical matter, and it is to the historical record that we turn shortly.

6.2.7   Enhancing the Strength of Conditionality

Even before proceeding to the empirical record, we can already make several points regarding ways to enhance the effectiveness of conditionality agreements. First, given the weakness of conditionality, the IMF and the World Bank probably undermine their effectiveness by signing too many (unrealistic) programs. In cases which appear particularly unrealistic, the IMF and World Bank can protect the conditionality process by requiring more prior actions on the part of the borrowing government, so that the government proves its resolve to carry through on the negotiated program (and is forced to build the domestic political base for the policy changes).

Second, if one source of unreality is the heavy burden represented by a large overhang of debt, the IMF and World Bank would increase the likelihood of success by endorsing some programs that allow for arrears to private-sector creditors, if those creditors are unprepared to allow for a realistic extent of debt relief. Furthermore, as we shall see, this point applies more generally to encouraging formal debt relief as part of overall IMF–World Bank programs.

6.3   The Recent Experience with Conditionality

The recent experience of the World Bank with high-conditionality lending in support of macroeconomic adjustment is rather limited, so that most of the discussion will focus on the outcomes of IMF programs. Moreover, measuring the success of Fund programs is a daunting task, because the inevitable refrain is "compared to what?" (See Williamson 1983, chap. 7, for an interesting discussion of possible bases for evaluation.) One useful standard, which I apply here, is to judge the programs in terms of the compliance of the debtor government with the terms of the IMF agreement. Even this limited type of assessment is difficult, both because compliance is multidimensional, and because many of the details of the programs (particularly the contents of the letters of intent) are typically beyond the public view. Because of this latter feature, we must rely almost wholly on studies of compliance undertaken by the Fund itself, or on case studies of individual countries by outside authors.

Of course the design of IMF conditionality loans, and to a lesser extent, World Bank Structural Adjustment Loans (SALs), have been subject to intense criticism and debate among policy makers and academic economists. These debates often make it appear that the fundamental diagnoses underlying such loans, and the conditions attached to them remain in serious dispute. However, the problem of diagnosis is almost surely not the main source of the problem with compliance. At a recent conference reviewing IMF conditionality (see Williamson 1983), Richard Cooper conjectured (pp. 571–73) that despite their differing theoretical views, the conference participants would find themselves in broad agreement in designing a stabilization program for any specific country other than their own. He went on to say that the chosen stabilization program would probably look quite like a "standard" IMF package. Notably, there were few demurrals, despite the wide range of theoretical positions represented at the conference.

In that conference (and in the country studies in the NBER Project on Developing Country Debt) there was much evidence for the prevailing IMF and World Bank views that (1) balance of payments problems typically reflect, inter alia, excessive money creation in support of fiscal deficits; (2) multiple exchange rate systems lead to serious resource misallocations, and are often a burden on public-sector budgets; (3) overvalued exchange rates, coupled with exchange controls, capital flight, and smuggling, represent a tax on exports that is detrimental to long-term development; and (4) allowing key prices (including real wages, public-sector prices, and interest rates) to respond to market conditions as part of an overall adjustment effort will improve efficiency and growth.

Ironically, though, there was one more point of agreement running through most of the analyses at the Williamson conference (and the NBER studies): IMF programs are very frequently, if not typically, unsuccessful in restoring stability and growth in countries beset with balance-of-payments and inflation problems. Aside from the cases of the developed country borrowers (Italy, the United Kingdom, and Portugal) discussed at the conference, several of the remaining programs that were described (Argentina, Brazil, Jamaica, Tanzania) were unsuccessful in meeting stated objectives. These findings of limited success are in accord with a growing number of other case studies and cross-sectional analyses of IMF stabilization programs, which in sum point to a mixed record, at the very best, in the compliance of countries with Fund programs. (Notably, however, in the cases where Fund programs were substantially implemented, the macroeconomic results seem to justify the conditions attached to the loans.)

Internal IMF reviews of compliance are similarly mixed. In a review of Fund programs supported by standby arrangements in upper-credit tranches during 1969–78, Beveridge and Kelley (1980) found that fiscal targets were achieved in about half the cases, but, "[b]y 1977 and 1978, expenditures were contained as planned in less than 20 percent of the programs, compared with over 50 percent in 1969 and 1970" (p. 213). Also, Beveridge and Kelley found that governments were not generally successful in meeting targets with respect to the composition of expenditure between current and capital outlays. In over 70 percent of the programs specifying a desire to expand capital outlays while constraining current outlays (exactly the form of conditionality considered in the theoretical model), "current expenditure in nominal terms exceeded the target or projection. In about half of these programs, capital outlays in nominal terms were lower than projected" (p. 214). With respect to the target on overall budget balance, as opposed to expenditures alone, budget targets were met in about 50 percent of the programs overall, but in less than 20 percent of the programs in 1978. Once again, a sharp downturn in compliance was noted. Doe's study (1983) has updated the Beveridge and Kelley results for Fund programs in 1980. Of the 18 programs surveyed that planned a reduction in the fiscal deficit, half of the programs did result in a reduced deficit, but in only 4 (22 percent) of the cases did the country actually meet the agreed-upon targets.

Stephan Haggard's (1985) recent review of IMF programs under the Extended Fund Facility (EFF) is no more heartening. The EFF was created in 1974 in the wake of the first oil shock as a way to enlarge the access of IMF member countries to Fund credits. The goals were similar to those enunciated for the Baker plan. In Haggard's words, the EFFs "are representative of a growing emphasis among development economists on the importance of microeconomic instruments and on the role of resource utilization and production as a basis for longer-term structural adjustment. EFFs often call for fundamental shifts in policy, such as liberalization of trade, decontrol of prices, and restructuring of public-sector corporations" (p. 508). The results of the EFFs were poor. According to Haggard, in his count, "of the thirty adjustment programs launched under the auspices of the Extended Fund Facility, twenty-four were renegotiated, or had payments interrupted, or were quietly allowed to lapse. Of these twenty-four, sixteen were formally cancelled by the IMF, virtually all for noncompliance" (pp. 505–6).

Haggard's bleak conclusions are echoed in a recent study by Remmer (1986), of IMF programs during 1954–84. It is worth quoting Remmer at length on the question of IMF conditionality:

Unsuccessful implementation of IMF recipes has been the norm in Latin America, not the exception. A high proportion of standby programs have failed to push key indicators of government finance and domestic credit even in the right direction. Moreover, examining the IMF standby programs on a before and after basis shows that changes in key indicators are more readily attributable to chance than to the operation of IMF stabilization programs. The obvious conclusion is that the economic, social, and political impact of IMF programs has been overstated. To describe the IMF as a "poverty broker," as does the title of a recent book, or to charge the Fund with undermining democracy is to engage in hyperbole. The power of the IMF remains a useful myth for governments seeking a scapegoat to explain difficult economic conditions associated with severe balance-of-payments disequilibria, but the ability of the IMF to impose programs from the outside is distinctly limited (p. 21).

Given all these unsatisfactory results, it is not surprising that the Fund has been unable to wean many countries away from IMF support, in spite of being only "temporarily available." Table 6.1, taken from Goode (1985), shows the list of 24 countries that have used Fund resources consecutively for a period of at least 10 years. Note that of these 24 cases, fully 19 are still using IMF resources as of 1984. In other words, the lengthy reliance on Fund loans is a contemporary feature of the system. This table, by definition, does not include even more problematic cases, in which the country's performance under Fund programs was so unsatisfactory that its access to further Fund credits was suspended.

The experience with the World Bank SALs is too brief to allow any such comparable review. By design these programs are intended to yield results only in the intermediate term (say 5–15 years), so that no comprehensive judgments can yet be made. However, there are already some very worrisome signs that the compliance with Bank conditionality is no better than with the Fund's. In a review of recent SAL experience, Berg and Batchelder (1985) note that three (Senegal, Guyana, Bolivia) of sixteen SAL countries have already experienced a clear breakdown of a program in process or a denial of a follow-up of SAL because of inadequate performance. These authors are also skeptical of the strength of Bank conditionality, pointing to the case of Senegal (whose SAL was cancelled in mid-1983) as an example of the nonenforceability of conditionality:

As noted earlier the Bank must shrink from the ultimate sanction, cancellation. Cessation of disbursements is too strong a response by

Table 6.1   **Members Making Prolonged Use of IMF Credit in the Period 1954–84[a]**

Member	Number of Continuous Years of Use	Period
Chile	27	1958–84
Egypt	27	1958–84
Sri Lanka	20	1963–84
Mali	20	1965–84
Sudan	20	1965–84
Pakistan	19	1966–84
Turkey	18	1954–71
Burma	17	1968–84
Nicaragua	16	1969–84
Philippines	16	1969–84
Guinea	15	1970–84
Chad	14	1971–84
Syria	14	1961–74
India	13	1958–70
Uganda	13	1972–84
Yugoslavia	13[b]	1972–84
Zambia	12	1972–84
Afghanistan	12	1965–76
Bangladesh	12	1973–84
Indonesia	12	1962–73
Kampuchea, Democratic	12	1973–84
Zaire	12	1973–84
Jamaica	11	1974–84
Romania	11	1974–84

Sources: From Goode (1985), table 3, which is based on International Monetary Fund, *International Financial Statistics: Supplement on Fund Accounts*, no. 3 (1982); IMF, *International Financial Statistics Yearbook, 1984;* IMF, *International Financial Statistics* (February 1985, p. 22–23).

[a]Periods of use are measured between the ends of calendar years and are, therefore, understated for all transactions occurring before 31 December of the years in question; the maximum understatement can approach two years.

[b]Yugoslavia also had an 11-year period of use from 1959 through 1969.

the Bank to banal acts of nonperformance. In the one case where this was done (Senegal), the SAL was replaced by new credits. Noncompliance, at least in the short run, was virtually costless to Senegal, whose share of Bank-IDA disbursements has been 50 percent higher, during July–February of fiscal 1984, than it was during fiscal 1981 and 1982. . . . [H]owever, new Bank-IDA commitments to Senegal have dropped off, and it is not clear when that decline will be reversed (p. 44).

The record of failed SAL programs (3 out of 16 countries) may well understate the failure rate in the longer term, particularly if the SALs become important for the Latin American countries. Many of the existing SALs cover the successful middle-income developing countries and the NICs, such as Thailand and Korea, rather than the problem cases of Peru, Chile, Argentina, Brazil, or Mexico.

6.4   External Debt and Conditionality

The theme of this section is that high external indebtedness can reduce the incentives for a country to undertake necessary macroeconomic adjustments, and thus further reduce the chance that the terms of a conditionality agreement will be fulfilled. Indeed, for very high levels of indebtedness, it may be useful for creditors to forgive some of the debt as an incentive for better performance, recognizing that such an incentive could actually *raise* the repayments to creditors in the long run. Before proceeding with this argument, a terminological point must be made. Creditors frequently "write down" the value of bad loans in their own books, without relieving the debtor of the legal obligation to make full repayments. The thrust of this section is not about writedowns (which may be wise from an accounting or regulatory point of view), but about explicit relief or forgiveness, in which the creditors reduce the legal obligations of repayment below the levels originally contracted.

6.4.1   The Basic Efficiency Case for Debt Relief

Let us see how debt forgiveness can work (once again the technical material is presented at the end of the chapter in appendix B). Suppose that a country has a large stock of debt due in the future. He will assume, for purposes of illustration, that the stock of debt is so large that the country lacks creditworthiness for any additional borrowing on international private markets. Moreover, to avoid complications, we will for the moment ignore conditionality lending. Finally, by assuming that the debt is due in the future rather than the present, we ignore issues relating to rescheduling.

The existing creditors have a choice this period: They can sit down with the country and negotiate some debt relief, or they can "hang tough" today, and hope to get fully repaid in the future. It might seem that, and it is often argued as if, the creditors should hold out for the maximum repayment, and take whatever they can get in the future. After all, why give up on full repayment today, before the debt is due? This is certainly the attitude of many banks, who recognize that they are unlikely to be repaid fully but have decided to sit tight until further developments occur. Unfortunately, this strategy may well ultimately leave the banks with smaller repayments than they would receive by negotiating forgiveness in some circumstances.

When the debt overhang is large enough, it can act as a major incentive against the very adjustments in the debtor country that would contribute to future debt servicing, as can be shown by a simple numerical example. Suppose that the country owes $150 million, but has a future capacity for debt servicing of only $100 million. Suppose also that in the future the country will repay (in present value terms) as much of the $150 million as possible, and will then default on the balance. Note that improvements in the country's future debt-servicing capacity (up to $150 million) would simply go to the creditors' benefit, and not the country's, since the overhang of debt is so large.

Suppose, for instance, that a wonderful investment opportunity is available for enhancing exports. If the debtor government sacrifices $10 million of current consumption and raises investments in the export sector, it will raise its future debt-servicing capacity from $100 million to $120 million. From the creditors' point of view this would be quite beneficial. But from the country's point of view, it would be highly irrational. The country would lose $10 million in consumption today, and would gain nothing in consumption in the future, since all of the added export earnings would go to the creditors, and the export earnings would still not be enough to repay the debt! The benefits of higher future production would fall entirely to the creditors.

Since the government will not undertake the investments in such circumstances, it is most likely that the debt-servicing capacity of the country will not be enhanced. The debtor will not adjust (i.e., the export-promoting investments will not be made). The future debt-servicing capacity will remain at $100 million, which is the amount that the creditors will receive in the future.

Now suppose instead that the creditors offer some debt relief. The creditors might agree to forgive $45 million, and to continue to demand $105 million of repayments (i.e., the creditors settle for 70 cents on the dollar). This could be done, for example, by a swap of the outstanding $150 million of debt for exit bonds with face value of $105 million. Now, if the country invests, it loses $10 million in consumption today, gains $20 million in additional export earnings in the future (total export earnings now equal $120 million), and repays $105 million in debt (i.e., the exit bonds would be fully serviced). Future consumption therefore rises by $15 million ($= $120 million $-$ $105 million), with a discounted utility gain of $-10 + 15/(1.3)$, or about $2 million. Since the government's rate of time discount is not too high, the opportunity to pay $10 million in current consumption in order to raise future consumption by $15 million is attractive, and the investment will be made.

In sum, *by agreeing to debt relief, the creditors raise the ultimate repayment from $100 million to $105 million.* The debtor is better off as well, since it accepts a short-run cut in consumption in return for a much larger future increase in consumption. The whole game is diagrammed in figure 6.2. With no debt relief, the equilibrium involves no investment and $100 million in debt repayment. With debt relief, the equilibrium involves investment with repayments of $105 million and an improved debtor utility of $2 million. Of course, the numbers used in this example are arbitrary, and the actual gains from debt relief for both the debtor and creditors could be far larger than shown.

This argument for debt relief would be misplaced if the debtor countries are actually in the range of indebtedness in which they will eventually service all of their debts at market terms. However, most of the direct and indirect evidence that we have on the market value of claims on the major debtor countries shows that the investors indeed believe that there is a significant chance that much of the debt will not be fully serviced in the long run. (See Sachs and Huizinga 1987 for further details on the market valuation of the outstanding debt).

If this analysis is correct, there may be significant welfare gains from forgiving some of the existing stock of debt, rather than piling up more debt in the form of new loans and reschedulings. The question of how

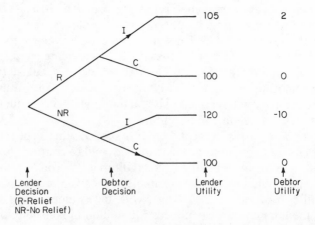

Lender
Decision
(R-Relief
NR-No Relief)   Debtor
Decision   Lender
Utility   Debtor
Utility

Fig. 6.2   The efficiency case for debt relief. Explanation: Without debt relief, the creditor is repaid $100 million, and the debtor consumes. Debtor utility in this case is set at 0.0, and utility in the other cases is measured as a deviation from this baseline, according to the formula $U = -I_1 + \max [0,100 + 2I_1 - D]/(1.3)$, where D is the amount of debt that is due. $D = 150$ in the case of no relief, and $D = 105$ in the case of relief. I_1 is 0.0, or $10 million. Lender utility is measured by the amount of repayment in the second period, and is equal to min $[100 + 2 I_1, D]$, which equals $100 million if $I_1 = 0$; $120 million if $I_1 = $10 million and no relief is granted; and $105 million if $I_1 = $10 million and D is reduced from $150 million to $105 million.

actually to engineer debt relief is a very difficult one. Equity and efficiency considerations will dictate that the existing creditors from all classes must coordinate any forgiveness. This will pose serious administrative and regulatory problems, since creditors in different countries and in different sectors would face very different costs and benefits. Commercial banks might even face shareholder lawsuits if they were to forgive some debt without adequate administrative support from the bank regulators and perhaps from the legislatures of the various creditor countries. Moreover, the debt relief must be designed in a way to limit the moral hazard problem of countries intentionally mismanaging their international economic policies for the sake of achieving debt relief.

Of course debt relief could come in all shapes and sizes, varying from an Alan Garcia–style cap on debt repayments relative to exports, to a conversion of existing debt into new securities with a lower contractual present value, to a rescheduling at below market interest rates, to a scheme in which each dollar of amortization reduces the debt outstanding by some multiple of a dollar (by agreement with the creditors), or finally to an explicit elimination of claims by the creditors without a quid pro quo (as in the cancellation of inter-allied war debts in the early 1930s). The relative advantages and disadvantages of these various methods are beyond the scope of this paper.

6.4.2 The Interaction of Debt Relief and Conditionality

There are really two linkages between a debt overhang and the effectiveness of conditionality, one obvious and the other a bit more subtle. The obvious linkage has already been made: In the absence of debt relief, a country may have no incentive to honor a conditionality agreement, and to carry through on an economic reform program. The foreign debt acts like a tax on adjustment. The debt relief removes the tax, and encourages the country to undertake efficient reforms.

The second linkage occurs when debt relief is a necessary but not sufficient condition for inducing the country to undertake needed reforms. In the previous numerical example, the country chooses to undertake reforms once debt relief is granted, even in the absence of conditionality. As soon as the debt is reduced from $150 million to $105 million, the country voluntarily reduces current consumption by $10 million in order to raise future consumption by $15 million. It might easily have been the case, however, that even with debt relief, the needed reforms would still look unattractive. This would happen, for example, if the government's rate of time discount is so high that an increase in future consumption of $15 million would not justify a cut in current consumption of $10 million.

In such a case, relief would not result in any improvement in the debtor country's economy, and so would be unattractive from the creditors' point of view. (In the formal modes, the creditors would be indifferent between relief and no relief: They would receive $100 million in either case. In reality, relief would only be granted if there were real expected gains, since in a world of uncertainty there is always some small chance that the loans can be repaid, and there is consequently an option value to the creditors in holding on to the face value of their claims. (See Krugman 1988 for a discussion of the value of this option in the model of uncertainty.) It might still be the case, however, that the combination of debt relief and conditionality would raise the welfare of both the creditors and the debtor, even though relief by itself and conditionality by itself, could not do so.

To see how this would work, suppose that the following high-conditionality loan package is put together:

1. Debt relief, which reduces the overhang of debt from $150 million to $105 million
2. IMF lending of $5 million to the country, and with repayment to the IMF of $5.5 million in the future
3. The country commits to undertake the export-enhancing reform, at the cost of $10 million today

Assuming that the conditionality is enforced, the country increases its future productive capacity from $100 million to $120 million. Current consumption falls by $5 million (since half of the cost of the investment is financed by the IMF loan). Future consumption goes up by $9.5 million ($120 million in exports minus $5.5 million in debt repayment to the IMF minus $105 million in debt repayment to the original creditors).

Now, instead of giving up $10 million today to get $15 million in the future, the government gives up only $5 million today to get $9.5 million in the future. As long as the rate of time discount is neither too low nor too high (specifically, as long as the discount rate is between 0.5 and 0.9), the country will reject the investment in the absence of the IMF–World Bank loan, but will accept the investment (with conditionality) if it comes with an official loan. In that case, the original creditors are better off, since their repayments rise by $5 million relative to the case of no reform. The debtor is better off by $9.5 million in the future. The IMF breaks even since its loan gets repaid.

And yet none of this would happen in the absence of debt relief (in which case the country reaps no benefit from reform), and in the absence of conditionality and new IMF lending (since the country would not undertake the investment without new lending, and would not get the new lending without a credible commitment to undertake the investment).

The key to this example is that the investment requires both new external financing and debt relief, and the external financing requires conditionality, since the country would prefer to borrow abroad and then not undertake the reform, as in the first example in figure 6.1. Again we can resort to a formal game analysis, as shown in figure 6.3. In figure 6.3a we have the case without debt relief. Any increase in debt service capacity goes to the benefit of the foreign creditors. The country will not undertake the investment, and will not consent to a conditionality package (or, more likely, the IMF loan will be made, but not adhered to). In figure 6.3b we have the case with relief, but without conditionality. Again, the country will not undertake the investment out of its own resources, but also will not get any new loans, since potential new lenders will correctly believe that new loans will be used for consumption purposes. Note that figure 6.3b is the same as figure 6.2, except for a higher rate of time discount in the debtor country. In figure 6.3c, we have the combination of debt relief and new external financing with conditionality.

This example belies two common views: That debt relief must hurt the creditors or that if debt relief helps the creditors, it will be achieved without official intervention. The example makes clear that both relief and official intervention by means of conditionality are necessary for a successful adjustment program to the mutual benefit of the debtor and its creditors.

6.5   Some Implications for the Pace and Phasing of Adjustment Programs

The postwar history of stabilization, liberalization, and conditionality can make a pessimist of the most tenacious optimist. Few stabilization and liberalization plans meet their initial objectives, and many fail miserably. We have seen that conditionality is inherently limited in its capacity to effect adjustment in the debtor countries, and that the limitations are even more severe in the presence of a debt overhang. In many cases, debt relief might have to be combined with conditionality to improve the likelihood of success of IMF and World Bank programs.

Given these limitations, it is important to make the objectives of conditionality consistent with the limited efficacy of conditionality. Programs of the IMF and World bank should be tailored according to a realistic assessment of the possible accomplishments. One of the most important issues in this regard is the balancing of the demands of stabilization with those of longer-term structural reform. Since the major debtor countries suffer from acute macroeconomic disequilibria (with inflation rates in Argentina, Brazil, and Mexico well exceeding 100 percent per year in 1987), a crucial issue is the balancing of macroeconomic stabilization with other types of structural reform.

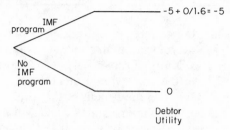

(a) No Debt Relief

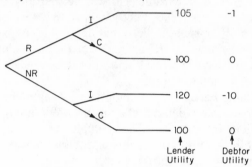

(b) Debt Relief, No New Lending
(Country discount rate assumed to equal 0.6)

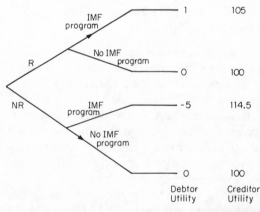

(c) Debt Relief, New IMF Lending cum Conditionality

Fig. 6.3 Debt relief with conditionality. Explanation: Without debt relief, the debtor's second period consumption is always 0.0. Thus, if it accepts the $5 million IMF loan, the utility effect is simply the change in C_1, which equals −$10 million ($= I_1$) + $5 million ($=$ IMF loan), or −$5 million. With debt relief, but no new lending, the benefit of investment is −$10 + ($120 − $105)/1.6, which is approximately −1. With debt relief *and* conditionality, the benefit of the IMF package is −$5 + [$120 − $5(1.1) − $105]/1.6 which is approximately 1. Note that $5(1.1) represents the repayment of the $5 million IMF loan at 10 percent interest.

The main theme of this section is that structural reform (especially a shift towards greater outward orientation and trade liberalization) is a very difficult process that takes many years to bring to fruition. The process is so difficult economically and politically that it is likely to fail under the best of macroeconomic circumstances, and is in general greatly jeopardized by a concurrent macroeconomic stabilization crisis. The historical record suggests that adjustment programs rarely succeed unless stabilization is their first step, with structural reforms proceeding gradually and mostly *after* macroeconomic balance has been restored.

The historical record points to a high failure rate in general regarding attempts at trade liberalization and a shift towards outward orientation. One thoroughly documented record of liberalization experiences can be found in the multicountry study on "Foreign Trade Regimes and Economic Development" directed by Jagdish Bhagwati and Anne Krueger at the National Bureau of Economic Research, and summarized in Krueger (1978). Krueger identified 22 attempts to liberalize from a situation of heavy reliance on quantitative restrictions and exchange controls (pp. 219–20). By her own count, 13 of these episodes were unsuccessful and 9 were successful. Even this count is too optimistic, however, since only 4 of the 9 "success" cases (measured as *four* years of successful liberalization) proved to be enduring until the time of Krueger's study (these cases are Brazil, 1964; South Korea, 1964; Israel, 1962; and Colombia, 1967). Perhaps most discouraging from the current policy vantage point is the fact that the Latin American countries show the most repeated failures in attempts at liberalization. And the legacy of past failures can have an important bearing on the success of any future plan, as I argue below.

Table 6.2 gives the breakdown of success and failure, with the dates of the program, and the inflation rate of the preceeding year. Two points stand out clearly. In almost all cases, the internal imbalances in the economy at the time of the liberalization attempts, as measured by the inflation rate, are far smaller than the crisis conditions now confronting the Latin American debtors. Second, a high inflation rate seems to be a serious hindrance in successful stabilization, since in four of the five cases in which liberalization was attempted with an inflation rate above 30 percent, the experiment failed. Of those five, only Brazil, in 1964, demonstrated a successful liberalization with stabilization. That episode might be the only modern case of the type of adjustment now demanded of the Latin American countries. It had its own special conditions that allowed a successful program, not the least of which was a strong military dictatorship that could sharply squeeze real wages in the period of disinflation, 1964–67.

The appropriate link between stabilization and liberalization may be the most important policy issue facing the World Bank in choosing a strategy for high-conditionality lending. The suggestion in table 6.2 that

Table 6.2   **Successful and Unsuccessful Liberalization Attempts, Krueger-Bhagwati NBER Study**

Cases	Year	Inflation Rate, Preceding Year
Successful		
Brazil	1964	66.7
Colombia	1967	19.8
Israel	1952	n.a.
Israel	1962	5.6
Korea	1964	19.7
Philippines	1960	−1.2
Philippines	1970	2.9
Turkey	1958	17.4
Turkey	1970	7.0
Unsuccessful		
Brazil	1957	
Brazil	1961	29.6
Chile	1956	83.8
Chile	1959	32.5
Chile	1965	46.0
Colombia	1951	n.a.
Colombia	1957	6.4
Colombia	1962	8.6
Colombia	1965	17.6
Egypt	1962	0.7
Ghana	1967	13.1
India	1966	9.2
South Korea	1961	10.2

Source: Krueger (1978, 219–20)

Notes: Note that the definition of success used here is rather modest: a Phase III liberalization is converted to a Phase IV liberalization for at least four years. Several of the success cases ultimately became failures, as qualitative restrictions (QRs) were reapplied. The precise definitions of Phases III and IV can be found in Krueger (1978 26–27). Phase III signifies a trade regime in which the exchange rate has been devalued "to reflect the de facto price of foreign exchange." QRs may be reduced in scope but will generally remain. Phase IV "features greater emphasis on price mechanisms than on quantitative restrictions in managing the balance of payments."

n.a. = not available.

an initially high inflation rate can do harm in a liberalization effort finds independent support in several quarters. First, Krueger herself notes that liberalization attempts are most successful in countries that are not at the same time pursuing anti-inflationary policies or policies to restrict the level of foreign borrowing. One clear reason is that the fear of inflation induced governments to undertake inadequate devaluations at the start of a liberalization exercise, and they then failed to keep the exchange rate adjusting downward in correction for a domestic inflation rate in excess of the world rate.

Unfortunately, this lesson was not learned in time for the recent Southern Cone stabilization exercises, which foundered exactly on this conflict of goals. In their excellent survey of these episodes in Argentina, Chile, and Uruguay, Corbo and de Melo (1985) conclude that "policy inconsistencies were the main reason for the eventual failure of the reforms" (p. 864), with the inconsistencies revolving first around the use of the exchange rate both to promote trade and restrict inflation, and second around the inconsistent application of tariff and regulatory policies. Even the tariff inconsistencies can often be traced to the anti-inflation program, since unexpected and unplanned tariff changes were often made (especially in Argentina) in an attempt to further reduce inflation.

The Southern Cone countries were attempting to pursue two targets, low inflation and liberalized trade, and had the freedom to relax a third constraint: external borrowing. In the late 1980s, the Latin American countries are being called upon to pursue three objectives simultaneously: lower inflation, liberalization, and reduced dependence on foreign borrowing. I am still searching in vain for an historical example in which all three targets were satisfied. (Even if one could be found for the 1960s, it would probably be possible to distinguish it from current circumstances by virtue of the buoyant growth in world trade in the 1960s.)

Brazil and Korea, in 1964, and Indonesia in 1967 come closest to being examples. It is clear, however, that certain factors disposed these cases to success. Brazil and Korea started out their programs with sharp real wage reductions, backed by a strong military regime (comparable real wage data for Indonesia are not available). Also, all proceeded gradually with liberalization, and after a few years (starting in the late 1960s) relied on increasing foreign borrowing in order to maintain the momentum of growth. Finally, Brazil and Korea began the episode with much smaller internal imbalances than are typical in Latin America today. Korea had an inflation rate of a mere 19.7 pecent in the year before the stabilization program began, and Brazil's rate of 66.7 percent, while very high, is still dwarfed by today's rates. (Indonesia's inflation rate reached a very high 1044 percent in 1965.)

Other research, by Killick et al. (1984) and Lin (1985), agrees with the proposition that the simultaneous application of stabilization and widespread liberalization is unlikely to be sustainable and successful. Killick notes that a degree of liberalization was sought alongside stabilization in at least 8 of 23 standby arrangements in 1978–79, with meagre results. He concludes "It does not seem that the means available to, or employed by, the Fund are strong enough to achieve its liberalisation objective in more than rare cases" (p. 238). Lin has made a persuasive case, this time based on a comparative economic history of East Asia and Latin America, that a reduction in inflation should take precedence over all other targets, including liberalization, when inflation rates are high and prone to rise. In a detailed comparison of the stabilization experiences of Latin American and East Asian countries, Lin argues that the success of the Asian cases was built on a reduction of inflation that preceded the liberalization attempts by 5 years or more:

> In both Chile and Argentina, the control of hyperinflation and the liberalization of the economy occurred at the same time [in the mid-1970s]. This greatly compounded the difficulties of the domestic industries by forcing them to cope with both the depressive effects of the stabilization policies and the increased competition of foreign producers at the same time. This contrasts sharply with the situation in Taiwan and South Korea, where the control of hyperinflation preceded intensive trade policy reforms by several years (chap. 4, p. 8).

Lin also points out at some length that inflation control was supported by a worsening rather than an improving of the trade balance, since foreign funds were used to support the governments of Taiwan and Korea after the resort to money creation was brought under control:

> In all of the cases mentioned, the eventual contraction of the inflationary process required the restoration of political stability and productive capacity, with the injection of massive foreign aid and the restriction of deficit financing by the central bank playing important roles (ibid.).

Lin is persuasive in arguing that improvements in the real economy have been unlikely to be long lasting when attempted in a setting of rapid inflation and large budget deficits. The analytical arguments in favor of giving anti-inflationary policies a strong priority include the following: (1) the damage to financial intermediation that occurs in a climate of high inflation, including bank failures, widespread disintermediation, the absence of financial instruments of long-term maturities, and capital flight; (2) the likelihood of major relative price distortions in an inflationary environment; (3) the damage to tax collection and public-sector finances; (4) the damage to real investment and financial institutions as governments implement increasingly onerous methods of collecting the inflation tax (e.g., raising reserve requirements on banks); (5) the likelihood of policy conflict and policy inconsistency in management of the exchange rate to meet both trade and inflation targets; (6) the high transaction costs that are incurred as individuals and firms economize on monetary transactions; and (7) the ever-present fear of the public that major new tax increases or capital levies will be used in order to close large public-sector deficits. Such fears will constrain the private sector from making the real investment expenditures necessary for a successful liberalization in the longer term.

6.6 Conclusions: Toward an Improved Use of Conditionality

We have noted that the efficacy of conditionality is inherently limited, and that the current overhang of debt greatly complicates the situation. In cases of extreme indebtedness, the debt itself might set up incentives that are adverse to significant adjustment or liberalization. In such a case, partial debt forgiveness can actually raise the expected repayments to the creditors, while at the same time giving greater incentive to the country for favorable adjustment. To be most successful, combining debt relief with IMF–World Bank conditionality would enhance the likelihood that the debt relief actually turns into economic reform.

The historical experience with liberalization alone, and with stabilization alone, are not very encouraging. The difficulties of combining the two policy initiatives are formidable. The historical record suggests that it is virtually impossible to bring inflation under control, while simultaneously trying to liberalize the economy. One is hard pressed to find an example of an economy which stabilized, liberalized, and improved the external position all at the same time. Only South Korea, Brazil, and Indonesia seem to provide examples of implementing the first two measures, and in those cases the programs were supported by a strong military government that substantially reduced real wages (at least in Brazil and South Korea) at the outset of the programs, and by favorable world conditions, including growing world trade, and after a few years, access to foreign borrowing in significant amounts.

These findings suggest that the IMF and World Bank should recognize the limited efficacy of conditionality. The following list of guidelines for improving the use of conditionality in future lending by the IMF and the World Bank would increase the chances of success for LOC adjustment programs and improve the effectiveness of conditionality:

1. Approve fewer programs.
2. Require more prior actions in cases where the efficacy of the conditionality is doubtful.
3. Encourage governments to enlist the necessary range of political support behind the terms of a high-conditionality program before the program is made final.
4. Approve programs which allow a buildup of arrears to private creditors in cases where the private creditors (a) fail to grant debt relief and (b) fail to provide sufficient amounts of new financing.
5. Encourage the use of debt relief schemes as a way to enhance the likely adherence to conditionality terms.
6. Narrow the goals of conditionality: Make macroeconomic stabilization the first step with structural reform to be implemented only as macroeconomic stability is restored.

Appendix A
A Formal Analysis of Conditionality

The model in this appendix provides a very simple illustration of the function of conditionality in international lending. Suppose that there are two periods ($t = 1,2$), and that a government of a small economy faces an allocation problem of consumption and investment. In the first period, the government can consume (C_1 or invest I_1 resources, subject to the budget constraint that total spending, ($C_1 + I_1$, must equal domestic output, Q_1, plus borrowing from abroad, D_1. The foreign loans carry an interest rate, r, so that repayments due in the second period are $(1 + r)D_1$. Output in the second period is a function of investment in the first. As a simple illustration, I assume a linear technology, with $Q_2 = Q_1 + (1 + g)I_1$, and also assume that investment opportunities are bounded by $I_1 \leq \bar{I}$. The utility function is $U = C_1 + C_2/(1 + d)$, where d is the rate of pure time preference. For purposes of illustration, I assume that we have the following relative parameter values: $d > g > r$. With this ordering, investments are profitable when evaluated at world interest rates, but not worthwhile when evaluated according to the subjective rate of time discount, d.

I assume that the country repays all of its foreign borrowing, subject to the constraint that $C_2 \geq 0$. If the debt is so large that full repayment would require $C_2 < 0$, then the country pays as much as possible, suspends further repayments, and consumes 0 in the second period. Under conditions of certainty, the lenders will ration credit such that $D_1 \leq Q_2/(1 + r)$. Of course $C_2 = 0$ should be taken figuratively. The model is virtually unchanged if the consumption constraint is $C_2 \geq M$ is some minimum level of consumption, based on political or economic constraints. Also, C_2 implicitly refers only to *tradable* goods (since only those goods can be used to finance debt servicing). With $C_2 = 0$ or $C_2 = M$, there could still be positive levels of nontradables consumption. However, to introduce nontradable goods at this point would unnecessarily complicate the model.

Now, to see the role of conditionality, suppose that private lenders must make loans *before* the country chooses the level of investment in the first period, while the IMF or the World Bank, to the contrary, can condition a loan on a particular level of investment. The private-sector creditor must determine how much investment the country will make once a loan is received, since the safe lending constraint $D_1 \leq Q_2/(1 + r)$ ties the sustainable debt D_1 to the level of Q_2.

It is easy to verify that for any level of debt D_1, the country will always prefer a zero level of investment, as long as we have the inequality that $d > g$. The reason is straightforward: an increment of investment reduces welfare by 1 in the first period and raises it in the second period by $(1 + g)/(1 + d)$ in terms of first period goods. Therefore, the welfare return from an increment of investment is negative. Since the country will choose $I_1 = 0$, Q_2 will equal Q_1, and the lending limit for the commercial banks is given by $Q_1/(1 + r)$.

It may be possible for the Fund or the Bank to lend more than this safely, if the new loans can be conditioned on investment expenditure. Suppose that the World Bank or the IMF can obtain a credible commitment of the country to invest $0 < I_1 \leq \bar{I}$ in return for a stabilization or adjustment loan. In such a case, the country will be able to support total foreign borrowing in the amount $[Q_1 + (1 + g)I_1]/(1 + r)$, which is $(1 + g)I_1/(1 + r)$ greater than in the absence of the program. Will the country agree to such a program? The answer is clearly yes, since first-period consumption rises by $(1 + g)I_1/(1 + r) - I_1$, and second-period consumption is unchanged (since the rise in income, $(1 + g)I_1$, equals the increase in debt servicing).

It is not necessary, in this scenario, for the World Bank or the IMF to actually make the conditionality loan in the amount $(1 + g)I_1/(1 + r)$. In principle, any smaller loan should attract additional private resources to make up the difference. The Fund or the Bank is important only in the "seal of good housekeeping" role rather than as a supplier of funds.

Appendix B
A Model of Debt Forgiveness

To see how a given stock of debt can interfere with conditionality, let us return to the simple two-period model presented in appendix A. We now amend the model in two important ways. First, the utility function is written in general form as $U = U(C_1, C_2)$, with the standard concavity conditions. Second, we assume that as of the first period, there is an existing stock of debt, inherited from the past and due in the second period. Let D be the legal amount due in the second period (interest plus principal), and let S denote the actual debt servicing in that period (S may be a stochastic variable as of the first period). The creditors might, we shall see, be willing to forgive some of the debt as of the first period, in which case we denote the post-forgiveness amount due as R. Thus, with $D > R$, there is some formal forgiveness of the debt as of the first period, and with $R > S$, there is a partial default in the second period (since as of the second period, R is due and only S is actually repaid). The production technology is as before: $Q_2 = Q_1 + (1 + g)I_1$, $I_1 \leq I$.

Suppose that the country is cut off from the world capital markets by virtue of the preexisting stock of debt, D, or by virtue of its general lack of creditworthiness, and ignore conditionality lending for the moment. All investment therefore comes from internal savings. We assume as before that as of the second period the country repays as much of the foreign debt as it can. If savings and consumption allocations are made by a central planner, then the planner's problem is:

$$\max_{I_1} \ U(C_1, C_2) \ \text{such that} \ C_1 = Q_1 - I_1$$

$$C_2 = Q_2(I_1) - S$$

$$S = \min(R, Q_2).$$

The creditors have a corresponding problem. Should they demand full repayment of the debt, D, or should they agree *as of the first period* to forgive part of the debt, and to demand a smaller repayment, $R < D$? Assuming that the creditor "moves first" by announcing the debt decision, and that the debtor country thereafter solves the optimal allocation problem, the creditor must solve the following:

$$\max_{R} \ S \ \text{such that} \ R \leq D \ \text{and}$$

S is the solution to the debtor problem given above.

In words, the debtor chooses the repayment level, R, that maximizes actual debt servicing, S, subject to the constraint that R be less than or equal to the original debt, D.

As noted in the text, it might seem, and it is often argued as if, the creditor should simply hold out for the maximum repayment, D, and take whatever he can get in the second period. Such a strategy, however, can be improved upon.

Consider the debtor's problem, taking R as a parameter. For low values of R, the debtor will repay everything, since it will turn out that $R < Q_2(I_1)$. Thus, the allocation problem becomes one of maximizing $U(C_1, C_2)$ such that $C_1 = Q_1 - I_1$, and $C_2 = Q_2(I_1) - R$. The interior solution to this problem sets the gross rate of return on investment, $(1 + g)$, equal to the marginal rate of substitution between first and second period consumption: U_1/U_2. Take, as an illustration, the special case of additively separable utility, $U(C_1, C_2) = U(C_1) + U(C_2)/(1 + d)$. The planner then sets $(1 + g) = (1 + d)U'(Q_1 - I_1)/U'[Q_2(I_1) - R]$. It is then easy to verify that I_1 is an increasing function of R in this range. In a sense, high debt repayments are a spur to adjustment. The social planner knows that there is a big reduction to real cash flow next period, because of the debt repayment, and therefore he smooths consumption across periods by saving today and investing more in order to raise second-period output.

For large values of R, however, it will be the case that $R > Q_2(I_1)$ so that the debtor will not make the full repayment, R. In that case, the allocation problem becomes one of maximizing $U(C_1, C_2)$ such that

$C_1 = Q_1 - I_1$ and $C_2 = 0$. Clearly, for very high levels of debt, the optimal policy is zero investment, since C_2 is fixed at 0! Let $R*$ be the minimum repayment due at which I_1 is set at zero. For $R \geq R*$, $I_1 = 0$. For R above $R*$, the entire increase in GDP due to higher investment would accrue to the existing creditors, rather than to the country itself. The debt is so high that the country works for the bank rather than for itself. The equilibrium level of utility is given as $U(Q_1,0)$. Call this threshhold level of utility $U*$. The country's utility can never fall below this level, since it is always feasible for the country to make no investments and to pay as much of the debt as is feasible, subject to the constraint $C_2 \geq 0$. At high levels of debt, the actual debt servicing is equal to $Q_2 [I_1 = 0] = Q_1$.

The key point from the creditor's point of view is that actual repayments, S, will fall when R increases above $R*$, since investment, I_1, falls to zero. The resource base from which the country makes debt repayments shrinks, so that actual repayments decline. Thus, for $R \leq R*$, we have $S = R$; for $R > R*$, we have $S < R* < R$.

Now let us return to the creditor's problem. For levels of debt, D, less than the threshhold $R*$, it is clear that the creditors should hold out for full repayment. Indeed, the higher the level of the debt, the greater will be the "adjustment" in the debtor country, with adjustment measured by the amount of first period investment. However, for $D > R*$, *it is a mistake to hold out for full repayment*. The creditors will get more repayment by agreeing in the first period to lower the required debt repayments in the second! Forgiving debt can be to the advantage of the creditors, by spurring investment in the debtor country, and thereby spurring the means of the debtor to service the debt.

The two-period model just explored lends itself to a standard diagrammatic analysis, as in figure 6.4. As usual, the X-axis measures production and consumption in the first period, and the Y-axis measures production and consumption in the second period. Note that since $C_1 = Q_1 - I_1$ and $C_2 = \max(0, Q_2 - D) = \max[0, Q_1 + (1 + g)I_1 - D]$, we can draw the consumption possibility frontier as $C_2 = \max[0, (2 + g)Q_1 - (1 + g)C_1 - D]$. When $D = 0$, the consumption frontier is given by the curve CC in figure 6.1(a). The point $Q = (Q_1,Q_1)$ is the consumption point when $I_1 = 0$; the CC curve has slope $- (1 + g)$, since each increment of foregone consumption in the first-period raises second-period consumption by $(1 + g)$.

When $D > 0$, the consumption frontier shifts downward as in figures 6.1(b) and 6.1(c). The curve shifts vertically downward by the amount D, except if D is so large that C_2 would turn negative if fully repaid. The resulting CC curve is shown for small levels of D ($< Q_1$) in figure 6.1(b), and for large level of debt D ($> Q_1$) in figure 6.1(c). In figure 6.1(c) note that the CC curve is kinked, because of the restriction that $C_2 \geq 0$.

The social planner picks the point on the CC schedule that maximizes domestic welfare. In figure 6.4(a), equilibrium is at the point A where CC is tangent to the indifference curve, U. Note that the horizontal distance between A and Q is the level of optimal first-period investment, I_1. In figure 6.4(b), equilibrium is at B. Note that the existence of a small amount of foreign debt, D, *spurs* investment (seen by the fact that the horizontal distance from B to Q, equal to I_1, exceeds the distance from A to Q). In this case, the foreign debt drives the social planner to smooth consumption by reducing C_1 in order to raise Q_2 enough to service the debt. In figure 6.4(c), the optimal policy is to set $I_1 = 0$, and to consume at the point E, with $C_1 = Q_1$, $C_2 = 0$. The point here is straightforward. Since D is so large that it will not be fully repaid, each increment of I_1 raises second-period output *without* raising second-period consumption. In such circumstances there is no incentive to invest! With zero investment, $Q_2 = Q_1$ and actual repayment in period 2 is $S = Q_1$, as shown.

The key point of this section is that in case (c) the creditors can raise the debt repayments through debt forgiveness. Instead of demanding D, they can instead demand a smaller amount, R. The result is a new equilibrium at point F. The country undertakes more investment and therefore has more resources with which to service the debt. As drawn, the debt writedown raises debt repayments (from S to R) and leaves the country's utility unchanged. It is obvious that a greater level of debt forgiveness could leave *both* the country and the creditors better off than at point E.

It might be objected that the foregoing model is artificial, in that it establishes a zone in which a high external debt level makes second-period investment *completely worthless* from the country's point of view. To see a more nuanced view, we could use the model of default and debt renegotiation in Sachs and Cohen (1985). Suppose that if the country defaults, the retaliation penalty from the creditors is a fraction, h, of national GDP. Thus, if the country repays the debt due, second period consumption is $Q_2 - R$. If instead it defaults, it saves repayments, R, but suffers a loss of GDP equal to hQ_2, so that second period consumption would be $C_2 = (1 - h)Q_2$. Clearly, the country would find default attractive whenever $R > hQ_2$. Finally, suppose that in lieu of default with retaliation, we can assume that in the second period if $R > hQ_2$, the creditors and debtor reach a *cooperative outcome* such that the debtors pay a fraction of the repayment due, in the amount hQ_2, and the creditors agree to forego any further retaliation.

In this case, the debtor's problem can be restated as follows:

$$\max \ U(C_1, C_2) \quad \text{such that} \quad C_1 = Q_1 - I_1$$

$$C_2 = Q_2(I_1) - S$$

$$S = \min \left[R, \ (1 - h)Q_2(I_1) \right].$$

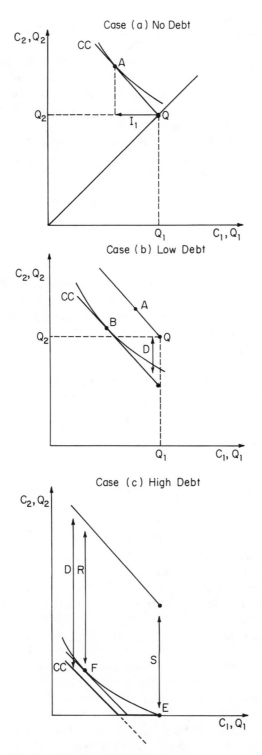

Fig. 6.4 Investment and external indebtedness

In this case, the marginal return to investment in the zone in which debt is fully repaid is simply $(1 + g)$. On the other hand, in the region in which debt is not fully repaid, the marginal return to investment is $(1 - h)(1 + g)$. The overhang of debt now imposes *a marginal tax of h percent* on the social return to investment. Once again, it is easy to show that explicit debt relief can in fact raise the creditors' eventual repayments, and can spur "adjustment" (i.e., investment) in the debtor country, by eliminating the implicit "marginal tax" on the returns to investment.

Appendix C
The Interaction of Debt Relief and Conditionality

In this appendix, we combine the models of appendix A and appendix B, to illustrate the case in which the *combination* of conditionality and debt relief is both necessary and sufficient for raising the welfare of both creditors and debtors.

For convenience, we work with the case of linear utility and linear technology. The government objective function is given as:

$$U = C_1 + C_2/(1 + d).$$

Production in period 2 is given as:

$$Q_2 = Q_1 + (1 + g)I_1 \qquad I_1 \le \bar{I}.$$

There is an initial overhang of debt in the second period, D_2, with

$$D_2 > Q_1 + (1 + g)\bar{I}.$$

In the absence of debt relief, the government will undertake zero investment spending in the first period. Moreover, the country would not agree to any binding package of new official lending *with* conditionality if the official lenders were financing anything less than 100 percent of the investment. Suppose that a share, s, of the investment could be financed with an IMF–World Bank loan. Then initial consumption would fall by $(1 - s) * I_1$, i.e., by the amount not financed externally. Future consumption would not rise at all, however, since after repayment to the IMF–World Bank, and partial repayment to the original creditors, nothing would be left over for the country.

Next, suppose that there is debt relief alone, without the involvement of the official institutions. Suppose, for example, that the debt is reduced to the level Q_1. Then, the country will surely repay the remaining debt in the second period. However, it will still choose to do no investment spending, as long as the rate of time discount, d, is greater than the return to investment, g. Moreover, in the absence of conditionality, it would not be safe to make new loans to the country even after the debt is written down to Q_1, since the country will use the loans for consumption, and not for investment.

Now, suppose that the debt relief is combined with a high-conditionality loan, in the following manner. The country undertakes to make investment, I_1, with the share, s, to be financed by the IMF–World Bank. The initial debt is reduced to $(Q_1 + e)$, where e is a small amount. First period consumption falls by $(1 - s) I_1$, and second period output rises by $(1 + g)I_1$. Second-period consumption now rises in the amount $(1 + g)I_1 - s (1 + r) I_1 - e$, which will surely be positive as long as e is sufficiently small. (Note that the rise in consumption equals the rise in output, minus the repayment to the IMF, minus the increment, e, in repayment to the original creditors above the level Q_1). Now, as long as the rate of time discount, d, is sufficiently small or the share of IMF–World Bank financing is sufficiently large, then the overall effect on the government's objective function is positive. Specifically, the condition for an improvement in the government's objective function is:

$$-(1 - s) I_1 + [(1 + g)I_1 - s I_1 (1 + r) - e]/(1 + d) > 0.$$

Since $g > r$, and e is close to 0.0, the condition for improvement is surely satisfied for s very close to 1.0, or d very close to 0.0, and may well be satisfied for intermediate values of s and d.

Note

1. Berg and Batchelder (1985) have done a very fine recent paper that reaches similar conclusions.

References

Berg, E., and A. Batchelder. 1985. Structural adjustment lending: A critical view. CPD Discussion Paper no. 1985-21, January. Washington, D.C.: The World Bank.

Beveridge, W. A., and M. R. Kelley. 1980. Fiscal content of financial programs supported by stand-by arrangements in the upper-credit tranches, 1969–78. IMF Staff Papers 27(2): 205–49.

Cline, William. 1984. *International debt: Systemic risk and policy response.* Washington, D.C.: Institute for International Economics.

Cooper, R., and J. Sachs. 1985. Borrowing abroad: The debtor's perspective. In *International debt and developing countries,* ed. G. W. Smith and J. T. Cuddington. Washington, D.C.: World Bank.

Corbo, V., and J. de Melo. 1985. Overview and summary: Liberalization with stabilization in the Southern Cone of Latin America. *World Development* 13(8): 863–66.

Diamond, Douglas W., and Philip H. Dybvig. 1983. Bank runs, deposit insurance, and liquidity. *Journal of Political Economy* 91(3): 401–19.

Doe, L. K. 1983. Fiscal policy and adjustment in the 1980 fund financial programs (departmental memoranda 83/52). Washington, D.C.: IMF.

Finch, David. 1988. Let the IMF be the IMF. *World Economy* (January/February): 126–29.

Goode, R. 1985. *Economic assistance to the developing countries through the IMF.* Washington, D.C.: Brookings Institution.

Haggard, S. 1985. The politics of adjustment. *International Organization* 39(3): 505–34.

Kelley, M. 1982. Fiscal adjustment and fund-supported programs, 1971–80. IMF Staff Papers 29(2): 561–602.

Killick, T., with G. Bird, J. Sharpley, and M. Sutton. 1984. *The quest for economic stabilization.* London: Overseas Development Institute.

Krueger, A. 1978. *Foreign trade regimes and economic development: Liberalization attempts and consequences.* Cambridge, Mass.: Ballinger Publishing Company.

Krugman, P. 1988. Financing versus forgiving a debt overhang. NBER Working Paper no. 2486 (January). Cambridge, Mass.: National Bureau of Economic Research.

Lin, Ching-yuan. 1985. Latin America and East Asia: A comparative development perspective. Unpublished ms., International Monetary Fund.

Remmer, Faren. 1986. The politics of economic stabilization: IMF standby programs in Latin America, 1954–84, *Comparative Politics* (October): 1–24.

Sachs, J. 1984. *Theoretical issues in international borrowing.* Princeton Studies in International Finance, no. 54. Princeton, N.J.: Princeton Univ. Press.

———. 1985. External debt and macroeconomic performance in Latin America and East Asia. *Brookings Papers on Economic Activity* 2: 523–73.

———. 1987. Trade and exchange rate policies in growth-oriented adjustment programs. In *Growth-oriented adjustment programs,* ed. V. Corbo, M. Goldstein, and M. Khan. Washington, D.C.: International Monetary Fund and the World Bank.

Sachs, J., and D. Cohen. 1985. LDC borrowing with default risk. *Kredit und Kapital,* Heft 8.

Sachs, J., and H. Huizinga. 1987. The U.S. commercial banks and the developing country debt crisis. *Brookings Papers on Economic Activity* 2: 555–601.

Short, R. P. 1983. The role of public enterprises: An international statistical comparison. IMF Fiscal Affairs Department, DM 83/134.

Von Furstenberg, G. M. 1985a. Adjustment with IMF lending. *Journal of International Money and Finance* 4 (June): 209–22.

———. 1985b. The IMF as marketmaker for official business between nations. Indiana University, processed.

Williamson, J., ed. 1983. *IMF conditionality.* Washington, D.C.: Institute for International Economics.

Yaeger, L. B. 1981. *Experiences with stopping inflation*. Washington, D.C.: American Enterprise Institute.

Yagci, F., S. Ramin, and V. Rosenbaum. 1985. Structural adjustment lending: An evaluation of program design. World Bank Staff Working Papers no. 735. Washington, D.C.: World Bank.

III   The International System

7   Private Capital Flows to Problem Debtors

Paul Krugman

7.1 Introduction

One of the key elements of the approach to the debt problem that has dominated official thinking since 1982 has been an effort to mobilize private flows of capital to countries with debt-servicing problems. The interest payments on LDC debt, it has been widely accepted, are more than the debtors can or, at any rate, will pay out of current export income. This gap between feasible resource transfer and interest due must be filled in some way. It could be filled by official lending, but this is an unlikely and probably undesirable prospect. It could also be filled by large-scale debt forgiveness, but the whole point of the US-IMF strategy has been to avoid forcing such drastic action. What remains is private capital flows. Bank lending was expected to provide most of the capital flow under the debt strategy as it first emerged in 1983, and it was supposed to play a major role under the Baker initiative of 1985.

Yet in fact private capital flows to problem debtors have consistently fallen far short of expectations. Even in 1983–84, the banner years of "concerted lending," much of the funding that came in the front door was lost through the back door. In the following two years, private capital flows to problem debtors were minor, despite a few highly visible injections of new money. To a first approximation, the debtors have made resource transfers equal to interest less official inflows. Since official inflows themselves have been fairly small, the end result has been that debtors have been forced to run massive trade surpluses.

Paul Krugman is a professor of economics at the Massachusetts Institute of Technology and a research associate of the National Bureau of Economic Research.

The purpose of this chapter is to reexamine the prospects for private capital flows to problem debtors. The central question is whether it is possible to induce sufficient capital inflows to aid substantially in the servicing of debt. To analyze this it necessary to ask, in particular, why efforts to mobilize private capital to date have been so disappointing. Thus the chapter focuses on the reasons for the stalling of the process of concerted lending after 1984 as a key test of the possibilities for inducing capital flows.

The chapter is divided as follows. Section 7.2 examines the rationale for private capital flows to countries that are already in debt trouble: Why should we ever expect to see new money provided to a country whose servicing of existing debt is in question? Section 7.3 reviews the experience with private capital flows since 1982, and examines alternative explanations of the failure of these flows to materialize on the scale that was originally envisaged. Section 7.4 examines the feasibility and desirability of attracting private capital through channels other than bank lending, notably through direct foreign investment or the currently popular option of debt-equity swaps. Finally, section 7.5 attempts to assess the prospects for generating private capital inflows in the future.

7.2 The Theory of Defensive Lending

To a man from Mars, or *The Wall Street Journal,* the proposition that new lending is essential to deal with the debt crisis seems extremely strange—a proposal to throw good money after bad. Yet private capital inflow has been a centerpiece of the official strategy for dealing with the debt crisis (although not of its execution—see section 7.3 below). To understand why this may be a good idea, it is necessary to appreciate two key points: the possibility that a country may have growing debt yet be growing more creditworthy over time, and the possibility that lending at a loss may be in the interest of the creditors if it defends the value of existing claims. On the other side, the problems that may block desirable capital inflow must be noted, as well as the potential role of official agencies in promoting such inflow.

7.2.1 The Analytics of Debt Growth and Creditworthiness

At the heart of the orthodox analysis of the debt problem, as represented for example by Cline (1983) and Feldstein (1986), is the analytical point that a country can simultaneously be increasing its debt and steadily improving its debt position as measured by such indicators as the ratio of debt to GNP or to export. The key point is that the debt indicators are *ratios,* whose denominators can be expected to grow over time. Thus it is possible for debt—the numerator—to grow while creditworthiness steadily improves, as long as it grows more slowly than GNP or exports—the denominator.

Consider the following numerical example, drawn from Feldstein et al. (1987). A country has a GNP of $200 billion, and an external debt of $100 billion (slightly above the average debt to GNP ratio for the IMF's category of "fifteen heavily indebted countries"). It must pay an interest rate of 9 percent on the debt. The world inflation rate is 4 percent, and the country's real GNP is expected to grow at an annual rate of 3 percent.

If the country were obliged to pay all interest out of current income then even if all principal were rescheduled it would be obliged to run a surplus on noninterest current account of $9 billion, or 4.5 percent of GNP. While such a surplus is not impossible to run, it is sufficiently large to impose substantial strains on the economic and political situation in debtor countries. A sustained resource transfer at this rate would raise risks that "debtor fatigue" will lead to increasing unwillingness of the debtor to pay. Thus some reduction in the size of the resource transfer is crucial.

Suppose, however, that the country is able to attract $4 billion of new money. Then it will need to run a noninterest surplus of only $5 billion, or 2.5 percent of GNP—a more tolerable number. It might at first seem that this simply puts the country even deeper into debt, which in a literal sense it does, since the debt grows by 4 percent. The country's real GNP, however, we have assumed will grow at 3 percent, which together with the price increase of 4 percent will imply a 7 percent growth in money GNP. Thus the ratio of debt to GNP will fall, and the country will be in a more favorable position, not a less favorable one, at the start of the next year.

In fact, if the country were merely seeking to stabilize its ratio of debt to GNP, it could borrow $7 billion, and make net payments of only $2 billion, or 1 percent of GNP. If it were able to borrow this much, and willing to devote 1 percent of GNP to net interest payments indefinitely, it could honor all its debt commitments. If the real interest rate were lower, or the growth rate higher, the necessary resource transfer would be even smaller. Calculations of this kind underlay the optimism of many economists about the debt of LDCs in the 1970s, and continue to be the basis of optimistic assessments now (again see Feldstein 1986).

If coping with debt seems relatively easy even given realistic levels of indebtedness, historically high real interest rates, and an assumed growth rate that is low by past standards, why is there a debt problem? The immediate answer is that the new money that in our example reduces the interest burden to an easily tolerable level has not been forthcoming. Lenders have not voluntarily lent to problem debtors (this is essentially the definition of a problem debtor), nor indeed have they provided much new money even under duress. This observation, however, only leads to the next question: Why does this favorable algebra not convince lenders to be willing to lend?

The main answer seems to be that while a modest annual rate of resource transfer to creditors will suffice to honor the debts even of countries that have high ratios of debt to GNP, this will only be the case if the resource transfer is very sustained. In the example we have just given—debt equal to half of GNP, growth at 3 percent, and a real interest rate of 5 percent—resource transfer at the rate of 2.5 percent of GNP would have to continue for 25 years to work off all the debt. If "debtor fatigue" were to set in before that, preventing further resource transfer, the debt would be worth less than par, even if the country were willing to run surpluses for quite a while. For example, even 10 years of resource transfer would provide a present value of resource transfer equal to only 45 percent of the value of the debt.

Doubt over whether debtors will be willing to run the trade surpluses needed to honor their debts for the very extended periods thus envisaged underlies the unwillingness of banks or other lenders to provide new money to the problem debtors. However, there remains a case for new lending by existing creditors to defend the value of their claims. This case for "involuntary," or perhaps more accurately, defensive lending, underlies the concept and rhetoric of the US-IMF debt strategy.

7.2.2 The Case for Defensive Lending

When a country's willingness to service its debts in full is uncertain, a potential lender with no existing stake in the country could be induced to lend only by being offered a high interest rate, which itself would provide an incentive for future nonpayment. Thus, in the case of problem debtors, new lending from the markets has dried up. Creditors may have an incentive to relend part of their interest due, however, as a way of protecting the value of the loans they have already made. This incentive forms the basis of the hopes for inducing bank lending to problem debtors.

When does it make sense to lend more money to a country already having trouble servicing its debt? The issue is often framed as one of liquidity versus solvency: The country is *illiquid,* that is, short of cash to pay its debt service, but it is *solvent,* that is, given time it will be able and (more important) willing to make resource transfers to its creditors equal in present value to its debt. However, it is quickly apparent upon reflection that this cannot be quite right; if a country were known to be merely illiquid, not insolvent, it would be able to attract voluntary lending to deal with its liquidity problem. It is only the possibility of a solvency problem that creates the liquidity problem.

The right way to think about the situation, as stressed by Cline (1983), Krugman (1985), and Sachs (1984), is as one of uncertainty in which defensive lending by existing creditors buys an option to collect on their claims in the future if the situation improves. Suppose that it is fairly likely that a country will fail to pay its debt in full even if it is able to avoid an immediate crisis; but that it is virtually certain that the country will repudiate an important part of its obligation if its creditors attempt to collect full interest immediately. Then new lending that reduces the interest burden, although a losing proposition in isolation, may be worthwhile because it improves the expected value of the initial debt.

Even under quite adverse circumstances this defensive lending argument can justify quite substantial increases in creditor exposure. To see why, consider the basic algebra of the situation. Let D be a country's outstanding debt, and d be the subjective discount that creditors place on that debt (which may be inferred from the secondary market price if that market is sufficiently well developed). Suppose that by relending part of the interest, and thus averting an immediate liquidity crisis, creditors can reduce the discount to some smaller amount, d'. Such a program will have a cost—the expected loss on the new lending—and a benefit—the increase in the value of existing claims. The cost will be $d'L$, where L is the value of new lending; while the benefit will be $(d - d')D$. Thus a program of defensive lending will be worth undertaking as long as

$$d'L < (d - d')D,$$

or

$$L/D < (d - d')/d'.$$

Now suppose that in the absence of a program of defensive lending the discount on claims would be 50 percent, while even with such a program the discount would be reduced only to 40 percent. Even with these fairly dismal numbers, it would be worthwhile for creditors to expand their exposure by 25 percent to protect their original investment.

The orthodox view of the debt problem, as exposited most famously by Cline (1983), was that this incentive for defensive lending could be used to mobilize new bank lending on a sufficient scale that, combined with adjustment efforts by the countries and an improving external environment, problem debtors could be returned to normal capital market access after a few years. It was recognized from the beginning, however, that there were serious obstacles to mobilization of capital flows from existing creditors; these obstacles now look more serious than was realized in 1983.

7.2.3 Obstacles to Defensive Lending: The Free-Rider Problem

The first obstacle to a program of defensive lending was immediately noted by many observers: There is a free-rider problem. The *collective* defensive lending of existing creditors raises the expected value of their *collective* claims, but for any *individual* creditor it would be preferable to opt out. In effect, the call for defensive lending from creditors asks that lenders, whom we suppose act competitively under normal circumstances, suddenly begin to act collusively once the country is in debt trouble.

Cline (1983) offered a convenient formulation of this issue, by supposing that the creditors consist of a collusive core and a competitive fringe. Defensive lending is undertaken only by the core that owns a fraction, f, of the outstanding claims. Assuming that it is possible to arrange for complete rescheduling of the principal of the fringe (which is a little optimistic; see section 7.3 below) the criterion for defensive lending now becomes

$$L/D = f(d - d')/d'$$

That is, the smaller the collusive core the less defensive lending will be worth undertaking.

In 1983 the hope was that this free-rider problem could be overcome through a variety of ad hoc means. First, while international capital markets may be highly competitive ex ante, the claims on any individual country are much more concentrated ex post. Second, most lending took the form of syndicated loans in which a certain amount of cooperative behavior was already built in. Third, the form of negotiations between a country and its creditors, in which an advisory committee represents the banks, itself tends to foster cooperative behavior among the creditors. Fourth, informal pressure from the central banks of creditors countries could be brought to bear on the smaller commercial banks to go along with collective lending packages. Fifth, official lending could reduce the extent of defensive lending required to an extent that would make the necessary cooperative behavior more feasible.

Does the limited extent of lending since 1984 show that these ad hoc means of overcoming the free-rider problem were inadequate? Before jumping to this conclusion, we need to recognize that free riding is not the only potential obstacle to defensive lending.

7.2.4 Obstacles to Defensive Lending: Bargaining and Conflict

To the extent that creditors are able to overcome their free-rider problems and act as a unit, they next find themselves in a situation of bilateral monopoly vis-à-vis the debtor country. There is a range of potential rates and terms of lending between the minimum acceptable to the country and the maximum acceptable to the banks. For the banks, any defensive lending that is less than the interest payments on existing debt—that is, any program that leads to a positive resource transfer from the country—is better than no payment at all. From the point of view of the country, there is a range of rates of resource transfer that is preferable to failure to reach an agreement, which would end the resource transfer but lead the banks to invoke penalties.

In general, economic theory does not offer any determinate outcome to bilateral monopoly. However, a useful light is shed on bilateral monopoly by recent developments in bargaining theory. The literature started by Rubinstein (1982) and applied to international debt by Bulow and Rogoff (1986) envisages a situation in which bargaining parties are able to make alternating offers, which continue until one party accepts. Each party pays some price for waiting. Such bargaining games have a simple and elegant solution: The first offer is in fact set at a level that will be accepted, with the terms of that offer depending on both the threat points of the players—the minimum settlement that each prefers to no agreement at all—and the cost to each of waiting.

While bargaining models are not easily applied to debt in a rigorous fashion, they suggest several useful points. First, it is a useful metaphor to think of capital flows from creditors to debtors as the outcome of a bargain. The determinants of that bargain are *not* the degree of optimism about the debtor's future, or the rewards for good behavior; they are the perceptions of each side about the level of welfare it can achieve without an agreement and the relative cost of delaying an agreement.

Second, by focussing attention on the bargaining aspect of the provision of new money, we are led to focus on the incentives for the parties to reach agreement. For the creditors the cost of failing to reach agreement is obvious—they do not get paid. For the debtor, however, the costs are more subtle and questionable: loss of future access to capital markets? disruption of trade? sanctions by creditor country governments? A key question in understanding the limited extent of capital flows is to ask why the rather fuzzy costs of failure to reach agreement have nonetheless left the countries in such an apparently weak bargaining position.

Third, the bargaining approach is a useful way to begin thinking about the problem of default. As Bulow and Rogoff have emphasized, the usual discussion, in which a country either pays or defaults, fails to capture the ongoing process of negotiation. On one side, a debt restructuring may considerably reduce the present value of debt obligations without any declarations of default or invocation of sanctions. On the other side, a country may fail to reach agreement with creditors, and be formally in default for a time, without precluding the possibility of eventually reaching an agreement. Thus rather than posing the question whether the country will pay or not, we need to ask *how much* it will pay, on one side, and how long it will take to reach agreement, on the other.

In the simplest bargaining models agreement is always reached immediately, because the first offer is set at a level that is just acceptable. However, this result depends on the parties having the same information. If one or both parties have private information—for example, if the country knows better than its creditors how costly it would be for it to go without an agreement, or the creditors are better informed about the consequences for them of having to declare loans nonperforming—then there is the possibility of a costly period of failure to reach agreement. The reason is that paying the costs of a temporary bargaining impasse may be the only way for either the debtor or the creditors to credibly establish bargaining strength. Brazil may feel that it is able to cope well with the consequences of not paying interest; if its creditors were convinced of this they would make concessions that would avert the need for Brazil to carry out its threat. A simple declaration of a tough posture, however, may not be enough; Brazil may need to go through a period of suffering the consequences of a debt moratorium to show that it really means it.

This point of view suggests that a failure to reach agreement should be viewed as a normal part of the bargaining process rather than a catastrophic event. It is not, however, necessarily appropriate for governments and official agencies to stand aside and allow the bargaining process to follow its bumpy path. Like the costs incurred to signal desirable attributes in other areas of economics, the cost incurred by a failure to reach agreement represent a real social cost (e.g., through disruption of trade, financial flows, political stability, etc.). It may be worthwhile for the Brazilians and their bankers to accept this cost in order to demonstrate their toughness, but it is preferable from the world's point of view, and possibily from the point of view of the parties themselves, if agreement can be reached more quickly. Thus there is a potential albeit problematic role for creditor country governments and multilateral agencies as facilitators of agreement.

7.2.5 The Contribution of Third Parties

Official agencies, such as the International Monetary Fund and the U.S. Treasury, can act to facilitate bank lending to problem debtors in several ways. To the extent that the free-rider problem is dominant, they can use indirect pressure to induce lending by reluctant banks, especially small potential free riders. They can also provide enough additional lending to make a defensive lending program by a collusive core worthwhile in circumstances where defensive lending is actually in the creditors' collective interest but not worthwhile for the collusive core alone.

The IMF and others can also enter into the bargaining process. Most benignly, the third party could simply serve as a mediator, making offers that serve as focal points for agreement. More problematically, it can use sticks and carrots to induce quicker agreement between the bargainers. If IMF resources are made available as a significant contribution to the pot, but only contingent on an agreement that also meets IMF terms, this provides an incentive for the players to forgo the costly process of signalling their toughness and to reach quick agreement. If the U.S. government implies that it will retaliate economically or politically against a country that fails to reach agreement with its bankers, this is also an incentive to reach an agreement quickly.

A bargaining perspective is again useful for examining this role. What it makes clear is that while an adroit intervention by third parties can facilitate the flow of private capital to a troubled debtor, a less adroit intervention can easily reduce that flow and perhaps even reduce the total capital flow to the country. Suppose, for example, that the country and its creditors would have reached agreement quickly without the carrot of official money; then provision of official money will not avoid any social costs, while it will typically be at least partly offset by a reduced supply of new money from the private creditors. (If the creditors make a take-it-or-leave-it offer to the country, then they will reduce the offer by the full amount of the official resources contributed. More generally, in a bargaining situation the country will get more but the banks will give less (see Bulow and Rogoff 1986).

If the third party threatens (or is perceived to threaten) sanctions against the country if agreement is not reached, this will make agreement take place more quickly, but it will also reduce the bargaining strength of the debtor. Thus while the risk of disruption as a result of hard bargaining goes down, so does the capital flow that eventually results. As I will argue below, U.S. policy may well have had this perverse effect, especially for some of the smaller debtors.

The point to be made is that the role of official agencies in a debt negotiation is, in economic terms, a second-best attempt to deal with a market failure. Like all second-best policies, its effect is sensitive to the details of the situation; a policy that does good in one case may do harm in an apparently similar case.

7.3   Bank Lending to Problem Debtors since 1982

I have now examined the rationale for continued bank lending to problem debtors. The theory suggests that there is an incentive for creditors to supply a continuing flow of funds, but that the process of lending may be hampered both by free-rider problems and by the efforts of parties to establish strength through bargaining. I now turn to the experience of bank lending since 1982, and its implications.

7.3.1   The Magnitude of Bank lending

Table 7.1 presents an overview of the lending of banks from the opening of the debt strategy at the end of 1982 to the end of 1986. Here two aggregates of debtor countries are considered: the IMF's group of "fifteen heavily indebted countries," and Latin America. The essential impression conveyed by the table is that the mobilization of private capital flows to debtors that was a central element of the debt strategy took place to a very limited extent in 1983 and 1984 and basically not at all since. Whether one looks at the broader aggregate of problem debtors or the narrower aggregate of Latin America, one sees that since 1982, and especially since 1984, debtor countries have run noninterest surpluses large enough to cover the bulk of their interest due, with a small contribution from official sources and very little from private new money. Only in 1986 was there a move toward current account deficit, which must have had capital inflow as its counterpart; more on this turn of events later.

Admittedly, this aggregative picture is somewhat misleading, for two reasons. First, it conceals differences among countries. While banks were on net withdrawing from some troubled but still relatively liquid debtors (e.g., Venezuela), they were significantly expanding their exposure in others. Second, the flow of funds reveals disbursements, but it is at least equally important to look at commitments, especially given the role of "concerted" lending for defensive purposes. Tables 7.2 and 7.3 provide some information on these issues.

Table 7.1   **Indicators of Bank Lending to Problem Debtors**

	1982	1983	1984	1985	1986
15 debtors					
Private debt	336.9	337.3	347.0	341.8	342.0
(growth rate)	—	0.1	2.8	−1.5	0.1
Current account	−50.6	−15.2	−0.6	−0.1	−11.8
Resource transfer	−12.8	21.0	38.3	37.4	21.1
Debt/GDP	41.7	47.0	46.8	46.3	48.4
Debt/exports	269.8	289.7	272.1	284.2	337.9
Latin America					
Private debt	291.9	292.1	303.2	303.8	308.0
(growth rate)	—	0.0	3.8	0.2	1.4
Bank debt (growth)	6.1	3.1	−0.1	2.7	0.9
Resource transfer	−42.4	−10.9	−2.6	−4.7	−16.1
Current account	−8.1	21.7	32.1	28.3	12.4
Debt/GDP	42.9	47.3	47.6	46.8	48.5
Debt/exports	273.8	290.3	277.1	295.5	354.7

Sources: International Monetary Fund (1987) and UNCTAD (1987).

Table 7.2   **Bank Lending to Selected Countries ($ billion)**

	1983	1984	1985	1985 1st half	1986 1st half
15 Heavily indebted countries	11.1	5.4	−1.9	−1.2	−3.4
Argentina	2.3	0.3	0.6	0.7	0.1
Brazil	5.2	5.2	−2.9	−1.0	−1.0
Korea	2.2	3.5	2.3	1.4	−0.2
Mexico	2.8	1.2	0.7	0.1	−0.8
Venezuela	−1.3	−2.2	0.4	−0.1	−0.3

Source: M. Watson., R. Kincaid, C. Atkinson, E. Kalter, and D. Folkerts-Landau, *International Capital Markets: Developments and Prospects,* International Monetary Fund, December 1986.

Table 7.3   **LDC Lending Commitments ($ billion)**

	1981	1982	1983	1984	1985	1984:1	1984:2	1985[a]	1986[a]
All capital importers	47.0	42.6	32.6	29.9	16.1	17.6	12.3	13.2	18.7
Latin America									
Total	25.2	23.0	15.3	15.4	2.5	11.4	4.0	2.4	7.9
Spontaneous	25.2	23.0	2.0	0.6	0.1	0.3	0.3	0.1	0.2
Concerted			13.3	14.8	2.4	11.1	3.7	2.3	7.7

Source: See table 7.2.
[a]First three quarters.

Table 7.2 offers some more detailed information on the financing of Latin nations. It shows that there was indeed more bank lending than the aggregates suggest, because in the aggregates the programs for Mexico, Brazil, and Argentina are masked by such events as the outflow from Venezuela and (in the larger aggregate) Korea's move toward current account surplus. For Argentina, Brazil, and Mexico, private capital did make a significant though modest contribution in 1983, and 1984 was not quite as bad as it seems in the aggregate. Nonetheless, the essential failure of bank lending to make much contribution after 1983 and especially 1984 remains apparent.

Table 7.3 looks at commitments rather than disbursements. By this measure the difference between 1983 and 1984 is less clear-cut; rather, the limited process of concerted lending seems to have run aground only in the second half of 1984. The table essentially reflects the conclusion of Brazilian and Mexican new-money packages in January and April of 1984 respectively, which were in effect the last large-scale attempts to mobilize new money until the desperation Mexican package of August 1986. The Mexican package is the main component of a sharp revival of concerted lending in 1986; the key question is whether this represents an aberration or the beginning of a new trend.

Taken together, these tables suggest the following summary of the effort to mobilize banks to provide new money for the debtors. First, even in 1983–84, when the new money was supposed to provide a major part of the solution, its supply was modest. Second, after mid-1984 new money from banks essentially ceased to be a recourse of the debtors.

The central question regarding the behavior of the banks, then, is why the seemingly forceful case for defensive lending generated only a brief, modest injection of new money. I will consider three possible explanations: that the creditors became unwillingly to lend because of unsatisfactory performance on the part of the debtors; that the free-rider problem blocked lending that was in the banks' collective interest; and that the absence of new money reflected an outcome of bargaining in which the countries were relatively weak and the banks strong.

7.3.2 Debtor Performance and the Supply of Funds

The bankers themselves prefer to ascribe their limited willingness to lend to the failure of the countries to show adequate progress in economic policy. One banker in conversation justified a lack of funding on the grounds that the debtor governments were "like children" who would simply waste any funds received. On this view the banks were in effect practicing conditionality, withholding funds contingent on reforms of economic policy.

This view raises two separate questions. First, is the indictment of the debtor governments correct? Second, and quite separate, is a judgment of debtor policies relevant to the explanation of limited lending? Do the volume and terms of lending to problem debtors depend positively on the performance of the countries' policymakers?

Policies in the Debtor Countries

The attack on the performance of the debtors faces in the first place the awkward fact that external adjustment, in the form of enormous trade surpluses, has been greater than anyone thought possible in 1983. This is of course the inevitable counterpart of the absence of new money, but it still means that the countries cannot be charged with having failed to make any adjustment. Instead the attack focusses on three issues: capital flight, budgetary adjustment, and the role of the private sector.

The attack on capital flight has come to assume a central place in the bankers' answer to charges that they have failed to deliver on their part of the debt strategy. For example, de Vries writes (in *World Financial Markets,* September 1986):

Psychologically, nothing has contributed more to the pervasive sense of frustration over the LDC debt problem than the realization that capital flight persisted, if on a much reduced scale, almost throughout the 1983–85 period of "involuntary" lending. Creditors, both private and official, are understandably reluctant to provide fresh funds unless the debtors put a stop to capital flight (p. 6).

To an outsider this attack on capital flight seems oddly timed, unless it is viewed more as a rationalization than a real explanation. The major period of capital flight was during the inception of the debt crisis rather than in the post-1983 period, and the structural causes of long-term capital flight—overvalued exchange rates and negative real interest rates—have actually been reversed, with very low real exchange rates and very high real interest rates in major debtors. Some capital flight does continue, because of a lack of confidence in the debtor's solvency. However, this is the same lack of confidence that prevents voluntary lending. There is no reason to expect domestic residents to be noticeably more willing to invest in a problem debtor, just because they happen to live there, than foreign investors. To demand that flight capital return before bank lending resumes is in effect to say that there will be no bank lending unless confidence is restored, i.e., that only voluntary lending will be provided. This ignores the whole point of the argument for defensive lending even when there is a perceived discount on claims on a country.

The second critique of debtor policies emphasizes the failure of budgetary adjustment, which manifests itself in particular in the problem of inflation. Here, while measurement issues can provide an endless source of debate, there is undoubtedly a valid point. One way to make this point is that the impressive external adjustment has come essentially at the expense of a decline in investment rather than a rise in saving, largely because of a failure to bring budgets under control. This is a useful point, because it suggests a focus on the fiscal aspect of the debt issue, which is a useful way to cut through some otherwise problematic issues, like the potential role of direct foreign investment and debt-equity swaps.

Finally, it is argued that debtor countries have failed to make essential moves toward freeing up their domestic economies, both in terms of internal liberalization and in terms of opening the way for foreign investment. In part this concern reflects the idea that direct foreign investment can serve as an alternative to bank lending for financing; in part it is related to the proposals for debt-equity conversion. Both of these topics are treated below. There is also an element of supply-side economics, in which countries are urged to pursue more market-oriented policies in order to achieve rapid economic growth, which will restore confidence and allow the debt problem to be resolved. This last argument requires a degree of certainty about the size and speed of the benefits of promarket policies that does not rest on hard evidence. It is also something new; demands for a radical shift to market-oriented policies were not on the table in 1983, when substantial bank lending was envisaged.

On balance, there are without question serious criticisms of the economic policies followed in each of the debtor countries. In any case, one need not condemn the policies of the debtors to be disheartened at the results. Whether or not one views debtor country policies as having been inadequate, the performance of the debtors has in one major respect been extremely unsatisfactory. One of the key premises of the case for involuntary lending was that countries could increase their debt while reducing the ratio of debt to GDP or exports, and thus become more creditworthy even as they continued to borrow. As table 7.1 makes clear, however, the debt ratios have either stagnated or worsened for major debtors, in spite of their having received far less financing than expected. This unfavorable result is largely due to weak world commodity prices and limited markets for debtors' exports, which have forced the trade adjustment to come primarily on the import side and also forced steep real devaluations that have reduced the dollar value of national income. If lenders are looking at the ratios, it is not surprising if they have become discouraged and are less willing to lend now than they were in 1983.

Although the debtors have thus dissatisfied their creditors with both their policies and their performance, it is questionable whether this dissatisfaction is the source of the unwillingness to lend. An alternative view dismisses complaints about the debtors' performance as rationalizations for the lack of bank financing, not its cause.

The Irrelevance of Debtor Policies

The basic point of this alternative view is that to advance the policy problems of debtors as an explanation of the absence of bank lending is to confuse defensive lending with free-market transactions. For a country that is borrowing from voluntary lenders on the open market, the ability to borrow does indeed depend on confidence in the country's management and prospects. When this confidence is lost, the country becomes a problem debtor. Once problem debtor status has been achieved, however, the new money provided through concerted action is not governed by the same motives. Provided that they are able to act cooperatively, creditors will lend as much as they have to in order to protect their investment, not as much as the country has earned or as much as it can be expected to service. It is by no means clear that good behavior will earn a country the right to more capital. If anything, good economic policies, by reducing the need for new capital, may weaken a country's bargaining position and lead to a *reduction* of the supply of new money and a worsening of its terms.

A perverse relationship between behavior and the terms of lending is apparent in recent events. Argentina and Mexico, both demanding and receiving new money, have been able to reschedule debt at 13/16 percent over LIBOR (the London interbank offer rate for dollar deposits). The Philippines, rescheduling without asking for new money, had to pay slightly more at 7/8 percent. Columbia, which has never needed to reschedule, recently paid 1 1/8 percent on a new loan (see *The Economist*, 25 April 1987, 77–78).

A perverse relationship between performance and the supply of new money can be seen in the case of Mexico. When Mexico was apparently able to run massive trade surpluses while resuming modest growth, it received no new money. When oil prices collapsed, the first new-money package in more than two years was negotiated.

The reason for pointing out these perversities is not to condemn the banks, or to suggest that their behavior is irrational. It is instead to emphasize that defensive lending is not the same thing as free-market lending. It is determined by what the traffic will bear, that is, by what is necessary to safeguard existing claims. If defensive lending falls off it is because the need for it, as perceived by the creditors, has declined. This means that the criticisms of debtor policies that have been offered to justify the lack of new money should be viewed as rationalizations rather than reasons. The question we need to answer is, why were the creditors able to get by with providing as little new money as they did?

7.3.3 The Free-Rider Problem

One prospect that raised fears in the early stages of the debt problem was that defensive lending by creditors would be paralyzed by the problem of getting collective action, especially by smaller banks. A possible interpretation of the stalling of lending to problem debtors is that the free-rider problem did in fact do just that. How much evidence is there for the free-rider problem's importance?

Data on U.S. banks does show evidence of a free-rider problem, albeit with some puzzles (table 7.4). The small regional banks have consistently either reduced their LDC exposure more or expanded it less than either the money center banks or the middle-sized banks. After 1983, the middle-sized banks have in turn consistently increased exposure less than the money center banks. (Somewhat puzzlingly, in 1982 and 1983 the money center banks accepted smaller exposure growth than the middle-sized banks.) Thus the burden has been borne disproportionately by the larger banks.

The real question, however, is how important the free-rider problem has actually been as an inhibition on bank lending. As a crude effort at answering this question, the last two lines of table 7.4 compare the actual growth rate of debt with the rate that would have obtained if middle-sized and regional banks had in fact been willing to expand their exposure as much as the large banks. In this hypothetical case exposure would have grown more rapidly in 1984, and fallen less rapidly in 1985 and 1986, but the basic qualitative fact of a near-stagnation in bank exposure would not have been altered. This reflects both the high initial concentration of claims in the hands of the larger banks and the fact that the withdrawal of smaller banks was a matter of gradual reductions in exposure rather than wholesale flight.

Now one might argue that had there been more cooperation from smaller banks the money center banks would have been willing to lend more themselves. The theoretical possibility that was raised in the first section of this paper was that the presence of a noncooperating fringe might make the whole enterprise of defensive lending unworthwhile from the point of view of the core of collusive creditors. However, this seems unlikely as an explanation of what happened in 1984–85. The nine largest banks hold about 60 percent of the total U.S. bank claims on problem debtors. Thus in terms of the criterion for justifiable defensive lending, f is about 0.6. It is hard to believe that the case for defensive lending rested on such a knife-edge that a 40 percent non-cooperative fringe made the difference (although if European and Japanese banks are also counted as free riders, the accounting changes dramatically). And as long as defensive lending remains worthwhile, free-riding should lead to *faster,* not slower growth in the exposure of the core banks.

One might also argue that the effect of the attempt to free ride by regionals is reflected not so much in their eventual exposure as in the delay they impose on the process. The recent Mexican new-money

Table 7.4   **Changes in Claims on Debtors (percent)**

	1982	1983	1984	1985	1986[a]
All capital importers					
Money center	8.7	3.6	−0.8	−7.1	−10.1
Medium-sized	11.4	8.1	0.9	−15.1	−21.5
Regionals	5.4	0.8	−7.7	−2.4	−11.6
Latin America					
Money center	8.5	2.1	4.7	−2.7	−4.8
Medium-sized	12.1	7.3	−0.6	−13.0	−13.5
Regionals	4.2	−1.4	−3.0	−2.5	−10.0
Total	8.2	2.3	1.9	−4.5	−7.5
Hypothetical	5.9	1.8	4.0	−2.5	−4.0

Sources: See table 7.2; and author's calculations.
[a]First three quarters.

package was held up for eight months because of the difficulties of getting the smaller banks on board. As we saw above, however, the cessation of capital flows to debtors after mid-1984 reflected an absence of new-money packages, not delays in approval and implementation of packages already negotiated.

The free-rider problem is a real issue, and may have contributed to the toughness of the stance of the large banks in negotiating a bargain with the debtors. However, the best explanation of the failure of the banks to lend is that this represented a collectively rational decision on their part: They lent as little as they did because they did not, as it turned out, need to lend more. This leads us to the third explanation of the lending shortfall, which locates its cause in the relative bargaining power of the creditors and the debtors.

7.3.4 Bargaining Power

The third, and I believe most persuasive, explanation for the stall in bank lending to problem debtors is that the banks did not lend because they did not have to: They found themselves in a strong enough bargaining position to extract full interest from the countries without a quid pro quo of new money. Defensive lending failed to take place because it was unnecessary. The corollary to this view is that the failure of the banks to come up with new money in 1984–86 does not show that they can never be induced to do so; the banks did not fail to act in their own interest.

The principal evidence for the view that banks were simply striking a hard bargain with the debtors is negative. There is no indication that banks were disappointed in the performance of debtors in 1984–85, leading to unwillingness to lend (and in any case we have already argued that there is if anything a perverse connection between performance and defensive lending). There were no cases of new-money packages scuttled by attempts of small banks to free ride. Most important, until 1986 there was no indication that the failure to provide new money was pushing countries to the edge of refusal to pay interest.

In a sense the question should be put the other way. It is not very puzzling that banks lent so little, since they seem to have judged correctly that they could do so without adverse consequences. The question is why the countries were so willing to acquiesce. This remains somewhat hard to understand; even *The Economist* confesses itself "baffled by the good behavior of the Brazilians and other debtor countries up to now." In the jargon of bargaining theory, it is hard to understand why the threat points of the debtor countries were set so low, or perhaps why the threat points of the banks were set so high. What were the threatened sanctions that made countries willing to service so much of their debt?

Bankers and theoretical analysts have both emphasized the importance of good behavior to future access to capital markets (Eaton and Gersovitz 1981). However, the prospects for a return to sustantial net inward resource transfer for the major debtors are distant at best. It would require a very low discount rate for Mexico or Brazil to regard it as worthwhile to make current resource transfers of 4–5 percent of GDP now in order to have a chance at receiving inward transfers of a few percent of GDP sometime in the next decade. There is also considerable question how much current bad behavior threatens future access to capital markets in any case (Kaletsky 1985).

An alternative possibility is that the debtor countries fear retaliation by creditors that would interfere with their trade. Such worries were widely expressed in 1982 and 1983, when it was argued that if a country were to default openly, the efforts of bankers to seize whatever they could would cut off not only trade credit but bank accounts, and even lead to seizure of cargoes in port. However, the experience since then has muted such images. At present eight Latin American countries are failing to service their debt; the consequences to their trade have not been readily apparent. Admittedly there may be longer-term damage because of the loss of reputation, but these costs are certainly diffuse. Also, it is possible to argue that banks have been reticent in invoking sanctions against small countries that are in extremely serious trouble, and that a major or more healthy debtor would finally feel the adverse effects of failing to behave properly. However, as time goes by in the Brazilian impasse without dramatic penalties this suggestion also becomes less plausible.

One point that may help explain the quiescence of the countries is the cynical but apparently valid political observation that only the recent rate of change of the economic situtation, not the level, matters for political purposes. By this criterion the debtors were, in 1984 and 1985, doing acceptably well; although their incomes had taken a severe beating in 1981–83, in 1984–85 Mexico achieved modest growth and Brazil rapid growth, despite the need to run very large trade surpluses. Again, impressionistically it seems that the countries felt that they were doing well enough to be unwilling to press their case with the bankers and set in motion unknown risks.

Finally, an important element in debtors' willingness to accept an unfavorable bargain has probably been the political pressure from creditor-country governments, especially the United States, carrying the implicit message that sanctions of nonfinancial kind will be imposed on debtors that fail to service their debt. These sanctions could include trade action, immigration policy, and changes in U.S. attitudes toward the internal political situation. Whether the creditor nations would actually use their powers to enforce penalties on Third World debtors is doubtful, but the belief that they might is an important element in the thinking of the debtors. As Dornbusch (1987) puts it, "the governments of the major industrialized countries have insisted on debt service and have managed a system of debt collection. . . [enforcing] the debts by behind-the-scenes political pressure."

7.3.5 Implications

The failure of the commercial banks to provide new money on the scale envisaged in 1983 has been seen by many observers, including myself, as a sign of the unworkability of the strategy of relying on concerted lending by existing creditors. That is, it has been viewed as showing that banks cannot be mobilized to provide new money, as proposed in such plans as the Banker initiative, even if the provision of new money is in their own interest.

This interpretation would be correct if the lack of new money essentially reflected an inability of the creditors to undertake collective action. The discussion here suggests, however, that this was not the case; that creditors *were* acting in a collectively rational fashion, and they lent so little because that was the strategy that made sense in their own interest. If this alternative explanation is correct, then a change in the situation can lead to a very different response from the banks. If the countries become tougher bargainers, or the banks less tough, than bank lending can still be provided, as the Mexican package illustrates.

This interpretation raises two questions: What would make the situation change, and how would the change take place? That is, will there be an extended period of debt moratoria, etc.? We return to these questions in the final section of the paper, but first it is necessary to examine the possibility that alternative sources of financing could obviate the need for bank financing.

7.4 Alternatives to Bank Financing

A number of analysts have suggested that the answer to the debt problem lies to a significant degree in encouraging other forms of capital inflow to substitute for bank financing. In particular, direct foreign investment would be a non-debt-creating flow that would decrease the "leveraging" of debtor countries, and potentially improve their situation. Recently debt-equity swaps have attracted much favorable attention as ways of making the contribution of direct investment not simply incremental but an immediate substitution for part of existing debt.

To assess the prospects for such alternatives to bank financing, it is necessary to start by asking more carefully than most analysts have exactly how new nondebt capital inflows help the debt problem—a subject that is more subtle than one might at first expect. Then we can turn to the prospects for increased direct foreign investment, and finally to the potential for productive debt conversion schemes.

7.4.1   Capital Inflows and the Debt Problem

Do nondebt capital inflows help a debtor country? It may seem odd to pose the question, since they of course reduce the size of trade surplus needed to service the debt. However, asking this question does force us to focus more clearly on the nature of the problem and the limits to what magic wands such as changes in the form of liabilities can do to resolve it.

The key point to be made is that the problem of a debtor country is not simply one of running a sufficient trade surplus to raise foreign exchange to service its external debt. In much discussion of the debt problem the fiction is adopted that the debtor country is a single unit, virtually a single individual, so that the debtor's problem is wholly one of dealing with external creditors—that is, it is purely a *foreign exchange* problem. This is a useful fiction for many purposes. However, when we get down to the level of proposing solutions it is essential to recognize that the debt problem is in the first instance a problem of debtor *governments*. That is, in addition to being a foreign exchange problem it is also, and perhaps even primarily, a more general *fiscal* problem. Most though not all of the debt problem is the problem that governments have in servicing their debt and the debt that they have guaranteed, both foreign and domestic.

Suppose that a debtor country succeeds in attracting a new flow of direct foreign investment. This clearly helps the foreign exchange problem. However, it does not make any direct contribution to the government's fiscal problem, except to the extent that over time the direct foreign investment may induce economic growth that raises the tax base. The only immediate favorable effect of direct foreign investment on the debtor's financial position is the extent to which it allows the government to issue more domestic debt with which to service its foreign debt.

Consider what happens to the consolidated accounts of a government and a central bank when a foreign firm makes a direct investment. The firm uses foreign currency to purchase domestic currency, with which it makes its investment. The central bank therefore sells domestic currency and acquires assets in the form of foreign exchange. However, the domestic currency that has been issued adds to the money supply, and may therefore have an inflationary impact. To sterilize the effect the government would have to withdraw the money through an issue of domestic debt. If it does this, the net effect on the balance sheet has been to swap an increase in domestic debt for an increase in foreign assets; the net debt position of the government has not changed.

Now it is possible and likely that the change in the government's portfolio will increase its freedom of action. To the extent that money issue has been constrained by defense of the exchange rate the increase in foreign assets will allow greater monetization of debt, in turn allowing lower real interest rates and higher investment. Alternatively, the availability of foreign exchange may allow the government to relax exchange controls, with beneficial results for economic growth. These are real benefits, but they hinge essentially on the proposition that for a problem debtor the shadow price on foreign exchange is less than the price the investor pays for it. This wedge provides the scope for gains from non-debt-creating capital flows, but these flows do not provide a panacea for the fiscal aspect of the debt problem. The point is that a million dollars invested in a new electronics plant in Mexico is *not* a perfect substitute for a million dollars worth of debt relief.

Thus even if the prospects for new capital flows other than bank credit are highly favorable, they provide at best an answer to only part of the problem. Nonetheless, we need to ask how favorable the prospects are.

7.4.2 Prospects for Direct Foreign Investment

Direct foreign investment occurs when foreign investors make two choices: to invest, and to finance by equity rather than debt. The prospects for attracting new flows of this kind depend on the incentives for both actions.

The prima facie case for foreign firms to increase investment in problem debtors is not strong. After all, actual investment in the debtors has fallen substantially, suggesting that local firms have not found it profitable. To suggest that there is an incentive for inward investment, one must argue for a difference in the incentives facing potential foreign investors and local firms.

One possible source of such a difference is capital costs. Real interest rates in the debtors have been very high, possibly reflecting the demands of the government on national saving with external financing cut off. For foreign investors who have a lower cost of capital, investment might still be profitable. It is possible to argue that rates of return on investment in the debtors are actually quite high; while protected import-substitution industries are depressed by the recessions in most debtors, the substantial real depreciations in many debtors since the onset of the crisis (table 7.5) have presumably made new export and/or import substitution activities more profitable than before.

Table 7.5   **Real Exchange Rates, April 1987 (1980–82 = 100)**

Argentina	53.3
Brazil	74.4
Mexico	62.9
Korea	72.5

Source: Morgan Guaranty Trust (1987).

On this argument, then, profitability of potential new investments has not declined; the fall-off in investment reflects instead a rise in the price of capital that does not apply to foreign firms. If firms had access to capital at world prices, the demand for investment would be sufficient to return debtors to their normal status of capital importers rather than exporters.

This argument raises the question, however, of why the high rates of return on financial instruments in debtor nations have not themselves attracted portfolio investment. The answer is presumably that the prospect of being able to realize these returns is less than certain; that the possibility of foreign exchange controls, inflation, or failure to pay fully on domestic debt is high enough to offset the seemingly high real interest rates in the eyes of international investors. But then the question is whether the same does not apply to the returns on investing in physical capital as well. Japanese residents are not buying Mexican Treasury bills, despite their high returns, because the risks outweigh the returns. Why does the same not hold true for Japanese investment in Mexican electronics plants?

Of course to date the answer has been precisely that foreign investors have regarded physical claims as risky, too. Despite the real depreciations there has not been a rush by foreign firms to manufacture in problem debtors. Hopes of inducing direct foreign investment on a substantial scale rest on the belief that investors can be induced to expect their claims to be treated differently from bank debt. Such a belief is not impossible to justify. Direct foreign investment (DFI), which makes a direct contribution to the economy and generates foreign investment income over a longer time horizon than debt service, could well receive more favorable treatment than debt, especially government debt. Furthermore, in the past DFI has been regarded with suspicion because of the perceived threat to national sovereignty, and it has been limited by restrictions. To the extent that debtor governments can credibly remove these restrictions, they may be able to induce new flows.

The major limitation on direct foreign investment for problem debtors is that foreign investors are potential victims of the fiscal problems that direct investment does little to resolve. As long as the expected ability of a debtor government to pay is less than its debt, there is, as Dooley

(1986) points out, an unallocated loss that may be expected to fall in part on owners of physical capital as well as on holders of debt. Unless this is resolved, the prospects for attracting large inward DFI are doubtful.

7.4.3 Debt Conversion Schemes

Financial industry experts have strongly pressed for the conversion of external debt into equity claims. Advocates of these swaps at first seemed to be claiming that such conversions would simultaneously reduce countries' external obligations and generate an inflow of direct foreign investment (see, for example, *Morgan Guaranty Trust* 1986). Some cooling of enthusiasm has occurred as careful analysis has shown that a debt-equity conversion in fact does neither. The advantages of debt-equity swaps are in fact fairly subtle, and there are potentially serious disadvantages.

Debt-equity swaps are actually part of a broader array of debt conversion schemes. The general characteristic of such schemes is that investors who have acquired some of a country's external debt at a discount on the secondary market are permitted to redeem the debt for some kind of domestic asset. In the largest program of debt conversion to date, that in Chile, more than half of the debt conversion has actually taken the form of sales of debt to the debtors, without any requirement that the proceeds be invested in equity (see Larrain 1986).

Investments made by means of debt conversion schemes in no case contribute to net capital inflow; the whole point is that they allow investors to acquire claims on a country through a transaction with the country's creditors rather than its residents. The potential benefits lie instead in the future effect on a country's stream of net investment income. First, debt, which carries with it an obligation to make a flat stream of nominal payments over time, may be replaced with other liabilities whose payment stream rises over time with growth and inflation. This serves the same aim of shifting the time profile of payments that defensive lending was supposed to accomplish. Second, in some circumstances debt conversion may serve as a back-door route to debt forgiveness; investors may be induced to acquire assets with an expected present value less than the face value of the converted debt.

Against these potential benefits must be set two possible costs. First is that a debt conversion scheme may divert capital inflow that would otherwise have taken place through other channels; since at best debt conversion makes no contribution to net capital inflow, *any* such diversion represents a net capital outflow. Second is the possibility that debt conversion schemes will have an adverse fiscal impact.

Although many debt conversion schemes are possible, the essential advantages and disadvantages may be understood by making two key distinctions. On one side is the distinction between debt-equity swaps, in which debt must be converted into equity and held in that form, and "debt-peso" swaps in which debt is converted into cash without a restriction on how that cash is to be invested (in the most significant program of debt conversion to date, that of Chile, this distinction corresponds to the distinction between chapter 19 and chapter 18 transactions respectively). On the other side is the distinction between conversions involving private debt, which have no fiscal impact, and those involving public or public-guaranteed debt.

1. *Conversions of private debt to equity:* The most favorable kind of debt conversion is one in which the debt of private firms is exchanged for equity (not necessarily of the same firms). Since dividends can be expected to rise over time with inflation and economic growth, this serves the desirable aim of tilting the time profile of a country's payments to foreign creditors in the direction of the time profile of its ability to pay. A secondary advantage is that to the extent that earnings on equity are related to the economic state of the country, this conversion shifts the country to a more equitable sharing of risk.

Even this most favorable form of debt conversion, however, can aggravate a country's foreign exchange constraint in the short run. To the extent that a purchase of equity through debt conversion substitutes for a purchase that would have taken place in any case—that is, to the extent that there is anything less than 100 percent additionality—the conversion reduces net capital inflows. One way to look at this is to say that a debt conversion that substitutes for capital inflows takes rescheduled debt—that is, debt that has been frozen into long-term claims—and de facto unfreezes it into short-term claims, undermining the purpose of the rescheduling. Since some substitution of debt-equity swaps for capital inflows is surely unavoidable, even this best case of debt conversion represents a trade-off of a worsened capital account now for a more favorable investment income profile in the future.

2. *Conversions of private debt to cash:* A sale of external debt back to the creditor, without a requirement that the proceeds be invested in equity, differs from a debt-equity swap both in being less likely to have favorable effects on the profile of future investment payments, and in running greater risks of worsening the capital account in the short run.

The best case of a "debt-peso" swap would be one in which domestic residents are induced to repatriate external assets that they would otherwise have retained outside the country. The initial capital account impact of this transaction would be zero. Future payments of interest and principal would be reduced. However, because the owners of the repatriated capital would presumably invest the funds domestically, they would in future substitute the income from these investments for additional repatriations. Thus the overall effect on the stream of resource transfers that the country must make to the rest of the world is uncertain; it depends on the planned domestic consumption of the investors.

The concern with debt conversations not tied to equity investment is that they offer greater opportunity than debt-equity swaps for actions that worsen the capital account. Most extreme would be the case where debt is converted into domestic currency, and this currency is then converted (legally or illegally) into foreign exchange and exported again. Such "round-tripping" would turn debt conversions into a device for facilitating capital flight. Less dramatically but equally harmful in its effect on the capital account is the use of debt conversions as a substitute channel for repatriation of earnings on overseas assets; the effect of this substitution is to reduce net capital inflows one-for-one.

The main justification that one might offer for unrestricted conversions of debt is that they may serve as an indirect way for a country to buy back its own debt at a discount; more on this below.

3. *Conversion of public debt:* Conversion of public debt, whether into equity or unrestricted, has the same effects as conversion of private debt, with an additional fiscal impact.

The conversion of external public debt into local currency, if not sterilized, will be inflationary. Thus it must be offset by an issue of domestic debt, which turns it from the point of view of the government into a swap of foreign for local currency debt. From a fiscal point of view, this is a definite disadvantage. The reason is that in problem debtors real interest rates on internal debt are far higher than on external. This in turn reflects the fact that the credibility of government promises to repay, both internal and external, is uncertain. In the case of external debt, however, rescheduling agreements have frozen creditors into holding claims at an interest rate well below what they would require to hold those claims voluntarily. A debt conversion unfreezes these claims and converts them into new, short-term claims on which the government must pay a high enough interest rate to compensate for risk of nonpayment. Thus a debt conversion involving public debt, even if it is structured so as not to worsen the capital account, trades off the benefit of an improved composition of external liabilities for the cost of a worsened fiscal situation.

This review of the effects of debt conversions does not convey a favorable impression. However, there is one other potential advantage of debt conversions that may be an important motivation: They offer an end run around some of the legal and institutional obstacles to debt forgiveness. Given the substantial discounts on secondary market sales of problem debtors' obligations, some governments may regard it as a worthwhile investment to buy back their own national debt. However, direct buy back at a discount raises legal problems. By inducing third parties to buy the debt, and then collecting some fee for the process, governments can achieve approximately the same result. Thus Chile has auctioned off rights to "debt-peso" conversions (though not debt-equity swaps), which in effect allows the government to buy back the debt at a discount equal to the auction premium. Other countries may achieve the same aim by specifying a different exchange rate for debt conversions than for other transactions.

At least so far, however, the debt forgiveness aspect has been limited. In the Chilean case the auction prices on debt-peso conversions have been much smaller than the secondary market discounts, presumably reflecting the fact that within Chile, with capital exports controlled, the shadow price of foreign exchange is higher than its official price. And debt-equity swaps are not auctioned off.

In summary, the idea of using debt-equity conversion as an alternative to defensive lending has been heavily oversold. Such conversions not only cannot eliminate the need for debt-creating capital inflows, they may easily increase rather than decrease the necessity for new borrowing.

7.5 "Financing" through Debt Forgiveness

Through most of this paper attention is focussed on the possibility of reducing the resource transfer burden through new capital inflows. However, an obvious alternative is to deal with the problems posed by an overhang of debt through an agreement by creditors to accept less repayment than originally specified in the loan contracts. That is, debt forgiveness is an alternative to financing. While debt relief proposals are dealt with in detail elsewhere in this volume, it is inevitable that the subject be tackled in this chapter, too. Three questions arise: First, what are the advantages of forgiving rather than financing a debt overhang? Second, what are the offsetting advantages of relying on new capital flows? Third, what operational difficulties might interfere with desirable programs of debt forgiveness?

7.5.1 Advantages of Debt Forgiveness

Debt forgiveness obviously offers a benefit to the country forgiven. However, proponents of debt forgiveness are not usually simply advocating a neutral redistribution of world wealth; they argue that debt forgiveness is in the interest of the creditors as well, or at least would raise world income as a whole. The usual reason given is the simple macroeconomic linkage: With the debt burden reduced, debtors would import more and thus stimulate world output. Except in the very short run, however, and maybe even then, output in the industrial countries is constrained by real or perceived supply limitations, not an inability to generate aggregate demand. The economic advantages of debt relief lie not in demand creation, but in eliminating the distortions of incentives generated by the overhang of problem debt.

One such distortion has already been mentioned, in the context of the bargaining game between debtors and creditors. As we noted, problem debtors and their creditors can be viewed as bargaining over the rate of resource transfer; in an effort to demonstrate their bargaining toughness, they may be led into actions that temporarily disrupt trade and financial markets, imposing costs on the world economy. One way to say this is to observe that as long as the debt remains too large to allow a return to normal debt service, the debt crisis remains at a continual simmer that must be expected occasionally to boil over. When this happens, the distributional struggle between debtors and creditors reduces the size of the overall pie. If it were possible by a program of debt forgiveness to reduce the remaining debt to a level that eliminated the need for this bargaining game, these costs could be avoided. This would represent a gain for the world economy as a whole, though it might still represent a loss from the point of view of the creditors.

A second distortion has been pointed out by Sachs (1986), and arises from the preverse relation between behavior and treatment of problem debtors. For a country that is engaged in a bargaining situation with its creditors, an enhancement of its economic situation will normally be reflected in a *reduction* in the inflow of new capital, i.e., in an increase in the rate of resource transfer necessary, and to a worsening of the terms on which that capital is made available. This amounts to a tax on the country's efforts to adjust its economy. Policies that expand export capacity, substitute for imports, increase an economy's flexibility, etc., typically are costly for governments to undertake, either because they require diversion of scarce resources or because they require challenging vested political interests. If the countries know that the net effect of such policies will largely be to benefit their creditors rather than themselves, the incentive to take desirable steps will be reduced.

Again, a program of debt relief that settles the issue once and for all can in principle eliminate this distortion. If debt is reduced to a level that countries expect to pay, any marginal improvement in a country's prospects once again accrues to the country rather than its creditors. Thus a successful once-and-for-all debt forgiveness would restore normal incentives, where a continuation of ad hoc financing that results from bargaining provides perverse incentives.

The combined advantages of avoiding costly future confrontations between creditors and debtors and eliminating the perverse incentives that a regime of involuntary lending gives to the debtors suggest that debt forgiveness would not only help the debtors but would tend to raise world income. Against these advantages, however, must be set the disadvantages, both those for the world as a whole and those for the creditors.

7.5.2 Disadvantages of Debt Forgiveness

From the point of view of the world as a whole, the main disadvantage of debt forgiveness is the moral hazard problem: If countries that ran up excessive debt levels in the past are able to get the debt forgiven, it will distort incentives in the future.

The nature of the distortion would depend on how debt relief is financed. If the debt relief were to come at the expense of creditor governments rather than private banks, the effect might be to encourage both irresponsible lending and irresponsible borrowing, as countries and banks conclude that OECD governments will bail them out in future crises. If (as is more plausible) the relief comes largely at the expense of the private creditors, lending will be constrained in the future, presumably to excessively low levels. However, though their borrowing would be constrained, countries might be tempted to behave irresponsibly in other ways. For example, countries that now have manageable levels of debt might be tempted to pursue policies that threaten their ability to service the debt, in the anticipation that if that should happen the debt would be forgiven. For that matter, debtors that received debt forgiveness once might be tempted to pursue policies that required a second round of forgiveness.

How important is this moral hazard issue? There is essentially no evidence that would let us evaluate it quantitatively. I would offer a purely intuitive guess that it is not, in the present case, very important. The ebt crisis of 1982 was a sufficiently unique event, both in terms of its global extent and in terms of the severe external shocks that debtor nations experienced, that debt forgiveness in this case would probably not be construed as setting a precedent for future debt negotiations. Also, if debt forgiveness can be negotiated at all, it will be such a difficult process that it will hardly facilitate further rounds of forgiveness. However, this is purely a judgement call. The moral hazard argument does make a global argument against debt forgiveness.

Probably a more relevant argument against debt forgiveness in practice is the fact that from the point of view of the creditors debt forgiveness now may reduce the expected value of their claims more than financing a debt overhang for the time being, even if they do not ever expect to be paid in full. The reason is that preserving the nominal debt on a country at its full value, even when it is subjectively viewed as being worth much less than this, gives creditors the opportunity to benefit from unexpected good fortune. Suppose that there are two possibilities: a country might in one state of the world be expected to repay 75 percent of its debt, in the other 25 percent. If these states are equally likely, debt would be valued at 50 percent of par. One might suppose that it would make sense to recognize the reality that the debt will not be fully repaid, and forgive the 50 percent of the debt that has already been discounted by the market. Yet to do this would prevent the creditors from collecting all 75 percent in the favorable state: The option value of the large nominal debt will have been sacrificed, and the reduced claims would be valued at only 37.5 percent of the original par.

The risks of future confrontation and the perverse incentive effects of a debt overhang work against the advantages of keeping nominal debt large, even for the creditors; they face a trade-off between the option value of financing without forgiveness and the incentive effects of forgiving rather than financing. Because they care about the distributional aspects, however, creditors can be expected to prefer a solution that involves less debt forgiveness than would be advocated by someone trying to maximize world income.

7.5.3   Operational Problems with Debt Forgiveness

Even if there should be a consensus that debt relief is desirable, it would be very difficult to put into practice. It might seem that the fact that debt is already discounted substantially on the market should offer possibilities for clever schemes to convert this discount into a reduction in countries' obligations. However, there are serious collective action and externality problems that block unilateral action on the part of both individual creditors and the debtors themselves.

Suppose first that creditors decide that it would actually be in their interests to offer a reduction in the obligations of a problem debtor. It is still not in the interest of an individual creditor to forgive debt, because this would simply reduce his own share of the claims while enhancing the value of other claims. Thus there may be a "prisoner's dilemma" in which it is in the collective interest of creditors to forgive part of the debt but no individual creditor has an incentive to act.

Suppose on the other hand that a debtor nation tries to take advantage of the secondary market to buy back some of its own debt at a discount (and we suppose that the legal obstacles are somehow waived). The problem in this case is that in the way the bargaining game that we have seen characterizes relationships between a problem debtor and its creditors, such a reduction in nominal debt outstanding will not reduce the country's expected future payments one for one. By reducing the outstanding debt, the country will have improved its objective position, and therefore *weakened* its bargaining strength vis-à-vis the remaining creditors. Conceivably a buyback of debt would serve only to raise the value of the remaining debt to creditors, with no benefit to the country at all. For example, suppose that a country has $10 billion of debt, but everyone knows that it can pay only $5 billion. If it buys back $1 billion of debt at 50 percent of par, it will have a nominal debt of only $9 billion remaining, but it will still be expected to pay $5 billion, and the buyback will have accomplished nothing from the country's point of view.

These problems mean that even if all parties agree that debt forgiveness in desirable, it cannot be achieved in a piecemeal fashion. A negotiation in which all or virtually all debt obligations are simultaneously reduced would be necessary. Such a negotiation could be forced by unilateral action by a debtor country; otherwise it would require a coordinating and mediating role by third parties, such as international organizations. At the present time there seems to be little inclination on the part of the major debtors to press for a once-and-for-all package of debt forgiveness, and even less inclination on the part of international organizations to take the lead in organizing such packages. That may change, but for the time being forgiveness does not seem about to displace financing as the key concern in the debt problem.

7.6 Outlook for Capital Flows

Direct foreign investment cannot be counted on to provide the financing that banks have failed to provide, and schemes like debt-equity swaps are much more problematic than their sponsors seem to have appreciated. The desirability of debt relief is still controversial, and in any case it poses operational difficulties that none of the actors in the debt situation seem at this point ready to take the lead in resolving. Thus the central question regarding financing for problem debtors is whether involuntary lending by banks can be restarted. This depends crucially on the interpretation of the problems with mobilizing lending so far. If the cessation of lending during 1984–86 really reflected an inability of the banks to act in their own interests, prospects are bleak. If it represented collectively rational behavior on the part of the banks, then the limits on bank lending tell us only that the banks chose not to, not that they will not.

The argument made here is that the evidence is most consistent with the view that low bank lending was the outcome of a bargaining process in which, for a variety of reasons, creditors had very high bargaining power compared with debtors. A shift in that bargaining process will produce a different result. Specifically, the bargain will shift if debtor countries come to realize that a return to normal market access is not imminent, that the internal political costs of continuing full debt service are high, that the external cost from a failure to reach agreement with the banks is low, and, perhaps, that the U.S. government will not take political revenge on deadbeats. Given a situation of this kind, creditors will prefer to negotiate some combination of de facto capitalization of interest and reduced rates rather than fail to reach any agreement.

What about the possibility of debt moratoria and sanctions against the debtors? If all parties were fully informed about each others' motives and opportunities, we would expect everyone immediately to reach a bargain that reflected the ability of the players to mete out and receive punishment, without any necessity for the actions actually to take place. However, given the uncertainty involved, it will probably be necessary for players to demonstrate their resolve by announcing debt moratoria, seizing assets, and so on. Ideally third parties would be able to mediate and avoid such open confrontations, which have real costs, although less than is often supposed. However, the important point if confrontations cannot be avoided—which will sometimes be the case—is to realize that periods in which debtors and creditors fail to reach agreement are a part of the game, not the end of it.

Thus the outlook, if this analysis is correct, is in fact for a revival of bank financing to the debtors. This financing may for a while take the form of arrearages, until the debtors and creditors reach agreement. Eventually it will be formalized in a new agreement. There will be new bank lending because the countries will need it: The moral of this paper is that the supply of capital to problem debtors is, in the end, driven by the demand.

References

Bulow, J., and K. Rogoff. 1986. A constant recontracting model of sovereign debt. Unpublished ms., Stanford University.

Cline, W. 1983. *International debt and the stability of the world economy.* Washington D.C.: Institute for International Economics.

Dooley, M. 1986. An analysis of the debt crisis. IMF Working Paper, WP/86/14. Washington, D.C.: International Monetary Fund.

Dornbusch, Rudiger. 1987. Our LDC debts. NBER Working Paper no. 2138. Cambridge, Mass.: National Bureau of Economic Research.

Eaton, J., and M. Gersovitz. 1981. Debt with potential repudiation. *Review of Economic Studies* 48: 289–309.

Feldstein, M. 1986. International debt service and economic growth: Some simple analytics. NBER Working Paper no. 2076. Cambridge, Mass.: National Bureau of Economic Research.

Feldstein, M., H. de Carmoy, P. Krugman, and K. Narusawa. 1987. Restoring growth in the debt-laden Third World. Prepared for the Trilateral Commission, New York.

International Monetary Fund. 1987. *World Economic Outlook* (April).

Kaletsky, A. 1985. *The costs of default.* New York: Priority Press.

Krugman, P. 1985. International debt strategies in an uncertain world. In *International debt and the developing countries,* ed. G. Smith and J. Cuddington. Washington, D.C.: World Bank.

Larrain, F. 1986. Market-based debt reduction schemes in Chile: A macroeconomic perspective. Catholic University, Santiago, Chile. Mimeo.

Morgan Guaranty Trust. 1986. *World Financial Markets* (September).

————. 1987. *World Financial Markets* (May).

Rubinstein, A. 1982. Perfect equilibrium in a bargaining model. *Econometrica* 50: 97–109.

Sachs, J. 1984. *Theoretical issues in international borrowing.* Princeton Studies in International Finance no. 54. Princeton, N. J.: Princeton University Press.

————. 1986. The debt overhang problem of developing countries. Paper presented at the conference in memorial to Carlos Díaz-Alejandro August 1986 at Helsinki, Finland.

UNCTAD. 1987. *Trade and development report.* United Nations Conference on Trade and Development.

Watson, M., D. Mathieson, R. Kincaid, and E. Kalter. 1986. *International Capital Markets: Developments and Prospects.* IMF Occasional Paper no. 43. Washington, D.C.: International Monetary Funds.

Watson, M., R. Kincaid, C. Atkinson, E. Kalter, and D. Folkerts-Landau. 1986. *International Capital Markets: Developments and Prospects.* IMF Economic and Financial Surveys (December). Washington, D.C.: International Monetary Fund.

World Bank. 1986. *World Development Report.*

8   Debt Problems and the World Macroeconomy

Rudiger Dornbusch

8.1   Introduction

This chapter discusses the role of world macroeconomic factors in contributing to the debt crisis. I investigate what role these factors—interest rates, commodity prices, growth—played in bringing on the debt crisis, and how they facilitated or complicated the first five years of adjustment. I also ask whether and in what way the world macroeconomy is likely to contribute to the solution of the debt problem in the next five years.

The chapter begins with the presentation of a conceptual framework and a review of the behavior of key macroeconomic variables in the past quarter of a century. I then proceed to a discussion of the origins of the debt crisis and a description of the adjustment period, 1982–87. The following part reviews alternative scenarios for the period 1987–90 and their bearing on debt questions. I also ask what contribution to expect from commercial policies. The chapter concludes pessimistically that for many debtors sufficient improvement cannot be expected from a good performance of the world economy. This makes it necessary to find mechanisms that would make it possible to reverse resource flows.

8.2   External Debt and the Debt Crisis

In this part of the chapter I set out a conceptual framework in which to discuss debt problems and present the macroeconomic background to the debt crisis of 1979–82.

The author is Ford International Professor of Economics at the Massachusetts Institute of Technology and a research associate of the National Bureau of Economic Research.

8.2.1   A Conceptual Framework

The balance of payments and national income accounts give us a basic framework for analysis. The identities and relations they contain, which are true by accounting definition, provide an objective conceptual setting.

There is a debt problem when a country cannot service its debt on the contracted schedule. Debt service difficulties may either be an inability to pay the principal of a maturing debt, as is the case for Colombia or Venezuela today, or an inability to pay both interest and principal. We focus here on debt difficulties of the more serious kind where interest cannot be paid. The reason is that difficulties in paying principal, when interest is regularly paid, should not present any problem since rolling over is a routine operation. The only reason difficulties with principal can become debt problems is if creditors wish to limit their regional exposure and hence insist on payment of principal even from those countries who are good debtors.

Focusing on interest payments, the current account of the balance of payments can be separated into two components: the noninterest current account (NICA), which includes trade in goods and in all services except interest payments on the external debt, and interest payments. Interest payments can be financed by noninterest surpluses or by net capital inflows:

(1)   Interest Payments = Noninterest Current Account
                                    + Net Capital Inflows

The category "net capital inflows" includes four components: reserve decumulation, direct foreign investment inflows, long-term portfolio inflows, and short- or medium-term borrowing abroad which is often called "new money." In the debt problems of the interwar period or the period preceding 1914, new money took the form of a "funding loan." Today it is concerted or involuntary lending by the commercial bank creditors and multilateral institutions.

Table 8.1 shows these current account components for problem debtor countries in the 1978–87 period.[1] It reveals the turn in the noninterest current account from a string of deficits until 1982 to a series of surpluses. In the period up to 1982 both interest payments and the noninterest deficit need financing and hence are reflected in a rapidly rising debt. Since 1983 a large part of interest is paid by noninterest surpluses and hence the increase in debt is sharply reduced. But debt is still rising, reflecting the financing of the remaining interest payments not met by the surplus and the financing of capital flight and reserve build-up.

Table 8.1   **The Current Account Deficit and External Debt: Countries with Recent Debt-Servicing Difficulties ($ billion)**

	Noninterest Current Account Deficit (Resource Transfer)	Interest Payments	Current Account Deficit	External Debt
1978	17.1	14.8	31.9	242
1979	10.1	21.8	31.9	292
1980	5.0	34.3	39.6	356
1981	20.2	47.5	67.7	430
1982	5.4	57.5	63.1	494
1983	−30.2	52.1	21.9	514
1984	−48.6	57.2	8.6	534
1985	−50.2	53.6	3.1	553
1986	−32.7	50.2	17.5	573
1987	−27.8	45.7	17.9	586

Source: IMF *World Economic Outlook.*

(2)   Interest Payments = Noninterest Current Account
                       + New Money + Other Net Capital Inflows

The category "Other Net Capital Inflows" is typically very small. There is little room for reserve decumulation, and long-term capital flows tend to be small. The only time other net capital inflows assume importance is in the case of capital flight or, less frequently, a repatriation of capital.

The discrepancy between the current account on one side and the sum of net borrowing plus non-debt-creating inflows (chiefly direct foreign investment and official aid) represents reserve changes and capital flight.

The noninterest deficit is often called the net resource transfer since it measures the net imports of goods and services (other than interest) over which a country acquires command. Noninterest deficits are the normal pattern for developing countries in which saving is low relative

Table 8.2   **Financing of Problem Debtors' Imbalances ($ billion)**

	1979–82[a]	1983–86[a]	1987
Current account deficit[b]	39.5	7.8	14.8
Non-debt-creating inflows	7.1	4.6	5.1
Net borrowing	49.4	11.6	16.3

[a]Period average.

[b]Deficit on goods, services, and private transfers.

to investment. Noninterest deficits are the channel through which re-sources are transferred from rich to poor countries to support capital formation and growth in the developing world. Private and public lend-ing forms the financial counterpart. Using the national accounts identi-ties we can represent the financing of investment from the resource point of view as follows:

(3)   Investment = Saving + Real Resource Transfer from Abroad

Table 8.3 shows the real resource transfers and the investment rates for Latin America. The table brings out strikingly the decline in in-vestment as a counterpart of the real resource transfer abroad. The shift in resource transfers is almost exactly matched by a decline in investment.

The essential distinction between pre-crisis and post-crisis is the turn of the net resource balance, with debtor countries now making net resource transfers to creditor countries.

8.2.2   Debt Crises

Any debt crisis involves the inability of debtors to meet timely pay-ments of interest and principal. Thus the gap between interest payments that are due and the noninterest current account is the chief charac-teristic of a debt problem. Four factors then can be identified as leading to a debt problem:

1. With an unchanged willingness to roll over debt and provide a given flow of new money, an increase in real interest rates raises the financing requirement. The imbalance between new money requirements and credit voluntarily supplied brings about a debt crisis.
2. A deterioration in the noninterest current account, because of domestic macroeconomics or because of a worsening in the terms of trade or a fall in export demand, opens a financing gap.
3. An increase in world inflation leads to an increase in nominal interest rates and hence to an early *real* amortization of the ex-ternal debt. Although real interest rates are unchanged there is a cash flow problem for debtors.
4. With an unchanged interest rate and noninterest current account, creditors decide that exposure is excessive and therefore limit

Table 8.3   **Resource Transfers and Investment as a Percentage of GDP**

	1973–82	1983–85
Gross investment	24.3	18.5
Noninterest surplus	−0.6	4.7

new money commitments and require that maturing principal be paid off.

I now proceed to identify the impact of world macroeconomic events on debtor countries. Specifically, given policies such as the real exchange rate and fiscal policy, how has the world macroeconomy been one of the factors leading to the debt crisis; how has it influenced the evolution of the debt problems since 1982; and what implications can be anticipated from alternative scenarios of the world economy in the coming years? World interest rates, growth, and commodity price trends are at the center of the discussion.

A special interest, however, attaches to their joint behavior. For example, what if the interest payments a country owes increase but the noninterest deficit also increases? And at the same time creditors become unwilling to increase their exposure? The financing equation then no longer adds up and something must give. When a debt crisis occurs and outright default or arrears are not the answer, creditors are often coerced into involuntary lending and debtors undergo adjustment programs to turn their noninterest deficits into surpluses. Creditworthiness must be reestablished. Now debtors have noninterest surpluses that finance the interest payments. But there may still be a part of interest payments financed by net capital inflows or "new money."

With this background in mind we can turn to the main world macroeconomic variables that had an influence in creating the debt crisis.

8.3 The World Macroeconomy: An Overview

Figures 8.1 to 8.4 highlight the chief external variables for debtor countries: the interest rate, the real interest rate, the real price of commodities, and world economic activity. Figure 8.1 shows the London interbank offer rate for dollar deposits (LIBOR). The contribution of interest rates to the debt crisis is shown by the peak level of an interest rate in excess of 18 percent in late 1981.

The interest rate effects appear through two separate channels. One is associated with the level of nominal rates, given the real rate of interest. When higher inflation increases the nominal interest rate the effect on debtors is a shortening of the effective maturity of the debt. The *real* value of the debt is amortized at a faster pace. As a result debtors may experience liquidity problems.

Interest rates also, of course, hurt debtors when real rates increase. In this context it must be decided in terms of at which rate of inflation the real interest rate should be assessed, and there is considerable difficulty in identifying the correct inflation rate. Alternative candidates might be the debtor countries' GNP deflator in dollars or the rate of

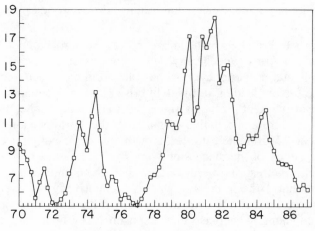

Fig. 8.1   The LIBOR rate

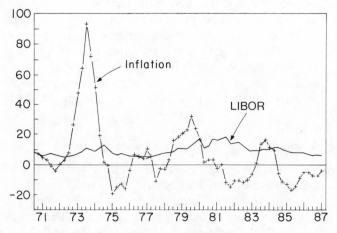

Fig. 8.2   Interest rates and commodity price inflation

inflation in world trade. We chose here the latter series, and it is shown in figure 8.2 together with the LIBOR rate. The behavior of the real rate is, of course, striking in that the sharp increase in nominal rates was accompanied by a falling level of prices in world trade. The combination implied that the real interest rate facing debtor countries was much higher than 20 percent per year.

Figure 8.3 shows the price of commodities. The series shown here is the IMF index of all (non-oil) commodities deflated by the export unit value of industrial countries. Commodity prices show a steady decline since their peak levels in 1973–74. By late 1986 they had fallen to only 40 percent of the peak level. But in the early 1980s, when the debt crisis first occurred, the real price of commodities did not show a dramatic deterioration. Commodity prices thus were not an immediate source of the crisis, but they did become relevant later in raising the costs of adjustment for several debtor countries.

Figure 8.4 shows world economic activity measured by the index of industrial production in the industrialized countries. The behavior of the index is relatively smooth. The events of the early 1980s do not appear striking even though there was a decline of about 5 percent. Figure 8.5, finally, focuses on the divergent behavior of nominal prices

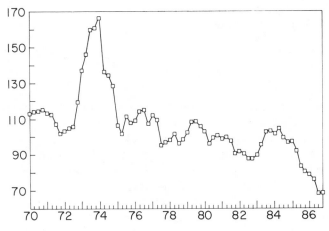

Fig. 8.3   Real commodity prices (Index 1980 = 100)

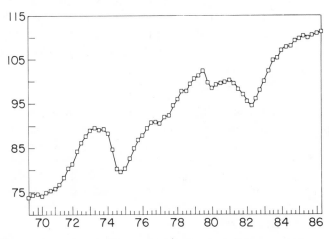

Fig. 8.4   World industrial production (Index 1980 = 100)

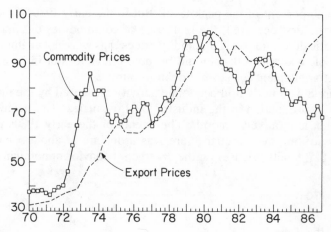

Fig. 8.5   Commodity prices and industrial countries' export prices
                    (Index 1980 = 100)

in world trade (the industrial countries' unit export value) and nominal
commodity prices.

Table 8.4 shows data for these aggregate indices. The table reports
the averages for the 1960s and 1970s and more detailed information on
the period of the debt crisis.

In addition to interest rates, real commodity prices, and economic
activity in industrial countries, a fourth external factor influences the
noninterest current account. This is commercial policy in developing
countries and its influence on market access and hence export performance. There are no good aggregate indicators of market access or of
changes in market access. But there is also no suggestion that this
factor would have been an important element in provoking the debt
crisis. Of course, that does not mean that protectionism did not increase
the costs and difficulties of debtor countries once the crisis had started.[2]

8.4   Examples of the Effect of the World Macro Shock

The overview of external factors gives little guidance as to what was
the impact on individual debtors. Their common factor is only to be
debtors and hence to be hurt by an increase in world interest rates.
But even that exposure differs significantly across countries depending
on their share of floating rate debt. At one end of the spectrum are
poor debtors with most of their debt at concessional rates; at the other
end are Brazil and Mexico for whom almost the entire debt has interest
rates linked to market rates.

But differences in trade structure also matter, and these imply differential effects of the movement of commodity prices in debtor coun-

Table 8.4   **Aggregate World Macroeconomic Indicators**

	Real Commodity Prices (1980 = 100)[a]	LIBOR (%)	Inflation[b] (%)	World Activity[c] (1980 = 100)
1960–69	115	5.2	1.0	56
1970–79	115	8.0	11.4	86
1980	100	14.4	13.0	100
1981	96	16.5	−4.1	100
1982	89	13.1	−3.5	96
1983	98	9.6	−3.3	99
1984	101	10.8	−2.5	106
1985	88	8.3	−0.4	110
1986	72	6.9	13.7	110
1987	63	6.8	12.8	112

Source: IMF and Economic Commission for Latin America.
[a]Measured in terms of manufactures export prices of industrial countries.
[b]Rate of inflation of industrial countries' unit export values.
[c]Industrial production.

tries or of economic activity in industrial countries. Korea, for example, imports commodities while Brazil and Argentina are net commodity exporters. To investigate the differential impacts of the 1980s external shock, the experiences of a number of individual countries will be examined.

Brazil: Brazil exports both commodities and manufactures. In the early 1980s the country had just become a predominant exporter of manufactures. Of a total of $24 billion in exports in 1981 nearly 38 percent were primary commodities (coffee, iron, soya, sugar) and the remainder manufactures. But much of manufactured exports had a high import content, as for example steel or orange juice. On the import side a striking 51 percent was oil. Of the external debt of $50 billion, 80 percent was at variable interest rates and more than 80 percent was dollar denominated.

For Brazil, therefore, oil prices and the world money market rate were the chief variables of interest. Being a net exporter of (non-oil) commodities, Brazil would on balance be hurt by a decline in real commodity prices. The concentration in exports on coffee, orange juice, soya, and iron ore is, however, important to note.

The external balance problem, of course, originated in the oil price increase of 1978–79. Oil imports increased from $4.5 billion in 1978 to $11.4 billion in 1981. This increase in the oil bill was automatically financed both in the budget and in the current account by the borrowing of the state enterprises in the world capital market.

The increase in world interest rates in 1979–81 added to the interest bill. In 1979 net interest payments amounted to $4.2 billion. By 1981 they had risen to $9.2 billion and in 1982 to $12.6 billion. At the end of 1978 the external debt was only $44 billion; by the end of 1981 it had risen to $61 billion and by the end of 1982 to $70 billion. The increase in LIBOR from 8.9 percent in 1978 to 12, 14, and 17 percent over the next three years added a cumulative $7 billion to the external debt. The combination of higher interest rates and higher oil prices "explains" almost the entire increase in debt between the end of 1978 and the end of 1981.

The fact that higher interest rates and higher oil prices explain the increase in debt can also be read to say that the failure to adjust to these external shocks, and the ability to borrow in world markets, meant that external debt was the means by which the country financed the impact of the external shock.

Mexico: The second oil price increase in 1978–79 provided an apparently sound basis on which to engage in a growth strategy. Petroleum export revenue increased from only $1 billion in 1977 to $14 billion in 1981. But spending increased far ahead of the increased revenues. The noninterest budget deficit, oil revenues notwithstanding, increased from 2 to more than 8 percent of GDP (see table 8.5). The current account deteriorated even though oil revenues doubled every year.

The strong domestic expansion, combined with a fixed exchange rate, encouraged overvaluation. The extent of overvaluation at no point became as extreme as it had been in Chile or Argentina. But even so it led to significant deterioration in the trade balance and to massive capital flight.

The capital flight was concentrated in the period 1981–82, in the final phase of the Lopez Portillo government. The deterioration in the external balance and the increasing difficulty in financing the deficit made it apparent that an exchange crisis was around the corner. Large wage increases led to an expectation of a sharp increase in inflation altogether incompatible with the maintenance of a fixed exchange rate. With no restrictions on capital flows there then occurred a massive flight into the dollar. In fact, the capital flight would have been much larger had it not been for the existence of domestic dollar deposits in the banking system. These Mex-dollar accounts absorbed a good part of the spec-

Table 8.5   **Mexico's Macroeconomy, 1977–81**

	1977	1978	1979	1980	1981	1982
Current account deficit (% of GDP)	2.3	3.1	4.1	4.4	5.8	3.8
Real exchange rate (1980–82 = 100)	93	94	98	104	114	83

Source: Morgan Guaranty Trust and Banco de Mexico.

ulation, although their holders ultimately did much worse than those who bought the real thing.

Estimates of the amount of capital flight from Mexico in 1978–82 differ. A recent study by Cuddington (1986) estimates a total of more than $25 billion whereas Morgan Guaranty Trust (1986) gives the higher number of $36 billion. Whatever the exact number, there is no question that somewhere between 10 and 15 percent of GDP went abroad in these critical years. And the reason is exclusively mismanagement since, unlike in the case of Argentina or Chile, there was no deterioration in external conditions until interest rates increased. On the contrary, the oil price increase had provided an extraordinary gain in real income and a potential improvement in the external balance.

Argentina: The Argentine external debt problems were largely due to a mismanagement of the exchange rate. The overvaluation of 1978–81, combined with the liberalization of capital flows, brought about massive capital flight.

Table 8.6 shows the basic data. Note the large real appreciation in 1978–80 and the terms of trade improvement up to 1981. The oil price increase which was important for Mexico, Brazil, and Korea had no effect on Argentina's terms of trade since the country is self-sufficient in oil.

The increase in external debt in Argentina far exceeds the cumulative current account. Therefore interest rate and terms of trade shocks cannot account for the major part of the debt problem before 1981. On the contrary, overvaluation and capital flight are the chief problems in this period. As we shall see below this is no longer the case after 1982 when the terms of trade deterioration becomes an important issue.

Korea: As an oil importer Korea experienced a major deterioration in the terms of trade (see table 8.7). The interest rate shock reinforced the external balance deterioration. Even so, by 1982 the external balance had already turned around and the deficit had become more moderate. In part this is a reflection of the real depreciation which restored competitiveness in the years following the crisis of 1980. In part it

Table 8.6   **Argentine Macroeconomic Variables, 1978–82**

	1978	1979	1980	1981	1982
Debt/GDP	23.9	30.2	37.3	48.1	60.3
Current account as % of GDP	4.0	−1.0	−7.6	−7.4	−3.8
Terms of trade[a]	84	88	100	114	99
Real exchange rate[a]	65	84	100	70	49

[a]Index 1980 = 100.

Table 8.7   **Korean Macroeconomic Variables**

	1978	1979	1980	1981	1982
Terms of trade[a]	118	115	100	98	102
Net exports of goods and nonfactor services[a]	−3.0	−7.3	−7.8	−5.4	−2.6
Net factor payments from abroad[b]	−1.3	−1.5	−3.3	−4.0	−4.1

[a]Index 1980 = 100.
[b]Percentage of GDP, National Income Accounts.

reflects a successful policy of exporting labor services to the oil-producing countries.

Chile: The Chilean case, just as that of Argentina and Mexico, reflects until 1982 primarily a mismanaged exchange rate rather than a predominance of external shocks. As shown in table 8.8 the terms of trade initially improve and the deterioration of the external balance is above all due to the extraordinary overvaluation.

Only in 1981–82 do international factors take over and cause the deterioration of the external balance by means of increased interest burdens. In 1981 the overvaluation and the external factors combine to yield record deficits. But by 1982 exchange rate adjustment and domestic restraint already compensate on the trade side and the current account deterioration only reflects increased interest rate burdens.

Conclusion: The examples illustrate that external factors were by no means the only influence in the debt crisis. On the contrary, domestic policies were an important, often the main, influence in bringing about a large accumulation of debt. External factors reinforced the impact of these debts in 1981–82 via the interest rate shock.

8.5   The Period 1982–87

This section investigates how the world macroeconomy influenced the debt problem in the period since 1982. I start with a review of the beliefs of 1982, namely that favorable trends in the world economy would significantly facilitate debt service. From there I go to a more detailed consideration of the actual evolution of the world economy to ask whether world macroeconomic conditions in fact facilitated debt service or added to the burden.

8.5.1   The Beliefs of 1982

When in 1982 Mexico, and shortly afterwards a host of other Latin American countries, encountered acute debt service problems, the pro-

Table 8.8   **Chilean Macroeconomic Variables**

	1978	1979	1980	1981	1982
Terms of trade[a]	94	106	100	86	77
Real exchange rate[b]	91	100	120	136	122
Trade balance[c]	−0.4	−0.4	−0.7	−2.7	0
Current account[c]	−1.1	−1.1	−2.0	−4.7	−2.3

Sources: CIEPLAN, Santiago, Chile, and Morgan Guaranty Trust.
[a]Index 1980 = 100.
[b]Index 1981–82 = 100.
[c]Billions of U.S. $.

cess of concerted or involuntary lending started. The basic philosophy of that process had three ingredients:

1. To assure an ultimate return to voluntary lending it was essential that debtor countries service their debts to the maximum extent possible, on commercial terms and without significant concessions other than with respect to the maturity of the debt principal.
2. Adjustments in debtor countries, specifically in the budget and exchange rates, would go far to bringing about a swing in the noninterest balance so as to service debt.
3. The world macroeconomy would make a substantial contribution in reducing the burden of debt servicing. From the vantage point of 1982 the macroeconomy could only improve. Debtor countries could anticipate higher growth in demand for their exports, lower interest rates, and improving terms of trade.

The question of adjustment in debtor countries is beyond the scope of this paper and has been amply dealt with elsewhere.[3] The issue of interest here is the contribution of the world macroeconomy. Certainly in 1982 the outlook must have been favorable:

1. The world economy was in the deepest recession since the 1930s. In the recovery period there had to be, accordingly, an expectation of growth significantly above trend. This growth would bring about two results. First it would mean an increase in demand for manufactures exports from debtor countries. Second it would translate into a cyclical upturn of real commodity prices. These stylized facts were quite beyond doubt, given the ample empirical evidence on the cyclical behavior of real commodity prices and export volumes.[4]
2. In respect to interest rates the outlook also had to be outright favorable. The short-term interest rate was at record high levels in American history. These high levels of interest rates were an

immediate result of a deliberate attempt to use monetary policy to stop the sharply accelerating U.S. inflation of the late 1970s and early 1980s. With the success of disinflation, interest rates would decline and hence the extraordinary debt service burdens of 1982 would come down.

3. Even though the dollar had appreciated already for more than a year there was not much discussion on this issue. The reason was presumably that dollar appreciation started from a very low point so that overvaluation was not yet a relevant notion. Nor was there an expectation of significant further appreciation. Discussion of a contribution of dollar depreciation to the debt crisis only occurred over the next three years as dollar overvalution became increasingly apparent.

The framework for analysis of debt problems rapidly became the Avramovic-Cline model of debt dynamics, which focuses on the ratio of debt to exports, b. The key question was whether the evolution of the world macroeconomy made declining ratios of debt to exports likely. The evolution of the debt-export ratio over time, b, can be developed in terms of several determinants, specifically interest rates, i, the growth rate of export prices, p_x, and the growth rate of export volume, x:

(4) $$\dot{b} = b(i - p_x - x) - v,$$

where v denotes the noninterest current account surplus as a ratio of exports.

Equation (4) highlights the debt problem in the sense of an ever rising debt to export ratio. Such a course is unlikely if the real interest rate, defined as nominal rates less the rate of inflation of export prices, is less than the growth rate of export volume and if there is a noninterest current account surplus. Table 8.9 shows the long-term averages for some of these variables for use as a benchmark.

With the data for problem debtors, and assuming a spread over LIBOR of 2.2 percent, we observe that the debt-export ratio would be

Table 8.9   **Long-term Average Growth Rates, 1969–78**

	LIBOR	Export Prices	Export Volume	Debt Ratio[a]
Asia	7.8	10.1	10.8	75.7
Western Hemisphere	7.8	13.9	1.7	197.7
Problem debtors	7.8	12.1	2.3	164.3

Source: IMF.

[a]Ratio of debt to exports of goods and services in 1979.

declining unless there was a noninterest current account deficit in excess of 7 percent of exports. Of course, in 1978–82 the deficits were in fact much larger.

The expectation of declining nominal interest rates and cyclically rising nominal and real export prices for debtor countries implied an expectation of low real interest rates. Recovery and sustained growth in the industrial countries were expected to translate into significant growth in export volumes.

Adjustment in debtor countries, both in terms of expenditure cutting and real depreciation, was expected to translate into significant export growth and into an increased noninterest current account surplus. Thus for every element in the debt dynamics equation a favorable scenario could easily be predicted. And if there was any pessimism on real interest rates and growth in export volume, the fact of noninterest current account surpluses provided the necessary leeway to make a trend reduction in debt burdens plausible.

Cline (1983) in particular expressed the view that the debt problem was largely under control. Using simulations for the major debtor countries, and assuming alternative scenarios for the world economy, he showed that for most debtor countries there was an expectation of declining debt-export ratios. Moreover, the gain in creditworthiness implied by a reduced debt-income ratio in several cases could be accompanied by significant growth in the debtor countries. Brazil, for example, could in Cline's simulations achieve both an average growth rate of 6 percent and a reduction in its debt-export ratio. The Cline analysis rightly emphasized the crucial role of oil prices in determining the relative performance of Mexico and Brazil. With the assumption of declining oil prices Mexico was a problem country and Brazil's prospects were relatively bright.

Table 8.10 shows a medium-term scenario developed by the IMF in 1982 as well as the actual outcome for the key variables. The IMF scenario assumed a strong internal adjustment in the debtor countries, continued inflation fighting in the industrial countries, a constant real price of oil at the 1982 level, and a sharply declining real LIBOR rate. Table 8.10 reports three scenarios: The base line scenario is labeled A, scenario B is pessimistic and hence imposes extra adjustment requirements on debtors, and scenario C is optimistic. The optimism and pessimism are judged in terms of the growth-inflation mix in industrial countries. There was apparently no recognition at the time of the real interest rate consequences of rapid disinflation and of the U.S. monetary-fiscal mix. The other respect in which the scenario is interesting is that there was a quite explicit confidence that current account imbalances could be financed.

Table 8.10   The 1982 IMF Scenarios for Non-Oil Developing Countries
(average annual rates for 1984–86 except as noted)

	A	B	C	Actual
Industrial country growth	3.2	2.2	4.3	3.1
Industrial country inflation	5.5	8.0	4.5	3.8
Real LIBOR Rate[a]	2.0	2.0	2.0	5.4
Net oil importers				
Export volume	7.6	5.9	9.2	8.1
Terms of trade	−0.5	−1.7	0.9	0.7
Net oil exporters				
Export volume	5.0	4.0	6.0	3.6
Terms of trade	0	−1.0	1.0	−10.0
1986 Current account[b]				
Net oil importers	−13.7	−19.4	−9.0	−1.4
Net oil exporters	−20.6	−27.0	−17.5	−16.8

Sources: IMF World Economic Outlook 1982 and April 1987.
[a]Using the U.S. GNP deflator.
[b]Percentage of exports of goods and services.

8.5.2   The Actual Experience since 1982

The actual outcome shown in table 8.10 differs from the IMF scenario in the following respects:

1. Real interest rates continued to be far higher than expected. The U.S. monetary-fiscal mix thus has strong implications for the performance of countries with high debt ratios and a high ratio of floating rate debt.
2. The real oil price fell dramatically and hence the relative performance of net oil exporters was due more to their adjustment efforts than to favorable terms of trade.
3. The assumption that debtor countries could afford to run significant current account deficits was overly optimistic. Financing constraints in fact limited these deficits.

Table 8.11 gives further details on commodity prices, nominal interest rates, and real oil prices, which were only addressed in the terms of trade category of table 8.10. Nominal interest rates did, indeed, decline significantly from their peak levels, and OECD growth showed somewhat above the 3 percent threshold that had been set as a benchmark for solving debt problems. The significant difference from the 1982 outlook was in respect to commodity prices. Rather than showing a recovery in nominal and real terms they in fact continued to decline. The decline was so significant that in 1986 they were at a lower level than at any time in the preceding quarter of a century, as already shown in figure 8.3 above. In nominal terms they had fallen back to the level of 1977.

Table 8.11   **Commodity Prices, Oil Prices, and Interest Rates (average annual percent)**

	Commodity Prices	Interest Rates[a]	Real Oil[b]
1969–78	9.8	7.8	
1980–82	−4.1	14.8	100
1983–86	−3.4	8.9	80

Source: IMF.
[a]LIBOR.
[b]Deflated by manufactures prices; Index 1980–82 = 100.

Creditworthiness

The belief that debt and debt service ratios would decline has not in fact been borne out, as is shown in table 8.12. On every measure of creditworthiness debtor countries today look worse than they did in 1982, excepting the debt service ratio. The reduction in interest rates since 1982 clearly helped reduce the service ratio as did the long-term restructuring of debts. But even though there is a marginal reduction in the debt service ratio, the extent of decline falls short of the 1982 expectations.

Favorable conditions in the world economy and the beneficial effects of adjustment programs on the part of debtors were expected to show in time an improvement in creditworthiness sufficient to warrant a return to voluntary lending. That remains the expectation, but the process is not on schedule. Abstracting from the oil shock, which improved the situation of Korea and Brazil while dramatically worsening that of Mexico, there has been as yet no improvement as dramatic as had been anticipated. Standard indicators of creditworthiness such as the ratio of debt to GDP or debt to exports have in fact worsened since 1982.

The return of voluntary lending was predicated on countries restoring their credit standing. While creditworthiness is a broad and vague idea, the operational concept was a reduction of ratios of debt to GDP and debt to exports. Table 8.12 shows that since 1982 creditworthiness

Table 8.12   **The Deterioration of Creditworthiness (percentage)**

	Debt/GDP			Debt/Exports			Debt Service		
	1978	1982	1986	1978	1982	1986	1978	1982	1986
All debtor LDCs	26	34	40	132	151	180	14	20	22
Problem debtors	31	43	49	180	254	282	28	40	38

Source: IMF, *World Economic Outlook.*

measured by these benchmark ratios has worsened or at least not improved, making the current adjustment effort of debtor countries entirely open-ended.

The Cline Projections

While the preceding discussion focuses on groups of countries, it is also of interest to see how forecasts fared in specific country cases. The analysis by Cline (1983) provides that possibility for the year 1985. Table 8.13 shows the results for Argentina, Brazil, and Mexico.

Three points stand out in these comparisons. First, that export revenues fall short of those predicted by Cline. Second, that import spending is much lower than Cline had predicted. Third, that interest payments are somewhat lower than predicted by Cline. Note, though, that the Brazilian current account surplus of 1985 was correctly predicted by Cline. Of course, by 1986 the differences are much more pronounced because of the vast influence of the decline in oil prices from $28 to $15 per barrel.

Extreme Cases

There are some countries that are outliers in the adjustment period since 1982. On one side are countries who are predominant exporters of commodities and borrow primarily from official sources. They would experience the large and continuing decline in commodity prices without the advantage of reduced interest burdens. Among the countries that come to mind in this category, Bolivia stands out. There interest payments have been as much as 70 percent at fixed rates, so the fall in world interest rates did not bring major benefits. But the terms of trade deteriorated over the period 1981–86 by 14 percent. The value of exports declined in 1984–86 cumulatively by 40 percent!

On the other side, the most striking improvement in the external debt position during the adjustment period has been made by Korea. Korea benefited from every one of the factors characterizing the 1982–87 period: lower commodity prices, lower oil prices, and lower interest rates. Each of these factors exerts a very significant impact on the

Table 8.13   **Cline Projections and Actual 1985 Outcomes ($ billion)**

	Argentina		Brazil		Mexico	
	Cline	Actual	Cline	Actual	Cline	Actual
Exports	10.4	8.4	29.5	25.6	23.6	21.9
Imports	6.4	3.8	18.2	13.2	16.0	13.5
Oil			7.0	5.7		
Interest	6.2	5.3	13.0	9.6	10.7	9.9

Source: Cline (1983) and various government publications.

external balance, and hence the combined effects—in conjunction with an aggressive exchange rate policy—produced a dramatic improvement in the external balance. The shift in the current account represents nearly 10 percent of GNP by 1986 and is still widening.

8.6 The Outlook

In this section I ask whether there are important shifts in the world macroeconomic outlook, and in the outlook for trade policies and the capital market, that promise to help overcome the debt problem or threaten to make its solution much more difficult. On the side of macroeconomics there is certainly a possibility of quite different scenarios depending on the way in which the U.S. budget problem is solved and the response of interest rates and the dollar to budget cuts when they do take place.

8.6.1   The 1987 IMF Scenario

A useful frame of reference for the world economic outlook is the 1987 IMF medium-term scenario shown in table 8.14. The central

Table 8.14   **The 1987 IMF World Economic Outlook**

	1987	1988	1989–91 Average
Industrial countries			
Growth	2.3	2.8	2.9
Real LIBOR	3.6	3.0	3.4
GDP deflator	2.9	3.4	3.2
World economy			
Manufactures prices	11.0	3.1	3.0
Oil prices	8.7	3.1	3.0
Non-oil commodities	−4.9	5.1	4.7
Problem debtors			
Real GDP	4.4	4.7	5.0
Terms of trade	−2.1	−1.0	—
Export volume	5.4	5.9	5.6
Import volume	2.5	3.6	5.7
Current account[a]	−1.5	−0.6	−0.6
Interest payments[a]	6.3	5.9	5.4
Latin America			
Real GDP	3.3	4.7	4.8
Terms of trade	−4.7	−0.6	0.2
Export volume	0.1	7.2	5.1
Import volume	−0.8	2.4	5.4
Current account[a]	−14.3	−9.3	−5.7
Interest payments[a]	25.3	23.1	20.5

Source: IMF, *World Economic Outlook,* April 1987.

[a]Percentage of exports of goods and services.

assumption of this scenario is a continued high real interest rate compensated by sustained growth in the world economy and in debtor country exports. There is an expectation of moderately rising real oil prices and no change in the terms of trade.

In terms of equation (4) above the IMF outlook places major reliance on continued large noninterest current account surpluses and on export volume growth to help contain or reduce debt problems. The scenarios allow for growth in imports at roughly the same rates as those of exports, which is possible because the starting point is a large noninterest surplus. Hence maintaining equal growth rates, with unchanged terms of trade, assures that noninterest surpluses are maintained. In other words the IMF assumes that in the period to 1991, problem debtors will continue to make real resource transfers to their creditors at present rates.

8.6.2   U.S. Adjustment: Implications for Debtor Countries

It is interesting to go beyond the IMF outlook and focus on the central development in the world economy in the next few years, namely U.S. adjustment of the twin deficits. Table 8.15 shows the U.S. macroeconomic data for the recent years. It is quite apparent that the large size of the U.S. external deficit is at least to some extent a counterpart of the ability of debtor countries to service their debts by noninterest surpluses. The extent to which debtor countries were able to shift their trade balance with the United States is apparent from table 8.16 which focuses on all goods and, specifically, on manufactures.

Table 8.16 shows that while the bilateral balance has not shifted when one considers all goods, the same is not true for manufactures where there is a shift of more than $50 billion. The difference resides in the fact that the decline in commodity and oil prices has tended to improve the balance for nonmanufacturing trade with developing countries.

The shift in the manufacturing trade balance is, of course, not only related to the debt crisis. In fact, much of it reflects the very strong

Table 8.15   **The U.S. External Balance and Net Investment Position
(billions of $ except as noted)**

	1982	1983	1984	1985	1986
Int'l. investment position	136.2	88.5	4.4	−107.4	−238
Current account					
Total	−9.2	−45.6	−112.5	−124.4	−147.7
Non-interest	−28.1	−37.0	−131.3	−149.6	−170.6
(% of GNP)	−0.9	−1.1	−3.5	−3.7	−4.1
Budget deficit (% of GNP)	−4.1	−5.6	−4.9	−5.1	−4.6

Sources: U.S. Department of Commerce, the Federal Reserve, and the IMF.

Table 8.16   U.S. Trade with Developing Countries ($ billion)

	All Goods			Manufactures		
	Imports	Exports	Balance	Imports	Exports	Balance
1980	122.6	79.6	− 43.0	29.5	55.6	26.1
1981	121.3	87.4	− 33.9	35.1	61.5	26.4
1982	103.7	80.7	− 23.0	37.0	55.5	18.5
1983	107.4	71.0	− 54.7	45.9	45.7	− 0.2
1984	125.9	72.7	− 53.2	61.8	47.5	− 14.3
1985	122.2	69.7	− 52.5	65.5	46.0	− 19.5
1986	124.8	68.3	− 56.5	77.3	49.4	− 27.9

Sources: GATT, Geneva, and the U.S. Department of Commerce.

performance of Asian exporters. Even there, however, in the case of Korea, for example, the export effort is not unrelated to the debt problems of the early 1980s. But whatever has been the role of the debt problem in contributing to the U.S. deficit, the question now is how U.S. adjustment policies will affect the external conditions of debtor countries.

Two features of U.S. adjustment can be highlighted as in table 8.17. One is whether there is a hard or soft landing. The hard landing scenario envisages a collapse of the dollar caused by a loss of confidence. The dollar collapse in turn translates into a sharp upturn of U.S. inflation and brings as a Federal Reserve response a severe tightening of monetary conditions. The result is recession and high real interest rates. The soft landing, by contrast, assumes that fiscal policy turns increasingly restrictive, and monetary policy accommodates with a decline in interest rates. The dollar falls and thus growth of output is sustained by an improvement in net exports. Growth thus is stable and inflation rises moderately. Real interest rates clearly decline.

The second dimension concerns trade policy. Here there are two possibilities: targeted restrictions on countries with large bilateral surpluses (Japan, Korea, Brazil, Mexico) or no significant change in trade policy.

Table 8.17 shows strikingly that the debt problem today remains wide open. Sustained U.S. growth with low real interest rates *and* unimpaired market access means debt problems will become significantly smaller. Continued ability to sell in the U.S. market, higher real commodity prices which come with dollar depreciation, and lower real interest rates all combine to create a scenario favorable for debtors. Of course, the counterpart of U.S. external balance improvement in this case is a worsening of the net exports of Europe and Japan. But lower real interest rates have a self-correcting property in that

Table 8.17   **Consequences for Debtors of U.S. Adjustment Scenarios**

	Soft Landing	Hard Landing
Trade restrictions	Moderate trouble	Debt default
No trade restrictions	Major improvement	Moratoria

debtor countries can reduce their noninterest surplus and yet improve their creditworthiness. This feature means that there is not necessarily a conflict between U.S. and debtor country objectives. When debtor countries argue for the need to reduce U.S. deficits they presumably have this scenario in mind.

The other extreme scenario is a hard landing with trade restrictions. The consequences are obvious: Recession and high real interest rates move debt service problems far beyond what debtor countries can be expected to make up for by domestic adjustments. Trade restrictions further worsen their ability to service debts. The almost certain consequence would be 1930s-style debt defaults or indefinite suspension of debt service.

World growth and real interest rates are central in judging the impact of alternative scenarios for debtor countries. On the side of growth, U.S. fiscal adjustment will tend to reduce growth in the world economy. If U.S. output growth is sustained this will mean that real depreciation sustains net exports and that accordingly foreign growth will tend to be less. It is very unlikely that Europe and Japan will provide an expansion in demand sufficient to keep world output growth constant. Thus on the growth side the expectation must be that the performance of the past few years cannot be sustained. But on the interest rate side there may be a favorable development. If the United States does adjust the budget and sustains growth by lower interest rates the dollar will depreciate and this is likely to force Europe and Japan into interest rate reductions even if that threatens monetary discipline.

The impact of interest rates on debtors' current account balances is, of course, very significant. Table 8.18 gives estimates of the impact on various Latin American countries of a 2.5 percent reduction in interest rates. It shows that the impact on individual debtor countries will depend both on their debt ratios and on the fraction of debt that is at floating rates.

The impact of interest rate changes on import availability is very significant for Mexico, Argentina, and Brazil, who are the large borrowers from commercial banks. For Latin America at large, a 2.5 per-

Table 8.18   Interest Saving from a 2.5 Percentage Point Fall in Interest Rates

	$Billion	Percentage of Imports
Latin America	6.0	7.8
Mexico	2.0	10.5
Venezuela	0.5	5.7
Bolivia	0.025	3.5
Chile	0.4	9.4
Argentina	0.8	15.7
Brazil	1.7	10.3
Peru	0.14	5.1

Source: United Nations Economic Commission for Latin America, Santiago, Chile.

cent reduction in interest rates would amount to a resource saving of nearly 8 percent of total imports. Hence the importance to debtors of the monetary policies that accompany the correction of the U.S. deficit.

Trade barriers might not be applied uniformly across U.S. trading partners. They might be applied only to industrial countries, specifically Japan, or only to *current account* surplus countries, rather than to countries with bilateral surpluses. For debtors the implication here is that an improvement in the debt service ability of countries like Mexico or Brazil might be paid for by extra restrictions on Korea or Taiwan. Thus developing countries as a group might experience an improvement while specific countries like Korea would bear the burden.

There is another way of looking at debtor countries and U.S. adjustment. Suppose that the United States in fact achieved a $100 billion reduction in the external deficit. Assume also that this had as a counterpart a $20 billion improvement in the U.S. bilateral *trade* balance with Latin America. How can Latin America experience a $20 billion deterioration in the external balance? There are only two ways: much lower interest rates or significant extra financing. Thus any hard landing scenario without default of necessity involves a dramatic change in financing availability which is not apparent today.

The focus on the U.S. adjustment problem throws a very different light on the links between world macroeconomics and debt problems. It suggests that the steady IMF scenario conceals that there is either good or bad news, but probably not the balanced no-news outlook implicit in table 8.14. Of course, it is possible that U.S. adjustment is a matter of the more distant future. In that case the IMF scenario would be more appropriate for the near term. But there would inevitably be an adjustment some time and that might be more nearly of the hard landing variety.

Is there a chance that debt problems will be solved in some other fashion by the world macroeconomy? Here one would look to a pattern of terms of trade, interest rates, and inflation of the 1970–73 variety. Since the United States is already at full employment, continuing depreciation and monetary accommodation, without fiscal contraction, will inevitably raise inflation while sustaining growth. This policy setting would ease debt problems significantly. The only question is whether the process of sliding gently into the soft landing option, with a few years' delay, can in fact be achieved. The monetary authorities would have to be sufficiently accommodating and impervious to inflation, and asset holders would have to be patient, sitting out dollar depreciation without a stampede. This does not seem to be a high-probability scenario.

8.6.3 The Commodity Price Problem

The final point to raise concerns the long-term behavior of commodity prices. Both figure 8.6 and table 8.19 show a long-term time series for the real price of commodities. Although exact comparisons across periods are impaired by the fact that these data are spliced from different series, the basic point is very striking.[5] Commodity prices in the mid-1980s have reached the lowest level in real terms since the Great Depression.

Several factors explain this low level of commodity prices. The high level of real interest rates is one and, until 1985–86, the high level of the dollar was another. But these factors are not sufficient to explain the large decline as discussed in Dornbusch (1985). Substitution toward resource-saving technologies on the demand side, and real depreciation and hence increased levels of output at given *world* real prices are often factors. Capacity expansions in many producing countries are further

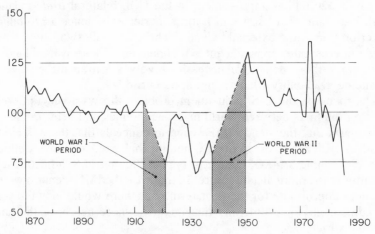

Fig. 8.6   The long-term trends of real commodity prices (Index 1980 = 100). *Source:* IMF (1987).

Table 8.19   **The Real Price of Commodities: 1950–87 (Index 1980 = 100, period averages)**

1950–54	124	1970–74	115	1985	85
1955–59	113	1975–79	104	1986	69
1960–64	106	1980–84	94	1987	64
1965–69	108				

Source: IMF (1987).

factors that reduce real prices. Finally, for agricultural commodities government support policies in industrial countries have played an important role.

But this large decline in real commodity prices, which has been a decisive factor in the debt performance of several countries, as for example Argentina, Bolivia, and Peru, may well have bottomed out. Moreover, the recovery of real commodity prices may turn out to be surprisingly large and rapid. Certainly the level of real commodity prices is unlikely to return to the high of the early 1970s because structural factors mitigate so large an increase. But a resumption of inflation and much lower real interest rates will drive up inventory demand and thus bring about a significant rise. Indeed, the signs of such an increase are already quite apparent except for food. In the one year to August 1987, the *Economist* index of all commodities increased in dollar terms by 22.1 percent, with industrial commodities rising by 46.4 percent. But that increase was not shared by food which showed a moderate decline.

8.7 Conclusion

World macroeconomic policies and variables were until 1981–82 not the major reason for the present debt crisis. Only in 1981–82 did the sharp increase in interest rates and the decline in growth help create a crisis in the aftermath of very poor policy performance in debtor countries.

Since 1982 the world macroeconomic environment has shown an improvement. Interest rates declined in nominal and real terms, and growth has been sustained, as was expected in 1982. The only surprises were that dollar overvaluation lasted as long as it did, a smaller decline in real interest rates, and a massive decline in the real prices of commodities. The world macroeconomic environment certainly did not provide a setting in which debtor countries could grow out of their debts by export booms and improving terms of trade.

Today, five years into the adjustment process, indicators of creditworthiness show a deterioration except for the ratio of debt service to exports. And even that indicator is barely below the 1982 level. Can we expect that the world economy in the years ahead will provide a distinctly more favorable setting? The IMF outlook for the period 1988– 91 shows a no-news setting: steady, moderate growth, no changes in the terms of trade, and an increase in real interest rates. In such an environment debtor countries would have to continue making massive real resource transfers to their creditors. Any improvement in their creditworthiness would have to come primarily from further domestic adjustments.

The no-news scenario conceals the wide variation of outcomes that lie ahead and depend on the nature of U.S. adjustment. Two extreme possibilities are (1) a soft landing with significant real interest rate reductions, improving terms of trade, and sustained growth and (2) a hard landing. The soft landing would ease debt service problems in the same way as happened in 1970–73. But the hard landing, with high real interest rates and recession, possibly reinforced by protection, would certainly preclude debt service on the scale that has taken place so far. U.S. external adjustment forces the question of how a reduction in debtor countries' noninterest balances is consistent with the lack of financing of debtors' interest payments. Without the financing there cannot be any reduction in surpluses except by moratoria or default. Thus U.S. trade adjustment poses a major unresolved issue for the international debt problem.

Notes

1. Countries in this group are characterized by having incurred arrears in 1983 and 1984 or rescheduled their debts in the 1982–85 period.

2. On the costs of protection in a situation of credit rationing, see Dornbusch (1985).

3. See, for example, Dornbusch (1985; 1986).

4. See International Monetary Fund, *World Economic Outlook* (1986) and Dornbusch (1985).

5. See IMF (1987, 90–91) for a discussion of the data.

References

Bergsten, F., W. Cline, and J. Williamson. 1985. *Bank lending to developing countries: The policy alternatives.* Washington, D.C.: Institute for International Economics, April.

Cline, W. 1983. *International debt and stability of the world economy.* Washington D.C.: Institute for International Economics, September.

Cuddington, J. 1986. *Capital flight: Estimates, issues and explanations.* Princeton Studies in International Finance no. 58 (December). Princeton, N.J.: Princeton University.

Dornbusch, R. 1985. Policy and performance links between LDC debtors and industrial countries. *Brookings Papers on Economic Activity* 2: 303–56.

———. 1986. International debt and economic instability. In *Debt, financial stability and public policy.* Kansas City, Mo.: Federal Reserve Bank of Kansas.

Feldstein, M. 1986. International debt service and economic growth: Some simple analytics. NBER Working Paper no. 2076. Cambridge, Mass.: National Bureau of Economic Research.

Goldbrough, D. and I. Zaidi. 1986. Transmission of economic influences from industrial to developing countries. In *Staff Studies for the World Economic Outlook* (July). Washington, D.C.: International Monetary Fund.

International Monetary Fund. *World Economic Outlook,* various issues.

———. 1987. *Primary commodities: Market developments and outlook* (May). Washington D.C.: IMF.

Krugman, P. 1985. International debt strategies in an uncertain world. In *International debt and the developing countries,* ed. G. Smith and J. Cuddington. Washington, D.C.: World Bank.

Maddison, A. 1985. *Two crises: Latin America and Asia, 1929–38 and 1973–83.* Washington, D.C.: Organization for Economic Cooperation and Development.

———, ed. 1986. *Latin America: The Caribbean and the OECD.* Paris: Organization for Economic Cooperation and Development.

Marquez, J. and C. McNeilly. 1986. Can debtor countries service their debts? Income and price elasticities for exports of developing countries. Board of Governors of the Federal Reserve, International Finance Discussion Papers no. 277. Washington, D.C.

Morgan Guaranty Trust. 1986. *World Financial Markets* (April).

OECD. 1986. *Financing and external debt of developing countries: 1985 Survey.* Paris: Organization for Economic Cooperation and Development.

———. 1987. *External debt statistics.* Paris: Organization for Economic Cooperation and Development.

Sachs, J. 1986. Managing the LDC Debt Crisis. *Brookings Papers on Economic Activity* 2: 397–432.

———. 1987. International policy coordination: The case of the developing country debt crisis. NBER Working Paper Series no. 2287. Cambridge, Mass.: National Bureau of Economic Research.

Sachs, J., and W. McKibbin. 1985. Macroeconomic policies in the OECD and LDC economic adjustment. Brookings Discussion Paper in International Economics (February). Washington, D.C.: The Brookings Institution.

Saunders, P., and A. Dean. 1986. The international debt situation and linkages between developing countries and the OECD. *OECD Economic Studies* (Autumn). Paris.

Truman, E. 1986. The international debt situation. International Discussion Papers no. 298. Board of Governors of the Federal Reserve (December). Washington, D.C.

World Bank. 1986. *A strategy for restoration of growth in middle-income countries that face debt-servicing difficulties.* Washington, D.C.: World Bank.

9   Resolving the International Debt Crisis

Stanley Fischer

9.1 Introduction

Since it was first recognized in August 1982, the international debt crisis has dominated economic policymaking in the developing countries, economic relations between the debtor and creditor countries, the attention of the multilateral institutions in their dealings with the debtor nations, and private sector decisions on lending to the developing countries.

Developments since 1980 are summarized in table 9.1, which presents data for the Baker fifteen of heavily indebted countries. The most significant fact is that the heavily indebted countries suffered reductions in per capita real GDP averaging 10 percent over the period 1981 to 1984, which wiped out most of the gain that had taken place since the mid-1970s.[1] There was an extraordinary turnaround in the current account of the balance of payments, which was in balance in 1985 as large trade surpluses were used to pay interest bills of about 5 percent of GDP. Improvement in the current account was matched by a decline in domestic investment,[2] implying a fall in net capital formation to half its previous share of GNP.

Developments on the trade and debt fronts are described in table 9.2. Net private capital inflows have virtually disappeared, and even total capital inflows have been much smaller since 1982 than interest payments abroad. The most remarkable feature of the debt strategy followed since 1982 is that the heavily indebted developing countries have been transferring real resources of close to 5 percent of their

Stanley Fischer is Chief Economist at the World Bank, a professor of economics at the Massachusetts Institute of Technology, and a research associate of the NBER.

The author is indebted to Geoffrey Carliner, Rudiger Dornbusch, and Allan Meltzer for helpful comments and discussions. This paper was completed before I joined the Bank; it is current to the end of 1987.

Table 9.1   Economic Performance, Fifteen Heavily Indebted Countries[a]

	1969–79	1980	1981	1982	1983	1984	1985	1986
Per capita real GDP growth	3.6	2.6	−1.6	−2.7	−5.5	−0.1	0.9	1.4
Current account ($billion)		−29.5	−50.3	−50.6	−15.2	−0.6	−0.1	−11.8
Interest payments ($billion)		25.1	37.0	45.5	41.5	46.0	44.0	38.2
Investment GDP (%)		24.7	24.5	22.3	18.2	17.4	16.5	16.8

Source: IMF, *World Economic Outlook,* April 1987, Statistical Appendix.

[a]Countries are Argentina, Bolivia, Brazil, Chile, Colombia, Ecuador, Ivory Coast, Mexico, Morocco, Nigeria, Peru, Philippines, Uruguay, Venezuela, Yugoslavia.

Table 9.2   Trade and Debt Data, Heavily Indebted Countries

	1969–79	1980	1981	1982	1983	1984	1985	1986
Total external debt ($billion)		269.3	330.8	383.1	394.2	410.9	417.2	434.4
Net private borrowing[a] ($billion)		43.2	57.3	30.7	−2.4	4.2	−2.7	−7.2
Debt/export ratio (%)		167.1	201.4	269.8	289.7	272.1	284.2	337.9
Terms-of-trade change (% p.a.)	4.4	13.4	−2.8	−4.1	−3.5	2.2	−1.9	−16.1
Non-oil commodities prices (% p.a.)	10.0	2.7	−14.1	−8.8	6.3	2.5	−10.8	1.5

Source: IMF, *World Economic Outlook,* April 1987, Statistical Appendix.

[a]Net external borrowing minus long-term borrowing from official creditors and reserve-related liabilities (short-term borrowing from foreign monetary authorities, and use of IMF credit).

p.a. = per annum.

income to the developed creditor countries. A solution of the debt crisis will either reverse the direction of this resource flow or at least significantly reduce it. Despite the virtual cessation of capital inflows, debt burden indicators, such as the debt-to-export ratio, have not improved:[3] the effects of the increased volume of exports and decreased volume of imports were offset by a worsening of the terms of trade.

The picture for the debtors is not entirely bleak. Real interest rates have fallen between 1982 and 1987. Net exports showed extraordinary growth. Budget deficits have been reduced despite falling incomes. In

1987 commodity prices have begun to recover. The period has seen a shift toward rather than away from democracy.

There has also been very real progress for the creditor banks and for the international financial system. Most important, neither the commercial nor central banks have had to deal with large-scale debt defaults. Balance sheets of creditor banks have been strengthened by additions to capital and loss reserves in the United States and Europe, by the weakening of the dollar for those foreign banks that lent in dollars, and by reductions in foreign exposure. There is an active secondary market in developing country debt, and debt-to-equity swaps are a reality. The optimist (for example, Feldstein 1987) can take solace in the failure of the worst fears of 1982—that there would be a worldwide financial crisis—to eventuate. He can also point to some successes, such as Korea and other southeast Asian countries, and the earlier problem case of Turkey.

But the fact remains that five years after it began, the debt crisis is very much alive. None of the major Latin American countries has restored normal access to the international capital markets. Even a country like Colombia, which has rigorously met its payments, finds it difficult to roll over its debts. At least one major debtor has been in trouble each year. In 1987 it is Brazil, whose moratorium could mark the beginning of a new phase of the crisis.[4]

In its brief life the international debt crisis has generated an impressive variety of proposed initiatives and solutions.[5] Least radical are proposals for procedural reform and changes in the nature of the claims on the existing debt. There have been several suggestions for the creation of a facility, or new institution, that would in specified ways deal with the overhang of existing debt. And finally, there are proposals for debt relief. I take up these possibilities in turn in sections 9.3 through 9.5. Preliminary questions about the nature of the debt problem and solutions to it are discussed in section 9.2.

9.2 The Meaning of a Solution

What would it mean for the debt crisis to be resolved? The simplest criterion is that the debt crisis will finally be over when the debtor countries have normal access to the international capital markets. Of course, normal access is itself difficult to define, both because it is quite normal that not all countries are able to raise funds on the same terms and that some of them may be credit rationed because lenders understand that raising interest rates to compensate for the risk of default may itself increase the probability of default.

More pragmatically, it will be clear that the debt crisis is moving towards a solution if the net outflow of resources from the developing debtor countries is significantly reduced, enabling most of them to run current account deficits. The resource inflows would finance investment to raise the growth rate and over time move living standards closer to those of the developed countries.

The assumption that a solution to the debt crisis would reduce resource flows from the debtors to the creditors is based in part on the view that investment opportunities in the debtor countries justify capital inflows. Although investment opportunities appear to warrant capital inflows in some debtors, such as Brazil, that may not be true of all debtor countries. Then the case for reducing their net resource outflows is fairness or the preservation of democracy or capitalism--and those are obviously both highly important and highly political issues.

Resolution of the debt crisis would enable developing country policymakers to base policy decisions on longer-term considerations than their effects on the forthcoming debt negotiations, and it would free up for more important purposes policymakers who are now preoccupied with debt negotiations. The private sector would be able to make investment plans with less uncertainty about the long term, in particular the availability of foreign exchange and investment financing.

If the debt crisis were resolved, banks would no longer have to make loans to developing countries merely to preserve their existing investments. The banks would eventually be able to reduce their exposure to the levels they would prefer—and after the experience of the eighties, these might be very low.

Resolution of the debt crisis would likely also see a change in the form of international lending. Both lenders and borrowers can now see that floating rate financing is a risky way for a country to finance its long-term development. Very likely, a resolution of the debt crisis would end with the debtor countries financed through long-term capital— bonds, equity, direct investment, and perhaps some forms of long-term indexed debt—rather than floating rate liabilities whose terms can change overnight.

Resolution of the debt crisis would mean also that the international institutions, the IMF and the World Bank, would be able to get back to their respective goals of promoting international monetary stability and economic development rather than preventing debt default.

9.2.1 Efficient Solutions

The debt crisis involves at least three parties: the debtor countries, the creditor countries, and the private banks and their stockholders. A more sophisticated view further distinguishes between the governments of debtor and creditor countries and their citizens, between the creditor governments and the international institutions, between workers in the debtor countries and portfolio holders who succeeded in moving their capital abroad, and between financial and manufacturing interests in the developed countries.

A solution to the debt crisis is efficient if it is not possible to make one of the parties better off without making another party worse off. There are many efficient solutions, involving trade-offs among the interests of the different parties. Although the point is rarely explicitly recognized, there is no avoiding the fact that alternative solutions imply different burdens for different groups involved in the crisis. Someone has to pay for past mistakes. It could be the bank stockholders, creditor country citizens, or citizens of debtor countries. Or the burden could be shared.

Up to 1987, most of the burden has been borne by wage earners in the debtor countries. Part has been borne by bank stockholders, who have seen the value of their shares rise less rapidly than the stock market as a whole. Some will be borne by the taxpayers of the creditor countries, as the banks record portfolio losses, lower profits, and lower taxes. The taxpayers of the creditor countries would pay more of the burden if their governments or the international institutions were to provide concessional aid to the debtors. It is of course entirely possible that a longer view of the interests of the developed countries would see benefits rather than burdens for their citizens in the provision of aid to the debtors, just as it might be possible that the unconditional provision of aid to their governments would make the citizens of debtor countries worse off in the long run.

Although the relative burdens are rarely explicitly discussed, the problem is implicitly recognized by proponents of plans who claim their plans to be in the best interests of everyone concerned. For instance, debtor countries are warned not to take unilateral action because future access to capital markets will be long delayed; or banks are urged to make concessions that will in the end enable them to collect more rather than less interest.

Why have the private markets not reached the optimal solution already? To start with, the underlying transactions were hardly private market loans in the first place. Many of the loans were made to governments, who, the lenders believed, simply would not default. Other loans were taken over from private firms by debtor governments on the view that default by a domestic firm would spill over to the credit terms for the country, or to protect domestic borrowers. Further, creditor governments and central banks were actively encouraging the recycling of petrodollars and, it might be expected, would support the banking system if any difficulties arose as a result of the large-scale foreign lending. Second, governments and governmental organizations—the IMF, the Fed, the U.S. Treasury, and other governments—

have been heavily involved since the crisis began.[6] Third, there is no single optimal solution. Solutions differ by who bears the burden.

But it is likely that improvements that could have been made by negotiation among the creditors and debtors have already been achieved. What remains to be discussed are changes that would shift the burden among the parties, and improvements that involve externalities, that is, actions that benefit more than the individuals making the direct transaction.

It is conventional in discussing the debt problem to focus on the restoration of debtor country growth as the ultimate aim. However, the *levels* of income and consumption cannot be overlooked. If it can repress living standards enough, a country can probably put itself in a position to begin growing again. Figure 9.1 illustrates. The country has been growing at a certain rate up to time, *T*, when the debt crisis strikes. The country has been living beyond its means, and has to reduce its living standards. By how much? By servicing the debt in full, it may move onto path *A*, cutting living standards sharply, suffering low growth for a while as the economy reallocates resources from production for domestic use to production for export and import competition, and then moving ahead. Alternatively the country may, perhaps through a moratorium, pay a lower price in terms of the initial reduction in the standard of living and move onto path *B*, starting at a higher level of income than on *A*, and as shown here, growing as fast.

If the growth rates on *A* and *B* are the same, and if income on *B* is higher by more than the interest on the additional debt on that path, the country gains from the moratorium. Corresponding to the lower standard of living on *A* is a larger transfer of resources to the creditor

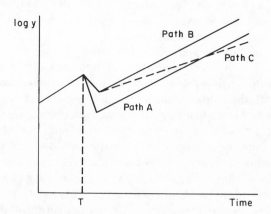

Fig. 9.1   Alternative growth paths

countries, ultimately to the stockholders of the creditor banks. The burden of adjustment on path A is greater than that on B, although both eventually lead to a restoration of growth. Eventual return to growth does not imply the success of a debt strategy. Quite possibly there were alternatives that would have resulted in higher levels of income or consumption in the debtor countries throughout.[7] The failure of the fifteen heavily indebted countries to restore consistent growth since 1982 has to be weighed in the balance in evaluating the debt strategy followed so far.

A major issue that has to be discussed in evaluating different debt strategies is whether the growth rate of real GNP for the debtor countries is the same on paths with deeper adjustment such as A, and paths with less adjustment such as B. If a moratorium or any policy other than full debt servicing reduces market access, it could also slow growth. If so, the relevant choice in figure 9.1 would not be between A and B, but between A and C, where C's low growth rate results from sanctions, explicit or implicit, that are imposed as a result of the failure to meet debt obligations in full, or by the incomplete adjustment of the economy to its new circumstances.

Before describing and evaluating plans to solve the debt problem, I make several stipulations about the nature of the problem and its solution:

1. The debt crisis will have to be resolved in a way that differentiates among countries. Bolivia's problem is different from Brazil's, and both are different from Tanzania's.
2. From the viewpoint of the stability of the U.S. banking system, the debt problem is dominated by just a few countries: over half of total U.S. banks' liabilities, and the liabilities of the nine money center banks, are in Mexico, Brazil and Venezuela. The concentration on the Baker fifteen with its heavily Latin American flavor is a result of those countries' debts being predominantly to the private sector. Similarly, the concentration in this paper is on private-sector capital flows and debts.
3. Concentration on the Baker fifteen overlooks the debt and growth problems of sub-Saharan Africa, which will have to be taken into account in any discussion of aid.
4. Just as the debt problem arrived unexpectedly as a result of changes in the international economy, it could quietly go away. Higher prices for commodity exports, and further reductions in real interest rates, would make the entire problem look manageable. It could also intensify quickly if the international trading system seizes up as a result of growing protectionism.

5. The concerned parties, the banks and the debtors, each have little interest in revealing the dimensions of whatever compromises they might ultimately be willing to make.

6. Finally, there are important political constraints on solutions to the debt problem. There is no well-defined economic sense in which a Brazil, Mexico, or Argentina is incapable of servicing and ultimately paying off its debt.[8] In none of these countries is the external debt to GNP ratio much more than 60 percent. Given long enough, and given a government powerful enough to reduce living standards sufficiently,[9] those countries would be capable of generating the trade surpluses that would enable them to regain normal access to the capital markets. However the new democratic governments in several of the heavily indebted countries are certainly too weak to achieve massive reductions in consumption. The question for both their own governments and the creditor governments is how far it is possible and politically wise to push their citizens to meet debt payments.

9.3   Procedural Reform and New Debt Instruments

Some debt plans would leave the present value of claims on the debtors unchanged while changing their form. Others would reduce the present value of claims on the debtors. Many of the proposals for new debt instruments are intended to maintain the present value of claims on the debtors while making it easier for them to pay, by adapting repayments schedules to the likely patterns of debtor foreign exchange receipts.

In this section I take up both procedural and regulatory reforms that could improve the bargaining process by which debt deals are reached and reduce obstacles to capital inflows to the debtors, and suggestions for new debt instruments. In neither case is the change designed to reduce the value of claims on the debtors.

9.3.1   Procedural Reform

Several procedural reforms are listed in table 9.3. There has already been progress in the implementation of a number of these reforms, including the first. The frequency of complicated debt negotiations has been a significant burden on the economic management teams of debtor nations. Because macroeconomic management skills are in short supply, reduction of the frequency of such negotiations would help improve the overall quality of macroeconomic management. Although the creditor banks value the short leash that more frequent negotiations provide, they can retain some of that control by using IMF Article IV consultations as a framework of evaluation of the country's economic progress and as a condition for further disbursement of funds. Multiyear

Table 9.3   **Procedural Reforms**

Change	Initiating Agency
1. Multiyear rescheduling	Banks and debtors
2. Reduced size of banking syndicates and exit option for small banks	Banks and debtors
3. Change accounting rules to allow partial writedowns and their gradual amortization	Bank examiners and accounting standards
4. U.S. information provision on foreign accounts	Bank regulators and IRS
5. U.S. taxation of foreign accounts	Congress

restructurings of the debt are becoming routine, for example for Mexico, Argentina, and the Philippines, and there appears to be no objection in principle to such agreements on the part of the banks.

The size of the banking syndicates involved in the debt negotiations and the need for hundreds of banks to agree to packages that have already been negotiated are obstacles both to efficient negotiation and to the rapid mobilization of capital after an agreement has been reached. After the September 1986 Mexican agreement it took nearly six months for all 500 banks to sign on. The desire of many of the small banks to leave the international debt business is well known. The exit vehicle may be either the interbank secondary markets or, as in the 1987 Argentine restructuring, special provisions to enable the small banks to leave the syndicates. For instance, it should be in the interests of both the large creditor banks and the debtor countries to agree to allow banks that collectively hold the last 3–5 percent of the debt to leave the syndicate. This could be achieved by the debtor selling them exit bonds that pay interest at a rate below the market rate, with an economic present value above the secondary market price of the country's debt but a face value equal to that of the original debt. Alternatively they might be allowed to leave the syndicate if they sell their claims in the secondary market.[10] In order to provide an exit vehicle for the smaller banks, it would also be necessary for the larger banks and the debtors to agree that sales of securities or purchases of long-term bonds of the debtors free the bank from the obligation to participate in future funding.

Two aspects of the accounting and tax treatment of sales of debt at less than face value have to be distinguished. First, it is unclear whether a bank selling part of its claims on a given country for less than book value has to write down its remaining claims to the same extent. That is a problem for those banks wishing to sell off part of their debts but not all, and presumably is not the main concern of the smaller banks that wish to leave the international debt business. Second, any bank taking a loss in a given period has to record it as a loss in current revenue and cannot amortize it over time.

To start with the second problem: It is not obvious that the value of a firm's stock is increased by amortizing a recognized loss over a prolonged period. Certainly markets responded well to the creation of large loss reserves by the leading banks in May and June of 1987, apparently placing a positive value on the explicit recognition of the possible loss. If nonetheless banks were convinced that amortization was preferable to a larger one-time loss, they could be allowed to write off the losses over a period of several years rather than immediately.

Uncertainty arises over the accounting treatment of debt whose market value is below face value when some of that debt is sold. One view is that banks have to write down the value of all the remaining debt of that type on their balance sheets. That would seem to be the rationale for banks' attempts to swap debt among themselves rather than buy and sell in the secondary market. However, some bankers believe that it is not necessary to write down all the debt of a given country if some of that debt is sold in the market, so long as a good case can be made that the bank is likely to collect on the remaining debt.[11] Certainly the creation of loss reserves against developing country debt has *not* forced the banks to carry the corresponding debt on their balance sheets at its market value.

The basic source of the accounting difficulties, if they exist, stems from the fact that debt is carried at more than market value in the first place. If for some reason it is appropriate to carry that debt at more than market value so long as it has not been sold, then the regulators should not have any difficulty allowing those parts of the debt that have not been sold to continue to be carried on the same basis as before.

Although some capital flight can be regarded as a natural attempt by portfolio-holders in developing countries to diversify internationally, much of it is a form of tax evasion. Procedural reforms 4 and 5 would help the debtors deal with the tax-evasion aspects of capital flight. U.S. and foreign developed-country banks that hold the accounts of citizens of other countries could be required to inform the tax authorities of those countries of the existence of the accounts. It is probably at present difficult to trace the home country of some depositors, but it should not be difficult to find a method of requiring those opening new accounts to give some proof of country of residence. This provision would have to be agreed to by other countries, and thus would take time to implement.

The United States could more easily impose a uniform tax on all interest on bank accounts, and indeed on other income generated from securities holdings, that are not those of United States taxpayers. Once again the effectiveness of such measures would depend on cooperation in introducing similar measures in other countries. By taxing the accounts itself, the U.S. government would be reducing the attraction of capital flight. An alternative would be for the taxes to be imposed by the country from which the capital fled, for which purpose the provision of better information about foreign-held bank accounts would assist the tax authorities in the debtor countries. Here too an international agreement would be needed if countries were not to compete for foreign capital by favorable tax treatment, as they do at present.

9.3.2 Changing the Nature of Claims

Many of the suggestions for dealing with the debt crisis involve changes in the nature of the claims on the debtors (see table 9.4). The driving force behind these suggestions is the conclusion that the structure of the debt in 1982 was partly responsible for the debt crisis. With virtually all payment flows linked to short-term interest rates abroad, the debtors were vulnerable to a rise in real interest rates in the developed countries, and had no protection against changes in the terms of trade. These suggestions are probably motivated also by the view that eventually the structure of debtor country liabilities should correspond more closely to the structure of underlying assets, and should

Table 9.4   **Changing the Nature of Claims**

Change	Initiating Agency
1. Development of secondary and insurance markets	Creditor financial institutions and official institutions
2. Indexed loans	Debtors and banks
3. Contingent lending obligations	Debtors, banks, and offical lenders
4. Longer debt maturities	Debtors and banks
5. Debt-equity swaps	Debtors and banks
6. Servicing of debt in local currency	Debtors and banks
7. Return of flight capital	Creditor and debtor governments, and banks
8. Country funds	Debtors and creditor financial intermediaries
9. Debt subordination	Debtors, existing and new lenders
10. Interest capitalization	Debtors and banks, plus creditor governments

have more long-term fixed interest debt, more equity, more direct investment, and less floating rate debt.[12] These arrangements would provide for more risk-sharing between lenders and borrowers than floating rate debt was expected to produce.[13]

The term securitization is often used to describe a process in which existing debt is taken off the books of the banks and turned into securities, for instance through sale in the secondary market. The same term can be used to describe potential changes in future private-sector financing of economic development, with the maturity and nature of the securities reflecting the underlying investments.

Secondary and Insurance Markets

It is often suggested that the development of secondary markets would help solve the debt crisis. Secondary markets have already developed to some extent, though trading in those markets is thin. Citibank's intention to use the secondary markets more intensively, announced in May 1987 in conjunction with the increase in its loss reserves, could increase the depth of those markets. Regulatory restrictions discouraging partial sales by the banks, or at least uncertainties about accounting and regulatory treatment of the sales, would have to be removed for these markets to develop.

The secondary market does little to solve the debt crisis other than to enable the banks—if they were to sell their claims—to reduce their vulnerability to default in particular countries. Banks have also engaged in debt swaps to strengthen their balance sheets, sometimes in conjunction with debt-equity swaps. The secondary market could eventually become the locus in which an international facility deals with the debt. And, if the market became deeper, prices in it could serve as the basis for debt renegotiation.

Private insurance of the debt is not in principle different from the provision of a secondary market, except that it would enable banks tied into the debt to reduce their vulnerability to default.[14] Insurance rates could be deduced from the discounts on debt in the secondary market, and would be extremely high for many countries. The public sector in the form of the Fed has implicitly been providing insurance to the banking system since the start of the debt crisis, but because the Fed is not obligated to come to the rescue of any particular bank, private insurance would remove uncertainty for creditor banks if it were available. Because the debt crisis and discounts on debt are so deep, it is difficult to see private insurance markets becoming large, or contributing significantly to a solution of the current debt crisis. But the emergence of such markets could facilitate future debt flows to developing countries.

There have also been proposals for public-sector provision of insurance of new capital flows, and perhaps through an agency associated with the IMF or World Bank.[15] Such an authority could help mobilize new private capital, perhaps at lower cost than through private insurance because the multilateral agencies have developed expertise in evaluating loans to developing countries. The agency need not necessarily subsidize the insurance rates; if it were to do so, it would have to decide if that was the most productive use of its subsidies rather than, for instance, providing them in the form of lower-cost loans to the borrowers. The provision of 100 percent insurance would create the type of moral hazard problem of inadequate monitoring of loans by lenders that contributed to the creation of the current debt crisis; the agency would therefore probably insist on significant levels of coinsurance with the lenders.

Indexed Loans

Any loan that ties payments from debtors to creditors to some objective criterion is an indexed loan. There are different motivations for such instruments. A proposal that countries should pay real interest on their debts, which would mean say 2–3 percent real, could imply a cash flow that starts out small and ends with a balloon payment at maturity when the inflation adjustment component is added to principal. But indexation of interest could also imply that the interest due in a given year is 2–3 percent plus that year's rate of inflation. The proposal to fix the real interest rate on the international debt was made with the aim of reducing short-term resource flows from the debtor countries, both by reducing the real rate below the extremely high levels implicit in then nominal rates, and in delaying some repayments until maturity. A reduction in the real rate would of course reduce the resource transfer from the developing countries. But given the possibility of supply shocks, debtors with real obligations could find themselves having to make high real transfers precisely when world trade and their export earnings are depressed. Of course, if the country is the beneficiary of the supply shock—for instance, the oil exporters during the first and second oil shocks—then the indexation helps it match its payments stream to its ability to pay. Similarly, if high inflation is caused by expansionary demand policies in the developed countries that raise commodity prices, indexation would create a closer match between the country's liabilities and its ability to pay.

Exchange participation notes suggested by Bailey (1983) tie payments to export earnings.[16] In a crude way Peru has instituted such notes by paying interest only up to a certain percentage of its export earnings. However creditors have not relinquished their unmet claims on Peru, whereas agreed-upon exchange earnings indexation could simply define the claim as a certain share of export earnings. In well-operating markets such claims could be priced and traded, and there is no difficulty in principle in envisaging their introduction.

Two objections to the indexation of interest payments to export earnings have emerged. First, if interest payments are indexed to export earnings—for instance, a country pays 20 percent of its foreign exchange earnings in interest—then that is like a tax on exports earnings, which discourages the country from exporting. Rather, it is argued, index the payments to a larger total, such as GNP, which would permit a lower "tax" rate and therefore a smaller disincentive effect. While the tax argument is correct (though its quantitative significance remains uncertain), it is not decisive: First, a country with export earnings has the foreign exchange to make payments to foreign creditors, whereas a country whose GNP is growing while its exports are not may not; second, the indexation of interest payments provides an incentive for the creditor governments not to restrict imports from the debtors, for in so doing they reduce the interest earned by their own banks.

The second objection to indexation of interest is that the bank regulators would have great difficulty handling the valuation of these quasi-equity claims and might forbid the banks from holding them. Other financial intermediaries, such as pension funds, might be willing to hold exchange participation notes. Further, debtor countries could attempt to sell such instruments as bonds. Oil-price indexed bonds have already been sold by both Mexico and a private company[17] and are an obvious indexed instrument that the oil exporters would presumably be willing to supply and for which a hedging demand in the developed countries is likely to exist.

It is sometimes suggested that the debtors would be unhappy to allow the payments on indexed notes or bonds to rise very high in the event the country suffers a bout of good luck. There is again no problem in principle for the capital markets to price indexed instruments with ceilings on payments. Of course the sellers of the bond pay a price for imposing the ceiling, but it may be a price they are willing to pay.

Direct swaps of debt for claims on commodities that the recipient exports are another form of indexed instrument. By tying the payoff of loans to a specific amount of the country's production, such agreements reduce the transfer problem.[18]

Contingent Lending Obligations

Contingent lending obligations are another variant of this type of proposal. Examples are the IMF's Compensatory Financing Facility and the 1986 agreement that Mexico will receive additional loans if oil prices fall. In all cases of contingent financing and interest payments the benefit for the recipient country is the assurance that it will automatically rather than after protracted negotiation receive financing in the event of need; the problem for the lender is the fear that good money may be thrown after bad. That can to some extent be compensated for by a higher interest rate, but higher interest rates increase the probability of default, which is the cause of rationing in credit markets.

Longer Debt Maturities

Moving on to item 4 in table 9.4, debt maturities are already quite long, from six to as many as twenty years, in many debt agreements. The long maturities protect the borrowers from having to roll over the debt frequently, but, because the loans are at floating rates, still leave them vulnerable to interest rate shocks. From the viewpoint of the banks, the lengthening of maturities is a lengthening of the rein on which the debtor countries are held, as indeed are other proposals in table 9.4 including indexed instruments, and therefore comes at a price.

Debt-Equity Swaps

Debt-equity swaps are the central element of most market-oriented debt restructurings, and they have also been implemented, for example in Mexico, Chile, and Argentina. The essential transaction is simply that a debt claim on a country is swapped by that country's central bank for local currency claims that should be invested in local firms.

If the domestic equity markets were working well, if there were no constraints on purchases of foreign exchange or domestic assets, and if there were no subsidies involved, such transactions would not attract any attention. But they do. The greatest attraction for the creditors is that debt-equity swaps often carry an implicit subsidy of the equity investment. Swaps may involve the purchase of debt in the secondary market at a discount, and redemption at face value. With secondary market discounts that even for the major debtors may be as high as 50 percent, the subsidy element can be very large.

However there is no inherent reason the debtor country has to subsidize the transaction to the extent set by the New York market price of the debt. If it wants to subsidize the transaction, it can do so by setting a price at which debt can be redeemed prematurely, at a level between the New York price and face value. Another approach has been used by Chile, which auctions off the right to exchange dollar debt for peso assets.

Obviously debt-equity swaps replace interest payments by dividend payments, and are not a source of new money for the debtor country. In addition, they may merely be subsidies for investment flows that would have taken place anyway. A further difficulty arises from the possibility of round-tripping, in which the debt-equity swapper succeeds in converting the purchased equity into foreign exchange at a rate close to the official rate. This is a result of the subsidy provided by carrying out the swap at a price for debt different from that in the secondary market, but can be mitigated by imposing minimum holding periods on the equity purchases.

None of these problems rules out debt-equity swaps as a useful supplement to handling the debt crisis. By swapping at a markup over the New York price, the debtor country in effect is able to buy back some of its debt for less than face value. The present value of the dividend outflow is probably similar to the expected present value of interest outflows on the debt, but does reduce the probability of debt default and does provide a payment stream that better matches the country's economic performance. For these reasons debt-equity swaps may be preferable from the viewpoint of the debtors to agreed direct purchases of their debt in the market at the same price as the swap is transacted. Argentina and other countries are attempting to ensure that the swaps produce new money by requiring swappers to demonstrate that they are in addition bringing in new funds.

Debt-equity swaps will to begin with play only a small part in solving the problem of the debt overhang. The amounts transacted have been small, perhaps approaching $4 billion in total, out of a debt of near $400 billion for the countries involved. Nonetheless, over time an increasing share of foreign investment may take equity form. As in the United States, the value of the equity will likely grow more from reinvestment of profits than as a result of fresh infusions of funds.[19] If the development of this form of financing also results in a strengthening of the domestic equity markets, that will be a bonus.

The substitution of domestic currency loans for foreign debt is part of the 1987 Philippines restructuring (Philippine Investment Notes). They may be used internally to buy equity. Unless the recipient can sell them directly for foreign currency, they appear to be a modified form of debt-equity swap.

Local Currency Servicing

Closely related to the notion of debt-equity swaps is the proposal from debtors that they be permitted to service their debt in local currency, with automatic reinvestment of the proceeds in the domestic economy. Part of the servicing might be made available to the government; the remainder would be relent to the private sector, in forms chosen by the creditors.

This proposal has the benefit for the debtors of reducing the need to generate foreign currency to service the debt. It has the advantage for creditors that their debt is serviced in full, but the disadvantage that they would be constrained from reducing their total exposure in any given country. The proposal is likely to receive consideration both as one means of automatically handling the transfer problem—the debtors' problem in transferring resources abroad—and because it establishes a simple formula by which all existing creditors provide continuing finance for a country.

Flight Capital

The return of flight capital is another item that has received considerable attention. Here the amounts involved may be large, of the order of half the Argentine and Mexican debts. Some debt-equity swaps probably represent the return of flight capital. Provided the subsidy element is kept small, this may be a useful vehicle for the return of flight capital. Similarly any measures the regulatory authorities in the developed countries are willing to take to enable countries to trace this capital would help the debtor governments tax it, and perhaps help bring it home.

The main advantage of flight capital over alternative sources of funding that might be available at lower rates is that it prevents the sale of the national patrimony to foreigners (Meltzer 1983). Flight capital might also be a preferable source of financing of domestic business because the local owners of flight capital have more specialized knowledge of local markets.

However it would be difficult to place flight capital as the centerpiece of any debt strategy. If it would come back for reasonable interest rates and small subsidization of debt-equity deals, it would not need any special attention. It is quite likely though that especially high rates of return would be needed, because the owners of flight capital would fear the imposition of ex post sanctions of some type.[20]

Flight capital left some countries, such as Argentina, completely legally. It left others that had exchange controls illegally. The possibility exists of providing an amnesty for the return of flight capital to those countries it left illegally, though here as with other aspects of the debt crisis, the fear of setting precedents would affect policy decisions.

Mutual Funds

Mutual fund investment in developing countries, the "Country X Fund," is a potential source of equity capital that would succeed in attracting some new capital, and help in the aim of changing the form of foreign investment in the debtor countries. The amounts involved here are, however, likely to be small initially. Such mutual funds would do more to encourage future capital flows to the developing countries than to deal with the existing debt problem.

Debt Subordination

Another suggestion to encourage new capital inflows is that existing debt claims be subordinated so that new lenders go to the front of the repayment line. Subordination is presumably ruled out without the permission of the existing lenders. If it were likely that substantial new capital could be tapped through subordination, the existing lenders could see an increase in the probability of their being repaid, and might be willing to agree. However with no obvious sources of new capital available, they are unlikely to do so.

Interest Capitalization

The last item in table 9.4, interest capitalization, could change resource transfers to the debtors quite radically and rapidly. Capitalization simply limits the amount of interest that has to be paid in any one year, perhaps to a given nominal interest rate on the debt, or to a given percentage of GNP, a given percentage of export earnings, or by some formula related to commodity prices. Whatever the criterion for the amount to be transferred in the given year, the remainder is capitalized and automatically added to the debt, to be paid off over a specified horizon.

Interest capitalization has the attraction of dealing very directly with the problem that current transfers from the debtors are so large as to inhibit growth. The obvious fear from the viewpoint of the creditors is that the process is unstable, that the amounts capitalized will grow too fast for the country ever to be able to pay all the interest without further capitalization. Whether that is a realistic fear depends entirely on the growth prospects of the country and the exact formula used for capitalization. But if every reasonable capitalization formula results in debt instability, then there is presumably no chance that current claims on the country can be collected in full. That is, interest capitalization is a simple substitute for rescheduling when the problem is liquidity, but not when it is solvency.

Table 9.5 presents calculations of the hypothetical path of the indebtedness of the fifteen heavily indebted countries under the assumption that interest capping began with the onset of the debt crisis in 1982 and continued to 1987. According to the real interest rate formula, the hypothetical payment from debtors to creditors each year was 3 percent plus the rate of inflation of the U.S. GNP deflator. According to the share-of-exports formula, the debtors made interest payments of 25 percent of their exports.[21] In each case it is assumed that the interest rate at which interest is accumulated is the average actual interest rate paid on the debt in that year. It is further assumed that the only capital inflows to the fifteen heavily indebted countries resulted from interest capping.

Table 9.5   **Results of Hypothetical Interest Capitalization**

Formula	Outstanding Debt ($billion)					
	1982	1983	1984	1985	1986	1987
Actual	383.1	394.2	410.9	417.2	434.2	464.9
3% real interest	383.1	392.6	409.8	427.3	443.9	451.5
25% of exports	383.1	400.7	414.4	429.6	443.8	457.4

Source: Underlying data are from IMF, *World Economic Outlook,* April 1987, Statistical Appendix.

The calculations in table 9.5 show that interest capping based on a 3 percent real interest rate would have produced a very similar pattern of capital inflows to the actual pattern, but it would have been produced automatically without the constant negotiation that has marked the period since 1982. The main difference between the first two rows of the table occurs in 1985, when capital inflows would have been substantially larger with a 3 percent interest rate cap, and in 1987 (for which the "actual" is in any event hypothetical) when the inflow would have been reduced. Interest capping under a formula that fixed actual payments at 25 percent of exports would have produced a larger inflow of capital in 1983 at the start of the crisis.

The assumption in table 9.5 is that exports and the interest rate at which interest is accumulated would have been the same under interest capping as actually occurred. It might be pointed out that with a 25 percent "tax" on earnings, exports would have been lower. That is possible, but note that actual interest is merely deferred by the capping, not forgiven. It is also possible that the dynamics of negotiation and thus the interest rate at which interest would have accrued would have been different under interest capping. However there is no presumption as to the direction of that effect.

The calculations presented in table 9.5 may thus be taken as indicative of the pattern that would have been seen under interest capping. The most interesting result in the table is that capping at a 3 percent real interest rate would have had only a small effect on the pattern of debt accumulation, and is thus a less radical proposal than it sounds.

Interest capitalization has received more support in Europe than in the United States. Capitalization maintains the banks' claims on the debtors, producing the prospect of eventual repayment, and would thus be preferred by the lenders to interest forgiveness. However it may suffer from accounting difficulties in the United States, with the issue being whether the debt has to be treated as non-performing when capitalization is triggered. Here U.S. regulators would have to change rules if capitalization were to become a practical option.

It has also been argued that capitalization is an unstable process because once introduced, it leads inevitably to the demand for more: If the first agreement is to capitalize 40 percent of interest, will the debtor not demand 60 percent next time, and so on. It is hard to see why the normal bargaining process is more unstable in this direction than in any other. Besides, agreements will almost certainly include an extra charge for the use of the capitalization feature.

As with the other types of change in the form of claims on the debtor countries, interest capitalization may be useful for some countries, in this case those clearly in temporary difficulties. The alternative of a rescheduling suffers the need to engage in a more complicated negotiation, which may bog down over the desire of the smaller banks to escape. But the reschedulings achieve some of the goals of interest capitalization in reducing immediate outward resource transfers from the debtors by providing a grace period before principal repayment is to resume.

Most of the proposals discussed in this section are for changes in the form of the debt that—except to some extent in the discussion of debt-equity swaps—do not reduce the present value of debtor country obligations. Alternative proposals do typically include elements of debt relief.

9.4 New Institutions

The overhang of the existing debt is the main obstacle to a renewal of resource inflows to the heavily indebted developing countries. Very early in the debt crisis both Kenen (1983) and Rohatyn (1983) proposed the formation of an international institution to buy debt at a price below the face value and provide relief to the debtor countries. Similar proposals have been made later, most recently in the 1987 U.S. trade bill.

Kenen's 1983 proposal was for the governments of the creditor nations to set up an International Debt Discount Corporation (IDDC) to which they would contribute capital. The IDDC would issue long-term bonds at a discount to the banks in exchange for their developing country debts. In 1983 Kenen suggested 90 cents on the dollar. It would in turn collect from the debtor countries, using some of the 10 cents to provide debt relief. If the IDDC misjudged and was unable to collect, the creditor governments would bear the losses.

The plan is elegantly simple in replacing developing country debt in banks' balance sheets with the liabilities of the IDDC, in effect requiring the banks to lend to the IDDC. Kenen proposed that the banks not be allowed to choose which debt they would sell, and that the debtor countries would have to agree that the IDDC was the successor debt holder. The IDDC could lengthen the maturity of the debt. He proposed only a modest discount, about 10 percent, on the debt; given the persistence of high interest rates and low commodity prices since 1983, and the large discounts in the secondary market, he would presumably currently suggest a larger discount.

Rohatyn suggested the setting up of an institution that would obtain resources by borrowing in the market, and from the creditor governments. It would then buy debt from the banks, at a discount, and pass the discount on to the debtor nations. He envisaged sufficient discounts to bring debt service burdens down to 25–30 percent of exports; they are currently 50 percent for the heavily indebted countries.

Weinert (1986–87) proposes that the World Bank and/or developed-country governments buy the debt from the banks in exchange for low-interest loans. Suppose that the debt relief is organized through an IDDC. The IDDC passes the same low interest rate on to the debtors. The interest rate is calculated so that the market value of IDDC bonds exchanged for a given country's debt is equal to the secondary market value of that country's debts. But because the face value is the same as that on the debts bought from the banks, the banks can in effect amortize their capital loss through lower profits over the life of the bonds.

Weinert assumes the operation can be carried out without government funds. Some source of capital, presumably governmental, would be needed in any case. Whether the governments retrieve their capital depends on whether the debtors succeed in paying off their reduced obligations. Possibly the creditor governments or the World Bank might decide that aid could be injected to reduce the burden of the debt on the debtors even beyond that implied by the purchase of the debt at secondary market prices.

There are several questions about IDDC type schemes. First, why would the banks agree, and would they all have to agree? At the right price, the banks collectively might agree to a scheme of this sort on the grounds that it transforms uncertain debt into more certain or perhaps even government-guaranteed debt.

The key operational issues in the setting up of an IDDC are the prices at which the IDDC buys debt from the banks, and the amount of relief it provides to the debtors. Unless the debt were auctioned off, it would be difficult to come up with the right price. Once the IDDC became a serious possibility, the secondary market price would reflect expectations about IDDC operations, and would not necessarily serve as an accurate indicator of value. But even though there appears at present to be little prospect of such an institution, the secondary market is thin and prices in it cannot be used as good indicators of the market value that would exist if the regulatory environment made it possible for the large banks to use that market freely.

How much debt would be offered by the banks? If the IDDC offered a high enough interest rate it would get all the banks to participate. At a sufficiently low interest rate no banks would take part. The IDDC could not force the banks to accept the offer unless perhaps it reached an agreement with the banking syndicate for each country. Unless there is some contribution of public money, the plan gets stuck if the banks will not buy debt at an interest rate that looks reasonable for the given country, or some other means is found of ensuring bank participation.

Any IDDC-type scheme creates a free-rider problem. If the IDDC buys up much of the developing country debt and makes some form of debt relief possible, then the credit standing of the debtors improves. Those creditors who stayed out of the IDDC agreement have a capital gain. For that reason an IDDC would have to find some means of ensuring almost complete participation by the creditors.

If it did not use secondary market prices, how would the IDDC proceed? It would have to calculate for each country the interest rate it regarded as right for that country, and then offer to exchange debt at that interest rate with the banks. There is no ready objective basis for calculating how much each country can afford to pay, or should pay. This will be an issue in all debt relief schemes, and will have to be settled on the basis of some combination of the country's per capita income level and the losses it has suffered in the debt crisis.[22]

Recently the Japanese commercial banks have, with government blessing, set up an intermediary to buy their holdings of developing country debt. The Japanese banks derive tax benefits from the sale of their assets at a discount. The U.S. tax laws appear not to afford the same advantages to U.S. banks taking discounts. The Japanese intermediary does not of course plan to forgive any of the developing country debt. But it does provide a precedent for half of the transaction an IDDC would undertake.

The IDDC notion is at the least interesting; if it could be carried off with relatively small injections of public money it would also be important. The key questions about each such plan are how large a write-down the banks should take, whether they would be willing, or could be made willing, to do so, and how much relief would be provided to the debtors. If there is to be an overall solution to the debt problem it will almost certainly involve an IDDC-type institution. But since the procedures it sets up for pricing debt will determine the burdens borne by both banks and debtors, and the possible extent of creditor nation government support, its operating rules and management are bound to be the subject of protracted negotiations. It might be possible in such a negotiation to separate technical discussions on the terms and methods of buying debt from aid discussions that determine the concessions that are given to each country.

One way to move ahead systematically on the debt issue is for the creditor and debtor countries to agree to exploratory talks on the setting up of such an institution.

9.5   Debt Relief

Debt relief could be given in the context of an IDDC. The case for relief is that debtor countries will be unable to grow unless they can increase imports, that no solution currently in sight permits them to do that without reducing income levels to politically unacceptable levels, and that ultimately they will in any case not pay most of their debts. If debt relief were not necessary, the creditor banks and debtors would already have got together on a plan, such as interest capitalization, that permits the resumption of growth while promising that the debt will eventually be paid off.

The case against debt relief is that of precedent, and the view that contracts that were voluntarily entered into should not be abrogated. The question of the precedent that would be set by giving debt relief is not simple. As Lindert and Morton (chap. 2 in this volume) point out, defaults have occurred quite regularly in the past, but that precedent has not made any of the major debtors default this time. Further, debt contracts involve both creditors and debtors, and the use of political authority to enforce the debts sets a precedent for creditors, whose incentives to exercise appropriate caution in lending are reduced.

Relief can come through direct negotiations between the creditor banks and each debtor country, or with the intervention of the international institutions and/or creditor governments. Or it may be imposed unilaterally by some of the debtor governments, either in the form of a moratorium that does not repudiate the debt, or in the form of unilateral action that leaves them to deal with the legal consequences of their actions. Or it could come in some combination of the above.

Negotiations between debtors and their creditor banks would not be direct unless the creditor governments and international institutions kept out. A negotiation in which a creditor government warns the debtor that any failure to pay 100 percent of the debt will affect political and aid relations is multilateral, not direct. In any direct negotiation the debtor nonetheless would have to weigh the legal and other consequences of not paying in full (Kaletsky 1985). If it can meaningfully threaten that, it should be able to reach an agreement that provides some relief.

Presumably the largest debtors, such as Brazil and Mexico, would have the negotiating power to reach an actual agreement on relief. The smaller debtors are in a weaker position with regard to reaching an agreement, although the case of Peru suggests the smaller countries may find it easier to set unilateral terms on which there is no formal agreement with the creditors. The most likely scenario in which smaller countries obtain agreed-upon relief in direct negotiations is that they reach agreements patterned on those of the larger debtors. Indeed, one of the fears of the creditor banks is that any concessions extended to one country will automatically have to be extended to others.

It might be possible for the major debtors to settle their own debt problems in direct negotiations. As in any real world bargaining situation, the outcome would be determined by the threats that each side could realistically make (Bulow and Rogoff 1986). Since neither debtors nor creditors can be sure of the consequences of default, the results of such bargaining are difficult to foresee. So long as the credit or countries permitted these negotiations to proceed without interference, and at critical stages were willing to help—for instance, by changing banking regulations—agreement is quite possible. The agreement would likely be conditional on the country's economic policies, and could involve the international institutions in monitoring roles.

However the free-rider problem among creditor banks is not trivial. If an overall agreement is reached in which creditor banks make concessions that help restore the debtor's growth, individual banks have the incentive to stay out to try to collect 100 percent of their debt. In the United States at least it appears to be extremely difficult to prevent this type of action, even by law, since the rights of the banks may be constitutionally protected.

Proposals to require relief, for instance by interest rate capping, or by debt forgiveness imposed by law, would likely also run into legal obstacles in the United States if not elsewhere. It might be possible to make relief more attractive to the creditors by providing further aid for the debtors, most likely in an IDDC context.

9.6 Scenarios

Three basic scenarios can be seen. The first is an evolution of the muddling-through strategy that has been followed to date. The basic element in the strategy is the negotiation of agreements from time to time between each country and its private creditors, with interest rates being set on a floating rate basis at some markup over LIBOR. The evolution would take place as new assets (such as oil-price indexed bonds, and exit bonds) were introduced, as banks swapped claims with each other and with the debtors (debt-equity swaps for example), and as the margins and fees on the existing debt change through negotiation. This is very much the mixture as before.

Its benefits were noted in the introduction: There has not been a world financial crisis, the banks have had time to improve their balance sheets, real interest rates have fallen, and possibly the world economic situation will become more favorable for the debtors. The difficulties with this strategy were also noted in the introduction: Growth has been slow or negative in the debtor countries and the crisis shows no signs of disappearing. If anything, debt negotiations appear to have become more rather than less difficult since 1982.

The second scenario would see a series of direct agreements between each debtor and its creditors, involving relief and substantial lengthening of the debt. The negotiations for such agreements would be protracted and possibly crisis-laden, and would likely involve the international institutions in monitoring roles. The benefit of such a solution is that it is a longer-term solution, which enables debtors to concentrate on domestic economic management, and gives creditors an opportunity to put their balance sheets in order. The chances of reaching such agreements may well have been enhanced by the creation of loss reserves by the creditor banks.

The third possibility is the setting up of a large international organization, the IDDC, to attempt to dispose of the debt problem. This too has the benefits of settling the crisis and enabling economic management teams to concentrate on policies for growth. It would also provide a longer-term solution for the banks. Such a scheme would likely require a net contribution of resources from creditor governments or the international institutions, and the political difficulties of reaching agreed upon formulas for debt relief would be formidable.

Of course, the scenarios are not mutually exclusive. The second and third possibilities could be combined, with the debt crisis eventually being resolved through a mixture of direct agreements between creditors and debtors, with extra relief being provided for the most impoverished countries though an IDDC or the existing international institutions. Elements of the first scenario would be seen in the evolution of international lending in the direction of more equity-like claims. In all cases the solutions would involve agreed-upon policy reforms in the debtor countries to attempt to ensure that the debt problem does not soon recur.

Notes

1. There are of course large differences among countries; for instance Argentina's per capita GDP fell almost 20 percent from 1981 to 1986, and was then still 10 percent below its 1975 level, while Brazil's 1986 per capita GDP was above its 1981 level and 20 percent above the 1975 level.

2. Total GDP for the fifteen heavy debtors is in the range $750–1,000 billion.

3. The debt to GNP ratio also increased over the period 1982–86.

4. However, the banks quickly moved to limit the system-wide effects of any unilateral Brazilian decisions by reaching agreements with other major debtors.

5. Dornbusch (1987), Feldstein et al. (1987), and Krugman (1986) present useful surveys of alternative solutions; the classification of debt initiatives used here is taken from Krugman.

6. It has been argued, for instance by Lindert and Morton (chap. 2 in the present volume), that the debt crisis would have been resolved far more rapidly without the government intervention.

7. A simple criterion by which to judge alternative strategies from the viewpoint of the debtors is the present discounted value of their consumption.

8. See Feldstein (1986) for a detailed scenario.

9. Of course it becomes harder for the debtors to meet their obligation if the creditor governments close markets to foreigners.

10. Obviously this would apply only to banks holding the last 3–5 percent of the country's debt as of a given exit date.

11. This was the position taken by a panel of the American Institute of CPAs in 1985 (see "The Outlook" column, *Wall Street Journal*, 26 October 1986).

12. Lessard and Williamson (1985) provide a very useful review of alternative proposals for changing the form of finance of the debtor countries. See also *World Bank* (1985) and *IMF*, (1986).

13. In the event, though, creditors have to some extent shared in the losses that higher interest rates imposed on borrowers.

14. In this paragraph I mainly discuss insurance of existing debt obligations.

15. National export credit agencies perform some of the same functions. The World Bank has provided some investment guarantees in the co-financing of projects with commercial lenders.

16. Lessard and Williamson (1985) analyze this and related proposals which they call "quasi-equity" investments.

17. Both Mexico and Petro-Lewis suffered subsequent reversals, and the Mexican oil bonds are not regarded as a success. Petro-Lewis's problems appear unrelated to the issue of indexed bonds.

18. In conversation Pentti Kouri has argued that the fact that Finnish reparations to the Soviet Union after World War II were specified in physical terms made the transfer of resources less burdensome than it would otherwise have been.

19. New equity issues usually account for only a small share of funds raised in U.S. capital markets; for instance in 1983, when equity issues were unusually large, they totalled $53 billion when total funds raised by private domestic nonfinancial business exceeded $400 billion.

20. The government of Turkey obtains funds from expatriate workers by borrowing in Germany at 3 percent above the Eurodollar rate (see Rodrik 1987 for details). Presumably debtor countries could set up similar schemes in foreign countries for capital held there. It might however be difficult for the government to justify paying higher interest to citizens who had invested abroad than to those who had kept their funds at home.

21. The 3 percent real interest rate and the 25 percent share of interest earnings were chosen to ensure that the hypothetical debt in 1987 was similar to the actual debt in 1987.

22. Sachs (1986) suggests per capita income declines since the start of the debt crisis as the basis for relief. This could give large amounts of relief to the

relatively rich borrowers. Since the provision of debt relief through public funds is in part a result of a sense of fairness, it is likely that relief would be based on the level of per capita income as well as (perhaps) debt-related indicators.

References

Bailey, Norman. 1983. A safety net for foreign lending. *Business Week*, 10 January.

Bulow, Jeremy, and Kenneth Rogoff. 1986. A constant recontracting model of sovereign debt. NBER Working Paper no. 2088. Cambridge, Mass.: National Bureau of Economic Research.

Dornbusch, Rudiger. 1987. The world debt problem: Anatomy and solutions. Report prepared for the Twentieth Century Fund, New York.

Feldstein, Martin. 1986. International debt service and economic growth: Some simple analytics. NBER Working Paper no. 2076. Cambridge, Mass.: National Bureau of Economic Research.

———. 1987. Latin America's debt: Muddling through can be just fine. *The Economist*, 27 June.

Feldstein, Martin, Herve de Carmoy, Koei Narusawa, and Paul Krugman. 1987. Restoring growth in the debt-laden Third World. New York: Tri-Lateral Commission, mimeo.

International Monetary Fund. 1986 and 1987. *World Economic Outlook* (April).

Kaletsky, Anatole. 1985. *The costs of default*. New York: Priority Press Publications.

Kenen, Peter. 1983. A bailout for the banks. *New York Times*, 6 March.

Krugman, Paul R. 1986. Prospects for international debt reform. Report to the Group of Twenty-Four, prepared for United Nations Conference on Trade and Development.

Lessard, Don, and John Williamson. 1985. *Financial intermediation beyond the debt crisis*. Washington, D.C.: Institute for International Economics.

Meltzer, Allan H. 1983. *International lending and the IMF*. Washington, D.C.: The Heritage Foundation.

Rodrik, Dani. 1987. External debt and economic performance in Turkey. Kennedy School, Harvard University. Mimeo.

Rohatyn, Felix. 1983. A plan for stretching out global debt. *Business Week*, 28 February.

Sachs, Jeffrey D. 1986. Managing the LDC debt crisis. *Brookings Papers on Economic Activity* 2: 397–432.

Weinert, Richard S. 1986–87. Swapping Third World debt. *Foreign Policy* (Winter): 85–97.

World Bank. 1985. *World Development Report*.

Contributors

Rudiger Dornbusch
Department of Economics
Massachusetts Institute of
    Technology
E52-357
Cambridge, MA 02139

Sebastian Edwards
Department of Economics
University of California
Bunch Hall, Room 8283
405 Hilgard Avenue
Los Angeles, CA 90024

Barry Eichengreen
Department of Economics
University of California
250 Barrows Hall
Berkeley, CA 94720

Stanley Fischer
S-9035
The World Bank
1818 H Street NW
Washington, D.C. 20433

Stephan Haggard
Center for International Affairs
Harvard University
1737 Cambridge Street
Cambridge, MA 02138

Robert Kaufman
Department of Political Science
Rutgers University
Hickman Hall, Douglass Campus
New Brunswick, NJ 08903

Paul Krugman
Department of Economics
Massachusetts Institute of
    Technology
E52-383A
Cambridge, MA 02139

Peter H. Lindert
Director
Agricultural History Center
University of California at Davis
Davis, CA 95615

Peter J. Morton
Department of Economics
Hofstra University
Hempstead, NY 11550

Jeffrey D. Sachs
Department of Economics
Harvard University
Littauer M-14
Cambridge, MA 02138

387

Name Index

Subject Index